34-00

Clive Hunt

Teatro de la Zarzuela
Teatro Calderón

MADRID THEATRES

- TEATRO DE LA ZARZUELA — c. de Jovellanos 4   1856
- TEATRO CALDERÓN — c. de Atocha 18   1917 opened as Odeon Theatre, then Teatro del Centro.
- TEATRO PAVÓN — c. de Embajadores 9   1925   Calderón 1929
- TEATRO APOLO — c. de Alcalá   cl. 1929
- TEATRO ESLAVA — c. de Arenal 11   1871   Now nightclub
- TEATRO REINA VICTORIA — Carrera de S. Jeronimo 24   1916
  (complicated — orig. nw S. Ginés)
- TEATRO IDEAL — c. Doctor Cortezo 6   1916. Adapted for zarzuela as cinema. 1990 Cinema 1932
- TEATRO REAL — Plaza de Isabel II   1850, closed 1925–1966
- TEATRO CIRCO —   complicated history
- TEATRO FELIPE — Paseo de Prado, later moved to Recoletos next to plaza de
- TEATRO DE LA LATINA — Plaza de la Cebada 2
- TEATRO FONTALBA   1924
- TEATRO CÓMICO — c. de Capillanes   rev. popular 1850
  (Teatro de Capillanes)   closed 1968, then demolished
- TEATRO FUENCARRAL — c. de Fuencarral 133   1918 – cinema
  1924 Theatre
  closed 1988.
- TEATRO ALBÉNIZ — c. de la Paz   c. 2009
- GRAN TEATRO — c. del Marques de la Ensenada 8   1902
  (Lyric Theatre)   cine in 1920, converted to residential use

- TEATRO PRICE
- TEATRO PRINCIPE ALFONSO
  (Teatro Circo de Rivas)

The Zarzuela Companion

Christopher Webber

The Scarecrow Press, Inc.
Lanham, Maryland, and Oxford
2002

SCARECROW PRESS, INC.

Published in the United States of America
by Scarecrow Press, Inc.
A Member of the Rowman & Littlefield Publishing Group
4720 Boston Way, Lanham, Maryland 20706
www.scarecrowpress.com

PO Box 317
Oxford
OX2 9RU, UK

Copyright © 2002 by Christopher Webber

All rights reserved. No part of this publication may be reproduced, stored in a retrieval system, or transmitted in any form or by any means, electronic, mechanical, photocopying, recording, or otherwise, without the prior permission of the publisher.

British Library Cataloguing in Publication Information Available

Library of Congress Control Number: 2002110168

ISBN 0-8108-4447-8 (cloth : alk. paper)

∞™ The paper used in this publication meets the minimum requirements of American National Standard for Information Sciences—Permanence of Paper for Printed Library Materials, ANSI/NISO Z39.48-1992.
Manufactured in the United States of America.

To my wife,
Sheila Webber

Contents

	Foreword, by Plácido Domingo	ix
	Preface	xi
1	Zarzuela: A Brief History	1
2	Zarzuela Today	7
3	Francisco Alonso	11
	La calesera	12
	Las leandras	15
	Me llaman la presumida	19
	La parranda	22
4	Emilio Arrieta	27
	Marina	28
5	Francisco Asenjo Barbieri	33
	El barberillo de Lavapiés	34
	Jugar con fuego	37
	Pan y toros	40
6	Tomás Bretón	47
	La verbena de la Paloma	48
7	Ruperto Chapí	53
	La bruja	54
	La patria chica	58
	La revoltosa	60
	El rey que rabió	63
	La tempestad	67
8	Federico Chueca	73
	Agua, azucarillos y aguardiente	74
	La alegría de la huerta	78
	El año pasado por agua	81
	El bateo	83
	El chaleco blanco	85
	La Gran Vía	87
9	Manuel Fernández Caballero	91
	El dúo de la africana	92
	Gigantes y cabezudos	95
	El señor Joaquín	98
	Los sobrinos del capitán Grant	100
	La viejecita	105

10	Joaquín Gaztambide	109
	El juramento	110
11	Gerónimo Giménez	117
	La tempranica ✓	118
12	Jacinto Guerrero	123
	Los gavilanes ✓†	124
	El huésped del Sevillano ✓†	127
	La montería ✓	131
	La rosa del azafrán ✓†	134
13	Jesús Guridi	139
	El caserío ✓†	140
14	Vicente Lleó	145
	La corte de Faraón ✓†	146
15	Pablo Luna	151
	El asombro de Damasco ✓†	152
	Molinos de viento ✓†	156
	El niño judío ✓ +(semi-staged)	159
	La pícara molinera ✓	162
16	Rafael Millán	167
	La dogaresa ✓	168
17	Federico Moreno Torroba	173
	La chulapona ✓†	174
	Luisa Fernanda ✓†	178
18	Manuel Penella	185
	Don Gil de Alcalá ✓	186
19	José Serrano	191
	Alma de Dios ✓†	192
	La canción del olvido ✓†	194
	Los Claveles ✓†	198
	La dolorosa ✓†	202
20	Pablo Sorozábal	207
	Black, el payaso ✓	208
	Don Manolito ✓	212
	Katiuska	215
	La del manojo de rosas ✓†	218
	La tabernera del puerto ✓	222
21	Reveriano Soutullo and Juan Vert	227
	La leyenda del beso ✓†	229
	La del soto del Parral ✓†	232

22	Tomás López Torregrosa	237
	La fiesta de San Antón	238
	El santo de la Isidra	240
23	José María Usandizaga	243
	Las golondrinas	244
24	Amadeu Vives	249
	Bohemios	250
	Doña Francisquita	253
	La Generala	257
	Maruxa	260
	La villana	263
25	Nineteenth Century	269
26	Twentieth Century	277
27	Catalan Sarsuela	283
28	Cuban Zarzuela	287
29	Writers	291
30	Singers	301

Appendices

A	Select Discography	313
B	Bibliography	323
C	Glossary	325

Index	329
About the Author	343

Foreword
Plácido Domingo

It is a great pleasure for me to be asked to introduce *The Zarzuela Companion*. We Spaniards have zarzuela in the blood. It is a very precious part of our heritage, and it is a joy to find that an increasing number of music and theatre lovers around the world respond to zarzuela, and wish to learn more about the stories, the composers, writers and singers who created these unique works.

For me, especially, zarzuela holds so many memories: of my parents, my early life and my career. My mother and father toured America in December 1946 with Torroba's zarzuela company, and the tour was so successful that when it was over they decided to remain in Mexico and form their own. You will read a little about my parents in this book. My mother enjoyed a long and distinguished stage career; and though by 1949, when I joined them in Mexico, my father had lost his voice prematurely, he too had been a fine singer. By then he was the producer and first actor of the company. Maestro Torroba, when we were working together on rehearsals for his opera *El poeta* (1980) told me that no one had ever sung Vidal's lines *"Ay mi morena, morena clara"* in his *Luisa Fernanda* so well and meaningfully as my father, and that my mother was the perfect Luisa.

Then I think of the many great colleagues with whom I have had the privilege of singing zarzuela in concert halls and theatres around the world. For all of us, this music means so much. My sister and I, for example, knew certain zarzuelas as well as we knew our paternosters—we could recite the whole of them by heart. For people nowadays, especially those outside the Spanish-speaking world, it is different. The information is not often to hand, and here in America I have often been asked the question: "Where can I read more about this wonderful music?"

Well, now I can answer them. Christopher Webber's book is a treasure trove of information on the great *zarzueleros* and their works, for the *aficionado* as well as the newcomer. I dare say that very few will be unable to discover something new to them here, or find some fresh light cast on old favorites. This book is an indispensable reference guide, a pleasure to read and browse because of its author's enthusiasm, skill and knowledge of his subject. Zarzuela is a very emotional matter for all my family because my parents dedicated their lives to bringing the best of this wonderful music not only to Spain, but also to the American continent. I salute Christopher Webber, and wish *The Zarzuela Companion* well.

Plácido Domingo
June 2002

Preface

This book has been born out of personal frustration. Falling in love with zarzuela is easy. Discovering what it's about is quite another matter, especially if you're unlucky enough to be living outside Spain. In Madrid it is assumed that everyone knows all about zarzuela anyway, so mostly inadequate CD sleeve notes and out-of-print literature make the task of learning about this extraordinary form far from simple. *The Zarzuela Companion* is aimed at anyone interested in these wonderful works, and the writers, composers and musicians who made them.

With ten thousand zarzuelas to choose from it cannot aim to be more than highly selective. The emphasis has been on works written after 1850, chosen for their popularity or intrinsic quality; and the sixty main synopses are pitched at the level of detail necessary for non-Spanish speakers to follow often quite long sections of spoken as well as sung action. There are also many mini-synopses, some contained in the four sections dealing with lesser Spanish composers (organized in two century-based chapters) as well as their Catalan and Cuban contemporaries. Finally there are short sections on the playwright-librettists, those men of the letters so much more important in zarzuela than in opera; and on the singers, who have brought zarzuela to life in the theatre and on record.

A select discography with current catalog reference numbers, a brief bilingual bibliography and a glossary of Spanish terms make up the Appendix. I hope *The Zarzuela Companion* will enhance the pleasure of the growing band from around the globe who, like myself, have been captivated by Spain's uniquely rich and colorful form of musical theatre.

What is zarzuela? It's been said that zarzuela means to Spain what operetta means to Vienna, Offenbach to Paris, Gilbert and Sullivan to London, and the musical to Broadway. Well yes, it means all of that—and much more. Zarzuelas range from simple, one-act farces through to three-act tragedies of blood, touching on just about every theatrical genre in between. Beyond the fact that nearly all of them employ spoken dialogue to a greater or lesser extent, there's little to define them more neatly. They aren't even necessarily in Spanish, as the tradition of Catalan *sarsuela* goes to show. The drama is often carried as much by the spoken as the sung texts, words and music held in an equilibrium unknown to opera. That is part of zarzuela's appeal, but also a source of frustration for many outside the Hispanic world—hence, *The Zarzuela Companion*.

I would not have been able to write it without the help of many people. First and foremost, I am deeply in the debt of my Madrid friends. Pedro Gómez Manzanares has taken endless time and trouble to share his insight and encyclopedic love of the repertoire with me. His critical input to the section on the writers has been vital, but his benign influence blesses the whole. María Luz González Peña, the Director of CEDOA at Sociedad General de Autores y Editores (SGAE) in Madrid, has been unstintingly kind and generous in providing me with most of the original material I have worked from, scores as well as texts. Here in England, I've been lucky to have Andrew Lamb's invaluable support, advice and practical help at every stage. As the authoritative sounding board on anything and everything to do with music theatre, he has given me the confidence to undertake this book.

I must also thank Derek Barnes for the music examples; Lucy Holliday of Music Sales Ltd. for providing material from the extensive Union Musical Ediciones (UME) archives; Alison Latham, editor of the *Oxford Companion to Music*; Michael Kaye; my editorial team—Bruce Phillips, Melissa Ray, Jessica McCleary and Jesse Goodman—for their help and encouragement; and the company of the London production of Sorozábal's *The Girl with the Roses* for the shared experience of zarzuela in performance. For the same reason, I'm grateful to Andrea Fellows Walters and Ellen Schlaefer of Santa Fe Opera, New Mexico, for giving me the opportunity to adapt *La dolorosa* and *Luisa Fernanda* into English for their highly popular, bilingual touring productions. I am specially grateful to Plácido Domingo for his helpful suggestions and gracious Foreword.

Last and not least, I owe a huge debt to the zarzuela singers, actors, directors and fellow *aficionados* that I've met through the 'Zarzuela!' internet website *www.nashwan.demon.co.uk*, where anyone who wishes to delve deeper will find many graphics, song texts, reviews, internet links and in-depth discussions of the recorded repertoire. Michael Hopf of Melbourne, Australia, and John Tombs of Mallorca have been especially kind in sending me zarzuela tapes, CDs and videos, some rarer than hen's teeth. The knowledge that there are so many people all round the world who have fallen in love with La Zarzuela, and would like a guide to her glories, has been my chief reason for writing one.

1
Zarzuela: A Brief History

Baroque Zarzuela

In 1657 at the Royal Palace of El Pardo near Madrid, King Philip IV of Spain, Queen Mariana and their court attended the first performance of a new comedy by Pedro Calderón de la Barca (1600–81) adorned with lavish music by Juan Hidalgo (1614–1685). Or so the legend goes: although it was by no means the first such entertainment *El laurel de Apolo* (Apollo's Laurel) traditionally symbolizes the birth of a new genre which soon became known as La Zarzuela, after one of the King's hunting lodges situated in a countryside thick with *zarzas* or brambles.

Tradition does not quite coincide with reality. In fact the first play with music Calderón wrote for the Palace had been *El jardín de Falerina* (Falerina's Garden) of 1648, although most would agree that *El golfo de las Sirenas* (The Sirens' Sea, 1657, music anonymous) and *El laurel de Apolo* (1657/8, with music reputedly by Hidalgo) were his earliest to be called zarzuelas from the start. Later, proven collaborations with the harpist-composer Hidalgo, such as *La púrpura de la rosa* (The Blood of the Rose, 1659/60) and *Celos aún del aire matan* (An Atmosphere of Jealousy Still Kills, 1660), enjoyed equal success. These zarzuelas were often revived at court and elsewhere, and some of the most impressive early zarzuela music to survive is the lavish new through-written score to *La púrpura de la rosa* provided in 1701 by Tomás de Torrejón y Velasco (1644–1728) for a production in Peru.

Why zarzuela? The hunting lodge was often visited by actors and clowns from the city; and the pieces Calderón provided, running the theatrical gamut from classical opera to low slapstick and popular *coplas y estribillos* (verses and refrains) perhaps reminded the courtiers of a typically mixed La Zarzuela performance. Some of these plays employed richly accompanied recitative rather than spoken dialogue; but all of them, like the later *El hijo del sol, Faetón* (Phaeton, Child of the Sun, 1661), *Eco y Narciso* (Echo and Narcissus, 1661) and *Ni Amor se libra de amor* (Cupid is not Exempt from Love, 1662) used mythological subjects from classical literature, interspersed with comic *intermedios* (interludes) of a popular nature. Calderón's writing was matched by scores of comparable sophistication and diversity, featuring *seguidillas*, light-footed popular dances and songs in triple time, as well as *arias* and *ariettes* in the Italian and French styles. The Spanish elements are essentially a spice to the main dish.

The courtly baroque zarzuela enjoyed a long and distinguished history. Sebastián Durón (1660–1781) took over the musical helm from Hidalgo, writing zarzuelas beginning with *Salir el amor del mundo* (Love Rules the World, 1696) in an even richer style. Durón's successor at court, Antonio de Literes (1673–1747), also provided zarzuelas such as the lively *El estrago en la fineza* (The Ravages of Goodness, 1718) for public performance. His famous *Acis y Galatea* (1708), in its stylistic diversity a signal contrast to Handel's masterpiece of ten years later, has been successfully revived. One of the finest late baroque zarzuelas is Antonio de Zamora's *Viento es la dicha de Amor* (Wind is the poetry of love, 1743) with music by José de Nebra (1702–68), a mixture of spoken blank verse and prose, opera arias, short choruses with a flavor of Monteverdi, popular songs with castanets and delectably orchestrated instrumental interludes.

Tonadilla

The onslaught of Italian opera gradually forced native opera into smaller compass, and from the late eighteenth century it was left to the short *tonadilla*—equivalent to the Italian *intermezzi* such as *La Serva Padrona* and *Pimpinone*—to keep Spanish lyric theatre alive. The outstanding writer of *tonadillas* and *sainetes* (at this time their spoken equivalent) was Ramón de la Cruz (1731–94), whose texts broke the mythological mold of earlier times by reflecting popular life and speech. Short, with little plot, character was the mainstay of the *tonadilla*, the bud which was to blossom into the all-conquering *género chico* late in the following century. Composers of famous *tonadillas* included the Catalan flautist Luis Misón (1727–76), who wrote over one hundred, and Blas de Laserna (1751–1816), who wrote seven times that number including the popular *La beata* (The Blessed Woman, 1781).

The few longer zarzuelas written by de la Cruz and others adopted Italian models as to versification, style and content. A delightful example is *La madrileña* (1778) an early work by Vicente Martín y Soler (1756–1806), who as "Padre Martín" was to find fame and fortune writing Italian operas in Vienna in rivalry with Mozart. The craze for Italian opera composers in Madrid made the native form with its spoken dialogue seem increasingly old-fashioned, although as late as 1786 Luigi Boccherini (1743–1805) wrote a two-act zarzuela for the palace of the Duke of Benavente Ossuna in Madrid. His *La Clementina* is a scandalously neglected masterpiece of Spanish lyric theatre, to a fine de la Cruz libretto. On occasion at least, the zarzuela was still worthy of the highest talents Spain could muster.

Enlightenment ideas came late to Spain, which in the late eighteenth century remained a deeply conservative country with a rigid hierarchy strongly resistant to change. The French Revolution and subsequent Napoleonic invasion had a seismic impact on Spanish life and culture: after Bonaparte's expulsion the country was subjected to a series of civil wars and revolutions which disrupted her social and cultural development. Little wonder that the early years of the nineteenth century were a fallow time for zarzuela. Composers Félix Máximo López (1742–1821); Ramón Carnicer (1789–1855) and, ironically, the Italian Basilio Basili (1767–1850) did something to keep Spanish Opera alive, but the zarzuela itself was submerged under a tide of comic *opera buffa* by Rossini and his lesser Italian contemporaries.

Romantic Zarzuela

Not until the early 1850s does the full-length native drama resurface. The rise of nationalist consciousness brought about the birth of the romantic zarzuela, a mighty movement in which a group of young writers including Ventura de la Vega (1807–65) and Luis de Olona (1823–73) were at least as proactive as their composer colleagues. The year 1851 saw them found a resident company at Madrid's Teatro del Circo, together with musicians led by Francisco Barbieri (1823–94) and Joaquín Gaztambide (1822–70). This was the crucial gamble: five years later, public and critical enthusiasm for their work led to the building by subscription of the Teatro de la Zarzuela in Calle Jovellanos, the horseshoe auditorium dedicated to lyric theatre in the Spanish language which remains the high temple of zarzuela even today.

France was the dominant political and cultural force of the time, and these playwrights drew their plots more or less from French romantic plays, posing amorous aristocrats with their servants in populist settings. Their chosen form was the three-act *zarzuela grande*. Their chosen literary means was elegant, formal verse. The music was largely Italianate, although in time Barbieri at least began slowly but surely to enrich his palette with Spanish popular song and dance forms. His *Jugar con fuego* written with Ventura de la Vega in 1851 was the first important romantic zarzuela, but its libretto is based on a French play and its delightful score could be by Rossini or Donizetti. It took thirteen years and many zarzuelas for Barbieri to grow confident enough to articulate a Spanish plot with essentially Spanish music: *Pan y toros* was the real watershed after which Madrid's musical life was liberated to follow its own course.

As with the Baroque, the essence of this romantic flowering was the artful mixture of elements, the inclusion of something to appeal to everyone. Many of these *género grande* ("large genre") three-act zarzuelas wedded operatic musical complexity to the subtlety of spoken drama, but even where the subject matter wasn't Spanish, there would be comic characters who recognizably were. Pragmatic nationalist musicians such as Barbieri and Cristóbal Oudrid (1825–77) faced constant intellectual and financial challenges, running the gauntlet between conservative composers such as Emilio Arrieta (1823–94), who doubted that Spanish music could bear the dramatic weight of the classic Italian forms, and populist entrepreneurs who wanted little more than novel frivolities to fill their theatres.

The most important of these managers, the actor Francisco Arderius (1835–86), adopted the parodistic, Parisian style of Offenbach for his theatre company, *Los bufos madrileños*. In 1866 he mounted *El joven Telémaco* (1866, music by José Rogel), written in a consciously light, frivolous, witty style which challenged the *zarzuela grande* head on. The younger *zarzueleros* led by Ventura's son Ricardo de la Vega (1839–1910) responded with a return to the aesthetic of Ramón de la Cruz, with his *tonadillas* and *sainetes*. They brought about another shift in the literary course of zarzuela, marrying the Spanish elements of the *zarzuela grande* with the light touch and short span of Arderius' *bufos*, and substituting the flavor of de la Cruz's realistic, everyday language for the exquisite verse drama of their elders.

In 1880 this new fusion, christened the *género chico*, had an epochal triumph with Ricardo de la Vega's *La canción de la Lola*. The short musical score, largely by Barbieri's heir Federico Chueca (1846–1908), became a *madrileño* mania within weeks, its songs pumped out by barrel organs and bar pianos all over the capital: the authorities even considered banning it. For the next twenty and more years, *género chico* ruled the roost; although the *zarzuela grande* never quite went away, and the *bufos* were to surface once again in the more sophisticated guise of Viennese operetta.

The genre is *chico* ("small") by virtue of length, not quality or potential complexity. Writers tended to conceive these theatre pieces or *sainetes* in a single act, lasting about an hour; two or three would make up the average theatre bill. Their subject matter is simple and comedic, mixing sentimental and cynical, romantic and realistic, *machismo* with submission to the superior intelligence of women. The prime characteristic of *género chico* is its root in *madrileño* culture, the life of the people, presented for the people. Poetic rhyme and meter are reserved for the *cantables*, or sung parts. The *chico* classics are a potent brew of sophisticated musical ensemble and poetic *romanzas* and *dúos* (operatic arias and duets) mixed with prose dialogue, popular songs and lowlife comedy characters. Others are *revistas*, satirical revues such as Chueca and Valverde's internationally famous *La Gran Vía* of 1886; still others short, often gently titillating one-act farces, mostly set in the less salubrious parts of Madrid—parts all too well known to many of the pleasure-seeking men in the audience, at least. In between these and the "respectable" *género grande* came a flood of zarzuelas in all shapes and sizes: it is estimated that in excess of ten thousand were written in the century after 1850.

Inevitably, many texts from this period are superficial, implausible and slipshod, relying on vulgarity and cheap laughs. Still, many good writers emerged during this Golden Age, often writing for the now vanished Teatro Apolo, *chico* rival to the Teatro de la Zarzuela where the *grande* tradition reigned supreme until the turn of the century. Writers of the quality of Carlos Arniches (1866–1943) and Miguel Echegaray (1845–1915) remain admirable for their fluent dialogue, clear characterization and verbal wit, as well as their facility to dovetail book and lyrics seamlessly. The great *sainete* composers, such as Chueca, wrote simply and directly, utilizing the forms of popular urban dances such as the chotis (schottische), mazurka, pasodoble and, from further afield, the Spanish American tango and habanera. Some versatile musicians such as Ruperto Chapí (1851–1909) and Manuel Fernández Caballero (1835–1906) were able to keep a foot in both camps, producing *chico* and *grande* zarzuelas as occasion demanded.

If there is a reason for the unique quality of this great outpouring of musical theatre, it lies in one word: Madrid. The spirit, sights and sounds of the capital pervade nearly all the great zarzuelas large or small from this classic period, and of many from the twentieth century. Even composers who came from outside the city or the country, from the Italian Boccherini through to the Basque Pablo Sorozábal, became steeped in its heady atmosphere, *madrileños* heart and soul just as surely as natives such as Chueca or the great novelist-chronicler of the epoch Benito Pérez Galdós (1843–1920). Many of the very finest zarzuelas, preeminently the classic *La verbena de la Paloma* by Tomás Bretón (1850–1923), Chapí's *La revoltosa* and Chueca's *Agua, azucarillos y aguardiente*, derive their richness from the presiding spirit of urban Madrid.

Twentieth Century

The first half of the new century saw the repertoire augmented by a huge quantity of work. After its first decade the literary focus of zarzuela again changed, as the influence of mainstream European and especially Viennese operetta with its exotic settings and situations pervaded the *madrileño género chico* and *zarzuela grande* alike. Longer libretti became the norm, the role of dance was expanded, new zarzuelas became more lavish scenically and musically, in contrast to the increasingly risqué *revistas* which were quickly written and performed to popular audiences without much thought as to artistic integrity. Composers such as Pablo Luna (1879–1942) and Amadeu Vives (1871–1932), more adept technically than many of the previous generation, became nationally famous for their operetta-zarzuelas. Others, notably the Valencian José Serrano (1870–1941), took a rather different tack, choosing to revivify the one-act *sainete* by an injection of Italian *verismo* with its emphasis on extreme romantic passions.

As the century wore on, these strands tended to merge together. The next generation of *zarzueleros*, among them Francisco Alonso (1887–1948) and Jacinto Guerrero (1895–1951), broadened the appeal of the form by combining sentimental plots with Pucciniesque musical fluency and regional Spanish *costumbrismo* (popular life and customs) from beyond Madrid's city boundaries; whilst librettists such as Federico Romero (1886–1976) and Guillermo Fernández Shaw (1893–1965) carried on the work of the best zarzuela playwrights, demonstrating advanced literary and theatrical craft, plus an awareness of the great traditions from which they had emerged. So it is that two of the most enduring works of the 1920s and 30s, Vives' *Doña Francisquita* and *Luisa Fernanda* by Federico Moreno Torroba (1891–1982), both to librettos by Romero and Shaw, self-consciously evoke both the older *madrileño género chico*, with its pasodobles and habaneras, and the broad scope and aristocratic fandangos of the old *zarzuela grande*. All this gives these complex masterworks universal appeal, as well as a flavor unlike anything else in the operatic or operetta repertoires.

If there was a late heir to Chueca and Serrano it was the Leipzig-trained Pablo Sorozábal (1897–1988), a composer who still polarizes opinion. With *La del manojo de rosas* (1934) he and his librettists pointed the zarzuela back firmly toward the direct, down-market modernity of Ricardo de la Vega and the 1890s *sainete*, reflecting the personal and political concerns of an increasingly unstable society with jazzy modern equivalents of the old *género chico* dance music.

With the cataclysm of the Civil War, the rich variety of Madrid's theatre life disappeared overnight. Despite Torroba's later efforts to foster a new spirit of *casticismo* (purity) in Spanish music, the zarzuela was more or less played out as a vital form. Only he and the evergreen, chameleon Sorozábal kept it artistically alive into the 1950's, and their later productions increasingly came to resemble Broadway musicals in verbal tone and orchestral timbre. Despite some valiant last-ditch attempts, such as Manuel Moreno Buendia's *Fuenteovejuna* (1981, based on Lope de Vega's play) the deaths of Torroba and Sorozábal in the 1980s marked the last rites of the romantic zarzuela tradition.

2
Zarzuela Today

The romantic zarzuela is Spain's distinctive contribution to lyric theatre; yet given its quality and diversity, the repertoire is still surprisingly little known outside the Hispanic world. The causes are many, various, and almost completely external to the works themselves. When they get the chance to experience zarzuela, whether in the original language with surtitles, bilingual production or translation, audiences the world over respond with enthusiasm, generally accompanied by the question "Why haven't we heard this before?" A handful are resistant to any mixture of spoken and operatic drama, but that's a debate which afflicts the reputation of Beethoven's *Fidelio* and "serious" musicals just as surely as zarzuela. Nor is the urban argot of *género chico* specially impervious to translation: indeed, Spanish humor, with its dry one-liners and double-entendres, is easier to render into English than its Italian, French or German equivalents.

Part of the problem has been relative ignorance of Spanish culture in general, a difficulty which is down to Spain's status as a closed nation for centuries before the Civil War of 1936. Due to her constant state of political turmoil, she hardly shared in the eighteenth-century Enlightenment or the libertarian movements of the nineteenth, but became increasingly isolated and self-absorbed. The only nineteenth-century work before recent years to make much impact in Europe was the short revue *La Gran Vía*, although zarzuela has always had a narrow bridgehead into the United States through the proximity of Spain's old colonies in Cuba, Mexico and Central America. In the 1920s and early 30s Barcelona and Madrid made a brief, doomed struggle to become more international in outlook; but the victory of Franco's forces nipped that in the bud, and once again the cultural and social barriers came down.

Inside Spain zarzuela soon recovered nearly all her old popularity; but visitors to Madrid CD shops are still surprised to see a healthy section marked Zarzuela rubbing shoulders with New Age, Classical and Rock/Pop. Although many older Spaniards in particular still take enormous pride in zarzuela, it no longer has the social or cultural dynamism of a contemporary art form; indeed, the Forty Plus generation tend to use *zarzuela* as an pejorative adjective implying "old-fashioned" or "establishment." Their offspring have no such reservations, and the Teatro de la Zarzuela's work with schoolchildren helps foster knowledge of their musical heritage in an energetic and practical way. Madrid may never again have thirty theatres playing zarzuela on any given night, as it did in the early 1900s; but there's no sense of a conservative tradition being preserved in aspic, here or in the rest of the country.

Festivals such as Oviedo, touring companies such as Antonio Amengual's Compañía Lírica Española, Spanish TV and radio—all are active and effective promoters of zarzuela. Professional and amateur performances proliferate, and Emilio Sagi's vibrant tenure as director at the Teatro de la Zarzuela itself raised production standards (and costs) to an international level. Abroad, José Tamayo's lavish and superbly drilled *Antología de la Zarzuela* song and dance spectacular toured Europe and the United States during the 1980s and 90s, alerting many music lovers to the glories of the repertoire. Its guest stars included Monserrat Caballé, José Carreras, and most significantly Plácido Domingo, who was born into a family of *zarzueleros* and whose personal crusade to raise the profile of this musical and theatrical treasure trove has had a major impact. Nowadays, many opera companies in the United States are starting to perform zarzuela regularly; and Japan, Australia, Britain, Germany, Austria and Holland have all mounted home-grown professional productions in the last year or so. Many Spaniards' pride in the revelation of their best-kept musical secret is still hedged about by a certain defensiveness ("Of course, it won't make any sense outside Spain"); but to their deep satisfaction, events are increasingly proving them wrong.

In the early twentieth century the intelligentsia was wary of zarzuela's cultural status, not because of its popular appeal, but because of the artistic difficulties posed by its heterogeneous form. No longer: Spanish musical circles have woken up to the durable quality of the classics. In particular, the Sociedad General de Autores y Editores (SGAE) does sterling work from its offices in Madrid and New York to facilitate performance and knowledge of zarzuela. Through their ICCMU imprint, full and vocal scores of many fine works are appearing in superb new critical editions: just as well, because the commercial Spanish music publishing industry has been lax in allowing most of them to go out of print. Librettos and scores are still ludicrously hard to find, even secondhand. These things, it seems, are passed down as treasured family heirlooms.

The recording companies, with the exception of the French Auvidis Valois, whose 1990s series of recordings sponsored by Domingo has been invaluable, have made very few new recordings of zarzuelas since the classic Alhambra, Hispavox and EMI collections of the 1950s and 60s. It is a pity that the repertoire is still defined by what great conductors such as Ataulfo Argenta were able to squeeze onto LP half a century ago. The reappearance of many historical recordings, often with original casts, is doing something to open people's eyes to zarzuela's immense strength in depth; but reinterpretation from today's generation of singing actors is a necessity if zarzuela is to bolster its living presence worldwide.

Baroque and Rococo zarzuela is enjoying an unprecedented number of revivals and recordings, thanks to the work of El Ayre Español and other committed groups; for the first time in three centuries composers such as Durón, Literes and Nebra are more than names in dusty encyclopedias. The Teatro de la Zarzuela has been particularly strong in its revivals of forgotten masterworks from its own past, by Gaztambide, Barbieri and others. The academic industry is gearing up for a major program of conservation and revaluation; and although the creative vein of romantic zarzuela is well and truly worked out, whilst there is so much half-buried material to revive La Zarzuela is no more likely than her elder sister La Opera to succumb through lack of novelty, variety or sheer staying power.

At root the prospects for zarzuela at home and abroad depend on one thing: the music. In quality, emotional range and diversity the best of these scores offer a musical experience distinct from any other, and this will continue to be zarzuela's great strength and appeal. As one delighted convert was heard to say after hearing *La verbena de la Paloma* for the first time: "It's *Carmen*, but the real thing." So it is. Like Bretón, most of the musicians discussed in the following chapters may be virtually unknown outside the Spanish-speaking world, where they are at least as familiar as Bernstein in America or Sullivan in England; but, to take three at a hazard, personalities such as Chueca, Serrano or Sorozábal are simply too strong not to make their mark in the wider world sooner or later. These composers were astute men of theatre, expert communicators, but above all distinctive voices whose music ensures a healthy future for the stage form to which they dedicated their remarkable talents.

3
Francisco Alonso
(1887–1948)

Francisco Alonso was born in Granada on 9th May 1887. His mother, a fine pianist, was supportive when her son's initial choice of a medical career was abandoned in favor of serious musical studies. By eighteen he was proficient enough to become musical director of the Cordova Regiment, and provide them with a popular success in the pasodoble *Pólvora sin humo*. About this time he also directed the Philharmonic Society orchestra of his native city, and wrote his first zarzuela *La niña de los cantares* (The Singing Girl) for the Teatro Cervantes.

Inevitable migration to the capital followed in 1911, but although Alonso made ready money writing *coplas* for fashionable salons, lasting theatrical success eluded him. Pieces such as the one-act *sainete Armas al hombro* (Shoulder Arms) were applauded only to vanish overnight, and it wasn't until 1916 that he achieved his first significant breakthrough, with *Música, luz y alegría* (Music, Light and Joy) at the Teatro Novedades. *La banderita* (The Bannerette, 1919), source of a much-played pasodoble, showed advances in orchestral sophistication and confident handling of his subject matter. Finally in 1924 came the first in his line of triumphs, *La linda tapada* (The Veiled Beauty) which enjoyed a highly successful run at the Teatro Cómico.

Both these were taken up with equal success in Latin America—some of the music was even heard in Parisian concerts—and from then on until almost the end of his career Alonso was able to pick and choose where and how he wanted to work, dividing his time between full-length zarzuelas and *revistas*. His three-act pieces include *La calesera* (1925), most famous of all with its swashbuckling romantic plot and immediately impressive score, *La parranda* (The Wayward Woman, 1928) and *La picarona* (The Villainess,

1930). *La morería* (Land of the Moors, 1928) written in collaboration with Rafael Millán enjoyed almost equal success. *Me llaman la presumida* (Call me Conceited, 1935) with its strongly contemporary atmosphere and jazz influences, is the third zarzuela in an unofficial *madrileño* trilogy (along with Serrano's *Los Claveles* and Sorozábal's *La del manojo de rosas*) which taken together give us a vivid portrait of the capital in the years before the Civil War. The *revistas* include the hugely entertaining *Las leandras* (1931).

After the civil war the zarzuela went into eclipse, and Alonso's career with it. Ever the chameleon, he tried to adapt his style to fashionable continental models, but neither *Rosa la pantalonera* (Rosa in Trousers, 1939) nor even the graceful *La zapaterita* (The Little Shoemaker, 1941) quite recapture his earlier strength. After this, he stuck mainly to *revistas*, with mixed success. Honors such as the Presidency of the Society of Spanish Authors (1947) came his way; and he died, still in harness, on 19th May 1948. His final stage work *La rumbosa* (The Splendid Woman) was eventually mounted late in 1951.

Many of Alonso's works display a generosity of spirit which places them far above many more obviously pretentious theatre pieces, and his colorful, exuberant bravura is as infectious now as ever it was. A highly-tuned theatrical awareness helped him to avoid simply presenting the mixture as before; and taken as a group, his longer zarzuelas present a wide-ranging geographical tapestry covering just about every part of the country, each with its own, distinct atmosphere. The *revistas*, notably *Las leandras* (1931) with its famous P*asodoble: "Por la calle de Alcalá"*, crackle with lively wit and good tunes, and demonstrate as surely as the full-length pieces the brilliance of Alonso's largely self-taught technique. A popular composer in the best sense, Francisco Alonso retains a well-merited place in the hearts of many of his compatriots.

La calesera
Zarzuela in three acts
(Madrid, Teatro de la Zarzuela, 12th December 1925)

Text: Emilio García del Castillo and Luis Martínez Román

Principal Characters: Maravillas "La calesera", a popular singer (soprano); Elena, Marquesa de Albas (mezzo-soprano); Calatrava, her major-domo (bass); Rafael Sanabria (baritone); Gangarilla, a comic actor (tenor); Pirulí, an actress (soprano).

ACT 1—A Madrid Café, during the revolutionary year of 1832. After a brief, extrovert *Preludio*, the curtain rises on Pedro García's theatrical company. While waiting to be paid off, the whole company—including their star singer Maravillas, nicknamed La calesera after the calesa (two-wheeled chaise) driven by her father—sing the amorous comedy story of *"Don Tadeo y doña Carlota"* to while away the time before her father arrives. A passing wedding procession with its *rondalla* band also serves to keep them amused. García arrives and the troupe clamors for its pay. It is left to Maravillas to keep the peace, and once harmony is restored she leads the company in a free-wheeling, improvisatory *Seguidillas: "Todos dicien que te quiero, calesera"*, reveling in her own power to attract lovers.

The comedian Gangarilla provokes a lively dialogue about the repressive government and the likelihood of a ban on the new *tonadilla* the troupe has in rehearsal. Maravillas is more concerned for the safety of Rafael Sanabria, an aristocratic liberal politician and her secret lover, especially when Gangarilla repeats a distressing rumor that he has become engaged to Elena, Marquesa de Albas. Another actor confronts a masked man who has been listening intently to their talk, but consternation turns to relief when the actors realize that it is none other than the famous libertarian bandit, Luis Candeles.

The wedding party enters the café, and the troupe takes advantage of the free drink on tap. Their next visitor is slightly less welcome: the Marquesa herself come to wait for Rafael, accompanied by her faithful majordomo, Calatrava. Having learned of the existence of her beautiful rival, Elena decides to warn her off. When she recognizes Maravillas as a woman who has helped their cause in the past, jealousy turns to subtle spite in their pointed *Dúo-Gavota*: *"Usía es damisela de mariñaque"*. There is a volley of shots and Rafael staggers in, slightly wounded. Elena quickly tends to him, and the couple sing of their affection in the face of the stricken Maravillas, who joins them in an expansive *Terceto: "No haste temer por mí"*. Rafael blames himself for his cowardice in surrendering to love when humanity is in chains, and sings a stirring song in praise of freedom (*Himno: "No hay bien más hermoso que la libertad"*). When Candeles and a comrade hasten in, asking the troupe to guard the banner of rebellion until the moment comes to raise it, even Maravillas is caught up in the fervor, raising the conspirators' spirits by waving the flag as the curtain falls.

ACT 2, SCENE 1—The Teatro del Príncipe. The players are anxiously waiting for news of the rising while rehearsing the new piece. The irrepressible Gangarilla and his fiancée Pirulí banter together in a flirtatious *Dúo Cómico*, until Maravillas brings disastrous news: the ruling powers have imprisoned the liberal leaders, and Rafael and Elena have escaped with her to the theatre with the police in hot pursuit. The troupe swiftly disguise the nobles and

Elena's faithful majordomo as actors. Calatrava even revels in his new career as a popular singer, venting an amusingly wooden song of gypsy love (*Canción: "Salto de mi carabela"*).

Rafael's gratitude to Maravillas awakens old feelings, and they confess to loving one another still, in their intensely felt *Dúo: "El veto, mi amor sincero ... Deja, que voy a olvidar"*. Two policemen duly arrive, but Maravillas and the players sing the swaggering *Pasacalle de los chisperos: "Yo no quiero querer a un chispero"* ("Pasacalle of the Bums") to put them off guard. The ruse works and the police are about to leave when a slip of the tongue by one of the actors leads to the trick being partly discovered. As Elena is unmasked Rafael swiftly steps forward to be arrested and taken off to prison instead, though not before leading a reprise of the great song of liberty (*"¡Libertad! Es el grito de la humanidad"*).

SCENE 2—Inside the prison. Rafael laments his fate in a brief *Carceleras*, or prisoner's song. Gangarilla has managed to impersonate a guard, and Pirulí and Maravillas pretend to be his sisters in order to gain access to Rafael. The situation is complicated by Elena's well-meaning majordomo. Sent to deliver a letter from his mistress and failing to gain entry, Calatrava attempts a robbery to get himself put in jail and so carry out his orders. Unfortunately his "victim" turns out to be Luis Candeles, who gives him money and sends him on his way. Another tale of marital mishap from the irrepressible comedians (*Dúo Cómico: "Críspulo se ha casado"*) distracts the real guards, enabling the conspirators to administer a sleeping potion and make good their escape with the nobleman.

ACT 3—An inn, on the highway to France. The troupe are in desperate flight, but decide to stop for a quick drink at a wayside inn. Led by Gangarilla and Pirulí they break into another song and dance tale (*Dúo y Coro: "Por mí dices, Elías"*). Maravillas is in torment, forced to listen as Rafael tells her of his plan to escape with Elena in his noble *Romanza: "Agua que río abajo marchó"*. When Luis Candeles joins them, she confesses that she has denounced their flight to the police, whose arrival to stop the fugitives is imminent.

Candeles does not pause to reveal her jealous treachery, but quickly organizes Rafael's departure with Elena, exchanging the nobleman's passport for a false one of his own; and though the lovers manage to escape Luis himself is caught and handcuffed. Over an orchestral *Final* recalling many of the most memorable themes of the zarzuela, Maravillas sighs that now she has nobody to love her; though before being led away Candeles finds time to whisper that he at least will always love the beautiful Calesera.

La calesera represents the high water mark of Alonso's brilliant career, artistic and commercial. Given the political ferment of Madrid at the time of the premiere, instant popularity was pretty well guaranteed for a work combining revolution and high romance, and *La calesera* scored high on both counts. Its passionate singer-heroine has taken the name of La calesera out of pride in her lowly origins, and is thoroughly embroiled in the liberal conspiracies that wracked absolutist Madrid at the time of the work's setting.

Sustained musical quality enables the work to retain that early popularity. Castillo and Román provided Alonso with a swashbuckling, three-act historical thriller which played directly to the composer's great strength: the facility to write colorful, "Spanish" music in a variety of regional flavors, which rarely descends into picture-postcard cheapness. Its melodic sweep and passionate vitality are manifest in almost every bar. Rafael's Song to Liberty has a noble power; and numbers such as Maravillas' first act *Seguidillas* and the *Pasacalle de los chisperos* have lost none of their intoxicating rhythmic and instrumental flamboyance.

Las leandras
Revista-zarzuela in two acts
(Madrid, Teatro Pavón, 12th November 1931)

Text: Emilio González del Castillo and Jose Muñoz Román

Principal Characters: Concha Valverde, a young singer (singer-actress); Aurora (soprano); Leandro (baritone); Francisco Morales (actor); Manuela, his wife (actress); Casildo, his nephew (actor); Porras, Aurora's father (actor).

PROLOGUE—The curtain rises on the triumphant finale of a Madrid *revista* starring Concha Valverde. Little more than a year ago Concha had been a schoolgirl. Her mother died, leaving her in the care of her Uncle Francisco from the Canary Isles, who sent the girl to a Madrid convent to complete her moral education, and promised Concha "something in the bank" once her studies were completed. Thrown out of the Convent School after causing a riot in the Botanical Gardens, Concha has gone into musical theatre, keeping up the pretence of study with the help of a couple of schoolfriends who pass on her letters.

Her pathologically jealous boyfriend Leandro, a shady property dealer of sorts with an eye to the main chance, examines the letters suspiciously before allowing them through. Concha is shocked to find one from her uncle, making it clear he's coming to Madrid accompanied by his nephew, a naval officer he intends to marry off to his niece. Leandro comes up with a bright idea: he has a hotel on his books which has been empty for three months, so why not put the chorus girls in uniform and set up a spurious Young Ladies' College for a few days? The girls enthusiastically agree to help out.

ACT 1—Entrance hall of the suburban Madrid hotel, now calling itself "Las leandras" after its founder. The "headmaster" himself, kitted out in mortarboard and gown, is helping his assistant Aurora to give the "pupils" an extremely dubious lesson in arithmetic, political economy, and urban transport, packed with entendres which are too overt even to qualify as double (*Coplas: "A dar lección"*). Manuela Morales, a wealthy if somewhat vulgar woman, brings her slow-witted daughter Fermina to learn cookery and other wifely duties to prepare for marriage with her cousin Casildo. Leandro explains that they also prepare for widowhood, as witness the lesson in progress—Concha and the girls, dressed as widows, running through a sequence from her new revista (*Vals: "Ay qué triste ser la viuda"*). Señora Morales is impressed by all this elegance, while Leandro is impressed by her daughter's well-developed figure, and by her money.

A short-sighted Postman arrives with some mail for another Concha, surnamed Martinez, previous manager of the hotel. Leandro learns from one of the letters that her "Beauty Parlor" was nothing more than a high-class brothel. The letter writer, Francisco Morales, canary-dealing husband to Manuela, promptly turns up with his son-in-law-to-be Casildo, a sexually inexperienced booby. Francisco is sure the letter he has sent to "Concha" (to whose professional services he is no stranger) will ensure Casildo some good experience before the wedding; given two Franciscos, two nephews, two Conchas, a Canary dealer and the Canary Isles, it's not long before the farce is in full flow.

In the midst of the confusions, the girls rehearse their next lesson—which is about Pichi, a boy doll popular at the time who featured in a series of Madrid magazine stories. Pichi presents himself in a sexily ambiguous *Chotis*, sung by Concha and the girls—the famous *"Pichi"*. The act ends with a tableau in honor of the false Uncle Francisco, this time with Concha as Clara Bow being entertained by sailors of different nationalities in the port of New York (*Final: "Clara Bow, gentil star"*).

ACT 2, SCENE 1—A telephone lobby off the main hall, later in the day. Aurora is scandalized by the behavior of "Uncle" Francisco, currently chatting up one of the dancing girls in his capacity as Visiting Professor. Manuela brings Fermina to enroll, although her daughter begs her not to give her away to the odious Casildo. Another visitor is ushered in, a highly respectable gentleman also called Don Francisco—the real one this time—come to visit his niece. While he is waiting to meet Headmaster Leandro, "Uncle" Francisco introduces himself to his putative fellow client, going on to complain that he's been here for two hours without being given a proper seeing-to. The hilarious verbal exchange that follows is completely at cross purposes. How's the music here? Worse than it was, they've moved the pianola. Much beating? Francisco hopes so. Don Francisco leaves to collect *his* nephew Ernesto, well satisfied with moral standards at the college. Casildo and "Uncle" are taken off to watch a tableau of steamy tropical love, which Concha and the chorus perform in honor of The Canaries (*Canción Canarías: "El bailar el tajaraste"*).

SCENE 2—The doorkeeper, Porras, enjoys a fantasy zarzuela scene. First a well-known local celebrity, the Old Mushroom Man, delivers a poetic prologue painting the scene outside the theatre with its florists and rose sellers, its streetwise boys and girls spending money and making love, on this verbena (festival) night of San Antonio. The curtain rises, and we see the street outside the Teatro Apolo, on the Calle de Alcalá, filled with a motley collection of hawkers including Aurelia, a lovely young flower-seller—Concha again—and a young dandy, El Gomoso. A scene in comically stilted verse follows, with Aurelia rejecting El Gomoso's advances in favour of Paco el Garboso (elegant)—who looks amazingly like Leandro! The lovers launch into the *Habanera Dúo: "Dile al gomoso ... la verbena de San Antonio"*, which parodies lovers' banter in earlier zarzuelas such as *La revoltosa*, and ends with them agreeing to go off to the verbena. The scene ends with Aurelia marching on at the head of a troop of flower girls, who conclude with the famous *Pasodoble de los nardos: "Por la calle de Alcalá"* (Pasodoble of the Roses) in praise of the erotic power of the blooms they sell on Madrid's favorite street.

SCENE 3—The hotel terrace. More farcical confusion ensues, especially when the false uncle discovers his wife has enrolled their daughter in the "school" to learn wifely duties. The booby Casildo of all people finally unravels the confusion over the Canary Uncle, and matters come to a head when the real Don Francisco reappears with his nephew Ernesto, the spruce young naval officer. Another uncle is too much for the jealous Leandro and he violently attacks the newcomer. Everyone else piles into the fracas on one side or the other, and the curtain falls on a scene of total mayhem.

SCENE 4—Evening. Confusion is compounded when Concha's uncle reveals that "something in the bank" meant just that: an offer to get her a job in a bank, as a typist! Sponsoring an artistic career for her is quite out of the question. Calling him a Scrooge, she goes off in tears, pursued by the attractive Ernesto. Leandro meanwhile cuts his losses and decides to marry Fermina: she is such an airhead that he needn't be jealous any more, and is a changed man. The booby Casildo consoles himself with Aurora, whose father Porras announces that the girls have prepared a final tableau for everyone's pleasure. The curtains open to reveal a glittering palace, and Concha and Ernesto mount the steps to the throne, finishing in an embrace—to the undisguised delight of the whole company.

If the glittering career of Madrid *revista* effectively began with *La Gran Vía* in 1886, it reached its apogee some forty-five years later here: if indeed *Las leandras* really is a revue, rather than a true zarzuela. Debate only demonstrates the fatuity of trying to pigeonhole these unique stage works as one thing or another; for however we choose to categorize it, the piece remains one of the brightest jewels in Spanish lyric theatre. The librettists' droll description ("a lyric comedy diversion in two acts, divided into a prologue, five scenes, several sub-scenes and apotheosis") thumbs a nose at dramatic pretension. *Las leandras* is a risqué little farce, full of double-entendres and what used to be called "sauciness," tricked out with musical numbers of more, or in most cases less, consequence to the plot. Its Political Incorrectness, so blatant to blushful modern sexual mores, takes nothing away from its sheer cleverness.

It was written to show off the talents of the great Argentine *chanteuse* Celia Gámez, to whom the piece is dedicated. Alonso's music is a piquant concoction of modern and traditional styles. The grand sweep of *La calesera* and *La parranda* is absent; but in its place we get a compendium of 1930s dances blended with traditional Madrid models, full of catchy tunes and sharply effective orchestration.

Numbers such as *Pichi*, the Lesson Scene, and above all the *Pasodoble de los nardos* with its haunting mix of sun and shade are still part of *madrileño* folklore, and the bust commemorating their composer can still be seen on Alcalá, with a good view down to the junction with La Gran Vía. *Las leandras* is proof that, in the right hands, *revista* could be transmuted into something of lasting value: both the chotis *Pichi* and *Los nardos* boast something rarely found in popular songs—truly memorable "B-section" tunes:

Me llaman la presumida
Sainete in two acts.
(Madrid, Teatro Ideal, 4th December 1935)

Text: Francisco Ramos de Castro and Anselmo Cuadrado Carreño

Principal Characters: Gracia "La presumida," a dressmaker (soprano); Pepe "Chevalier," a young actor (tenor); Paco, a jeweler's assistant (baritone); Doña Olga, a greengrocer (mezzo-soprano); Pepa, her daughter (soprano); Don Basilio, a photographer (bass); Cayetano, his nephew (tenor).

ACT 1—1935. A small square in downtown Madrid, with a photographer's, greengrocer's, junk shop, jeweler's, and fashion shop. A lively opening *Escena: "Por una chica del barrio"* introduces the inhabitants of the Square; notably Doña Olga, the greengrocer, bantering with some customers; and Paco, the shy young jeweler's assistant, pining for love of his neighbor Gracia, handsome but conceited supervisor of the fashion shop. Although secretly returning his feelings she jeers at him for his pains, despite the sympathy of the other dressmaker's girls, Lola and Carmen, and of the greengrocer's daughter, Pepa.

The photographer Don Basilio and his nephew Cayetano use their profession as a means of getting their hands on young ladies—for strictly "artistic" purposes of course—but things go awry for Cayetano, who is chased out of the shop by a bridal party for having suggested some distinctly unusual wedding poses. Three city slickers turn up to pay court to Gracia, and are given short shrift by the proud beauty in a jaunty *Pasacalle: "Una mujer madrileña"*.

The girls are leaving for lunch when the handsome heart-throb actor Pepe "Chevalier" comes in, coolly inviting them all to a local bar to drink fashionable "vermut." Only Gracia pretends to be unimpressed. When the girls leave, Paco manages a quiet word with his friend Pepe. Paco is in love with Gracia, but the words don't come out right and she only laughs at him. Will his sophisticated friend sound her out on his behalf? Indeed he will, and when Gracia appears Pepe tries to tell her of a man who loves her dearly. She mistakenly thinks he is speaking for himself and, flattered by his attentions, responds with warm ardor. Pepe's initial embarrassment turns to enthusiasm, and he ultimately makes a declaration of love on his own behalf in a sensual *Dúo: "Hace tiempo que he leído"*.

Don Basilio successfully tries out one of his nephew's chat lines ("Think of me not as a photographer, but as a doctor") on an attractive young woman, much to Cayetano's amusement; and though Pepa is uncomfortable with her lover's loose morals he half convinces her that is exactly how a sophisticated modern couple should behave. Marriage, for example, is impossibly old-fashioned. But when the smooth radio-announcer Heterodino pretends to announce his engagement to Pepa over the air, the boot is on the other foot and Cayetano becomes violently jealous. A shame-faced Pepe returns, and when Paco asks him anxiously for news he is too tongue-tied to answer his friend clearly (*Mazurka-dúo: "La cosa fue"*).

Pepe is put out of his misery when the girls come back from lunch, and Gracia announces publicly that though they may call her La presumida (conceited), she has given her heart after all—to Pepe! As the brief *Final* begins, the shocked and angry Paco tries to attack his friend, but his master Eugenio holds him back. Before he leaves, he tells Gracia that one day he will gain her love, but La presumida merely laughs at his threats.

ACT 2, SCENE 1—The square, two months later. Things are going along much as usual: Gracia and Pepe have been fighting constantly; Lola, now involved in the arts, is a cause of jealousy between them, spending far too much time with Pepe despite being warned off by La presumida. Cayetano, too, is still enjoying handling the clientele—when Uncle Basilio doesn't get in first. The old photographer and Eugenio the jeweler reassure Paco that everything will turn out for the best, and he sings of his unquenchable hope in a suave *Romanza: "Madrileña graciosa"*.

The ever-hopeful radio-freak Heterodino makes a pass at Gracia, and is warned off in no uncertain terms by Paco. When Gracia mockingly asks him why he has bothered to concern himself, Paco tells her that he has made peace with Pepe and puts loyalty to his friend above any feeling for her. Gracia, impressed, leaves quietly. The older inhabitants confer with Paco and Cayetano about the authorities' warning of possible poison gas attacks on the city from the air. No joke: it seems a full-scale defense exercise is to be held next day, and Paco has already bought his gas mask. Cayetano worries about how a gas attack might affect his inheritance, and he and Pepa agree to have a good time while they have the chance, going dancing and drinking exotic foreign spirits such as whisky and Pernod (*Dúo cómico: "Yo soy una mujer"*).

Gracia taxes Pepe with two-timing and their row develops into a smoldering *Habanera-terceto: "Me llaman la presumida"* in which Paco subtly challenges the girl by seeming to take his friend's side. Eventually Paco persuades her to stay with the actor, much to his own distress. The scene ends as old Don Basilio gets his comeuppance from the Herculean Santi, fiancé of one of his "artistic" sitters.

SCENE 2—Gracia and Paco's adjacent balconies in a downtown tenement, early next morning. It is the day of the civic defense exercise, and Paco and Gracia are getting ready to go out. They enjoy a sparring conversation over her pet bird, and reminisce about the lost chance they had to get together in the gently pointed *Dúo chotis: "Si presumo es porque puedo"*.

SCENE 3—The square, later in the day. The gas attack exercise gets underway. Olga's greengrocery has been transformed into a Red Cross station, while she and the younger women are to act as nurses, supervised by Pepe, though when the siren sounds to start the exercise he and Lola soon disappear. Olga gives Gracia some honest advice: if she will swallow her conceit and forget the feckless actor, Paco is still hers for the asking. Though for how long? She advises Gracia that she must move fast. More busy comings and goings ensue, and when Gracia returns Lola shamefacedly admits that she and Pepe are carrying on an affair. Basilio comes out of the photography shop, wearing his gas mask, for fear of an attack—not from the air but from the local Hercules, who has sworn to break his neck. Olga takes him to task for being a silly, lecherous old man in a lively *Foxtrot: "Un socio le busca"*. Though he can only reply with indistinct sounds from inside his gas mask, deep down he knows he'd be better off with a mature wife like Olga; after all by night "all cats look like leopards"!

The exercise continues, and Cayetano runs on wounded—by a lady client who has given him a twisted arm for his pains. He finally gives in to his fate, making it up with Pepa and agreeing to marry her. Gracia forgives Pepe, who is to marry Lola. An "injured" man is carried in wearing a gas mask. It is Paco, who soon overhears Gracia admitting that she really loved him after all. As the second siren sounds to mark the end of the "gas attack" he removes his mask, Gracia falls into his arms and all the happy couples embrace. Even the announcer Heterodino is left with a good story for his radio report …

The final work in Anselmo Carreño's modern Madrid Trilogy, *Me llaman la presumida* (Call Me Conceited) was the second to be written in partnership with Francisco Ramos de Castro. Not surprisingly, *Me llaman* draws heavily on its predecessor *La del manojo de rosas* (1934) for settings, situations and characters. Both zarzuelas, for example, feature second-act *romanzas* in which a patient baritone hero apostrophizes an errant heroine, Sorozábal's *"Madrileña bonita"* mirrored by Alonso's *"Madrileña graciosa"*. The sense of déjà vu is heightened by further resemblances to the first part of the triptych, *Los Claveles* (1929), whose sharp-tongued shop floor supervisor Rosa is the clear source for Gracia La presumida herself.

In spite of all this, Alonso's *sainete lírico* remains a landmark. The premiere of *Me llaman* was one of the very last before the long-feared Civil War broke out in earnest, and if their writing is more fractured than in the earlier masterpiece, Castro and Carreño vividly depict the carnival atmosphere of the capital just before Madrid was plunged into the vortex. With its gas masks, sirens and air of frantic decadence, *Me llaman* is a work on the edge, a feverish comedy whose characters are in the grip of contrary obsessions, craving both hedonistic freedom and the security of conventional married life.

Given the correspondences between *Me llaman la presumida* and the earlier zarzuela, comparisons between the two scores are inevitable. Though Alonso's music is undeniably simpler and less personal than Sorozábal's, his theatrical and melodic gifts make him very much his own man. With its jazzy riffs, blaring saxophones and blend of modern and traditional dance forms, *Me llaman* is a pivotal work in the composer's output, pointing forward to the lighter style he adopted after the Civil War. The emotional counterpoise of the Act 1 *dúos* and the habanera for the three principals in Act 2 make for a remarkable work which manages to be both diverting and disturbing.

La parranda
Zarzuela in three acts
(Madrid, Teatro Calderon, 28th April 1928)

Text: Luis Fernández Ardavín

Principal Characters: Miguel, a potter (baritone); Aurora, a pottery worker (soprano); Carmela, her friend (soprano); El Retrasao, Carmela's boyfriend (tenor); Manuel, owner of the pottery (actor); Don Cucu, an old usurer (actor).

ACT 1, SCENE 1—The courtyard of a pottery factory in Murcia, in the last decade of the nineteenth century. Following a short, energetic *Preludio*, the curtain rises on a group of workers praising the glorious spring weather on this fiesta day. The owner Manuel, an aging roué, has taken a fancy to Aurora, one of the laborers. Although she is clearly uncomfortable about his attentions, her coldness merely spurs him on. The girl lives alone, and Manuel is fascinated by rumors of a secret past whence she acquired her nickname La parranda: "The Wayward Woman."

Her friend the simple worker Carmela, supported by her even more simple boyfriend El Retrasao ("backward"), reassures Aurora that all will be well. Together with six *botijeros*—makers of those quintessentially Spanish, huge earthenware drinking pots—the couple sing a lively song *"Dame el dineriquio, que yo te guarde"* to cheer Aurora's spirits. A young potter, Miguel, listens thoughtfully, glancing from time to time at Aurora, who seems to return his interest.

SCENE 2—The workshop, some time later. The others have disappeared for their fiesta, and Miguel is working quietly alone. When Aurora appears he takes the opportunity to speak out seriously, and in a passionate *Dúo: "Mirandome en tus pupilas"* they confess their mutual love. Manuel interrupts their idyll, and tries to bully the young woman into compliance. With a rush of blood, the infuriated Miguel runs to her defense, and only the intervention of Carmela and El Retrasao saves the foolhardy boss from serious injury. Naturally he sacks Miguel on the spot, and Aurora bravely decides to leave with him.

Carmela, El Retrasao and the popular local moneylender Don Cuco express their glee at the couple's escape in a *Terceto: "Esta parejita ya me va escamando"*. Manuel, however, determines that he will find out more about this enigmatic beauty. He asks Don Cuco, who seems to know more about the mystery than anybody else, to reveal the truth. This the old usurer tentatively agrees to do—for a price, of course.

ACT 2—Some months later, in the yard of Miguel's farm. The former potter's new calling has prospered, and it is the morning of his wedding to Aurora. Following a subtle *Preludio-nocturno* featuring violin and cello solos, Miguel appears with a festive *rondalla* band. After a noble *Alborada* shared with the leader of the band, the bridegroom launches into his famous song in praise of Murcia (*Canto a Murcia: "En la huerta del segura"*). His bride is dressing for the wedding, and her young friends chaff Aurora on the onerous duties of a married wife as she sings a gentle *Romanza: "Campanitas de la ermita"*.

Aurora is nervous about going through with the ceremony, partly for fear of what her old boss Manuel may be planning. She is about to run away, but Don Cuco prevents her, reassuring her that he knows her secret, and will find a way to put her mind at ease.

The secret is a simple one. When little more than a girl, Aurora was married off by her impoverished parents to a wealthy old man. On the day of the wedding, her drunken husband responded to a compliment from a young buck to his wife by cutting the boy's throat, and has been an imprisoned murderer ever since. Aurora's parents died, and she moved away to start a new life. The marriage was never consummated, as she confesses to the local Curé, Don Vicente. He has no hesitation in declaring the marriage dissolved, and agrees to officiate at the wedding with Miguel. The old workshop boss is still intent on preventing the wedding, but Cuco has been won over by the young couple and tries to frighten Manuel off by mentioning a large debt the man owes. Rather than bear the pain of watching the wedding ceremony, Manuel leaves, swearing to have his revenge: he thinks he already knows enough to act.

Awaiting the bridal pair's return from church, Carmela sings a vocal "Offering" or *Ofrenda*: *"Un regalo a la novia quieren hacer"*. They are greeted with a festive choral ensemble *"Boda de rumbo es esta boda"*, which incorporates the refrain of the happy couple's earlier *dúo*, as well as a catchy song from El Retrasao bawdily insinuating the joys of the wedding night. Aurora's secret is still gnawing at her conscience, though Miguel tries to raise her spirits with an elegantly turned *Romanza* in which he praises his wife's smile as a jewel above price: *"Diga usted, señor platero"*.

Celebrations reach a climax in the traditional Murcian song and dance *las parrandas*, but are rudely cut short by the arrival of Manuel, accompanied by the local police, to publicly accuse Aurora of bigamy. Miguel tries to prevent his wife's arrest, but to no avail. To save her husband from committing violence, Aurora confesses. Don Vicente's assurance that the marriage had ecclesiastical dispensation is not enough to save her from detention. The officials take Aurora away to prison until the situation can be clarified.

ACT 3—The Farm, some days later. Miguel and the villagers are sunk in despair, though they receive a surprising visit from Manuel, now racked with guilt and repenting his jealous action. A general prayer for Aurora's safety is sung to the solemn accompaniment of bells and organ. Aurora herself appears. Don Cuco has saved the situation by obtaining a Papal Edict confirming the dissolution of her first marriage. Finally, news comes that Aurora's first husband has died in jail. The young couple can face the future without a shadow over their marriage. The *rondalla* band strike up again, Miguel gives thanks for his luck in having his lovely wife restored, and the curtain falls as the whole company sing the proud refrain of the *Canto a Murcia*.

La parranda is Alonso's homage to the rich Murcian plain, a riot of flowers and fruit, reflected in music of strong contrasts and vibrant colors. Ardavín's libretto may be little more than conventional rustic melodrama, but it does contain a kernel of strong, convincing motivation for the major characters and good opportunities for the comedy actors. Most importantly, it offered the composer a robust framework on which to hang his tapestry of lively, rural dance rhythms and songs.

Indeed, this is a choral zarzuela *par excellence*, with a generous, theatrical sweep which disarms criticism. The title carries typical double meaning, referring to the heroine's nickname (roughly approximating to "Wayward Woman") as well as *las parrandas*, the Murcian dance which features in the Wedding celebrations of Aurora and Miguel. The music, as with the earlier *La calesera*, sees Alonso's melodic gift at full tide. The inspiration in *La parranda* is just as consistent, the orchestration if anything more subtle and varied. Besides the nap hand of thrilling choruses, there is a fine love duet;

and best of all the gorgeous melodies of the bridal scene, especially the r*ondalla alborada* (dawn serenade) and the powerful, virile Song to Murcia:

La linda tapada (The Veiled Beauty, 1924)
Author José Tellaeche chose seventeenth century Salamanca, with its great university, as the setting for a full-length Castilian romantic drama centering on a mysterious, veiled lady. The varied cast includes the nobility, the military and local militia, as well as groups of actors and students, in a comedy of mistaken identity with happy endings all round. Alonso's varied music is in his happiest vein, and the hero's gypsy-inspired *Canción del Gitano: "En la carcel de villa"* is one of the standards of the baritone repertoire.

La picarona (The Villainess, 1930)
A highly attractive three-act work set in the Segovia region, in the troubled days before the fall of Isabel II (1868). The melodramatic plot centers on a group of bandits led by Maribel, villainess of the title, and her lover Ginés, who are determined to steal the property of the local mayor, Montiel. He himself is in reality a Marquis about to lead the liberal revolt against the Queen, and with the success of the rising all is forgiven. Ginés (tenor) is given the memorable "Song to Segovia," but all three major characters are given fine opportunities by Alonso's characteristic score, darker and more poetic in tone than either *La calesera* or *La parranda*.

La zapaterita (The Little Shoemaker, 1941)
If much of Alonso's work after the Civil War was not at the level of his earlier zarzuelas, *La zapaterita* is something of an exception. Set in eighteenth century Aranjuez and Madrid, the story of Casanova's ultimately unsuccessful attempt on the virtue of a Madrid shoemaker's daughter is a sprightly one—despite the sentimentality of the end, when the virtuous heroine, Marolo, is rewarded by marriage with a rich Castilian nobleman. Alonso's music is elegant and witty in his lighter style. The poetic evocation of nocturnal Madrid sung by Casanova, *"Mujeres de España"*, and a virile choral homage to Vives' famous fandango from *Doña Francisquita* are outstanding.

4
Emilio Arrieta
(1821–94)

The son of a country landowner, Pascual Emilio Arrieta y Corera was born in Puente la Reina, Navarra, on 21st October 1821. Several adventurous trips to Italy culminated in an extended period of study at the Milan Conservatory (1841–5) under various *maestri* including Vaccai. There he became friends with Amilcare Ponchielli, composer of *La Gioconda*, winning First Prize on his graduation and writing *Ildegonda* (1846), a three-act opera to an Italian libretto by the fashionable Temistocle Solera which was successfully performed in several Italian cities.

He returned to Madrid the same year, becoming a fast favorite of the Queen, Isabel II. She appointed the young composer to a succession of posts, culminating in his investiture as first director of the Teatro Real in December 1849, two months after the presentation of *Ildegonda* at the new theatre. A second Italian opera *La Conquista de Granada* followed in 1850, again to a text by Solera. He taught at the Madrid Conservatory from 1857, becoming director after the "Glorious" Revolution of 1868; his leading pupils were Chapí and Bretón, but after the final deposition of Isabel II his influence gradually declined. Two years after suffering a stroke he died at his home in Madrid on 11 February 1894.

Conservative in his politics, passionately Italianate in his musical tastes, Arrieta took little part in the initial establishment of the Teatro de la Zarzuela, though he did contribute a short work *El sonámbulo* (The Sleepwalker) to the new venture in 1856 as well as having a hand in several other pieces. In spite of this he remained a significant rallying figure for artistic opposition to his exact contemporary Barbieri and the other founders of the national school. They in their turn suspected him of subverting their efforts to foster musical theatre in the vernacular, although in time personal relations between Barbieri and Arrieta mellowed.

Not surprisingly, many of his zarzuelas are written in a more Italianate style than those of his contemporaries. *Romanzas* from *El grumete* (The Cabin Boy) and *El dominó azul* (The Blue Domino, both 1853) are occasionally heard; but many of his later successes, such as *El conjuro* (The Conjuror, 1866), *La vuelta del Corsario* (The Corsair's Return, 1861) and *La Guerra Santa* (The Holy War, 1879, based on Jules Verne's novel *Miguel Strogoff*) have sunk without trace. His last significant success was *San Franco de Sena* (Saint Francis of Siena, 1883) to a fine text by his friend and regular collaborator, the great poetic dramatist Adelardo López de Ayala (1828–79).

The eternally popular three-act opera *Marina* (1871, adapted from a two-act zarzuela of 1855) is the one work keeping his reputation alive today. It remains an admirable barometer of Arrieta's artistic personality. Gently mellifluous, elegant and gracious after Donizetti's lighter manner, it offers great opportunities for the leading soprano and tenor, but leaves little space for the more pungent popular musical song and dance forms found in the works of Barbieri and Oudrid. *Marina* certainly requires star singers to bring it to life, and this may be felt nowadays a token of its limitations rather than its undoubted strengths.

Marina
Opera in three acts
(Madrid, Teatro Real, 16th March 1871)

Text: rev. Miguel Ramos Carrión, from the 1855 zarzuela by Francisco Camprodón.

Principal Characters: Jorge, a captain (tenor); Marina, his ward (soprano); Roque, his first mate (baritone); Pascual, a ship's fitter (bass).

ACT 1—First light in Lloret de Mar, a seaside village on the Costa Brava. After a *Preludio* which presents the main themes of the opera, fishermen out to sea are heard singing a song to the dawn. Marina, orphaned daughter of a merchant captain, awaits the return of Jorge, the man who took her in after her father's death. She is in love with him, but as he is older and her guardian she has never dared tell him the truth (*Barcarola: "Brilla el mar engalanado"*). She confesses all to her friend Teresa in the sweetly poised *aria: "Pensar en él"*, before the news that Jorge's ship has been sighted launches her into a *Cabaleta: "Ya sus ojos divisan la playa"*.

Another captain, Alberto, Teresa's father and a friend of Marina's, tells the girls he is sailing away that evening. Marina asks him to give her a letter he had from her father, which she would like to keep as a memento. Alberto gladly agrees and their fond farewells are misinterpreted by Marina's jealous suitor, the ships' fitter Pascual, who considers himself virtually engaged to her. Pascual tells Marina that his rough ways stop him expressing the depth of his love for her, while she admits that the young man's efforts fail to move her. In exasperation she tells Pascual to ask her guardian for her hand: if Jorge agrees, then she will marry him. In reality of course, Marina hopes this will force Jorge into revealing his own feelings for her.

The men and women of the village witness Jorge's landing, and soon enough he arrives with an enthusiastic greeting to his beloved sea coast (*Salida: "Costa la de Levante"*). He recalls his beloved Marina in a gentle *Romanza: "No es verdad que con la ausencia"* before asking where she is. The villagers explain that she has gone to pray for his safe return, and as she runs in he praises her devotion in a lilting *Siciliano: "Al ver en la inmensa"* while Marina prays that her feeling for him may be returned.

Pascual loses no time in telling Jorge that he intends to get married, and just as the older man heartily tells him that he has had the same thought, Pascual names Marina—to Jorge's shock and consternation. Marina is equally hurt that Jorge apparently wants to marry someone else, while Jorge's cynical boatswain Roque comments on the ironies of the situation: anyone who embarks with a woman goes by boat to hell (*Cuarteto: "Alma mía, que has soñado"*). Pascual takes the tearful Marina away to give the news to his mother, and Jorge is left with Roque to bemoan the apparent fickleness of women.

ACT 2—The fitter's yard on the seashore, noon. Pascual's workers sing happily as they work (*Coro: "Marinero, marinero"*). Their master gives them his news, and a holiday to prepare for the wedding. Marina is scarcely able to conceal her distress, and though the workers can see that all is not well, they congratulate her, finish their work and leave, muttering in a Donizettian undertone (*"La novia no parece muy satisfecha"*). After they have gone Marina pours out her heart in a delicate *Romanza: "¡Oh! grato bien querido"*. Alberto reassures her that he will send her father's letter ashore before he leaves, and once again the jealous Pascual misinterprets his concern and rudely cuts him short.

A group of townspeople rush in to praise the happy pair (*Coro: "Cumplido parabién la gratitud"*). Jorge and Roque join them, and the four once more express their conflicting emotions—Jorge bitter, Marina sad, Pascual triumphant and Roque worldly-wise and cynical—in another quartet (*Concertante:*

"Mi mal exapera"). Pascual asks Marina to come with him to tend to her crippled future mother-in-law, and the act ends with Jorge and Marina praying that, in spite of appearances, their hopes may be fulfilled in the end.

ACT 3—A bodega near the beach, that evening. After a poetic orchestral *Preludio* Jorge, Roque and a group of young sailors are discovered drinking themselves stupid to drown their sorrows (*Brindis: "A beber, a beber y a ahogar"*). The sailors leave, and a tearful Jorge tells Roque he can't stand any more. Marina appears, and Jorge asks her savagely if she knows the ungrateful woman who robbed him of his heart. Marina, deeply hurt by her inability to dry Jorge's tears, still fails to realize the cause of his pain. He taunts her by asking bitterly whether she loves him, while Marina asks Roque what woman can possibly have reduced Jorge to this state; but the boatswain is too sozzled to comprehend what is going on.

Pascual and a group of friends appear, with the idea of serenading the bride-to-be. The sleeping Roque, disturbed by the noise, grabs a guitar and sings some suggestive *Seguidillas* with the men which steal the moody fitter's thunder. The boatswain and his friends tell Pascual they're going off to sleep—though not before they finish proceedings up with a lively *Tango: "Dichoso aquél que tiene"*.

Pascual intercepts one of Alberto's crew bringing the letter from her father to Marina; and seeing it is a declaration of eternal love he leaps to the obvious conclusion, curses Marina bluntly and breaks off the engagement before rushing away into the night. Jorge appears, and soon understands Pascual's mistake and the innocence of the letter. When he hints that he will be leaving tomorrow, Marina can no longer avoid giving away the identity of the man she really loves, and in a brief *Dúo* they admit their love for one another. Roque ushers on the villagers, who ask Marina what is going on: is there to be a wedding or not? She replies that only the bridegroom has changed, and leads the company in a joyful *Rondo-final: "Rayo de luz encantadora"*.

On hearing the original 1855 version, Gaztambide wrote to the poet López de Ayala: "Emilio's new zarzuela *Marina* is most outstanding; a true Spanish Opera sure to please the crowd; it will, I'm sure, be much liked." Indeed it was, and when the great tenor Enrico Tamberlick expressed a wish to play Jorge at the Teatro Real, Arrieta had no hesitation in agreeing to expand it into the through-written, three-act form familiar today. Although there is some question whether *Marina*'s charms were improved by the inflation or merely diluted, the operatic version proved an even more resounding success. The plot is a wafer-thin romance, but the perturbations of Marina, her timid lover Jorge, surly fiancé Pascual and the drunken Roque proved so popular that many later zarzuelas, notably Chapí's *La tempestad* (also to a Carrión libretto) and Sorozábal's *La tabernera del puerto*, adopted *Marina*'s maritime setting and romantic ambience.

Arrieta's music is notable for easy charm rather than dramatic thrust. The Act 3 *Preludio* is outstanding, a delicate nocturne featuring a brooding solo for French horn. Roque's *Seguidillas* and the sleepy *Tango* impart a little Spanish seasoning, but the other major characters converse musically at least in the purest Italian. Yet, despite its musical and theatrical limitations, *Marina* obstinately refuses to lie down and die. Much of its appeal is down to the vocal fireworks Arrieta offers his soprano and tenor. Marina's *"Pensar en él"* and final *Rondo* are effective showpieces for any agile lyric soprano, but Jorge in particular has attracted great singers from Tamberlick himself down to Alfredo Kraus. *"Costa la de Levante"* has indeed been called the Spanish equivalent of Otello's entrance in Verdi's masterpiece, a claim which is supported by its need for clarion delivery and stratospheric security.

El dominó azul (The Blue Domino, 1853)
Like many three-act zarzuelas of the period, Arrieta's first notable success in his native language was based on a French original; in this case a Scribe libretto originally set by Auber, with its court intrigues and romantic disguises transplanted to seventeenth-century Madrid during the reign of Philip IV. The best known number is a jeweled, Italianate *Romanza* for the tenor hero, Herman: *"Cuando sus ojos lánguidos"*.

El grumete (The Cabin Boy, 1853)
A sentimental drama in one act, set on the coast of Cantabria, *El grumete* chronicles the love trials of Serafín, the poor cabin boy of the title, and his beloved Luisa, betrothed to a wealthy suitor by her well-meaning father. In the end their problems are sorted out by the intervention of Tomás, the boy's wealthy uncle, and all ends happily. Serafín is an early Spanish "breeches" role; and this mezzo-soprano hero is given the gem of the score, the expressive *Canción "No iré yo al río"*, notable for its insistent barcarolle rhythm and sensitive word setting. Seldom seen nowadays, *El grumete* well merits revival for this and much else in its delightful score.

5
Francisco Asenjo Barbieri
(1823–94)

Francisco Asenjo, born 3rd August 1823 in Madrid, later came to prefer the name of Barbieri in remembrance of his maternal grandfather, manager of the Teatro de la Cruz where the young boy first came into contact with theatre and music. In 1837 he entered the Madrid Conservatory, studying clarinet, piano, vocal and compositional studies, these last under the influential composer Ramón Carnicer. After 1841 he made a living as a peripatetic singer, musician, translator and copyist, writing his first opera *Il Buontempone* (1847). This was in Italian, but later in the same year he founded La España Musical, a society to promote native Spanish opera, and his true life's work began.

As a major step toward his ideal of creating a distinctively Spanish theatrical form he abandoned Italian opera, writing his first zarzuela in 1850. He was central to a group of composers including Oudrid, Gaztambide and Arrieta working from 1851 at the Teatro del Circo, directing the chorus as well as providing many original stage works. The year 1856 saw the founding of the Teatro de la Zarzuela, and from the 1860's Barbieri broadened his activities even further, founding the Society for Orchestral Music (1866) and introducing much of the German symphonic repertoire to Madrid.

He looked to the past as well as the future: his publication of the *Cancionero de Palacio* (1890), a large collection of nearly 500 songs of the fifteenth and sixteenth centuries, served to reawaken interest in the Golden Age of Spanish polyphony. Like Berlioz, he supplemented his tireless musical crusade by publishing a wide variety of books, articles and reviews on music, politics and other topics. He died, honored at home and abroad as the father figure of Spanish music, on 19th February 1894 in his beloved Madrid.

Barbieri's contribution to the renaissance of the nation's cultural life cannot be overemphasized. He was the most influential Spanish composer of the nineteenth century, cultivating the growth of a national musical style quite distinct from its Italianate roots though his series of *zarzuelas grandes* that followed the groundbreaking *Jugar con fuego* (Playing with Fire) of 1851. His music is uneven, but works of the quality of *Los diamantes de la corona* (The Diamonds of the Crown, 1854), *El diablo en el poder* (The Devil in Power, 1856) and *Entre mi mujer y el negro* (My Wife and the Negro, 1859) exhibit increasing dramatic confidence and melodic power. The series culminated in the magnificent national epic *Pan y toros* (Bread and Bulls, 1864); though his comic masterpiece is the peerless *El barberillo de Lavapiés* (The Little Barber of Lavapiés, 1874), a miracle of raw popular spirit, musical subtlety, ironic wit and political fervor which remains one of the best-known zarzuelas at home and abroad. The influence he had over later composers may justly be compared to Glinka's in Russia, revealing new possibilities and paths toward a genuinely Spanish style of composition in all musical fields.

El barberillo de Lavapiés
Zarzuela grande in three acts
(Madrid, Teatro de la Zarzuela, 19th December 1874)

Text: Luis Mariano de Larra

Principal Characters: Estrella, Marquesita of Bierzo (soprano); Don Luis de Haro, her fiancé; Paloma, a seamstress (mezzo-soprano); Lamparilla, a barber (high baritone).

ACT 1—Lavapiés, downtown Madrid, during the summer fiesta of St. Eugene. An ebullient group of street-sellers, young courting couples and students are enjoying the holiday. Lamparilla, local rogue and dentist-barber, amuses the crowd with the story of his checkered career before going on to make some trenchant criticisms of the government of the day: there is a crisis, and the Chief Minister Grimaldi has ordered night patrols and bright street lamps to dampen trouble.

The seamstress Paloma, Lamparilla's girlfriend and another popular figure, arrives with a gracious *Seguidillas* in which she compares her fate favorably with those of the doves after which she is named: *"Como nací en la calle de la Paloma"*. Don Juan de Peralta and Estrella, Marquesita of Bierzo enter in disguise. They are plotting the downfall of Grimaldi on behalf of Count

Floridablanca, but before they can join their fellow conspirators at a nearby inn the Marquesita's fiancé Don Luis de Haro appears. He assumes the worst, but as he is a nephew of Grimaldi the Marquesita cannot tell him what she and Don Juan are really up to (*Terceto: "La mujer que quiere a un hombre"*). The Marquesita and Don Juan slip into the inn under cover of the arrival of a group of *majas* and students; Don Luis, his suspicions apparently confirmed, decides to fetch in the Walloon Guards to investigate and challenges his "rival" to a duel.

The Marquesita comes out of hiding to ask help from her dressmaker and confidante Paloma. She explains the political delicacy of the situation, asking Paloma to introduce her into the fiesta as an obscure cousin and get Lamparilla to take her safely home. When Don Luis and his Walloons are sighted, the Marquesita is saved from discovery by the wily barber, who offers his arm to the veiled lady and takes her into the house opposite. The Guards march in doggedly and surround the inn, but Lamparilla talks Don Luis into a state of numbness before going inside to organize further distractions. As the crowd gathers Don Pedro, Captain of the Guard, has a curtained sedan chair brought up to remove the Marquesita without attracting too much attention. The Walloons rush the inn, and do indeed end up with a prisoner; but the head poking out through the curtains as the act ends belongs—of course—to the ubiquitous Lamparilla!

ACT 2—The piazza in front of Lamparilla's barber shop. The Walloon Guards continue their night patrols, and Lamparilla's customers complain about the disasters that have befallen them at the hands of the barber's assistants during his absence. To their delight, the barber appears; though he is far from clear about how he was allowed to escape (*Canción: "Por salvar ... yo no sé como"*). He boasts that he was imprisoned for breaking the new street lamps; but the truth is that the Marquesita bribed the jailor to set him free, and she again asks Paloma to persuade Lamparilla to join the conspiracy. She will even pay for their wedding; but Paloma, grateful to the Marquesita for providing financial help to her dying mother, wants no payment. In any case the aim of the conspiracy is peaceable: to force Grimaldi to accept a meeting between the King and Floridablanca, so that the latter can explain his ideas of reform. The Marquesita wants Lamparilla to bribe some troublemakers to break the street lamps as a diversion whilst the real action goes ahead. Don Luis questions his fiancée again, but when the Marquesita begs his indulgence for a few more days of silence, he pretends to concede (*Dúo: "En una casa solariega"*) before watching her enter her house across the square to join the other conspirators.

Paloma calls on Lamparilla, and after a poised *Dúo Cómico: "Una mujer que quiere"* ripe with double-entendre, she enters the shop to explain the plan further. Don Luis returns quietly with Don Pedro and his Walloons, who settle down to watch the Marquesita's house and await the right moment to break in and seize the conspirators. Don Luis tries to intercede for his fiancée, but Don Pedro is adamant that everyone must be captured. As the crowd of troublemakers gather, Lamparilla launches into a hyperactive *Seguidillas: "En el templo de Marte"* to disarm the suspicions of the Walloons as they make ready to storm the house; but by now the Marquesita and her friends have had the opportunity to escape through to the shop next door and thence across the roofs to freedom. The act ends in chaos as the Walloons come out of the Marquesita's house, confused as to whether they should be pursuing the conspirators or collaring Lamparilla's rioters, who start smashing the street lamps with enthusiasm as the curtain falls.

ACT 3—Paloma's room in the Calle de Toledo, some days after the failure of the conspiracy. The seamstresses working for Paloma are finishing some skirts. They sing a sweetly bawdy song, ostensibly about Paloma's goldfinch, *"Parajito que estás entre faldas"*, ("Little bird amongst the skirts"). Paloma has been shut up in her house since the failure of the conspiracy, unable to work for her aristocratic clients. Nevertheless, she keeps quiet about her plan to help the Marquesita and Don Luis escape from the city dressed as *majos*. Lamparilla has finalized arrangements, and when the Marquesita appears in her costume Paloma gives her good advice about playing the part. Don Luis is led in by Lamparilla and all four prepare to head for the countryside (*Cuarteto y Caleseras: "El sombrero hasta las cejas"*). Hearing footsteps, they head for Paloma's bedroom just before Don Pedro and the Walloon Guards break in to the mockery of the seamstresses. Moments later, however, the two aristocrats and Paloma are ferreted out. At last Lamparilla, who got away across the roof, bursts in triumphantly with great news—Floridablanca has met the king and been made Chief Minister after all! Don Luis, as nephew of the fallen Grimaldi, must go into exile. The Marquesita will keep faith with her fiancé and go with him, but Lamparilla and Paloma look forward to a happy future together in Madrid as the zarzuela ends in festive rejoicing.

El barberillo de Lavapiés (The Little Barber of Lavapiés) represents at once the finest flowering of the *zarzuela grande* and an evolution away from it. De Larra's text is a well-tailored combination of upstairs and downstairs intrigue, in equal measure passionate, witty and satirical; but his romantic aristocrats are significantly upstaged by their servants in a manner recalling both the Italian *buffo* tradition of *Il Barbiere di Siviglia* and Ramón de la Cruz's *tonadillas*. Initially Lamparilla was to have been a bullfighter by profession, but Barbieri's worry that this would remind audiences too much of the earlier *Pan y toros* (1864) led to his transmogrification into the barber who irresistibly evokes not only Rossini's Figaro, but also the composer's own name. Like Barbieri, the "Little Barber" is a musician, poet and organist — in fact, like his creator, "a bit of everything."

The plot of *El barberillo* is nicely poised between romantic melodrama and scenes drawn from the lives of the common people of Madrid; and its dramatic life comes from this strong sense of place as much as from Barbieri's theatrical use of tuneful popular idioms. Significantly, even the Marquesita and Don Luis are eventually disguised and drawn into the world of the *majos*, so full of that energized, outdoor music peculiar to Spain that is symbolized by the *seguidillas*. Lamparilla's exhilarating example as he and his friends prepare to smash the Italian-style street lamps is representative, a real roller-coaster ride of spirited, nervous energy:

El barberillo is contemporary with the masterpieces of Johann Strauss Jr. in Vienna and Arthur Sullivan in London. Like the latter, Barbieri mixed a potent brew of musical ingredients ranging from Rossini through to the popular music of his own time and place. Indeed, the Walloon Guards with their funny, lumbering bassoon tune have more than a passing musical and dramatic similarity to their first cousins the Police in Gilbert and Sullivan's near-contemporary *The Pirates of Penzance* (1879); and it's little wonder that *El barberillo* has achieved a parallel place in musical history, not only as the comic cornerstone of its national tradition, but also as a universally recognized masterwork of musical theatre.

Jugar con fuego
Zarzuela grande in three acts
(Madrid, Teatro del Circo, 6th October 1851)

Text: Ventura de la Vega

Principal Characters: Duchess of Medina (soprano); Duke of Alburquerque, her father (bass); Marquis of Caravaca (baritone), her foolish admirer; Félix (tenor), her lover.

ACT 1—The Manzanares river in Madrid, sometime in the mid-eighteenth century. It is a summer night, the Festival of Saint John, and well-bred ladies and gentlemen mingle with the crowd on the wooded banks of the river. The young, widowed Duchess of Medina is among them, veiled and disguised as a chambermaid to meet with a young admirer. She is harassed by the Marquis of Caravaca, a foolish, bullying braggart who believes that every woman he meets has only to set eyes on his fashionable clothes and ample figure to fall in love with him. He has seen through the Duchess's disguise, and smugly offers his amorous services, a suggestion which she laughingly rejects (*Dúo: "Si te place de este bosque"*). Her father the elderly Duke of Alburquerque appears, enabling her to melt back into the crowd and leaving the Marquis to boast mendaciously about his new conquest.

Two impoverished hidalgos, Félix and his cousin Antonio, greet the aristocrats. Félix is here for a nocturnal tryst with an unknown veiled beauty who calls herself Leonor. The Duke is cynical, the Marquis starts to put two and two together; but Félix is simply madly in love (*Romanza: "La vi por vez primera"*). The Duke promises to do his best to seek preferment for the young men, and leaves with the Marquis. "Leonor" appears, and when Félix confesses that he is too poor to aspire to her hand, she explains that she is only a poor chambermaid to the Duchess of Medina. Nonetheless, she refuses to permit him too many familiarities as they sing their witty *Dúo: "Hay un palacio junto al prado"*.

When the Marquis blunders into view, Félix sneaks away to order a carriage for "Leonor." She runs straight into her father, and as the *Final* begins is forced to masquerade as a Court Lady to obtain his dubious protection. When the Marquis and some courtiers arrive by torchlight to reveal the veiled lady's identity, the Duke defends her at sword point, but before he can claim his reward Félix has spirited her away, leaving the courtiers to mock the disappointed pair of lecherous aristocrats.

ACT 2—A salon in the Royal Palace of Buen Retiro. Over an orchestral *Introducción* the Duchess discusses her narrow escape with her friend the Countess. The courtiers mock the ludicrous Marquis, who responds with pointed threats to the Duchess. The Countess warns her friend how dangerous an enemy the Marquis may prove. Though she sympathizes with the Duchess's feeling for Félix, she warns her that the difference in rank will surely doom their love.

Félix and Antonio arrive to attend upon the Duke. The Marquis slyly asks Félix how his amorous affairs are progressing, and is gratified when the young man is rendered virtually speechless by seeing that the Duchess of Medina is one and the same with his adored Leonor. The Marquis presents the couple to one another and maliciously enjoys their mutual discomfiture. When questioned by her father, the Duchess denies she knows the young man, who confusedly apologizes for his mistake. However, once alone with the Marquis, Félix complains that the Duchess has played him a cruel trick, and shows his presumed friend a letter she has written to him. The Marquis confirms it is the Duchess's hand, and promises to confront her with it if the young man agrees to watch silently from the gallery above.

The Duchess enters, and is promptly blackmailed by the Marquis. Unless she agrees to marry him, he will reveal all to her father. Once he shows her the letter she has no alternative but compliance, to save both her own reputation and her beloved Félix. Yet though she falls into his arms, she vows to use her feminine wiles to trick this odious enemy (*Dúo: "Por temor de otra imprudencia"*). Félix has seen everything, and utters a cry of despair from the gallery as the *Concertante Final* begins. He confronts the Duchess with her apparent treachery (*"¡Oh, maldad!"*), and despite her pleas calls in her father and the whole court before denouncing her. The Duke decides the only way to save his daughter's reputation is to lock up the distraught young man as a lunatic, a course to which the heartbroken Félix readily agrees. The Duchess herself has no option but to go along with her father's decision, and the Act ends as the gloating Marquis sees his rival dragged away to the madhouse amidst popular enthusiasm.

ACT 3—The central courtyard of the madhouse. Antonio has come to visit his cousin, but while he is waiting in the courtyard the lunatics set on him (*Coro: "¡Suelte, pícaro sastre!"*). He is finally rescued by the Keeper, and when Félix emerges Antonio tells him that he will be freed if he will only sign a declaration admitting his mistake. This the proud nobleman resolutely refuses to do. When Antonio takes him inside the building, two women appear, the Countess and the Duchess, once again in her maidservant's clothes. She pours out her guilt and her determination to right her lover's wrongs in a *Romanza: "Un tiempo fue"*.

When Félix appears, he is amazed to see "Leonor". She half convinces him that she is indeed not the Duchess, and that he should sign the declaration to that effect; but when the Marquis is announced she confesses the truth and her enlightened lover decides to deal with his Machiavellian rival. The Marquis is duly astonished when Félix tells him that the veiled lady is waiting for him in the next room. The Marquis goes to find her, only to be set upon by the lunatics and stripped virtually naked. When the inmates come into the courtyard to auction off his clothes, Félix, Antonio and the Duchess prepare to flee in the confusion—only to be stopped by the Duke, who orders his daughter to cease this shameful folly. She declares that as a wealthy widow she is free to marry whomsoever she likes. Her father retorts that if so, Félix will be locked up for ever. At this impasse the Countess returns bearing a letter from the King. In gratitude for the services of the Medinas to the crown, he has given his blessing to the Duchess's union with Félix. The general joy is augmented when the Marquis rushes in half-naked, pursued by the lunatics and shouting for help. Nobody pays any attention, and the zarzuela ends with his humiliation at the hands of the lunatics and his vow to take revenge on his persecutors (*Final: "¡Quién me socorre!"*).

The night of 6th October 1851 was a watershed in the development of zarzuela. *Jugar con fuego* (Playing with Fire) wasn't quite Barbieri's first zarzuela, but its three-act form and substantial content were immediately recognized to be a significant step forward on the road toward a truly national art form. Objectively, *Jugar con fuego* is a forced marriage of French play to Italian music, yet for the first time a piece in the vernacular proved it could hold the stage as well as any imported opera, and from then on Barbieri was to be hailed as the torchbearer for his country's musical renaissance. Ventura de la Vega was a crucial literary figure in this revival. An habitual borrower from French models, he based his plot and characters very squarely on *La Comtesse d'Egmont* (1833) by Ancelot and Decomberousse. The result may be coarser, more trivial and less plausible than the French *comédie*, but his supple verse and fluid stage sense provided Barbieri with some excellent opportunities for musical drama which the composer grasped with both hands.

Anybody looking for hints of a Spanish style in the score of *Jugar con fuego* will be largely disappointed. The music is almost wholly Rossinian in melodic cut and orchestral texture, though equally energetic, brilliant and tuneful throughout. Barbieri's growing stage sense is readily apparent in the swift-moving and neatly proportioned finales to the first two acts, as well as the marvelously effective closing scene with its burlesque shades of *The Rake's Progress*. Despite the success of his ensembles and choruses, Barbieri's most distinctive musical number is the Duchess's *Romanza "Un tiempo fue"*, a true avatar of things to come with its pronounced tendency toward the melancholy minor, and its lilting bolero rhythms. A sequel focusing on the lovable villain of the piece, *El marqués de Caravaca* (1853) did not meet with lasting success.

Pan y toros
Zarzuela grande in three acts
(Madrid, Teatro de la Zarzuela, 22nd December 1864)

Text: José Picón

Principal Characters: Doña Pepita, the King's mistress (soprano); Princess de Luzán (mezzo-soprano); Captain Peñaranda (baritone); Abbot Ciruele (tenor); The Corregidor of Madrid (bass); Goya, the painter (baritone).

Much of the action of *Pan y toros* revolves around the political crisis in Spain just before the French Revolution in the early 1790s. In the zarzuela, this is simply portrayed as a power struggle between the pro-French party led by Carlos IV's Prime Minister Godoy, keen to sign a peace even at the expense of independence; and the liberal, nationalist wing led by the patriotic Jovellanos, who as the action begins has been packed off as Ambassador to Russia in order to reduce his influence.

ACT 1—The Corregidor's Meadow on the banks of the River Manzanares in Madrid, with Goya's house and studio in the background. After a passionate *Preludio* incorporating the melody of the "Marseillaise," the curtain rises to reveal an animated crowd of *manolos* and *manolas*, young Madrid folk. A family of Blind Beggars cry for alms, a fake Palmer offers blessings from a plaster-cast footprint of Christ, and street-sellers hawk their wares. Despite Jovellanos's absence, the Madrid Corregidor (magistrate) is worried about the increasing activism of the patriotic alliance. He asks the beggars, whose blindness is a ruse, for news. They tell him that a consignment of guns has been taken into Goya's house. The influential royal mistress Doña Pepita comes out of the house and makes her report to the Corregidor: Goya has been entertaining the usual mix of dissident literary and theatre people, aristocrats and bullfighters. The political situation is delicately poised, and the virtuous Princess de Luzán is influencing the populace with ideas taken from the revolutionary philosophies of Rousseau and Voltaire. Their ally General Cruzalcobas suggests the suppression of fiesta processions, but the Corregidor replies that this would work disastrously against them. On the contrary, he himself is arranging a *corrida* in the Plaza Mayor to distract the populace, while soldiers are sent in to root out artists and rebels:

"¡Pan y toros!	"Bread and bulls
a pueblo y aristocracia,	for the people and the nobility!
y en vez de universidades	and in place of universities,
escuelas de tauromaquia."	bullfighting schools."

Pepita discovers from the Duchess of Alba that the Princess's love for one Captain Peñaranda, whom she anonymously nursed back to health in an army hospital, caused her to give up her religious vocation. Perhaps this may be used against her. The crowd surges back accompanying three rival *toreros*, Costillares, Pepe-Hillo and Romero, to the *rondalla* sound of mandolins and guitars. Goya joins the Corregidor while the glozing Abbot Ciruele watches with the Ladies. In a well-known chorus *"Al son de las guitarras"* the crowd truculently greets the Corregidor, and the three bullfighters make their varied pleas for the honor of election as President of the *corrida*. Finally, in a lottery rigged by the Abbot in favor of the Duchess' favorite, Romero is chosen and the Corregidor orders the crowd to disperse.

Captain Peñaranda has returned hot-foot from France with reports warning the King of Godoy's intended treachery. He greets his old friends Goya and the Abbot, a fellow student at Salamanca. The latter explains in a virtuoso, bolero-style song *"Como lleva en el bolsillo"* how he managed to worm his way up to the dignified rank of Abbot. Goya reveals how his art depends on painting not just the aristocracy but the common people, and actresses like the Abbot's mistress La Tirana, going on to lament the mercenary nature of the coterie which is now in power. Their policy of *"Pan y toros"* will make Spain a French colony.

Doña Pepita has been spying on them to discover the Captain's purpose. Coming forward veiled, she insinuates that she is the mysterious lady who nursed him in France; but although the Captain is taken in, he will not yield up his papers. Furious, Pepita reveals her true identity, and the Captain indignantly enters Goya's house. Pepita reports back to the Corregidor and the General, and when the Captain reappears he delivers an impassioned speech decrying the decay into which Spain has fallen. A fight with the General is averted by the sudden arrival of the Princess of Luzán herself. She calms the situation and offers to protect Peñaranda, despite the muttered threats and imprecations of her enemies; and when a chorus of children appears to plead for the life of a condemned soldier the Princess undertakes to raise the matter personally with the Queen. She is hailed as a heroine and led off in triumph as the curtain falls, accompanied by Goya and the whole crowd.

ACT 2—A dark street in Madrid, by moonlight. We can make out the Blind Beggars' cottage, a tavern and a statue of the Virgin. The balcony of a brightly-lit palace is also visible. The fake Blind Beggar and Palmer are drinking outside the tavern, while an aristocratic crowd in the palace makes merry to the strains of a French Contredanse, adorned by subtly smutty verses sung by the Abbot from the balcony: *"La grave contradanza la gusta don Manuel"*. Meanwhile outside the tavern, the bullfighters Romero and Costillares sing a popular song of the time, *"El perulillo"*.

In a scene spoken over music the Beggar tells the Palmer that if he is willing to help murder a certain military man, he will be well paid. The Palmer agrees, but before the two of them can set off, the hellfire rantings of a wandering madman El del Pecado Mortal ("Mortal Sin") strike the Palmer deeply. He has second thoughts, but when the Beggar shakes a purse at him he allows himself to be led away to plan the murder.

Pepita and the Corregidor enter. He has bribed the Beggar's family to allow use of their hovel for a secret meeting of the liberal conspirators. Pepe-Hillo has been badly gored during the *corrida*, and if Madrid were to be distracted by his "accidental" death, it would be easy to act quietly and imprison these self-styled patriots. If the Captain can be eliminated before he sees the King, false reports can be substituted for the truth and the peace with France can be signed.

The Abbot enters the hovel with his fellow conspirators, Goya, the Captain and the Princess herself. Goya urges the necessity of dealing with Godoy's coterie by force to stop the French Treaty, and though the Princess is horrified she agrees it is the only option. The Abbot adds fuel to the fire, pointing out that they must act before Jovellanos has crossed the border on his way to Russia. Goya explains the details of the coup to be carried out by himself, the Captain and a hand-picked band of *manolos*. The terrified Abbot leaves with him to fetch his beloved Tirana out of harm's way. Left alone with Peñaranda, the Princess orders the Captain not to sacrifice his life, but he replies that, despite his gratitude, patriotic duty must come first. She is too proud to urge her love for him, but does offer him the nun's scapular she wore while tending him in the hospital and which she has treasured since as a keepsake. He accepts it fervently in the *Dúo: "Este santo escapulario"*.

Goya returns with his *manolos*, and the Abbot with La Tirana. The Princess begs them to pray to the Virgin before going into action, but as they finish the prayer *"¡Oh reina de los ángeles!"* the Corregidor bursts in with Pepita, the General and his troops. To the coterie's fury, the Captain produces a safe conduct from the King, allowing him to go free. The Princess, however, is to be detained in her Palace, and the rest of the rebels imprisoned.

Everyone except the Captain departs. In another scene spoken over music, he is approached by the Palmer, who begs for his white military cloak to shield a poor man from the cold night airs. Before the would-be murderer can act, Brother Mortal Sin again crosses the stage, confusing him. The Captain hands over his cloak and leaves, just before the Blind Beggar steps from behind the Statue of the Virgin—and stabs the unsuccessful Palmer in the back. The Corregidor is soon on the scene, and finding the evidence of the bloody cloak, announces to all and sundry that "a soldier has been murdered."

ACT 3—Next morning. A state room in the Princess's palace, hung with rich tapestries by Goya. The Princess's waiting women have heard rumors that their mistress is set to enter the royal convent of Las Descalzas; and although the Abbot has not quite given up hope, he cannot deny the truth of the rumors. La Tirana, let out of prison with Goya and the other conspirators by order of the King, tells the Abbot that the Captain has been found dead outside the hovel. Goya enters with Jovellanos himself, who having obtained proof of the coterie's treachery can place his evidence before the King. Even he cannot dissuade the Princess from the determination to take her vows, although he plants a doubt in her mind to the effect that the tales of the Captain's death may prove false.

Pepita arrives, feigning friendship, to make sure the Princess will be firm to her vows. The Princess openly despises her and her politics, but in a magnificent coloratura *Dúo: "Quien cogida es infraganti"*, Pepita argues that as the Princess was caught *in flagrante* with the Captain in a beggar's hovel, her only course is to retire from the world. The Princess accepts her fate, and leaves to prepare for her last journey. Pepita is joined by the Corregidor and the General, who have brought the Town Council to escort the Princess to Las Descalzas. Next on the scene are the Abbot, with the three bullfighters and the *manolos* disguised as a prior and monks, come to stop the incarceration of their beloved Princess. She warns them to attempt no uprising on her behalf as she has finally made up her mind.

The Corregidor, threatened by the *manolos*, produces the bloodstained cloak as final proof of the Captain's death. The last ensemble begins as Pepita and the General congratulate the Corregidor on his cunning, while the Abbot swears vengeance for the death of his friend. The people of Madrid are equally furious with the crimes of Godoy's coterie, and the heartbroken Princess remains determined to retire from the world. Fortunately, at the crucial moment the voice of the Captain is heard offstage, singing the theme associated with the Holy Scapular, which again has protected him from death. The lovers are united, despite the furious threats of Pepita and the coterie.

At length Goya rushes in to announce that the King has appointed Jovellanos Chief Minister in place of the disgraced Godoy. The Captain's disappearance was necessary to catch the ruling clique off guard, and he begs the Princess's pardon, which is readily granted. Jovellanos himself announces that no peace with France will be signed, and that the Corregidor, Pepita, the General and the rest of the coterie are to be arrested. Spain is saved and the lovers finally united, as the curtain falls to the strains of the opening *Preludio* with its insistent reminders of the "Marseillaise."

Pan y toros (Bread and Bulls, equivalent to the proverbial Roman "Bread and Circuses") is in many ways Barbieri's most important work. *El barberillo de Lavapiés* is better loved and much more regularly performed, but *Pan y toros* marked the coming of age of the romantic zarzuela. Picón and Barbieri freed themselves here from those French and Italian textual and musical models upon which they and their colleagues had previously relied; and although the complicated plot remains centered on aristocratic intrigue, *Pan y toros* is a work notable for panoramic social sweep and nationalist fervor as much as for musical originality. Madrid's high and low life are strongly represented; and some vignettes, such as the eerie scenes involving "Brother Mortal Sin," have powerful dramatic resonance.

The three famous bullfighters, Costillares, Pedro Romero and Pepe-Hillo, are most interestingly treated of the large *dramatis personae*. Though bullfighting is seen as a symbol of the decadent state of the nation, the toreros themselves are portrayed as men of the people, whose hearts are very much in the right place. They and some of the other characters are familiar from the canvases of Goya, who himself appears as a highly proactive supporter of the patriotic opposition, and the text presents a vivid portrait of the capital in a tumultuous era.

As for the music, although Barbieri still relies as heavily on Italian forms as in *Jugar con fuego* there is a genuine sense of new wine being poured into the old bottles. Spanish popular dance rhythms, melodic turns and harmonies stand out boldly against the stiffer contredanse and gavotte associated with the French Ancien Régime. Barbieri's use of melodrama (spoken dialogue over music) is strikingly effective, and the whole score—alas, too much of it absent from the one available recording—has that fresh energy common to the best of Barbieri's later work. This music clearly gave Chueca and other composers of the younger generation the confidence to strike out more deeply into the specially Spanish musical terrain that Barbieri had opened up. As a nationalist music drama, *Pan y toros* is a considerable achievement in its own right.

Los diamantes de la corona (The Diamonds of the Crown, 1854)
An early Barbieri zarzuela based on a libretto written for Auber by the leading French dramatist Scribe, *Los diamantes de la corona* has retained much of its early popularity, thanks to a score of superior quality; including one number, the *Bolero: "Niñas que a vender flores"*, which holds its place among the most popular in the repertoire. The story, set in late eighteenth-century Portugal, centers on Princess Maria, the heir to the throne. As "Catalina," she consorts with bandits and pawns her father's crown jewels to give aid to the poor. The zarzuela ends with mass celebrations as Maria is crowned Queen and finally weds the love of her life, the Marqués de Sandoval.

El diablo en el poder (The Devil in Power, 1856)
Francisco Camprodón's complex web of Machiavellian political intrigue, set in seventeenth-century Madrid, is not without its satirical edge. The clever youth Ubilla pretends to be the devil in order to gain the hand of the woman he loves; and his eventual success prompts the thought that Spain would perhaps be better off with such a clever devil as this in power. Barbieri's Italianate score is full of good things, notably the elegant, gently perfumed *Romanza: "En mi ausencia y mis duelos"* sung by the baritone "devil" himself in the first of the three acts.

6
Tomás Bretón
(1850–1923)

One of the pillars of the Spanish musical establishment during the last two decades of the nineteenth century, Bretón was born in Salamanca on 29th December 1850. From the age of fourteen he trained at the Madrid Conservatory, notably under Arrieta, while at the same time acting as music director of an equestrian circus. The 1872 first prize for composition was awarded jointly to him and his future great rival, Ruperto Chapí. After graduation Bretón worked as a violinist at the Teatro de la Zarzuela and in Barbieri's orchestral Sociedad de Conciertos, later gaining experience as a conductor at Arderius' *Los bufos* and with other companies in Madrid and Barcelona.

Eventually he became a leading academic and director of the Madrid Conservatory, director of the Sociedad de Conciertos, and founder-director of the Orquesta de la Unión Artísto-Musical. His orchestral works include the popular suite *Escenas andaluzas*, two fine symphonies and the tone poem *Salamanca* (1916); whilst his serenade *En la Alhambra* (1888) is one of the best works to emerge from *alhambrismo*, the movement which sought to forge the romantic allure of Moorish architecture and culture into a truly Spanish musical style. He also wrote an oratorio *El apocalipsis*, and a quantity of estimable chamber music including the Piano Trio in E minor and String Quartet in D major.

His first opera was *Guzmán el Bueno* (Guzman the Good), performed at the Teatro Apolo in 1875, followed among others by *Los amantes de Teruel* (The Lovers of Teruel, 1889) and *La Dolores* (1895), both of which are occasionally revived in Spain. His many zarzuelas include *El domingo de Ramos* (Ramos' Sunday, 1894); *El reloj de cuco* (The Cuckoo Clock, 1898); *La cariñosa* (The Best Beloved) and *El clavel rojo* (The Red Carnation, both 1899); *Las percheleras* (The Fowlers, 1911) and *Los husares del Zar* (The

Czar's Hussars, 1914). He even collaborated with the popular Chueca and Valverde, in *Bonito país* (Wonderful Land, 1877).

His influence on later Spanish composers has been slight, and his austere, fatalistic melancholy was legendary. On the opening night of his great zarzuela *La verbena de la Paloma* (The Festival of La Paloma, 1894) as the glum composer-conductor arrived in the orchestra pit and took up his baton, he leant down toward the concert master and murmured audibly, "This time I've made a big mistake." He hadn't. Nowadays he is remembered almost exclusively for this one zarzuela that stands as the *locus classicus* of the *género chico*, rivaled only by Chapí's *La revoltosa*. For his orchestral brilliance, tasteful technique and sustained quality of invention, Bretón is justly revered, and *La verbena* presents an unrivaled musical portrait of Madrid in the last years of the century. A follow-up to another text by de la Vega, *Al fin se casa la Nieves* (Nieves Marries at Last, 1895) better gratified the composer's pessimism, proving a complete failure.

La verbena de la Paloma
Sainete lírico in one act
(Madrid, Teatro de Apolo, 17th February 1894)

Text: Ricardo de la Vega

Principal Characters: Julián, a young printer (tenor or high baritone); Rita, his godmother (mezzo-soprano); Susana, a Madrid *chulapa* (soprano); Casta, her sister (soprano); Tía Antonia, her aunt (actress); Don Hilarión, a chemist (comic baritone); Don Sebastián, a shopkeeper (baritone).

SCENE 1—A busy Madrid street, with a chemist's shop, bakery and wine bar. It is the evening of August 14th during the verbena of la Paloma. After a *Preludio* presenting several of the main themes of the zarzuela, the scene opens with Don Hilarión and his old chum Don Sebastián discussing their ailments, the barbarity of modern science, and the insufferable heat in front of the chemist's shop (*"El aceite de ricino"*). Julián and Rita, the barkeeper's wife, converse about the young printer's fatal obsession with the capricious Susana while her husband plays cards. In a heartfelt solo Julián bemoans his jealousy (*"Tambien la gente del pueblo"*) and Rita tries to console him. A janitor and his wife wrangle about putting their child to bed on such a hot evening, some flashily dressed individuals buy doughnuts, *churros* (fritters) and drinks in the bakery opposite. The scene culminates in a celebratory *Seguidillas* as everyone prepares to enjoy the verbena: *"Por ser la Virgen de la Paloma"*.

Julián explains to Rita that he saw Susana riding with a man in a carriage that morning, and that he's determined to make a scene about it. Rita calms him down and after a perfunctory goodbye to her husband drags the young printer off to the verbena. When Don Sebastián accuses the chemist of being a randy old goat, Don Hilarión reveals to his friend his personal philosophy of sex: he doesn't give a fig for public opinion, likes women, and is prepared to pay for his pleasures. They're only too glad to provide them, so everybody's happy (*Coplas: "Tiene razon Don Sebastián"*). In particular he is in pursuit of a pair of sisters, one blonde, one dark, Casta and Susana by name. Left alone, the barkeeper heads off after his wife accompanied by two lady friends.

SCENE 2—A street in the Latina quarter. Casta and Susana sit in the Café de Melilla with their common old aunty Antonia, some neighbors and a couple of policemen, half listening to a *Soledad* sung by a flamenco singer to piano accompaniment (*"¡Ay! En Chiclana me crié"*). The girls compare the rival attractions of Julián and Don Hilarión, before a racket from Antonia's dogs sends them scuttling back to the house.

Night falls. A night watchman and two policemen grumble about local politics as they halfheartedly go about their evening duties (*Nocturno: "¡Buena está la política!"*). Don Hilarión trips in to take the two girls off to the verbena, but before they go he takes a drink with old Antonia and dances to a *Mazurka* played by a violin-piano duo inside the café (*"¡Oh, qué noche me espera!"*). The barkeeper arrives with his friends, then Rita with Julián, fired up to go straight into Susana's house. Rita's sensible advice is that if Susana wants to ditch him there's no point making a fuss about it, so why not let her console him instead? (*Dúo: "Ya estas frente a la casa"*). The printer is incredulous when he sees the two girls flirting with the chemist, and Rita has to hold him back (*Quinteto: "Linda Susana"*). Finally Julián breaks free, and sweeping Susana away from the indignant Don Hilarión asks with heavy irony just where she thinks she is going. A moment of silence—and we are launched into the famous *Habanera Concertante: "¿Donde vas con manton de Manila?"*. Susana gives as good as she gets, Antonia threatens to set the dogs on Julián, and everyone else intervenes to stop him lashing out at the old chemist. Susana continues to taunt the hapless printer, until finally the whole company sweeps off to the verbena.

SCENE 3—The verbena, outside Don Sebastián's shop. Everyone is enjoying dancing to the sound of a barrel organ. Don Sebastián gets trouble from his wife, daughter and the servants, who want to go out to join the party. The printer is scouring the crowd for Don Hilarión, who quickly takes refuge in his friend's shop. The distressed Rita searches for Julián, but Antonia and her dogs find him first, and manage to get arrested by the police for drunken insolence as a fight ensues. Don Sebastián intervenes on behalf of Julián, who goes into the shop to change his trousers which have been torn by the dogs. A moment later the old chemist rushes out, chased by his furious rival. Eventually Susana, Rita and Casta calm him down, the lovers are reconciled, and the verbena finishes in comparative peace as the crowd repeat their lively *Seguidillas: "Por ser la Virgen de la Paloma"*.

Perhaps the greatest zarzuela of all, *La verbena de la Paloma* is an original work by Ricardo de la Vega, whose father had written libretti for Barbieri and his contemporaries. He originally offered it to Chapí, who saw its outstanding possibilities but was unable to set it because of a legal wrangle with his publishers. Chapí's great rival wrote his whole score in only nineteen days, despite its near-operatic intricacy. He later wrote: "I composed it in cafés, taverns, even on benches in the street." Its success was instantaneous and enormous, and *La verbena* has since been performed countless times all over Spain, as well as the Americas. Phrases such as *"¿Donde vas con manton de Manila?"* ("Where are you going in your Manila shawl?") and *"Tiene razon Don Sebastián"* ("You're right, Don Sebastián") have been as proverbial in Spain as Gilbert's "What never? Well, hardly ever!" in England and the United States.

Paloma is a Madrid street, famous for a statuette of the Virgin which performed popularly attested miracles in the late eighteenth century. This was celebrated by an annual verbena, or local religious festival spilling over into dancing and street carnival revelry. Vega's text presents us with a slice of life on such a hot, carnival night, and his characters are drawn from the working people he'd have observed any and every day in Madrid. We meet *chulapas*, young working-class girls smartly dressed for a night on the town; lecherous, well-to-do tradesmen; and Julián, typesetter in a printing works, a model of the educated working-class young man whose honesty and intelligence set him apart from the mob. Perhaps the most vivid creation of all is Seña (Señora) Rita, the sympathetic older woman more concerned for the happiness of her young, former lover—if that's what Julián is—than for her own. All which, of course, is presented in the popular language of the day, and this immediacy is the source of the direct appeal of *La verbena de la Paloma*.

The music is unusually advanced in design and generous in scope for a short *género chico* zarzuela. The complexity of the long first scene reflects Bretón's study of Wagnerian and late Verdian methods, though his material is purely Spanish in rhythmic and melodic cut:

The later ensembles, such as the steamy *Soledad* with its bar piano and hypnotic rhythms, and the ubiquitous *Habanera Concertante*, are even more absorbing musically:

(habanera)

¿Dón - de vas con man - tón de Ma - ni - la? ¿Dón - de vas con ves - ti - do chi- né?

Yet Bretón knows exactly when to make an effect through the simplest means, as in Don Hilarión's little *Coplas*:

Tie - ne ra - zón Don Se - bas- tián,   tie - ne mu - chí- si - ma ra - zón.

The honky-tonk *Mazurka* and the breathtaking *Nocturno*, where the most ordinary of conversations is supported by magical string melismas and flecks of woodwind color, are equally unforgettable. Typically for zarzuela, there is virtually no original music provided for the last scene, but despite this—by operatic standards—imbalance, *La verbena de la Paloma* remains the brightest jewel of the repertoire.

7
Ruperto Chapí
(1851–1909)

Ruperto Chapí y Lorente was born on 27th March 1851 in Villena near Alicante, the son of the village barber. As a true Valencian, Chapí was soon involved in band music, both as a cornet player and—by the age of nine—as a composer and arranger. By fifteen he was conducting the Alicante town band, going to the Madrid Conservatory a year later and studying with Arrieta, his first great champion. Short of funds, he made ends meet playing the cornet in various theatre orchestras, and composed his first zarzuela *Abel y Caín* for the Teatro Circe de Price, where his future great rival Tomás Bretón was an orchestral colleague.

The two shared the First Prize for Composition in 1872, and with Arrieta's help Chapí obtained a commission from the Teatro Real for an opera, *Las naves de Cortés* (Cortés' Ships, 1874) in which the great tenor Tamberlick took part. This is turn produced a scholarship to the Paris Conservatoire; and after the obligatory trip to Rome Chapí returned to Madrid in 1878, where another opera *La hija de Jefté* (Jeptha's Daughter) had been performed two years earlier, and settled into a comfortably successful career.

Chapí's later operas *Roger de Flor* (1878), *La serenata* (1881) and the ambitious *Circe* (1902) have not lasted—unlike some of his orchestral works, notably the exotic orchestral *Fantasía morisca* (Moorish Fantasy), a cogent symphony and a strikingly adventurous tone poem *Los gnomos de la Alhambra* (The Gnomes of the Alhambra). He also wrote chamber music and songs, as well as an oratorio *Los ángeles* (The Angels). In 1889 he had refused to join the Academia de Bellas Artes, partly because of their lax attitude toward royalties, and his 1899 founding of the Sociedad de Autores to protect and administer performing rights remains one of his most durable achievements. He was taken ill while conducting his last opera *Margarita la tornera*

(Margarita the Doorkeeper, 1909) at the Teatro Real and died shortly after, two days before his fifty-eighth birthday.

This last opera is occasionally resurrected, but Chapí's fame largely rests on the best of his many zarzuelas, notably *La tempestad* (The Tempest, 1882), *La bruja* (The Witch, 1887) and *El rey que rabió* (The Raving King, 1891) all of which are three-act *género grande* works. When the shorter *género chico* became fashionable Chapí successfully cut his cloth to match with *El tambor de granaderos* (The Grenadiers' Drummer, 1894), *Las bravías* (The Viragos, 1896) and—certainly his best-loved work—*La revoltosa* (The Troublemaker, 1897). After this his stage works became progressively diluted in quality; though several, especially *La patria chica* (The Little Homeland, 1907), contain much worthwhile music.

If Chapí's musical inspiration rarely runs at a consistently high voltage, his impact on the development of zarzuela and Spanish music in general cannot be overstated. Frequent reminders of contemporary Italian and French taste, wedded to unfailing technical security, lend a smooth finish to his work. Chapí's own musical personality may not be very pronounced, but his strongest music—the famous *preludios* to *El tambor de granaderos* and *La patria chica*, the folksongs and dances of *La bruja*, the whole of *La revoltosa*—has in abundance that spiced, vibrant energy which effortlessly evokes Spain for listeners all over the world. At his considerable best, Chapí remains among the most accessible of the great zarzuela composers.

La bruja
Zarzuela in three acts
(Madrid, Teatro de la Zarzuela, 10th December 1887)

Text: Miguel Ramos Carrión and Vital Aza

Principal Characters: The Witch (mezzo-soprano); Magdalena, an innkeeper (mezzo-soprano); Rosalía, her daughter (soprano); Leonardo, her stepson (tenor); Tomillo, a shepherd (tenor).

ACT 1—Magdalena's Inn in the Vale of Roncal, Navarra, 1697. A *Preludio*, based on the main themes from the work, leads into the first scene. Women are spinning, the men are drinking and playing cards with the local Curé and the young shepherd Tomillo, a lodger at the Inn. His sweetheart Rosalía, Magdalena's daughter, is prevailed upon to sing the tale of the beautiful

Princess Zulima, daughter of a Moorish King of Granada, whose Christian lover contrived to bear her away from the Alhambra with the miraculous aid of the Virgin (*Canción: "Pues señor, este era un rey"*). When Tomillo responds with a story about his encounter with an old Witch who lives at the nearby castle the Curé is horrified, but the shepherd defends the woman, who has saved a sick child and does nothing but good. The Curé leaves, and the inhabitants of the Inn settle down for the night. Eventually Magdalena dozes off, giving the young lovers the chance to flirt together (*Terceto* and *Dúo: "Chito, que ya mi madre ... Hora que en calma"*). Magdalena sneezes and wakes up, telling Tomillo once and for all that if he cannot raise at least a hundred doubloons, he will never marry her daughter.

Leonardo, Magdalena's stepson and heir to the inn, comes in fresh from hunting. He tells Tomillo why he has been so distracted lately. Sleeping on the riverbank, he had a vision of a beautiful woman bathing. She fled into the forest, but since then he cannot get her beauty out of his mind (*Relato: "En una noche plácida"*). Tomillo tells him to forget his dream, but Leonardo assures him that the Witch has told him that he will win both love and fortune. So Leonardo has spoken with the Witch, too? Yes, she cured him from a fever he contracted after seeing his vision, and comes to help him every time he blows three blasts on his horn. After Leonardo falls asleep, Rosalía creeps in to ask Tomillo how they should avert her mother's threat. Tomillo bravely steals Leonardo's horn and sounds it three times before his friend is awake enough to stop him. The old Witch materializes. She agrees to help the couple, producing a bag of gold from thin air containing the necessary hundred doubloons and more. Leonardo is strangely moved by her kindness, and Tomillo and Rosalía offer extravagant thanks before they leave (*Cuarteto: "Cual siempre a tu llamada"*).

The Witch confesses to Leonardo that she is the girl of his dream, and tells him her story. As Blanca de Olvedo, a young girl at Court, she attracted the attentions of four noble suitors but rejected them all. In revenge, they paid a sorceress to enchant her by adding their combined ages to her own. Although she looks ancient, her heart is still that of a young girl of sixteen, and the spell may be broken if a man does great deeds for love of her alone. Leonardo swears to win fame and fortune with the Spanish army in Italy, and thus free her from the enchantment. To help him on his way the Witch gives him a ring to show to the General, the Duke of Savoy (*Dúo: "¡Así, así te quiero yo!"*). In a solo passage of extraordinary beauty (*"Adiós, risueños campos"*) Leonardo expresses his deep regret at having to leave the land where he had thought to live and die; but he is resolved to free her from the enchantment, or perish in the attempt.

When the Witch hears musicians approaching to celebrate the union of Tomillo and Rosalía, she disappears up the chimney. Leonardo announces that he must leave for the wars, much to everybody's surprise, and the Act ends with his famous *Jota navarrese:* "¡*Ay, canto alegre de mi país!*", in which melancholy praise of his lost homeland alternates with the wildly energetic celebrations of the villagers.

ACT 2, SCENE 1—The village, two years later. The villagers are celebrating the midsummer fiesta, and the bells of the little church ring in honor of the Virgin. Tomillo emerges from the church praying God to stop sending him children: Rosalía is so fertile she's already provided him with three. The villagers congratulate the happy parents, and Magdalena invites them back to the Inn to celebrate the fiesta. There is talk of the King's sickness. He has apparently been enchanted, and they wonder whether their local Witch might be responsible, though Tomillo defends her stoutly. After the opposing *pelota* teams of Roncal and Biscay sing together in friendly rivalry, the villagers leave to watch the game.

Leonardo appears, now a brave captain. He sings of his joy at finding the village unchanged (*Romanza: "Todo está igual"*). Leonardo tells Tomillo how he has proved himself worthy of the love of the Witch, whose story was well known to the General, and sets off for the castle. The villagers celebrate the victory of their team, but their zortzico dance is interrupted by the arrival of an Inquisitor and six constables, asking the way to the Curé's house. As he unwillingly tells the villagers to guide the Inquisitor to the castle to arrest the Witch, Tomillo and Rosalía go swiftly ahead to warn their benefactress.

SCENE 2—Leonardo arrives at the castle and blows his horn. The Witch, delighted that her champion has succeeded in his quest, feels her blood stirring and youth returning (*Dúo: "Circula en mis venas"*). Their joy is interrupted by the arrival of Tomillo and Rosalía, who warn the Witch about the approach of the Inquisitor and his minions. She retires into the castle as the Inquisitor's party arrives. When he calls for the doors to be opened in the name of the Holy Office, a beautiful young woman appears, dressed in white. It is the Witch, transformed back to her proper shape as Blanca de Acevedo, who chose to live here in her ruined family castle rather than go into hiding when she became bewitched. The Inquisitor says she must answer the accusations of witchcraft, and she gives herself up, warning the frantic Leonardo to put his faith in God's mercy. Blanca is taken away to the city of Pamplona, leaving Leonardo and his friends in despair.

ACT 3, SCENE 1—The citadel of Pamplona, two nights later. Army officers are enjoying a drinking bout to celebrate the peace, and though Leonardo feels very far from happy he leads them in a *Brindis: "La dicha y la calma"*. Leonardo tells his fellow officers that due to the machinations of the Inquisition Blanca has been condemned to penance for life as a nun in a nearby convent, and they offer to help him rescue her before she takes her final vows.

Rosalía and Magdalena bring news. They have been unable to see Blanca, but have discovered from a friendly Sacristan that the whole convent has been in a hysterical uproar since her arrival. The Sacristan has told the Mother Superior that a holy friar is on his way to exorcise the girl. Thus disguised, Leonardo is to visit Blanca and assure her that help is on the way, leaving the rest to Tomillo, who now arrives, also dressed as a friar. The conspirators disperse as the soldiers return to celebrate the evening retreat with a rousing "Rataplan" *Coro: "Retírase el soldado"*.

SCENE 2—The dormitory of the convent. The young pupils and their teachers pray that the devil may be cast out, and in a whispering chorus they chatter about a demon and three witches who have been seen flying around the walls. "Friar" Tomillo comes in with Rosalía and Magdalena, bearing a letter for the Mother Superior asking her to accept Rosalía as a postulant. They discover the exact whereabouts of Blanca's cell as the pupils announce the holy friar's arrival—Leonardo, dressed as a Franciscan. Explaining he must be alone with the girl, he opens Blanca's cell and lets her out. She feels that she must submit to becoming the Bride of Christ; but Leonardo begs her to keep faith in his love, while Tomillo leads the prayers for Blanca's soul and reports to the nuns on the successful progress of the "exorcism." When Leonardo leaves, Tomillo frightens the girls by telling them that now Blanca's demons are on the loose, they'd better lock their doors at night. The Mother Superior asks Rosalía and her mother to stay overnight with Tomillo within the convent walls, before she and the pupils retire nervously to their cells.

Blanca prays alone in her cell (*Plegaria: "Inquieto late el pecho mío"*). A bell rings, and the frightened pupils quickly lock their doors. Tomillo, Rosalía and Magdalena enter disguised as witches. They sing and dance to frighten the girls thoroughly before knocking on Bianca's door. She comes out draped in black, and the "witches" whisk her out of the convent (*Terceto: "¡Zahorí! ¡Zahorá!"*). The pupils rouse the Mother Superior and the nuns, telling them that Blanca has been spirited away by three witches. The nuns go to ring all the bells, but are interrupted by a cannon shot from the citadel. Captain Leonardo enters with Tomillo and a troop of soldiers. The cannons are announcing the death of the old King and rise to power of Philip V; and when the Mother Superior implores him to help find the girl who has been captured by the witches, Leonardo tells her that the age of witches and demons is over—the girl who occupied the cell was the last ever witch, and the Age of Enlightenment has arrived! The nuns disperse to pray for the soul of the late King, and the curtain falls to a recapitulation of the Inquisitor's music from the previous act.

Carrión's *La bruja* (The Witch), written in a mixture of lively prose and the Italian-decked verse of the day, is a strong mixture of rustic comedy, high romance and the supernatural. The writer was unable to make up his mind about how to finish his zarzuela, and left it to his friend Vital Aza to provide the cheaply farcical conclusion. Perhaps Carrión was unwilling to subject his sympathetic Witch to a tragic fate, but the tongue-in-cheek rationality of the happy ending sorts ill with the supernatural frissons of the earlier action.

In spite of this flaw *La bruja* is one of Chapí's most admired scores, a pinnacle of the *zarzuela grande* tradition. It is dedicated to the great violinist Pablo Sarasate, "Pride of Navarra, glory of Spain and darling of Europe," praise which might be accorded the work as truly as the dedicatee. *La bruja* proved sufficiently large in scope and conventional in its operatic forms to enjoy something of a vogue outside Spain, at least for a few years. Chapí's music maintains a high standard of excellence through to the none-too-bitter end. All of it is intelligent, theatrical, and solidly constructed. Two numbers, the first *dúo* for Leonardo and the Witch, and the impressive *Jota navarrese*, are considerably more than that, containing music of high imaginative power. Chapí's trick in both cases is to conjure up a shimmer of uncertain tonality under repeated semitonal shifts in the melody, to hauntingly memorable effect. Little wonder that the *Jota navarrese* in particular remains one of most admired of all zarzuela numbers:

La patria chica

Sainete in one act
(Madrid, Teatro de la Zarzuela, 15th October 1907)

Text: Serafín & Joaquín Álvarez Quintero

Principal Characters: José Luis, a painter (tenor); Españita (comic tenor); Mariano (baritone); Pastora (soprano); Pilar (mezzo-soprano); Ansúrez (comic baritone); Mr. Blay (actor).

SCENE 1—After a substantial *Preludio*, recalling Spain's proud history, the curtain rises to reveal a garret in turn-of-the-century Paris, home and studio of a young Spanish painter, José Luis Romero. The painter is trying to put the final touches to a canvas requested by a rich Englishman (*Romanza: "Mujer de vulgar historia"*) but is distracted by the antics of Españita, an old Spaniard long domiciled in Paris who often visits the attic to get away from the taunts of a sharp-tongued wife. The two men discuss the enigmatic character of the rich Englishman Mr. Blay, who so admired one of José Luis's early Spanish portraits that he promised money to the impoverished painter if he agreed to make this copy for him. The evocative figure makes Españita homesick for the Andalucia of his birth.

More Spanish émigrés arrive in search of the painter. Pastora, Pilar, Mariano and Ansúrez are four members of a flamenco troupe brought to Paris by an unscrupulous impresario. After the failure of the show, the performers were left to fend for themselves. Penniless and hungry, the four have no means of returning to Spain and have come to appeal to the painter for help. He calms them down, and explains that their best hope is to allow him to finish his painting and sell it to the Englishman.

To while away the time Españita sings the visitors a Spanish song which he has written to console himself in his troubles (*Coplas y Quinteto cómico: "Yo soy español"*). Fired by his patriotism, Mariano and Pastora argue passionately as to whose part of Spain has the best landscapes, festivals and songs, he in Aragonese *jota* style and she in an Andalucian *soleares* (*Dúo: "Pom pom ..."*).

José Luis finishes his painting just as Mr. Blay arrives. The émigrés crowd round, begging him to buy it and enable them to return to their beloved Spain. The Englishman is not impressed, especially when Ansúrez sings a frantic gypsy song in order to persuade him to part with his cash (*Canción castiza: "Un dolorcito que tengo no lo curan melecinas"*) and its cool reception only deepens their plight. Pilar fares little better with a modest prayer to the Virgin (*Plegaria: "Al virgen santo del Pilar"*) and it is only when Pastora throws caution to the winds and sings him a teasing little love song (*Canción: "Te quiero"*) that Mr. Blay changes his mind. He will pay for their repatriation—on condition that Pastora stays with him in Paris.

The proud Aragonese Mariano objects on behalf of his erstwhile sparring partner, and appeals to the Englishman's sense of fair play: the Spaniard's way is all for one and one for all, so if Pastora cannot leave, none of them will. They will not buy their freedom with her dishonor. Blay is impressed by this demonstration of Spanish pride and changes his mind. He will defray their expenses and accompany them himself, attempting to win Pastora's heart through his own merits. The *sainete* ends with a brief but ecstatic finale, led by Mariano, with all the Spaniards singing the tune of the trumpet call from the *Preludio* (*Final: "A que hable mal de España"*).

Few openings are more evocative than the distant trumpet calls of Chapí's *Preludio* for *La patria chica* (The Little Homeland); and though the Álvarez

Quinteros' slight one-act *sainete* is set in contemporary Paris, it is intensely redolent of all things Spanish. No wonder that the characters' little recreation of their homeland in a cold French garret has gained a special place in the hearts of émigrés around the world.

The score was Chapí's last major success. Like many of his later zarzuelas it makes up in solid construction what it lacks in fresh melodic inspiration. Having said which, the thrilling *Preludio* is among his most masterly orchestral essays in thematic as well as formal power. Although the succeeding solo numbers do not match this level there is much attractive music, notably Pastora's epigrammatic *"Te quiero"*, one of the deftest songs in the repertoire and a guaranteed encore triumph for any Spanish soprano up to its tricky technical demands.

La revoltosa

Sainete in one act
(Madrid, Teatro Apolo, 25th November 1897)

Text: José López Silva and Carlos Fernández Shaw

Principal Characters: Mari-Pepa "La revoltosa" (soprano); Felipe (baritone); Cándido (baritone); Gorgonia, his wife (actress); Tiberio (tenor); Encarnacion, his wife (actress); Atenedoro (baritone); Soledad, his fiancée (soprano); Candelas, a police officer (actor).

SCENE 1—After a spirited orchestral *Preludio*, based on the main musical themes of the zarzuela, the curtain rises on the courtyard of a tenement building in the poor quarter of Madrid, on the night of the summer verbena. We meet three couples, the tailor Cándido and Gorgonia, Tiberio and Encarnacion, Atenedoro and Soledad; and a highly attractive, provocative young woman called Mari-Pepa. Without really intending to, she has alienated the affections of the three males, who vie for her favors in reasonably friendly rivalry. Their wives, led by the outspoken Gorgonia, are not surprisingly on the warpath against this girl they call La revoltosa ("troublemaker"). Her other admirers among the residents include the local officer of the *Guardia*, old Signor Candelas, and an unattached young man, Felipe.

Cándido, Atenedoro and Tiberio are playing cards with Felipe in the cool of the evening, delicately evoked by the orchestra. As soon as they think their wives are out of the way, Atenedoro gets out his guitar and plays a

LA CORRALA, LAVAPIÉS MADRID

SGAE

EN EL ESCENARIO DE UNA CORRALA COMO ESTA
NACIO LA REVOLTOSA
LOPEZ SILVA, FERNANDEZ SHAW
Y EL MAESTRO CHAPI LA INMORTALIZARON
LA SOCIEDAD GENERAL DE AUTORES DE ESPAÑA
HONRA LA MEMORIA DEL INSIGNE COMPOSITOR
RUPERTO CHAPI
EN EL 75 ANIVERSARIO DE SU MUERTE
MCMLXXXIV

serenade under Mari-Pepa's window (*Seguidillas: "Al pie de tu ventana"*). Gorgonia overhears the men and shouts at them to shut up, and the neighbors take up her mockery. When Mari-Pepa herself emerges onto a balcony and throws some of the sarcasm back into the women's faces, things threaten to turn nasty. Felipe tries to calm things down, but the jibes turn into a general verbal altercation between all the men and their women. Candelas emerges from his room in full uniform to break up the racket, ordering everyone to disperse. He pompously lectures the card-players about their marital duty, is soundly jeered at and indignantly retreats. The men continue to play, the women light the lamps outside their houses and bid each other good night.

Felipe mocks his neighbors for their obsession with a worthless, amoral cat like Mari-Pepa when they have such beautiful, intelligent and loving wives (or fiancées: Atenedoro is still only engaged to his Soledad). They ridicule him for his failure to appreciate Mari-Pepa's stunning looks and great body. When she comes down the stairs and starts flirting with the other three, Felipe throws in his hand and leaves in disgust. The men vie for Mari-Pepa's favours in a pleasingly patterned *Quarteto: "La pobrecilla"*. She teases them mercilessly, playing each one off against the others as their suggestive insinuations become more and more outrageous. After working them up into a sexual frenzy, she agrees to give them an answer "soon," and goes back inside.

The women have had enough. They come back down to try and bully their men back into line. Gorgonia pleads with Candelas to lay down the law to the destructive trollop, and he agrees to lecture Mari-Pepa, despite objections from the men. When it comes to the point, however, La revoltosa twists the old official round her little finger, and soon has him more besotted than the rest. The furious women give her a tongue-lashing, though Mari-Pepa gives as good as she gets, until Felipe comes out to restore peace by flattering the wives at La revoltosa's expense. She, of course, is maddened by his cool indifference. Meanwhile Gorgonia is hatching a mysterious plot with Candido's apprentice boy Chupitos, and the scene ends with the women determined to band together to defeat their dangerous rival and put the men in their place.

SCENE 2—Later that evening, outside a doughnut shop. Mari-Pepa is riled by the sight of Felipe chatting up two young *chulapas* over a doughnut. She frightens them off and the two combatants exchange a brilliant series of studied taunts and veiled come-ons. They each describe the lover of their dreams, and enjoy their sparring match so much that when they separate, it is with some reluctance. The next couple to appear on the scene are less happy: Cándido has been lurking in the doughnut shop following Mari-Pepa, and is caught sneaking out by the vigilant Gorgonia. His wheedling and her incensed fury afford a contrast to the lively wit of the younger pair, until finally Cándido is dragged back home under a rain of blows.

SCENE 3—The tenement courtyard that night. After the popular *Intermedio*, a fast and furious orchestral dance, the final scene begins calmly with the distant voice of Soledad, heard singing a lively street song lamenting the treachery of the male once the woman has given him her all (*Guajira: "Eso le pasa a las hembras"*). All the inhabitants are enjoying the evening, singing and dancing (*Coro: "¡Olé los niños con esbeltez!"*). Candelas is coming on to Soledad, and Chupitos is putting Gorgonia's plan into action, secretly whispering to the eager three and Candelas that Mari-Pepa will meet them privately in her room at ten o'clock. Soledad sings another two verses of her song (*Guajira: "Cuando clava mi moreno"*) as the chorus clap and sing along with her. The errant husbands and hypocritical Candelas give various excuses to hang around outside, while Chupitos and the three wives pretend to go into the street to join their neighbors at the verbena.

Felipe appears. He can't stop thinking of Mari-Pepa, but how far can he trust such a woman? Is she really as bad as she seems? She comes in suddenly, and taken unawares the pair drop all reserve, and admit their true feelings in a warmly sensual *Dúo: "Por qué de mis ojos"*, which moves from hesitant probing to a triumphant celebration of mutual passion. Soon, however, Felipe's jealousy reasserts itself, Mari-Pepa's pride is stung, and the two are at one another's throats again before storming off to their respective rooms.

It is nearly ten o'clock. Chupitos looks round the street door. Seeing the coast is clear, he ushers the wives back up to Soledad's apartment to enjoy the fun (*Escena: "No hay nadie, adentro"*). The four Lotharios, sneaking toward Mari-Pepa's room, run up against one another in the dark, and suspiciously separate again. Felipe, despairing at the thought of losing his love, comes out in time to spy Candelas creeping back along the balcony. When the old lecher knocks on Mari-Pepa's door Felipe goes for him, and an immense row erupts, involving a frightened Mari-Pepa, Candido, Tiberio and Atenedoro as well as their three women, Chupitos and all the neighbors, who run back in to see what the trouble's about. Before Felipe can do murder, Gorgonia explains: Mari-Pepa is innocent, the whole thing is a plot to trap their husbands and the disgraceful Guardian of the Peace. The domestic drama is done. The women look likely to forgive their men, Candelas reasserts his shredded dignity, and the two young lovers bring down the curtain at the end of the *sainete* with a plea to the audience to "pardon its many faults."

Three years after Bretón launched *La verbena de la Paloma*, his great rival Chapí produced a highly effective counter-thrust with *La revoltosa*. These two masterly *sainetes* are the inseparable heavenly twins of zarzuela, comparable in popularity to their Italian equivalents *Cavalleria Rusticana* and *Pagliacci*; and it might well be argued that the Spanish works match the Italians in originality, theatricality and substance. *La revoltosa* shares with *La verbena* a contemporary setting, a combative central passion between two well-suited lovers, and a rich farcical underlay of *madrileño* low-life lechery.

The text of *La verbena* had to be passed on to Bretón due to contractual difficulties, much to Chapí's chagrin; but the story that much of *La revoltosa*'s music was composed earlier with de la Vega's libretto in mind is alas untrue (if anything, it would have ended up in the contemporary *El tambor de granaderos*). The difference between the two great works is one of musical scale. Bretón's music is integral to the play, and has muscle enough to stand by itself. The score of *La revoltosa* lasts only thirty-five minutes, and a fair amount of that is given over to orchestral interludes and street songs, though the substantial and sophisticated *dúo* for the sparring lovers lies at its musical heart:

The libretto is of classic quality, brilliantly combining Shaw's poetic sensibility with Silva's boisterous street argot, but it needs the stage to bring it to full life. Nonetheless, Chapí's atmospheric music has wit and huge vitality, so *La revoltosa* has enjoyed constant and well-merited popularity. It has been the inspiration for several films as well as providing the template for a whole hatful of highly enjoyable *género chico* imitations. Mari-Pepa herself has been a role model for Madrid's justly proud women for more than 100 years, even down to having clothing, cakes and fizzy drinks named after her!

El rey que rabió
Zarzuela in three acts
(Madrid, Teatro de la Zarzuela, 21st April 1891)

Text: Miguel Ramos Carrión and Vital Aza

Principal Characters: The King (soprano, or tenor); Rosa (soprano); Jeremías, her cousin (comic tenor); The General (baritone).

ACT 1, SCENE 1—A room in the palace of the King of an imaginary country. The courtiers enthusiastically greet their King, newly returned from a royal progress through his domain (*Coro: "Al monarca esperamos"*). He relates that everyone in the realm seems content, and the courtiers echo his satisfaction (*Coplas: "¡Cuándo el alma se recrea!"*); but left in private with his Chief Minister, Treasurer, Admiral and General he demands the truth about the state of the nation. Rather than contradict their rosy reports he resolves to undertake another journey, this time incognito, on foot as a peasant. When the horrified ministers refuse his request he leaves them with a threat: if they cannot approve, he will accept their resignations. In a delicious quartet the ministers reflect on the terrible consequences resignation would bring, at least to them personally, and decide they won't stand on principle after all (*Cuarteto: "¡La dimisión!"*).

The General has a further bright idea: rather than resign, he will accompany the King on his travels, quietly arranging matters to keep up the appearance of a happy, benign state. The Admiral and Treasurer gossip about the King's foolishness, and their indignation at being overheard by a simple shepherd turns into embarrassment when this turns out to be the King himself in disguise. Ignoring them, he sings a "Pastoral Idyll" in which he praises the simple life of the fields, quietly undermined by the two ministers (*Idilio pastoril: "Soy un pastor sencillo"*).

The General appears, disguised as a cowherd. In an act of supreme self-sacrifice, he has shaved off his moustache, and is roundly mocked by the others for his pains in a "Laughing Quartet" (*Cuarteto de la risa: "¿Quién es?"*). The King orders the ministers to keep silent: the army in particular must know nothing about his journey. With cries of "Long live freedom!" he and the General set off on their travels.

SCENE 2—A town square. Outside the Town Hall the people are protesting noisily against increased taxes. Their Alcalde (Mayor) proves unable to pacify them, and agrees to plead on their behalf with the provincial Governor. The foolish innkeeper's boy Jeremías is crying because he has been called up for military service. His cousin and fiancée the Alcalde's daughter Rosa comes in carrying a pitcher to the well, and the pair join in a romantic verbal colloquy, by the end of which Jeremías is once again crying: this time for joy as Rosa renews her promise to marry him.

The disguised King and General praise the tranquil peace of the town square, and when the King overhears Rosa's sweet singing as she returns from the well he addresses some romantic couplets to her—much to Jeremías' jealous sorrow (*Cuarteto: "El chorro de la fuente"*).

The people stream out of the Town Hall singing the praises of the Governor, who has remitted their taxes as promised and proclaimed a holiday.

The King joins in a zortzico dance with Rosa, Jeremías weeps loudly and the General waxes indignant. Before he can pull the King away, a platoon of soldiers arrive to collect the new recruits. Jeremías points out the "shepherd" as another likely lad, and much to Rosa's horror her new lover is pressed to join. The General loyally volunteers too, and all three march off with the soldiers as the act ends (*Final: "Ahí llega ya la música"*).

ACT 2, SCENE 1—A castle courtyard at dawn. Reveille sounds. The General asks how his monarch slept in the barracks: "Sound as a dormouse" comes the depressing reply. The Alcalde arrives with Rosa, come to steal a word with her shepherd on the pretext of visiting her cousin. She sings of her changing emotions in the poised *Romanza: "Mi tío se figura"*. The King slips out to join her, and they avow their determination to overcome all obstacles in a radiant *Dúo: "Mientras con los reclutas"* before absconding.

When the news breaks Jeremías starts crying and runs after them. The tormented General reveals his true identity and that of the deserting soldier to the Captain of the troop—who responds by putting him on a charge as a drunken liar and sending him off to jail! In the nick of time the Governor arrives, the long-suffering General is freed, and everyone goes off in pursuit of the errant King.

SCENE 2—The courtyard of a farm. A group of reapers are heard in the distance, singing of the joy of harvesting, and they are soon welcomed by Juan and María, the farmer and his wife (*Coro y solos: "Andando, segadores"*). The fugitive lovers are among them, and Rosa sings a spirited harvest song (*Canción: "Por entre las mieses"*). Seeing the King and his love canoodling, María firmly instructs the foreman to make sure that the men go to the haystacks to sleep, the women to the kitchen.

Over a poetic *Preludio nocturno* the reapers leave. María locks the door and looses her dog, which barks furiously when a stranger comes knocking at the door. It is Jeremías, pursued by his Captain and urgently seeking sanctuary in the farmhouse (*Raconto: "¡Por Dios! ¡Por la Virgen!"*). María agrees to hide the lad in the dog's kennel, and when the disgruntled animal bites him hard Jeremías screams out for help, a moment before his Captain arrives with the General searching for a deserter (*Quinteto: "Buenas noches"*).

When María gives the game away the Governor and General depart, leaving it to their junior officer to recapture the King, despite the fact that the Captain does not know him by sight. The King, overhearing from the haystack, points out Jeremías as the "deserter," and when the Captain reverently asks Jeremías to return to the palace by carriage the bitten and baffled youngster obliges. Juan accompanies them, carrying the dog to be tested for rabies by the court physicians.

ACT 3, SCENE 1—The palace garden. The court pages comment on the King's absence, and four of their number pass on the gossip that the King has been carried back in a carriage, with a rabid dog which is to be sent off for examination by the Royal Physicians (*Coro de pajes: "Compañeros venid"*). The General greets his fellow ministers and fills them in on the adventure. The dog is produced, and the doctors immediately get to work examining it with learned certitude and unanimous agreement: either the dog is rabid or it is not (*Coro de doctores: "Juzgando por los síntomas"*).

SCENE 2—An antechamber. The real King has returned, determined to continue the deception until he is sure his beloved will accept him for what he is. He sings of his hopes and fears in an ardent *Romanza: "¡Intranquilo estoy!"*. Rosa is ushered in, determined come what may to plead with the King for the life of her beloved shepherd. Jeremías is brought in by the Captain, and bewails his confusion at being brought here with all the courtesy due to a king. Rosa agrees to ask the King to pardon him as well as her shepherd; but when the King eventually enters, to the shock of Jeremías and shame of Rosa herself, it is he who begs her pardon for the deception (*Terceto: "Mi amor, mi bien, mi dueño"*).

When the ministers and courtiers come in, the King clears up any remaining confusion: after all, if once upon a time there might have been *"El rey que rabió"* (a "raving" or "rabid king"), such a thing is surely impossible in the modern world. Even the dog is given a royally clean bill of health! When the Treasurer announces that three foreign embassies have come to offer suitable brides, the King threatens to go mad for real; but he calms down quickly, and agrees to behave in statesmanlike fashion.

SCENE 3—The throne room. The King receives ambassadors from Scotland, Italy and Russia, each bearing portraits of lovely prospective brides. He replies gracefully but finally interrupts the charade by claiming Rosa as his Queen. "Impossible," cry the ministers, "she isn't even an aristocrat!" The King answers that he has made her a Countess, and the ministers bow to the inevitable as soon as the word "resignation" is mentioned. Jeremías, though glad that the dog isn't rabid after all, goes out crying, but the zarzuela ends in a brief hymn of praise to the King and his bride.

Ruritanian romance is a staple subject for light musical theatre, whatever the language. Three-act *zarzuela grande* boasts its fair share of good operettas; and of these *El rey que rabió* (The Raving—or Rabid—King), has deservedly held its place of honor. Carrión's text, completed like *La bruja* by Aza, is a sophisticated mix of gentle satire, broad comedy and genuine romance with a strong debt to French *opéra comique*. The characters are clearly delineated individuals, the plot is clever, the structure sound; and Carrión certainly inspired his composer once again to give of his entertaining best.

Although he was more of a musical chameleon than his most distinctive contemporaries, Chapí's theatrical range was perhaps greater; and it is hard to credit that the hand which penned the fantastic, poetic *La bruja* could also be responsible for the brooding melodrama of *La tempestad*, let alone this subtly seasoned comedy. *El rey que rabió* is perhaps more varied in mood than any of his scores. The poised *romanzas* and *dúos* for the King and Rosa; the witty choruses of pages, and doctors examining the luckless dog; the poetry of the Reaper's scene; the desperate patter-song for the comedy tenor—all are among his most distinguished pieces. The "breeches" title role was written for the popular soprano Almerinda Soler, although today it is more often sung by a tenor or baritone. It's also worth noting that the pivotal role of the Dog was originally played not by a canine actor, but by one Prieto, a member of the Teatro de la Zarzuela chorus!

La tempestad
Zarzuela in three acts
(Madrid, Teatro de la Zarzuela, 11th March 1882)

Text: Miguel Ramos Carrión

Principal Characters: Simón, an innkeeper (baritone); Angela, his ward (soprano); Roberto, a sailor (soprano); Claudio Beltrán, a wealthy stranger (tenor); Mateo, a sailor (comic tenor).

The action of *La tempestad* takes place in a port village in Brittany, during the early years of the nineteenth century. It centers on the death of a rich merchant arriving from the West Indies during a tempest some twenty years earlier, murdered and robbed as he struggled to land with his baby daughter. She was left in the care of the miserly, taciturn innkeeper, Simón, who claimed to have seen a young villager commit the crime. By next morning the man had fled, never to be seen again.

ACT 1—Inside Simón's Inn. After a *Preludio* depicting a violent tempest, the curtain rises to reveal the women of the village. They pray to the Virgin for the safety of their menfolk, whose voices are heard out to sea as they struggle to bring their boats safely into port (*Coro: "Estrella de los mares"*). To everyone's relief the storm eases, the boats land safely, and the cheerful Mateo leads the other sailors in a spirited drinking song (*Coplas: "La carga y el pasaje salváronse por fin"*).

The sailors praise the young fisherman, Roberto, for bravely saving the life of a passenger on a stricken barkentine. He modestly replies that the sea was his cradle, so why should he be afraid of it? (*Estrofas: "Hijo soy del mar salobre"*). The villagers carry him away in triumph, and Mateo describes his heroism in ludicrously graphic detail to Simón's housekeeper Margarita. The local Justice and Town Clerk, sheltering from the storm, recall the unsolved crime, which took place in weather similar to today's. Margarita tells them that the orphaned child of the wreck, Angela, is now grown to a fine young woman and the brave Roberto's sweetheart. The storm blows itself out, and everyone goes about their business.

Simón, who had locked himself away during the tempest, reveals in a brooding monologue that, though the skies have cleared, his own soul is still wracked with the storms of guilt (*Monólogo: "La lluvia ha cesado"*). He jealously opposes Roberto's plans for his adopted daughter, but once the old man leaves the youngsters take advantage of his absence to indulge their dream of love in the mellifluous *Dúo: "Cuando en las noches del estío"*, with its gentle barcarolle rhythm.

When Simón interrupts their idyll, making it clear that he will not give his treasure up to a penniless sailor boy, Roberto tells the heartbroken Angela that he must seek his fortune in the New World. They leave, and the gray-haired passenger Roberto saved from the wreck comes in. He is Claudio Beltrán, the man who fled the village as the suspected murderer that fatal night, but who now returns with a fortune from the West Indies. In a deeply felt, graceful *Romanza* he blesses the coast of his birth, despite the pain it has cost him (*"Salve, costa de Bretaña"*).

Angela is drawn to the stranger, and when he discovers the reason for her sadness Beltrán agrees to endow Roberto with a large sum of money in order to allow them to marry. The sullen Simón feels powerless to prevent the good deed, but is disturbed by the stranger's look: where can he have seen him before? (*Cuarteto Final: "Un hombre soy que debe"*).

ACT 2—Outside the Inn. Wedding preparations are underway, and the villagers gather to honor the happy bride with a dawn serenade (*Alborada: "Llegad, llegad ... Despierta, niña despierta"*). Mateo sings a *Coplas: "Ha comprado veinte casas"* extolling—and exaggerating—the catalogue of Beltrán's wealth and generosity. He is keen to press his own suit with Margarita, but she wishes to remain loyal to her bitter old master. Simón refuses to have anything to do with Angela's marriage, and in a spoken monologue he reveals his increasing unease. Beltrán gently pleads with him to attend the church ceremony, but is answered scornfully.

The bridegroom, Roberto, arrives with his friends. In the freshly delicate *Coro: "En busca de su novia"* they greet the bride and bridesmaids. Despite Simón's objections, the marriage has taken place, much to Beltrán's delight. He presents Angela with a beautiful collar of Brazilian diamonds, though she feels that her face is better reflected in Roberto's eyes (*Terceto: "Diamantes brasileños"*).

The Justice gives his blessing, but Simón stands out as the specter at the feast by contributing a doleful ballad about the drowning of a pair of newlyweds in a tempest (*Balada fantástica: "¡Din, don! ¡Din, dan!"*). The villagers, sickened by his black humor, go off to dance, while Beltrán finally tells something of his story to Simón and the Justice. The innkeeper is horrified, realizing his only course is to deflect suspicion away from himself by revealing Beltrán as the fugitive murderer.

In a dramatic interruption of the dance, Simon accuses Beltrán, whom the Justice has no option but to take into custody. In the impressive ensemble which follows, Beltrán's passionate declaration of innocence is seconded by the prayers of Roberto, Angela and the villagers. Only the haunted Simón knows the truth (*Final: "En tanto que los novios salen acá"*).

ACT 3, SCENE 1—The steps of the village courtroom. The villagers solemnly describe the scene as Beltrán is brought in by the gendarmes; and in the lively passage that follows the women go on to describe the bad dreams that his likely fate—death by guillotine—has given them (*Coro: "Esa es la puerta ... En cuanto me acuesto"*). Roberto and Mateo are determined to free Beltrán once the verdict goes against him, by breaking into his cell through the wall of the Inn.

In her reflective *Romanza: "Con él mi esperanza va"*, the heartbroken Angela reflects on the dangers Roberto is running for their erstwhile benefactor, who after all apparently killed her own father. The verdict is brought in, and Beltrán emerges to proclaim that he dies innocent. Joined by Roberto and Angela, he puts his faith in God and blesses the young couple in a final embrace (*Terceto: "Al borde del sepulcro"*).

SCENE 2—Inside the inn. It is the middle of the night, and Simón broods sleeplessly over the horror of his compounded guilt. A tempest seems to howl in the air, and he has a vivid dream of Angela's dead father and his own terrible crime, graphically described in a stormy *Intermedio*. The vision recedes, leaving Simón in a fitful sleep. Mateo enters through a hole in the wall with Beltrán, and tries to persuade him to hide until Roberto has a boat ready for their flight; but the honorable man will not agree to place the others in jeopardy by escaping, and goes back to his cell. Mateo, left alone with the sleeping Simón, is shocked to hear a full confession from the old innkeeper, still in the grip of his dream. He runs to tell the Justice what he has heard.

SCENE 3—The courtroom. Simón fiercely protests his innocence, but the recurrent vision of the dead man forces him to break down and confess all. He is taken away to be judged, and as the innocent Beltrán is restored to the arms of Mateo and the devoted young couple the zarzuela ends with a brief orchestral *Final*.

Carrión always denied hotly that his well-made play owed anything to Erckmann-Chatrian's *Le Juif Polonais*, the sensational novel which was the source for Leopold Lewis's famous Victorian drama *The Bells* (1871). The guilt-wracked Simón is certainly close kin to burgomaster Mathias, the role which made Henry Irving the most famous English actor of his time; but in fairness Carrión's plot with its maritime flavor derives little more from the novel, so perhaps his righteous indignation was justified. Though Simón is much the most memorable, Carrión's romantic and comic characters are uniformly strong and attractive—though admittedly the saintly behavior of Beltrán may stretch modern credulity.

La tempestad is the earliest of Chapí's major scores to remain in the repertoire. As with the libretto, commentators have pointed out its reliance on French sources; and indeed the lilting saxophone tune in the *Preludio* (from the lovers' Act 1 *dúo*) strongly recalls Bizet's use of the instrument in *L'Arlésienne*. True, there's no special flavor here to differentiate Chapí's music from many operas of the time; but nowadays reminiscences of Meyerbeer and Gounod are not so obvious as the composer's nodding acquaintance with Wagner's *Der Fliegende Holländer*, happily recalled by his fresh, lively choral writing and intensely theatrical storm music.

The most original music in this attractive score is Simón's Act 1 monologue, *"La lluvia ha cesado"*, with its reminders of Rigoletto's *"Pari siamo"* in its gradual evolution from brooding recitative to halting, lyrical arioso:

¿Por qué,___ por qué tem-blar?   ¿Por qué,___ por qué tem-blar?

The young hero Roberto is a "breeches" role, and his exquisite *Barcarola* with Angela is one of a very small number of soprano duets in the repertoire. The tenor's *Romanza* in salute to his beloved coast is equally memorable; the choruses and ensembles are varied and well put together. Altogether, *La tempestad* is several musical notches up on Arrieta's not dissimilar *Marina*; only its melodramatic tone and the scenic demands of the last act account for its comparative neglect.

El barquillero (The Wafer Seller, 1900)
With its hero Pepillo torn between his poor wafer-seller's apron and the attractive uniform of a soldier, this gentle *sainete* effectively mixes the low-life Madrid of *La revoltosa* with the military vigor of *El tambor de granaderos*. The heroine, Socorro, goes against her mother's wishes in preferring Pepillo to a rich cad, a dilemma which prompts her *"Cuando el amor se apodera del alma de una mujer"*, the finest number in the score—and indeed in its understated nobility and subtly insistent syncopations, one of the most hauntingly memorable *romanzas* in the entire zarzuela repertoire.

Las bravías (The Viragos, 1896)
Shakespeare's *The Taming of the Shrew* is relocated to contemporary Madrid in this slight but effective *sainete* by the authors of *La revoltosa*. Patro is the *madrileño* Kate, Lucio her Petruchio. The joy of *Las bravías* is its colloquial, realistic language and general vivacity rather than any special musical distinction. Much of the writing is spare; although the music Chapí provides for a mocking chorus of laundresses is memorably spiteful, and there is an epicurean duet for the pair of subsidiary lovers, Primorosa and Gurriato, lightly accompanied by pizzicato strings.

La chavala (The Lass, 1898)
Written by José López Silva and Carlos Fernández Shaw, the team responsible for *La revoltosa*, this one-act *sainete* has many of the virtues of the earlier masterpiece, though its plot is slight. Its portrayal of contemporary lower-class Madrid life is equally pungent, its characters sharply three-dimensional. Unfairly, it owes its survival to just one song, the *Canción de la gitana: "Fue mi mare la gitana"* sung by the heroine Concha, whose mother, a gypsy from Seville, never forgot the memory of her beautiful homeland through many years of cruel drudgery in the capital city.

Curro Vargas (1898)
The theme of "The Indian"—the young village boy seeking his fortune in the New World and returning rich to his native soil—is exploited in several zarzuelas, of which Chapí's three-act tragedy is the most famous nineteenth-century example. The dramatic quality, range and variety of his score has led many critics to consider it the crowning achievement of the whole *zarzuela grande* tradition, which makes its subsequent neglect all the more regrettable. The *Preludio*, with its pronounced Andalusian flavor, is occasionally heard; as is the poetic tenor *Romanza: "Soledad mía"*, in which the returning hero addresses his former fiancée, married in his absence to a rival suitor.

Las hijas del Zebedeo (The Daughters of Zebedeo, 1889)
The confusions of this neat little two-act farce center round the true identity of the illegitimate daughter of Zebedeo, a Madrid restaurateur. Luisa, the scatterbrained heroine at the centre of the imbroglio, cannot be played by an equally scatterbrained singer; for Chapí gives his soprano one of his most technically challenging and effective songs, the *Carceleras: "Al pensar en el dueño de mis amores"*. A *carceleras* was originally a prison lament, but Chapí's witty conceit is to turn it into a breathless song of amorous frustration. His song has been a guaranteed showstopper for Spanish *divas* ever since.

El milagro de la Virgen (The Miracle of the Virgin, 1884)
Chapí's most operatic three-act zarzuela has a sensational plot encompassing rape, sudden death, destitution, murder and a blinding—or so it seems. All is revealed in the last scene to have been the heroine's dream while under the influence of a sleeping draught administered midway through the First Act, and everyone ends happily. Alas, this farrago is the reason for the eclipse of some of Chapí's best music. Only the hero's *"Flores purísimas"*, an exquisite *Romanza* recorded by many great tenors including Caruso and Kraus, keeps the zarzuela's name alive today.

Música clásica (Classical Music, 1880)
This early comic skit takes its tone and style from the eighteenth century Spanish *tonadilla* tradition. The wily Paca tricks her father, Tadeo, into sanctioning her marriage with the ne'er-do-well Cucufate, by convincing the music-mad old man that her lover is a great composer. This allows Chapí the latitude to drag Beethoven's *Pastoral* Symphony, Mendelssohn's *A Midsummer Night's Dream* and several other heavyweight classics into his score; as well as some delightfully light, Rossiniesque numbers of his own.

El puñao de rosas (The Handful of Roses, 1902)
With its Cordovan country setting and colorful score, this one-act piece is among Chapí's most immediately attractive works. Stylistically it looks forward to the *verismo* simplicity of Serrano's zarzuelas. The lilting rhythms of the *Intermedio*, and the following offstage chorus of muleteers replete with mule bells and drivers' cries, are most evocative; so also are the Andalusian-flavored songs and *dúos*. The plot, in which the simple Tarugo ("Blockhead") saves his girl from the clutches of a predatory Gentleman, partly centers on the boy's well-meaning theft of a bunch of roses from the altar of a local hermitage.

El tambor de granaderos (The Grenadiers' Drummer, 1894)
The bracing, martial opening of the *Preludio* to *El tambor de granaderos* remains one of the most instantly recognizable in the repertoire; its military spirit imbues the whole plot of this dashing romantic comedy, set in the turbulent last days of the Napoleonic occupation of 1808. The patriotic drummer-hero escapes execution when Napoleon's brother, José I, familiarly known to *madrileños* as Pepe Botella ("Bottle") is deposed in favor of the Bourbon King Ferdinand VII. Chapí's music is in his most direct and lively vein, and his integration of the familiar tunes of the *Intermedio* within the single act of the zarzuela itself is most expertly accomplished.

La venta de Don Quijote (Don Quijote at the Inn, 1902)
Reputedly Chapí's own favorite amongst his many zarzuelas, this one-act comedy brings together the original Quijote and his creator at a La Mancha inn, which the confused gentleman mistakes for a magnificent castle, its sluttish maidservant Maritornes for a princess. The adventure inspires Cervantes (who also appears in Guerrero's *El huésped del Sevillano*) to begin writing his great epic. Chapí incorporates some earlier music intended for a symphonic work on the subject, and finishes the zarzuela in grand style with a musical representation of Don Quijote's later assault on the La Mancha windmills.

8
Federico Chueca
(1846–1908)

Chueca was born 5th May 1846 in Madrid's Casa de los Lujanes, a squat tower in the ancient Plaza de la Villa where his father was caretaker. At the age of eight he was enrolled at the Madrid Conservatory, and by the following year some of his little piano pieces were attracting the attention of the local press. Nonetheless, on leaving school he adopted a less chancy career, starting medical studies at the San Carlos in 1862. Managing like many other students to get arrested in the infamous Saint Daniel's Night Uprising of 1865 (an event recalled in Galdós' great novel *Fortunata y Jacinta*) he used his time in jail to compose a waltz sequence boldly called *A Prisoner's Lament*. Barbieri heard this, liked it well enough to orchestrate it, and changing the title to the more urbane *Cupido y Esculapio* (Cupid and Esculapius) introduced it at the outdoor Teatro Rossini to great effect.

Chueca's adoption of Barbieri as a father figure is thus hardly surprising. The death from cholera of his earthly parents in 1867 forced Chueca to give up medicine and rejoin the Conservatory, where he paid for his studies by playing piano at the Café de Zaragoza. In 1868 he composed a *Hymn to General Prim*, which as the March from *Cádiz* was finally adopted as a quasi-national anthem by the military in 1896.

In 1874 Chueca became conductor of the Teatro de Variedades, and shortly afterward began a fruitful collaboration with Joaquín Valverde in the brief *El sobrino del difunto* (The Deceased's Cousin, 1875). The many works they wrote together over the next fifteen or so years include the three-act *Los barrios bajos* (The Low Suburbs, 1878); the hugely successful *La canción de la Lola* (Lola's Song, 1880); *Fiesta Nacional* (National Holiday, 1882); the patriotic two-act *Cádiz* (1886); *El año pasado por agua* (The Year Under

Water, 1889); and most influential of all *La Gran Vía* (1886), which celebrated the construction of Madrid's fashionable new thoroughfare in an original mix of satire, popular song and dance.

In 1885 he became conductor of the Teatro Apolo, increasingly working alone, and devoting much time to the infant art of photography, of which he was a skilled exponent. The best of his later zarzuelas include *El chaleco blanco* (The White Waistcoat, 1890); *Las zapatillas* (The Slippers, 1895); *La alegría de la huerta* (The Pride of La Huerta, 1900) and his last major success *El bateo* (The Baptism, 1901). He died of complications arising from diabetes on June 20th 1908, to be buried with great pomp and circumstance at the Cemetery of St Justo, a man nationally mourned and admired. The Madrid Plaza which bears his name is situated next to the Calle Barbieri, a token of his friendship with "My Father in Music" of which Chueca would have been justly proud.

Chueca's training was piecemeal, his grasp of compositional technique imperfect. But what he lacks in musicianship he makes up for in melodic verve, wit and sheer cheek. His partnership with Valverde is one of the most successful in nineteenth-century theatre music, and perhaps the main role of the older composer was to add a patina of orchestral polish to Chueca's lively inspiration. At all events the sheer *joie de vivre* of their zarzuelas is irresistible, especially the famous "street party" of *La Gran Vía* with its string of popular dance forms: polka, waltz, tango, jota, mazurka and chotis. The greatest of the post-Valverde pieces is the scintillating *Agua, azucarillos y aguardiente* (Water, Meringues and Spirits, 1897), a vivid celebration of streetwise Madrid that sounds as fresh now as the day it was written. If one composer can be said to embody the Spirit of Madrid, Chueca is that man.

Agua, azucarillos y aguardiente
Sainete in one act
(Madrid, Teatro Apolo, 23rd June 1897)

Text: Miguel Ramos Carrión

Principal Characters: Asia, a young poetess (soprano); Doña Simona, her mother (mezzo-soprano); Don Aquilino, their landlord (actor); Serafín, Asia's admirer (comic tenor); Pepa, a stallkeeper (soprano); Manuela, a water seller (soprano); Lorenzo and Vicente, their lovers (baritones).

SCENE 1—After a vivacious *Preludio* the curtain rises on an ordinary Madrid lodging room. Asia, an ardent young woman with literary ambitions, is reciting her latest poem to a pet goldfinch. An unsuccessful addiction to publication has led her and her mother, Doña Simona, into financial difficulties; and Simona is relieved to have received a letter from Asia's rich uncle, ready to tear up their IOUs on condition that Asia agrees to marry his bumpkin of a son. The furious Asia pronounces that she belongs either to her beloved Serafín, or to the tomb. Mama, however, entertains serious doubts as to Serafín's intentions. True, he has taken them both out for evening treats in the Recoletos Gardens, including the *azucarillos* (meringues) to which she is so partial, but there has been no mention of that vital little word "marriage." If he says nothing tonight they must leave Madrid for good, and go to the rich uncle in the sticks whether Asia likes it or not.

Their waggish landlord Don Aquilino comes to demand the long overdue rent. Doña Simona tells him that Asia has written a poem in praise of the *botijo* (Madrid's special drinking pot) which is bound to be a big hit in one of the Madrid comics. Don Aquilino counters that unless he gets something on account by next day he will send in the bailiffs. Doña Simona desperately pleads that Asia's fiancé Serafín, the son of a former minister, will bail them out. Aquilino knows Serafín well—he lent him four thousand pesetas himself only yesterday! The fellow will be rich when his father dies, but until then he too is living off IOUs, paid for by his grandmother. The landlord congratulates them a little guardedly on their good fortune, and leaves. So there it is: Asia sees that Serafín must prove his devotion to her in practical, not poetic terms: "Oh how Horrible is the Prose of Life!" The drop curtain falls, and we read Asia's ludicrously effusive sonnet "The Apotheosis of the Botijo" during the orchestral *Intermedio*.

SCENE 2—A drinks stall in Recoletos Gardens. It is a warm evening, and the gas lamps are lit. The scene opens with the brilliant and varied Chorus of Nannies (*Coro de Niñeras: "Tanto vestio blanco"*) in which a harassed group of nannies and wet-nurses bewail the fact that they've been forced to bring their troublesome young charges to the Park by "the señoras," while the children variously shout at them, sing songs, and demand to be taken to the rest room. Finally the harassed nannies drag the truculent infants away.

The stallholder Pepa and her boyfriend, out of work picador Lorenzo, are in dire straits. They, too, owe Don Aquilino the rent, and if they haven't paid by tomorrow they will lose the stall. Lorenzo is insanely jealous of Pepa's customers especially the "young whelp" Serafín, who spoke very intimately with her the night before. She explains that he was offering her a hundred pesetas to lace Doña Simona's meringue with a sleeping draught, to give him the chance to abduct Asia. She refused indignantly, but Lorenzo points out that the money would cover the overdue rent. If only they could find a way of getting the money without doing the deed ...

Serafín eventually appears. He reveals that the carriage for abducting Asia is already arranged, and Lorenzo blackmails the "whelp" into handing over double the money he offered to Pepa before he will agree to administer the opium draught to Doña Simona. Vicente, a former lover of Pepa's, comes to parley with the picador. There have been angry scenes between her and his jealous new girlfriend Manuela, an itinerant spirit vendor, but Vicente promises that Manuela won't cause any more trouble and wheedles Lorenzo into accompanying him to the gambling club where Vicente is doorman. The two men sneak away quietly, taking half the money with them.

Manuela herself is next on the scene, bawling out her wares: *"¡Agua, azucarillos y aguardiente!"* ("Water, meringues and spirits!"). She is spoiling for a fight, and her verbal duel with Pepa is threatening to get out of hand when the appearance of two policemen puts a stop to the row. Manuela beats a retreat, and the policemen, though complaining vehemently about the rule not allowing them to drink on duty, have to make do with glasses of water from the law-abiding Pepa. They leave as Doña Simona and Asia arrive for the assignation with Serafín. Simona has decided to ask him for a large loan to see them out of their trouble: as he's unlikely to pay anyway, she might just as well be hung for a sheep as a lamb. A group of *barquilleros* (boy wafer sellers, played by the female chorus) march on. They describe their working methods and clientele in the celebrated and shockingly naughty *Coro de barquilleros: "Vivimos en la Ronda de Embajadores"* before prancing off to make new sales.

Pepa breaks the news of Serafín's dastardly abduction plan to the horrified women, who agree to play along while Pepa administers the opium to him instead. The "whelp" arrives, and Pepa whispers that Mama has already eaten her laced meringue. When Simona starts to feign drowsiness, the lovers take the opportunity to drink *zarza* (blackberry liqueur) together, Pepa having poured the drug into Serafín's glass. In the delectable Waltz-Quartet which follows, Serafín charms Asia back into a state of doubt, while Simona and Pepa become increasingly incensed by his villainy (*Vals: "¿Está dormida?"*). Doña Simona pretends she fancies a little walk to clear her head, Serafín starts to yawn uncontrollably, and the three of them leave the stall.

Don Aquilino sees them going, and gloats that tomorrow he will effectively get his own money back from Simona with interest! Pepa calls him over and redeems her own IOU with another of the bank notes he lent to Serafín. Drawing the conclusion that Pepa must be another of Serafín's women, the chuckling Aquilino goes off home elated with his good luck. Asia and her mother return, reporting that the drug has taken effect and Serafín has slumped unconscious onto a bench. Asia, tragically disillusioned, accepts she must resort to those hated relations in the country, much to Doña Simona's relief. They leave quickly.

The long *Final* begins with a chorus of theatergoers grumbling about the interminable length of the evening's play (*Mazurka: "Ya es más de la una y media"*). A little Italian beggar boy breaks into a cheap Neapolitan song to his own harp accompaniment, but the crowd find Pepa's Spanish singing more entertaining, and curtly tell him to get lost. Manuela comes back, and there is another verbal duel between her and Pepa, which everyone enjoys hugely (*Panaderos: "Ya esta ahí la Manuela"*). Violence is imminent when Lorenzo and Vicente reappear (*Cuarteto: "Vamos a ver, ¿qué ha paso?"*) but the two men quickly calm their women down. There are tears and embraces, and all is made well between them. The men's gambling luck has been in; they have redeemed a pair of their girlfriends' manila shawls and suggest they all go off to enjoy the San Lorenzo verbena, an idea which is joyfully accepted (*Pasacalle: "Pa que veas, Manuela"*).

As the street lights dim, three shadowy figures appear (to the pickpockets' theme from *La Gran Vía*) carrying Serafín's waistcoat, trousers and jacket. Discovering his wallet, they gleefully scamper off just as the "whelp" himself is hauled in by the shocked policemen—wearing just his underwear! The zarzuela ends with the befuddled, unwitting exhibitionist being dragged off to enjoy a night in the cells.

"*Agua, azucarillos y aguardiente*" was a common cry of street vendors in turn of the century Madrid, and Carrión's great *sainete* evokes its time with matchless verve (the American version's *Water, Candy and Brandy* captures the flavor well). The virtue of his unpretentious one-act social comedy lies in the simple, unsentimental thrust of its action. Though the satire is genial enough, the writer was not afraid to hold up the pretentious hypocrisy of the literary middle classes to ridicule; and in a world where everyone seems financially up against it, the down-to-earth, cynical practicality of the street vendors—and even Don Aquilino the money-lender—comes across as comparatively honest. *Agua* ... may be lighter in tone than the other two great zarzuelas written at about the same time, *La revoltosa* and *La verbena de la Paloma*, but it yields nothing to them in generosity of spirit.

Chueca's music is appropriately direct and tuneful, and none the less evocative for that. Modern musicologists have pointed out the unobtrusive skill with which the various numbers—pasodoble, waltz, pasacalle, mazurka—effectively make up an integrated dance suite. Nobody has ever needed to point out Chueca's tight theatricality and musical zest. The street cries, choruses and ensembles give the score of *Agua, azucarillos y aguardiente* a perennial appeal which a century has not dimmed. The brilliant waltz-quartet is typical of its freshness:

The street cry *"Agua, azucarillos y aguardiente!"* itself is memorably bawled out from behind the curtain toward the end of the popular medley-overture—and in case anyone is curious about *azucarillos*, they are substantial meringues delicately flavored with cinnamon, lemon and other fruits, then folded into the shape of boats. What's more, they are still available for ready money in at least one shop in Madrid's Calle Mayor!

La alegría de la huerta
Sainete in one act
(Madrid, Teatro Eslava, 20th January 1900)

Text: Antonio Paso and Enrique García Álvarez

Principal Characters: Carola (soprano); Alegrías (tenor); Juan Francisco (baritone); Troncho (actor); Heriberto, a musician (actor); La Angustias, a gypsy (mezzo-soprano).

The action takes place in Murcia's rich agricultural heartland, La Huerta, during the Fiesta of the Virgin of Fuensanta, Patron of the region. Carola *"la alegría de la huerta"* ("pride of La Huerta") and Alegrías are drawn to one another, but the young man has been too respectful of the girl's feelings to declare his love.

SCENE 1—Verdant countryside in La Huerta of Murcia. After a substantial *Preludio* the curtain rises to reveal a typical country scene. Women are washing clothes in a stream, while a group of gypsies dance and sing (*Coro y zambra: "Arza, gitana"*). One of the gypsies, María de la Angustias, sings a passionate flamenco *Canción: "Erase el 'churumbel' más bonico"*) before they pack up and leave.

The waggish Troncho and old tío (uncle) Pipporo discuss Alegrías' failure to act, over a bottle or three of wine. They agree that there will be trouble unless the pair make a match very soon. Trouble duly arrives, in the shape of Heriberto, talentless director of the local *charanga* (wind band) who is taking advantage of Alegrías' hesitancy to divert Carola's attentions toward Juan Francisco, son of the District Deputy. Heriberto has deluded himself into thinking that this good office, together with the dedication of his latest pasodoble to the young man, will procure for him the directorship of the great San Bernardino band in Madrid. Carola brings her washing from the stream, hoping that Alegrías will at long last speak out to her; but though she hears him singing of his own unhappiness, he does not approach her directly, and she is left hurt and alone (*Dúo: "Corre, mulilla torda"*).

Troncho, clarinetist in the band, is fully awake to his bandmaster's machinations and determines to speak up for his friend. Stung by this well-meaning but clumsy intervention, Carola accepts Juan Francisco's proposal, agreeing to be formally betrothed at the Hermitage of Fuensanta before the Fiesta procession. Alegrías comes in, determined at last to speak; but it is all too late, and he leaves heartbroken. Heriberto is triumphant, and Troncho decides to make him pay for his treachery by spoiling the performance of the new pasodoble.

SCENE 2—A wooded part of La Huerta. Heriberto and his band march in to rehearse their pasodoble. The oddly assorted bunch include a lame flautist and a deaf drummer as well as Troncho and his clarinet. In a comic interlude reminiscent of the rustics' rehearsal from *A Midsummer Night's Dream*, the nervous composer puts his amusingly incompetent players through their musical paces, with the mischievous Troncho causing all the trouble he can. At length Heriberto is satisfied by a reasonable performance of the *Pasodoble* (played by the orchestra in the pit!) and his virtuosi march off toward the Hermitage.

SCENE 3—The Hermitage of Fuensanta. Hawkers are selling their wares outside the church, and a blind man begs for alms (*Solo y Coro: "Una limosnita"*). A bell tolls and the people are heard within singing a Hymn to the Virgin, which concludes with the lovely melody familiar from the *Preludio* (*Coro: "Señora Reina de los cielos"*). A group of pious women dressed demurely in black leave the church discussing the lovely sermon they have just heard, and gossiping about the worldly prayers they would like answered (*Coro: "¡Qué sermón escuché!"*).

Convinced that Troncho is planning something unpleasant for the performance, Heriberto informs Piporro that he is going to make sure the villager due to play the *cabezudo* (carnival dwarf) in the procession displaces the treacherous clarinetist in the band. He rushes off to arrange matters; but the wily Troncho, guessing his plan, bribes the villager to hand over his costume. When Heriberto flatters the *cabezudo* by gratuitously insulting the original clarinetist and his talents, Troncho is unable to keep his temper and a fight develops. Luckily, the other musicians and an officer of the *guardia* intervene before Troncho's cover is blown, and Heriberto's swap is duly effected. Meanwhile Alegrías has told Piporro that he cannot bear to see his beloved married to another, and must leave La Huerta for good.

Juan Francisco comes in with Carola. He is sensitively concerned at her evident distraction (*Dúo: "¿Por qué estas triste?"*); but before Carola can allay his doubts Alegrías appears with the *rondalla* of guitars and bandurrias to sing a lively jota, in which he blesses his beloved girl of La Huerta (*Jota: "¡Huertanica de mi vida!"*) Juan Francisco is impressed by his rival's magnanimity, but when Alegrías comes out to wish Carola luck and take his leave of her for ever, she finally breaks down and confesses her true feeling. The generous Juan Francisco releases her from her promise, and Piporro leads a toast to the happy couple as they and the villagers sing the thrilling *Jota* once again.

The Fiesta procession begins, and Heriberto's signal to the band is the cue for a series of unmusical screeches from the disguised Troncho and his clarinet. When Heriberto, thoroughly mortified, mistakenly starts beating the innocent *cabezudo*, the crowd laughs heartily. Once Troncho realises that Alegrías has won his Carola after all he begs pardon of Heriberto, and the zarzuela ends with the *Pasodoble* played to its creator's evident satisfaction.

In *La alegría de la huerta* Chueca for once moved away from the capital into a country setting, the lovely and varied agricultural area of Murcia known as La Huerta (Orchard). García Álvarez and Paso put together a tightly effective text, in which most of the characters speak in naturalistic Murcian dialect. Piporro's sage-sounding but vacuous pronouncements poke subtle fun at the ideal of the wise village elder, undefiled by urban sophistication; and there is more verbal fun to be had from Heriberto, a Shakespearian creation reminiscent of Berlioz's Somarone in *Beatrice et Benedict*, who lards his pretentious speeches with the affected Italianisms of an overweening rural musician.

The real composer at least allowed Heriberto to "write" a really catchy pasodoble, one of the highlights of this brief but varied score. Despite the nominal setting, Chueca's music does not move far away from his beloved Madrid, at least until the magnificent final *Jota* which provides the dramatic as well as musical climax to the action:

Instead of typical Murcian dances such as the parranda, Chueca gives us a pasacalle, a chotis and that pasodoble with which Heriberto hopes to gain his own engagement in the capital. Apart from the *Jota* the best tunes are all in the fine *Preludio*—notably the heart-lifting melody later associated with the Virgin of Fuensanta.

El año pasado por agua
Revista in one act, music in collaboration with Joaquín Valverde
(Madrid, Teatro Apolo, 1st March 1889)

Text: Ricardo de la Vega

Principal Characters: Julio Ruiz, as himself (tenor); A modiste (mezzo-soprano); The Year 1889 (actor); Neptune (tenor); La menegilda (mezzo-soprano); An emigrant (tenor); The Republic (mezzo-soprano).

SCENE 1—After a brief orchestral *Introducción*, the curtain rises to reveal a Madrid street. It is pouring with rain, and the soaked crowd of *madrileños* sing a traditional rhyme about the tiresome inevitability of the wet weather (*Coro: "Que llueva, que llueva"*). The famous actor-singer Julio Ruiz enters, escorting a fashionable modiste. Both carry umbrellas, and his suggestion that they share one between them to go off for lunch and whatever comes after is accepted by the lady, on condition that Julio pays. The flirtatious Umbrella Mazurka (*Mazurka de los paraguas: "Hágame usté el favor de oirme dos palabras"*) swiftly became the most popular number in the *revista*, and retains all its wit and charm today.

An actor representing the New Year 1889 enters in conversation with Mariano, a city policeman. 1889 wonders why his predecessor left Madrid in such a shocking state, and Mariano explains that 1888 was truly *"El año pasado por agua"* ("Last year under water") as he will happily demonstrate.

SCENE 2—A flooded quarter of Madrid. The crowd hails 1889, hoping that he will be drier than his older brother, and that the municipal authorities will manage him rather better. The familiar figure of Neptune appears in his impressive chariot, escaped from his stone fountain near the Prado Museum and wearing a fashionable brown suit. To an infectious waltz tune he glories in the new freedom available to him in the flooded streets, though the crowd reflects that there are some dangerous fish in Madrid who would scare even the Ruler of the Waves (*Vals de Neptuno: "De los mares rey me llaman"*).

1889 and Neptune are joined, in a dialogue heavy with contemporary social and political satire, by allegorical representatives of various leading newspapers. Eventually Neptune agrees to solve all their problems at a dance he will give that night for the Ministers of the Crown. A procession arrives from the bullring, singing a joyous pasacalle in praise of the various quarters of the city (*Coro: "¡Aquí viene la flor de Maravillas!"*) The crowd is joined by a *madrileño* gentleman, and La Menegilda (servant girl) from *La Gran Vía*.

In a sensuous habanera she tells Neptune and his friends how the different quarters of Madrid contributed to the development of her dubious career, which has culminated in the post of mistress to a pallid, rich Englishman (*Habanera: "Oiga usté, caballero"*).

A gondola floats on, in which are seated the lead tenor and soprano from Carrión and Chapí's zarzuela *La bruja*. They throw off their costumes and are revealed as allegorical representations of an Emigrant and the Republic. In a delectable parody of Carrión's verse, the couple regret their need for parting, watched by a chorus of constables and the Inquisitor from the 1887 zarzuela (*Zortzico: "¡Ay, niña de mis ojos!"*). The Inquisitor bewails the threat that Emigration brings to the Republic, and exhorts the constables to catch and imprison the felon in a lugubrious *Chotis: "¡Ay de mi! ¡Qué cruel situación!"*. Eventually the Emigrant and The Republic float off happily together in their gondola, to the despair of the cleric and constabulary.

SCENES 3 and 4—At the Liceo Ríus, three Municipal Guards bewail the fact their policemen's lot is not a happy one (*Polka: "¡Traemos los cuerpos trunzaus!"*), and a *chulo* and *chula*—Madrid teenagers—indulge in a love scene exposing the intellectual poverty of the city. A final tableau presents a decorative frieze extolling the successful Universal Exposition of Barcelona in 1888, as all hail Neptune and the New Year 1889 in a Grand Apotheosis *Final*.

1888 had been a wet year in Madrid. So wet in fact, that the circumstance gave rise to this sparkling follow-up to Chueca and Valverde's highly successful *revista La Gran Vía*. Ricardo de la Vega was to go on to write the incomparable *La verbena de la Paloma* with Bretón. His deft little revue is no less brilliantly observed; but though municipal indolence is still with us, many satirical targets of this water-drenched revue have sunk beneath the waves of time. *El año pasado por agua* (Last Year Under Water) survives through Chueca's diamond of a score, with its parade of dance forms, local, regional and international, and host of good melodies—not least the evergreen Umbrella Mazurka, one of the Granny's Favorites of the repertoire, with its jaunty, hat-tipping main tune:

El bateo
Sainete in one act
(Madrid, Teatro de la Zarzuela, 7th November 1901)

Text: Antonio Paso & Antonio Domínguez

Principal Characters: Nieves (actress); Lolo, her fiancé (actor); Pamplinas, her former sweetheart (actor); Valeriana, her mother (actress); Wamba, a republican (comic tenor); Visita, a neighbor (soprano); Virginio, Visita's admirer (tenor).

SCENE 1—A street in the poor suburbs of Madrid. After a lively *Preludio*, we see guests arriving for a celebration hosted by Señora Valeriana. They join in a spontaneous *Seguidillas:* "*No quiere el Municipio regar*", after which the droll republican Wamba entertains the crowd with his guitar playing and some zany satirical *coplas* about the political state of the nation, full of extremist factions warring at the expense of ordinary people: what it surely needs is a new Robespierre to sort matters out (*Zapateado: "El día menos pensado pasa un barbaridad"*).

The reason for the gathering is the baptism of the natural child of Valeriana's daughter Nieves. The father, Lolo, has honorable intentions toward his girlfriend, and the atheistic Wamba is to be the unwilling godfather. Trouble is brewing through the interference of an old sweetheart of Nieves, Don Tancredo Pamplinas, who believes he has proof that the lady has been receiving visits at night from a strange man. A skittish neighbor, Visita, confirms that she has seen a man climbing in over Nieves' balcony, as does her well-heeled, doting admirer, Virginio. This ill-assorted pair sing a substantial duet, in which Visita's duplicitous greed is fully matched by her lover's foolishness (*Dúo habanera: "Yo me llamo Virginio Lechuga"*).

Visita breaks the news of the rumors to Lolo, who is torn between jealous fury and disbelief. A major row with Nieves ensues; though Wamba, sure that the misunderstanding will be sorted out, eventually calms things down. At his suggestion everyone agrees at least to move off to the church of San Antonio de la Florida to get the baptism over and done with, whether or not the marriage is to follow. A crowd of cheeky street urchins joins the crowd as the party marches off to the church (*Coro: "Bateo pelao"*).

SCENE 2—Another side street. A group of organ-boys (female chorus) has decided to go on strike for better conditions. To the tune of a catchy *Mazurka* they explain that Madrid will be stuck with Beethoven, Verdi and Mozart from now on, and give the audience a final taste of their popular repertoire (including fragments of tunes from *La alegría de la huerta* and Giménez's *La tempranica*) before marching off to join the pickets (*Coro de organilleros: "Somos los organilleros"*).

SCENE 3—The vestry of San Antonio de la Florida. The punctilious sacristan, Celestino, is meticulously preparing the parish ledger for the baptism helped by his even slower assistant Expedito, while the curate can be heard in the church calling for them to hurry up. Wamba, standing fast by his republican principles, is unwilling to sit in the church to fulfill his duties as godparent, but finally he succumbs to everyone's pleas. At length the details of the child's parentage are about to be registered; but as Lolo claims paternity Pamplinas storms in, accusing him of being a liar, and the scene ends in confusion.

SCENE 4—Don Pascual's restaurant near the church. A frenchified photographer struggles to pose the family group, disrupting the luncheon service in the process (*Polka: "¡Qué grupo más bonito!"*). In the absence of the organ-boys, a group of serious musicians try to play an old-fashioned French minuet for the guests to dance to, with predictably ludicrous results as everyone tries to converse in French and even English (*Gavota: "Pianísimo ese re"*).

Before the celebratory lunch can be served, the row breaks out again. Pamplinas's motives were mixed, but he genuinely does not want Lolo to take responsibility for a child that is not his, and all are stunned by the presumed infidelity of Nieves. At last the truth comes out: Wamba was the man seen climbing in over the balcony, visiting not Nieves, but her mother Valeriana! Amicable relations are restored all round, and the baptism meal is finally served by Don Pascual as the curtain falls to a final reminder of the organ-boys' *Mazurka* from the orchestra.

El bateo (The Baptism), premiered at the Teatro de la Zarzuela, was the last of Chueca's great successes. The theatre is significant: for the first time Madrid's most truly popular musical hero had been invited to provide a *género chico* piece for the respectable home of three-act zarzuela. His librettists, the experienced Paso and talented newcomer Domínguez, provided the composer with a vivid, naturalistic slice of life, not without some satirical thrusts at extremist politics and middle-class "foreign" fads, but in all essentials an optimistic little farce about ordinary people's capacity to forgive and forget.

Chueca's score delighted the discerning patrons of the Teatro de la Zarzuela. As an enthusiastic amateur of the art, the composer must have relished the opportunity to provide music for the hilarious photography scene, and altogether *El bateo* is one of his happiest inspirations. Once again, it effectively takes the form of a popular dance suite, with its catchy seguidillas, tango, habanera and the rest. Many of these are quoted in the rhythmically brilliant *Preludio,* which hits the ground running with Wamba's catchy *Zapateado*:

There is even a mini suite-within-a-suite in the potpourri of the organ-boys, who play a mazurka and vals before finishing with a "new" pasodoble incorporating quotations from popular scores by Giménez and Chueca himself. The street boys are played by the *tiples* (sopranos) of the chorus, an example of a titillating convention associated with several *género chico* and zarzuela-operetta classics.

El chaleco blanco
Sainete in one act
(Madrid, Teatro Felipe, 26th June 1890)

Text: Miguel Ramos Carrión

Principal Characters: Pérez, a lodging-house keeper (comic tenor); Casta, his wife (actress); Tecla, his daughter (soprano) ; Rosa, their servant (actress); David, a lodger (tenor); Don Quintín, another lodger (actor); Don Ventura, yet another lodger (actor).

SCENE 1—The dining room of a small lodging house, run by Pérez and his wife Doña Casta. After a lively *Preludio* the curtain rises to reveal the master of the house polishing boots, humming as he works (*"Polka del limpiabotas"*). He chats to Rosa, who has come to collect the day's laundry, until Doña Casta admonishes her for using too much soap on the clothes and sending them back in rags. Rosa leaves with the clothes. One of the lodgers, Don Quintín, sneaks in and explains to Pérez that he has borrowed some of the other residents' better clothes, for a meeting he has to secure himself a job. Pérez's daughter Tecla comes on the scene with another lodger, her lover David, a young musician of limited talents and prospects who also happens to be way behind with the rent. If only he could be composing beautiful fantasias instead of having to play rubbish like *La Gran Vía* all the time, all would be well! Pérez, unlike Doña Casta, has taken to the young man, but points out that it will be the worse for him if his wife catches them billing and cooing like this (*Terceto-Mazurka: "Tengo muche que contarte"*).

A third lodger, the fat Don Ventura, complains to Pérez that his frockcoat has vanished: another of Don Quintín's borrowings. Meanwhile, Doña Casta plans to throw David out to make room for a possible rich suitor to Tecla, but all plans are thrown into turmoil by David's reappearance with astounding news: he has won a fortune in *el gordo* ("the fat one"), Madrid's biggest lottery. That is, he will have, when he retrieves the lucky ticket from his white waistcoat. Mass consternation ensues when it is discovered that his white waistcoat is apparently one of the articles Rosa has taken away to wash, and there is a mad scramble for hats and coats as they all rush off in search of the ticket. Their *Quinteto: "Vamos todos, vamos presto"* features an extended quote from Manrico's *"Di quella pira"* from Verdi's *Il Trovatore*, the difference being that young David is hastening to rescue, not his mother from the fire, but his lottery ticket from the water.

SCENE 2—The banks of the Manzanares River, near the laundry. Rosa and the other laundresses are going about their business with a will (*Coro Seguidillas: "Pa sortijas y gracia"*). They stop work to buy their lunch from the baker in another animated ensemble, the so-called Underwear Mazurka (*Mazurka: "¡El bollero!"*). This leads into a lively *Pasodoble: "Rataplan"*, led by a Drum-Corporal. Eventually David and the rest breathlessly reach the river, only to find that Rosa isn't in her usual place. By the time they find her it is too late: the clothes are already in the washing lye, and all seems lost!

Don Quintín, fresh from a highly satisfactory job interview, is surprised to find no response to his good news. Ventura spots his frockcoat, and takes it back, revealing beneath it—a white waistcoat! It is David's, and the whole company set on Quintín to rip off the garment, from which David triumphantly extracts the winning lottery ticket. David gets his Tecla, and all ends happily with an orchestral reminder of the *Seguidillas*.

El chaleco blanco is a classic *género chico sainete*, a small-scale musical play in one act, centered on the everyday life and hand-to-mouth existence of the *madrileños* themselves. Carrión's witty little farce had an original genesis. A group of writers were dining together one evening when it was suggested that they should draw a random title from a hat. Anyone who didn't produce a playscript within a month had to stand supper to the rest. Spared such intractable gems as "Sleeves and Hoods" and "Pelota in the Attic," Carrión drew *El chaleco blanco* (The White Waistcoat). Somehow all the writers managed to produce something within the thirty days, but only *El chaleco blanco* has stood the test of time.

Chueca, working without his long-term musical collaborator Valverde, produced a sparkling gem of a score. The nine short musical numbers once more form a kind of vocal suite taking in many of Madrid's favorite dances, polka, seguidillas, pasodoble and mazurka. No work of Chueca's captures the atmosphere of its time and place more perfectly, a Madrid where a lottery ticket can make all the difference between happiness and abject misery.

La Gran Vía
Revista in one act, music in collaboration with Joaquín Valverde
(Madrid, Teatro Felipe, 2nd July 1886)

Text: Felipe Pérez y Gonzalez

Principal Characters: El Caballero de Gracia (baritone); El paseante (actor); La menegilda (mezzo-soprano); Doña Virtudes (mezzo-soprano); Three pickpockets (singers); La Elíseo (soprano).

This synopsis follows the original version of the score, which is the one most generally heard today. Many changes to music and text were made during *La Gran Vía*'s original run, including the additions of a *Vals de la Seguridad* (Waltz of the Security Police) and *Pasodoble de los Sargentos* (Sergeants' Pasodoble) poking further fun at the lazy incompetence of Madrid's police.

SCENE 1—An assortment of threatened Madrid streets and squares appear, singing and dancing. They have gathered to complain about the announcement of the birth of a new thoroughfare, La Gran Vía or "Main Street," which is going to result in their demolition (*Introducción y Polka de las Calles: "Somos las calles"*—Polka of the Streets).

Off La Gran Vía even today, we may still find a seedy little alley somewhat grandly named Caballero de Gracia (Graceful Gentleman). This worthy now appears, common, ridiculous and affected, boasting about his amorous conquests. His swaggering mock-Viennese waltz is mocked by the other streets and squares (*Vals del Caballero de Gracia: "Caballero de Gracia me llaman"*—Waltz of the Graceful Gentleman).

El paseante (Idler) joins the Caballero in conversation, and a medical official, Don Comadrón (Male Midwife) appears, announcing that the birth of the new street must be delayed for an indefinite time, due to lack of funding and corporate wrangling.

SCENE 2—After a brief orchestral *Interludio* we find ourselves in a small plaza on the outskirts of central Madrid. The Caballero and El paseante discuss the political incompetence which has brought about the current impasse, before La menegilda (Housemaid) appears. In what is perhaps the most famous song in the entire zarzuela repertoire, she relates the dubious course of her brief career under the Lady of the House and beyond (*Tango de la menegilda: "Pobre chica"*—Housemaid's Tango). No sooner has she finished than Doña Virtudes (Virtue) the Lady of the House herself appears, to put her audience right on the true course of events, to the same infectious tango tune (*Tango de Doña Virtudes: "Pobres amas"*—Doña Virtudes' Tango). After a violent altercation, both ladies leave.

Three more semi-allegorical figures, taking their names from quarters of the city, emerge to plague the Caballero and El paseante: Prosperidad (Prosperity) begging alms; Pacífico (Pacifism) fermenting discord; and Injurias (Damages) hurling insults. A brief orchestral *Allegro* is followed by another satirical scene, as two characters representing Petroleum and Gas argue over their superior power—and profitability! They are followed by three Ratas (Pickpockets), who boast of their thieving skills while cheekily eluding capture by two incompetent Policemen (*Jota de las Ratas: "Soy el Rata primero"*—Pickpockets' Jota).

SCENE 3—In Puerta del Sol, then as now Madrid's busiest square, Doña Sinceridad (Sincerity) is mocked by her children. The Caballero and El paseante listen to the woeful story of the Fountain in the middle of the plaza, as she complains that the Town Council is going to knock her down to make room for a tramcar route. A Paleto (Bumpkin) robs the Caballero and El paseante while they continue to debate the advances in civic responsibility and government policy. A group of Marineritos (Little Midshipmen, played by the female chorus) have come to Madrid to admire the architecture, but the heavy double entendres of their song suggest other possibilities (*Mazurka de los Marineritos: "Somos los marineritos"*—Midshipmen's Mazurka).

SCENE 4—The Caballero and El paseante find themselves at the *Elíseo madrileño* (Madrid Elysium), a disreputable dancehall frequented by maids, porters and cooks, and another impending victim of the civic developments. The ladylike Elíseo herself leads the company in a surprisingly poised and elegant dance (*Chotis del Elíseo: "Yo soy un baile de criadas"*—The Elysium Schottische).

At the end of the dance, Don Comadrón the midwife rushes in and excitedly announces the new birthdate for La Gran Vía—the 30th February ... if it exists!

SCENE 5—A plaza on La Gran Vía itself. A general celebration ensues to mark the birth of the wonderful new thoroughfare, as a futuristic vision of the City rises in the background (*Marcha y desfile general*—March and Walkdown Parade).

For many *La Gran Vía* is the essential *género chico* zarzuela. Yet, strictly speaking, *La Gran Vía* isn't a zarzuela at all, but a *revista* or revue. There's virtually no plot, and the characters are either archetypal or named after Madrid streets. Felipe Pérez's script is a bold mixture of comic fantasy, social comment and political satire, centered on the creation of Madrid's answer to New York's Main Street or London's Piccadilly. The demolition of older streets and suburbs to make way for the grandiose modern thoroughfare proved as controversial as the massive funding put aside for the project, which effectively reformed the centre of the city.

Chueca and Valverde had been collaborating since 1875, and though they had already enjoyed huge success before, *La Gran Vía* was to eclipse even the controversial *La canción de la Lola* in popularity. Like many of Chueca's scores, *La Gran Vía* was conceived as a suite of songs and choruses based on popular dance forms—polka, waltz, tango, jota, mazurka, chotis and march. As for Valverde, current musicological opinion suggests his contribution was primarily the addition of orchestral polish.

Chueca's melodic and rhythmic vitality are as potent today as ever they were, and many of the numbers still retain their status as popular hits—notably the sleazy, ubiquitous Housemaid's Tango, an unsentimental narrative of social and sexual exploitation which packs a punch fully the equal of anything in Weill and Brecht's *Die Dreigroschenoper*:

Taking Madrid by storm, *La Gran Vía* transferred to the larger Teatro Apolo when the Teatro Felipe closed, gradually evolving for many months after. It also made its way successfully to Paris, Prague and Vienna, where it hugely impressed the philosopher Friedrich Nietzsche by its brevity and direct musical freshness; and even in a fashion to London and New York, where Chueca's music provided the substance for Spanish revues not remotely akin to Pérez's original script. By turns simple and sophisticated, musically direct but subtly organized, its vitality and popularity are undimmed by time.

Cádiz (1886, with Joaquín Valverde)
Patriotic zarzuela in two acts to a libretto by Javier de Burgos, produced the same year as *La Gran Vía* and for a time almost as famous. The romantic action takes place during the Napoleonic siege of Cádiz by French forces, culminating in the relief of the city by the British. The score includes many brilliant dance numbers, as well as a dramatic *Preludio*; but the only numbers to retain their popularity are a lively *Jota*, and the famous March—itself the inspiration for a later zarzuela by Valverde's son "Quinito" and Ramón Estellés (*La marcha de Cádiz*, 1896) and still very much a staple part of national and military celebrations.

La canción de la Lola (Lola's Song, 1880, with Joaquín Valverde)
The first great triumph of *género chico*, to a libretto by the young Ricardo de la Vega, *La canción de la Lola* is an epochal work that inspired many later works (most obviously *La revoltosa*) in its contemporary milieu, popular subject matter and realistic treatment. Set in a Madrid tenement courtyard the action concerns the rivalry for Lola's hand and heart between El Chulo (The Lad) and El Chato (Flat-nose), whose wealth and slick sophistication look set to win the day—despite the fact that he is the father of a child by Lola's neighbor Genara. The desperate Chulo steals Lola's wedding clothes (the original, rejected title was *La camisa de la Lola*, or Lola's Shift) and after an almighty row, all ends well. The simple but effective musical score set the tone for Chueca and Valverde's more sophisticated later *sainetes*. It proved so dangerously popular that, as Benito Pérez Galdós relates in his great novel *Fortunata y Jacinta* (1886), the authorities seriously considered banning it from public places!

9
Manuel Fernández Caballero
(1835–1906)

Born after the death of his father in Murcia on 14th March 1835, Caballero began musical studies very early with his brother-in-law Julián Gil, director of the local theatre orchestra. He also sang as a chorister in the city's Augustinian Monastery. At the age of ten, he was sent to Madrid to continue studies with another brother-in-law, Rafael Palazón; and in 1850 he decided to settle permanently in the capital, entering the Conservatory and studying a wide variety of disciplines, notably with the respected composer Hilarión Eslava. In 1856 he won the First Prize for Composition.

As early as 1853 he had been working as a violinist at the Teatro Real, and conducting at the Teatro de Variedades where he wrote quantities of orchestral overtures, incidental and ballet music. The following year he moved on to the Teatro Lope de Vega, where he wrote his first zarzuela, *Tres madres para una hija* (Three Mothers for One Daughter, 1854). Despite signal successes with zarzuelas like *La jardinera* (The Gardener, 1857) the path to prosperity proved elusive. Seven years and about 30 zarzuelas on, disillusioned and underemployed, he formed a company to go out to Cuba where he worked until 1871.

On his return to Madrid the tide turned, and Caballero soon became a household name with a string of successes starting with *El primer día feliz* (The First Happy Day, 1872). Among his best-known works over the next thirty-five years *La Marsellesa* (The Marseillaise, 1876); the extravagant *Los sobrinos del capitán Grant* (Captain Grant's Nephews, 1877); *Chateau-Margaux* (1887); *El dúo de la africana* (The Duet from L'Africaine, 1893) and *El cabo primero* (The First Corporal, 1895) deserve particular mention, as does *La viejecita* (The Little Old Lady, 1897) From 1882 he was a regular conductor with the Artístico-Musical Orchestra, whilst his zarzuela company continued to tour with great success as far afield as Buenos Aires and Montevideo (1884–5).

From 1894 encroaching blindness increasingly curtailed Caballero's compositional activities, though a cataract operation in 1902 restored his sight sufficiently for him to read an acceptance speech on election to the Academia—significantly, on the theme of Spanish popular song. Of his later works written with the help of amanuenses, *El señor Joaquín* (1898) has undeservedly lost the toehold it once held on the repertoire; but the superb *Gigantes y cabezudos* (Carnival Giants and Dwarves) from later the same year, after the Spanish defeat in Cuba, retains its immense popularity as a patriotic celebration of the *jota aragonesa*. He died on 26th February 1906 in Madrid.

Caballero was a fine all-round musician, whose work boasts unfailing technical security as well as musical interest. Toward the end of his working life he followed the trend of placing popular Spanish song at the heart of the drama; but even though his earlier scores may lack picture-postcard color, they are possessed of an elegant élan which distinguishes them from their Italian and French models. Indeed his later scores have a strength and passion which marks him out as mentor to Serrano's school of Spanish *verismo*, and his orchestration has comparably simple vigor. His Cuban years bore fruit, too—he was largely responsible for popularizing Spanish-American song and dance forms such as the habanera in mainstream Spanish music—and without doubt he must be accounted one of the finest composers of the romantic zarzuela movement.

El dúo de la africana
Sainete in one act
(Madrid, Teatro Apolo, 18th May 1893)

Text: Miguel Echegaray

Principal Characters: Querubini, an opera impresario (baritone); Antonia "La Antonelli," his wife (soprano); Giussepini (tenor); Amina, Querubini's daughter (actress); Pérez, the Stage Manager (actor).

SCENE 1—The rehearsal room of a theatre. After a gentle *Preludio*, partly based on the theme of Meyerbeer's famous duet from *L'Africaine*, Pérez the Stage Manager greets the chorus for the morning rehearsal. They are a lively lot, full of gossip and flirtatious banter, and he has difficulty getting them settled down ready for a rehearsal of *L'Africaine* which they are to perform that evening (*Coro: "Buenos días, Inocente"*).

The Italian impresario, Querubini, berates Pérez in an amusing mixture of Italian and imperfect Spanish for wasting time rehearsing, when they haven't even sorted out scenery and costumes for the evening. He feels that the set from *La Gran Vía* is somehow not quite right, but is unwilling to pay a painter to convert the gardens of the Madrid Retiro into an African jungle. Left alone, the impresario indulges in a verse soliloquy to the audience. His chief concern is money. Fortunately his new wife, Antonia "La Antonelli," is *prima donna* of the company, and his daughter Amina the leading soubrette, so he doesn't have to pay them. What's better, the new tenor Giussepini, though possessed of a magnificent voice, doesn't want paying either but sings for love of Art. All of which makes for a cheap company and a healthy bank balance.

The spiteful Amina tells her father the truth: Giussepini is singing not for love of Art but rather for love of La Antonelli. No sooner has Querubini gone to his office to ponder his situation, than the tenor comes in to rehearse with the Ladies' Chorus. They are joined by La Antonelli with the men, and the two principals banter about their favorite opera roles. Giussepini praises the women of Seville (which happens to be Antonia's birthplace) while she is loud in favor of the lusty men of Aragón, the tenor's homeland (*Coro y solos: "Amigas mías y compañeros"*).

Querubini storms in, soon to be subdued by his masterful wife, and they begin to rehearse the Meyerbeer Duet. Amina directs her father's attention to the way in which Giussepini is passionately overstepping the mark, but when Querubini jealously interferes Giussepini complains that he is ruining his Art. The impresario drags his wife away, and the tenor leaves with a flourish from *"La donna è mobile"* (*Melodrama: "Oh mía Selika"*). The company has thoroughly enjoyed the offstage drama, and comments on the situation with quiet glee in a gossipy number (*Coro de la murmuración: "Se marcha furioso"*), which deliciously echoes the chorus *"Saria possibile?"* from Donizetti's *L'Elisir d'Amore*.

SCENE 2—Querubini's office, before the performance. The company's leading Bass is pursuing Amina, but she mocks his *basso profondo* ardor and teases him into a frenzy. Querubini comes in to investigate the disturbance, and complains that Amina is as frail as her mother, a Neapolitan who ran off with a policeman. A perfect solution suggests itself: he will offer his daughter's hand to Giussepini, thus safeguarding wife and daughter at a stroke. Under a thin veneer of friendship he makes his offer, but the tenor will have none of it, claiming his vocal powers will diminish with the duties of matrimony. In a witty duet the surface politeness of the two men is contrasted with the jealousy and scorn that lie beneath (*Dúo: "Casa mia figlia"*).

Querubini leaves to greet the audience, and Giussepini tries to persuade La Antonelli to elope with him; though she is tempted she resists his amorous pleas (*Dúo: "Comprendo lo grave de mi situación"*). The tenor sings a passionate Aragonese *Jota: "No cantes más La Africana"* in a last attempt to make her change her mind, but she holds firm.

Amina has spotted them together and reports the fact to her father, who is unwilling to cancel the performance as there is a full house, but becomes frantic with jealousy when he thinks about what may happen in the Duet. A wealthy aristocrat, Doña Serafina, comes in looking for her son Pepe who she claims has run off to join the opera company. It becomes clear to the impresario that this errant son is none other than Giussepini, and that the furious mother is intent on dragging him away before the performance. He accepts a bribe in exchange for an agreement that Giussepini will not sing, but double-crosses Serafina, pocketing both her money and the takings by allowing the tenor to sing after all. Amina comes in, still pursued by her Bass, to tell Querubini that the big Duet is about to get underway. He rushes off in a whirlwind of conflicting emotions to watch the outcome, while Serafina vows to punish his duplicity.

SCENE 3—Backstage in the wings of the theatre, during the Fourth Act of *L'Africaine*. The stage is visible, and Giussepini has reached the infamous phrase *"Oh, mia Selika!"*. Carried away by the emotion of the moment, his hands begin to stray. Querubini cannot restrain his jealousy. He runs onto the stage to try to murder the tenor, but Pérez quickly brings down the curtain and the chorus separate the combatants. A Police Inspector has been called, and as he vainly attempts to ascertain the facts of the situation, Pérez saves the day by pushing the two singers out onto the stage to finish their famous Duet.

The score of *El dúo de la africana* (The Duet from L'Africaine) was only just finished in time for its premiere. Little wonder. Echegaray had read his *sainete* at a Café Inglés *tertulia* barely two months earlier, and the composer hadn't found the theatrically demanding text at all easy to set. Perhaps this haste was a blessing in disguise, for *El dúo* has a spontaneity and uncomplicated lightness of tone which ensured an initial run of over two hundred performances and has kept it firmly in the repertoire ever since. A sequel entitled *Los africanistas* (1894) failed and has never been revived.

Echegaray pokes gentle fun at the grandiloquence of Italian opera, singers and entrepreneurs, though his back-stage action centers on a performance of a famous French opera of the time, Meyerbeer's *L'Africaine* (1865), which portrays a romantic liaison between Vasco da Gama and an African girl, Selika. The climax of the farcical action is an avatar of the Marx Brothers' film *A Night at the Opera*, with relatives and police invading the stage during the famous duet. Caballero's tuneful music may quote Meyerbeer's theme and use Italianate forms, but as always he retains his distinctively Spanish dash and subtle humor. The *Jota* in particular, remains one of the favorites of the select zarzuela repertoire of *dúos* for tenor and soprano:

Gigantes y cabezudos
Zarzuela in one act
(Madrid, Teatro de la Zarzuela, 29th November 1898)

Text: Miguel Echegaray

Principal Characters: Pilar (soprano); Antonia (mezzo-soprano); Isidro (actor); Timoteo (singer); Jesús (tenor); A Sergeant (actor).

SCENE 1—The market square of Zaragoza in Aragon. A short *Introducción* giving a taste of many of the zarzuela's themes precedes the opening scene. Antonia and Juana with other market women and their customers argue heatedly over prices, until the popular butcher Isidro appears and calms everybody down (*Coro: "Hay que separarlas"*). Timoteo, the timorous local *guardia* officer, nails up a decree announcing that the Municipal Council are going to double local taxes. As the husband of the fiery Antonia, he has the tricky task of trying to balance his official duties against personal loyalty (*Salida: "El Ayuntamiento"*). Not surprisingly he is attacked by the women in the combative *Jota: "Anda, vé y dile Alcalde"*. Pilar, Isidro's adopted niece and assistant, argues most fiercely on the butcher's behalf. Several men have fallen for the passionate girl, and one in particular—an Andalusian Sergeant—is determined to capture her by force; or more likely subterfuge, as the girl remains staunch to her beloved Jesús, a conscript fighting with the army in Cuba.

Pilar only lives to receive a letter from her sweetheart. Finally the postman delivers it, and in a touching *Romanza: "Esta es su carta"*, she despairingly regrets the fact that as she cannot read, she must rely on other people to give her his news. Is he surviving the heat and dangers of Cuba? Does he still love her? Will he ever return? Antonia tries to help her, but can't make out the meaning either, and in the end the girl has to ask Pascual, a young man known to all as "Jeremiah" owing to his melancholy sighing for Pilar, to read the letter. Jesús is well, and as the war is going badly he hopes to be sent home soon.

The Sergeant tells her that he has had a more recent letter, telling him that Jesús has married a Cuban woman and advising Pilar to seek the protection of his "best friend": the Sergeant himself. Pilar is unsettled, though she doesn't really believe the man and finally tells him that she would rather wait for Jesús to become a widower. The market women meanwhile have decided that enough is enough, and Pilar leads them in revolt against the new taxes in another powerful *Jota: "Si las mujeres mandasen"*. The scene ends in colorful riot as Timoteo, frightened by his wife's threats of marital disharmony, breaks his sword and leaves the *guardia*.

SCENE 2—By the river Ebro, on the fiesta day of the Pilarica, Zaragoza's basilica-cathedral. Poor Timoteo has gone fishing to try and catch something to eat. The first repatriated troops land from Cuba, more dead than alive (*Coro de repatriados: "Por fin te miro, Ebro famoso"*). Jesús is amongst them. He cannot wait to greet his mother and beloved Pilar once again (*Solo: "Por la patria te dejé, ay de mí"*).

SCENE 3—The main square, in front of the Cathedral. In the *Coro: "Por ver a la Pilarica"* a group of bumpkins from the local farms joyfully anticipate the traditional parade of elaborately dressed stilt-walkers (*gigantes*) and huge-headed carnival dwarfs (*cabezudos*). Soon the huge and gaudy monsters appear in the *Salida de los gigantes y cabezudos*, with its colorful, rustic instrumentation. Pilar, come to celebrate her nameday festival as best she can, leads the praise of the Aragonese carnival in another tremendous *Jota: "Luchando tercos y rudos"*.

The Sergeant pursues his stratagem, telling Jesús that Pilar, tired of waiting, has married a rich American. In despair the boy decides to collect his kit from the barracks and leave the city for good. Sure she has heard Jesús' voice in the throng, Pilar plays a trick on the Sergeant. Producing an old letter, she asks the Andalucian to read it to her. He tells her that Jesús has been killed in an enemy ambush and died begging Pilar to marry "my good friend, the Sergeant," so revealing his plot as a pack of lies. Ashamed, he confesses the truth and Pilar, sorry for his pathetic machinations, forgives him. The Sergeant in his turn goes to find Jesús at the barracks and tell him to meet his beloved at the door of the basilica. Things are looking up: even Timoteo is to get his old job back.

The Carnival figures return, and the zarzuela ends combining the song of the returning soldiers with a grand musical *Final apoteósico: "Salve a la Virgen del Pilar"* in praise of the Virgin of the Basilica, and by extension the staunchly faithful girl who shares its name. At last Jesús runs to meet his Pilar, and the lovers are reunited.

At first sight, it might be tempting to explain away the success of *Gigantes y Cabezudos*, (Carnival Giants and Dwarves) as something of a sentimental freak, a work which undoubtedly owed its huge initial popularity to two circumstances. In a time of shame over the military defeat by the United States that had led to the loss of Cuba and massive repatriations earlier in the year, the subject matter reflected Spain's need to reassert national pride in her popular culture and the values of simple human decency. It also marked a personal triumph over adversity for Caballero, at a point when encroaching blindness seemed certain to terminate his career.

Echegaray's libretto offered the revered maestro a tightly constructed storyline in a carnival setting, which allowed Caballero to include a liberal helping of popular song and dance: not for nothing has *Gigantes y cabezudos* been called "The Apotheosis of the Jota." With the aid of his sons and amanuensis José Serrano, who worked with him on the orchestration, he produced a score which is at least as colorful, passionate and musically coherent as any of his earlier works. The instrumentation is a wonderful blend of popular elements and almost Tchaikovskian richness.

Pilar's *"Esta es su carta"* calls for special mention. The simple dignity of her words is matched by music of poignant, delicate subtlety; and the sympathy of the blind composer for the girl who cannot read results in a wonderful *Romanza* as touching and beautiful as any in the zarzuela repertoire:

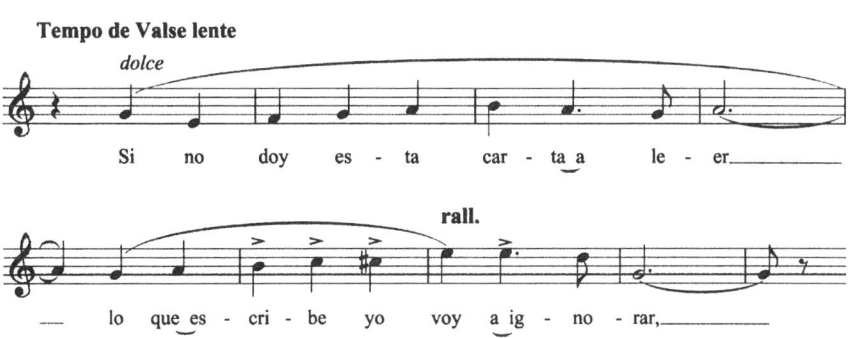

El señor Joaquín
Lyric Comedy in one act
(Madrid, Teatro de la Zarzuela, 18th February 1898)

Text: Julián Romea

Principal Characters: Joaquín, a Madrid grocer (actor); Vicenta, his wife (soprano); Trini, his daughter (soprano); Manuel, his bookkeeper (baritone); Chisco, his apprentice (comic tenor).

SCENE 1—Madrid, during the heat wave of August 1897, on the eve of the verbena of San Joaquín. Following a *Preludio* which draws on the main musical themes of the work, the curtain rises on the back parlor of Señor Joaquín's shop. The grocer has two women in his life; his second wife Vicenta, and Trini, his daughter by the previous marriage. Because the two are almost the same age, they are more like sisters than stepmother and stepdaughter. Just now they are nominally engaged in housekeeping, while Manuel, the personable young man who does the accounting for Señor Joaquín, busies himself with some paperwork. Trini indulges in some mocking flirtation with Manuel, until Señor Joaquín comes in and levity ceases.

He asks Manuel to hand him an invoice, and is surprised to discover on the back of the paper some amorous doggerel addressed to "a lovely woman." Manuel respectfully denies having written them. In fact the verses have been penned by the gawky, foolish apprentice Chisco, a foundling whom Joaquín has kindly taken in, and who is hopelessly in love with Trini. She treats the whole thing as a joke and goes off to help him and her father in the shop.

Left alone together, Manuel pours out his love to Vicenta, who gently reproaches him and rejects his advances (*Dúo: "Vicenta, yo me muero"*). It emerges that the two were engaged some years ago, before Vicenta met and fell in love with Señor Joaquín. When her husband surprises the two of them in intimate conversation, he generously concludes that Manuel must be in love with Trini but afraid to speak for himself, a theory which the terrified young man is quick to go along with. The flustered Vicenta leaves. Joaquín is well pleased by the prospective match, as is Trini when he calls her in to tell her the news, though she shows her high spirits by mocking Manuel even more than usual. Chisco calls his boss out to deal with an important customer, leaving Manuel to haltingly declare his love to Trini. She continues to make fun of him in their *Dúo: "Quien mi cariño pretenda"*, a clever sequence of mazurka, tango and zapateado rhythms. Joaquín reappears and calls for

Chisco, who is coming out of the cellar carrying a pile of tin cans. On hearing of the "engagement" he tumbles down the stairs in his shock, and the scene ends with the cacophony of the falling cans.

SCENE 2—Outside the shop. It is dusk, and a chorus of street sellers are offering their wares, stationery, buttons and hairpins, flowers and *azucarillos* or meringues. A band of blind beggars join them (*Chotis de los ciegos: "Pobrecitos degraciados"*) before launching into some once-notorious couplets mocking the city authorities *(Coplas: "Cachirulipón en las coplas que canto")*. A policeman tells them all to move on, and after the crowd has dispersed he tells Joaquín he will return soon to celebrate the shopkeeper's name day. Trini is out taking the air, and Chisco has time to present her with a rose before he is called back in by her father. Before the girl can go back inside, Vicenta appears with Manuel. Trini hides, and overhears the bookkeeper announce his resolve to leave the shop for good. Not only is he giving pain to them both, but now he is also in danger of breaking Trini's heart. He feels guilty for using her, and determines not to hurt the girl any more. After the unhappy Vicenta forgives him he goes back inside to pack his bags. Trini steps forward to confront her stepmother, who explains everything and consoles the poor girl, before leading her sadly back into the house. A street band comes in with a crowd, who dance the lively *Polka* which ends the scene.

SCENE 3—The grocer's shop, that night. A party is in progress to celebrate Joaquín's name day. Food and drink is served, and Trini takes advantage of the lull to explain to her father that she doesn't love Manuel after all but Chisco, a story which Joaquín finds hard to credit. When Manuel tells him that he wishes to give his notice and leave immediately, and that his supposed love for Trini was all a mistake, the shopkeeper's jealous suspicions are finally aroused. Vicenta reassures him, explaining that Manuel really wishes to leave because he is ambitious and work in a shop is no life for him. Joaquín unhesitatingly believes her, fondly embracing his wife to everyone's satisfaction. It's time for music, and Trini offers to sing an *Alborada* she learned while staying in the Galician town of Orense the previous year (*Balada y alborada: "Noche pura y serena"*). Choosing his moment, Manuel leaves quietly, spotted only by Trini who valiantly keeps singing. After he has gone her strength gives out, and Trini faints into the arms of her stepmother, leaving her song unfinished. The zarzuela ends abruptly with the guests attributing her collapse to the heat and youthful nerves.

El señor Joaquín was initially one of the most popular of all zarzuelas. Nowadays it is almost forgotten, although it boasts some of Caballero's best work, notably Trini's haunting *Alborada* (dawn serenade), which features some subtle use of *alhambrismo*, the decorative Moorish-style music which so attracted Spanish composers of the time. Sorozábal later paid homage to this lovely number, quoting it in *La del manojo de rosas* at the moment where his own hero—another Joaquín—is mentioned for the first time:

No - che pu - ra y se - re - na, no - che de a - mor,

Undoubtedly the Blind Beggars' famous *Coplas* satirizing the municipal authorities of the day has lost most of its bite, but a deeper reason for the zarzuela's neglect is the distinctly downbeat sentimentality of Julián Romea's little domestic drama. The conclusion, though crowned by the *Alborada*, is neither uplifting nor tragic, merely slightly sad. One interesting detail: the title role of Señor Joaquin, trusting *paterfamilias* of the household, was first played by the multi-talented author: actor, playwright, and even on occasion zarzuela composer himself.

Los sobrinos del capitán Grant

Zarzuela in four acts
(Madrid, Teatro Príncipe Alfonso, 25th August 1877)

Text: Miguel Ramos Carrión

Principal Characters: Mochila, a retired infantryman (baritone); Soledad, a young Madrid girl (soprano); Escolastico, her fiancé (tenor); Sir Edward Clyron, a Scots magnate (actor); Lady Ketty, his "niece" (soprano); Doctor Mirabel, a botanist (actor); Jaime, a Catalan forger turned Australian outlaw (baritone); Captain Grant (actor).

ACT 1, SCENE 1—The courtyard of a tenement house in Madrid. The residents dance and sing noisily (*Coro: "Ya llegó la murga"*) until Lieutenant Mochila ("knapsack") comes out of his apartment and fires his gun, which scatters them. Another inhabitant, the pretty young dancer Soledad, is in love with the student Escolastico. He has won some money in the lottery, and goes to tell Soledad of his plans to abandon his studies. Mochila reappears, an impoverished ex-infantryman given to wild daydreaming (*Canción: "Soy un hombre que está desesperado"*). He calls his neighbors to tell them of a mysterious plan, which will win them all fame and fortune—if they'll only provide him with a little capital (*Solo y Coro: "¡Vecinos! ¡Vecinas, al patio bajad!"*). No one listens to the crazy old officer except Soledad, who offers to help him. Mochila tells her about a bottle he has found in the belly of a sea-bream, which contains a message from one Captain Grant, detailing his shipwreck off the coast of Patagonia. His brig the *Veloz* ("Swift") sank, and he himself was taken prisoner by natives. A rich treasure trove awaits any adventurer who finds it, according to this last, despairing message.

A Scots magnate, Sir Edward Clyron, appears in response to a cryptic advertisement Mochila placed in the local newspaper. Captain Grant once saved Clyron's life, and he agrees to put his sailing yacht, the *Scotland*, at Mochila's disposal if the old soldier will help discover the fate of his savior. Soledad, pretending to be a niece of the shipwrecked Captain, vouches for Mochila's selfless disinterest in the matter. After a little gentle persuasion, his "nephew" Scolastico agrees to join the party, as does Clyron's shy "niece" Lady Ketty (Katy), whose Spanish is sadly limited. The generous Escolastico agrees at once to act as tutor to this pretty English rose. Enjoining secrecy, Clyron leaves with Ketty, and the three *madrileños* celebrate their cunning in a breathless patter trio (*Terceto: "Vuestro tío se ha salvado"*).

SCENE 2—On board the *Scotland*. As the passengers embark, the mariners make final preparations to cast off with a gently nostalgic tango, the *Coro: "Así escuchando de la mar"*. At the last minute they are joined by the absent-minded Doctor Mirabel, anxious to study the flora and fauna of the Philippines. He meant to have sailed there with the *Ireland* but discovers his celtic confusion too late as the *Scotland* casts off for the long voyage to Patagonia. The act ends with a brief English shanty from the sailors (*"La enseña de Inglaterra"*).

ACT 2, SCENE 1—The main square of Talcahuano in Chile. It is fiesta, and the picturesque townsfolk are taking the air (*Coro: "Hoy celebra Chile"*). A posse of local women extol the virtues of smoking in a habanera tinged with seductive double entendre: it may be a vice for men, but it is fashionable and elegant for ladies (*Coro fumandar: "Si es en el hombre un vicio"*). The entire populace join in the exhilarating *Samba: "Oigan las guitarras"* which heralds the arrival of Clyron and his party. It becomes clear that the lovely Ketty, whose Spanish is improving no end under Escolastico's tender pedagogy, is really Clyron's fiancée—rather to the relief of Soledad. Mochila, who had gone in search of details of the wreck, returns with the disheartening news that no Spanish boat has been sunk in Chilean waters for over ten years. The rescue party decide that Captain Grant must be a prisoner of the Indians, and decide to press inland to look for him. Doctor Mirabel, unable to find a passage to the Philippines, decides to tag along.

SCENE 2—A rocky mountain pass in the foothills of the Andes. A Patagonian native guide offers his services to the adventurers, which they accept gladly. Lady Ketty has discovered, slightly to her disappointment, that the Spanish "cousins" are really lovers. She has heard passionate whisperings which are a great mystery to such a well-bred British maiden—do all Spanish lovers behave like that? Ketty and Soledad compare notes as to national style in love-making in the delightful *Dúo: "En Inglaterra los amantes"*, featuring the English (?) refrain *"Yes you love mi, very, very morning star, my dear"*. After this charming interlude, the whole party set off up the pass on pack mules.

SCENE 3—The high peaks of the Andes. Our heroes congratulate themselves on reaching the summit, but celebrations are cut short by subterranean rumblings; and all start tumbling down the mountain as a devastating earthquake, represented by a violent orchestral *Intermedio*, knocks the entire Andes range flat!

SCENE 4—The intrepid travelers have rolled down to the Argentine Pampas, where they soon recover from their exertions. But where is the Doctor? Horrified, they see him being carried off in the claws of an enormous condor, which the quick-thinking guide manages to shoot out of the sky. The doctor is fortunately dropped into a nearby tree, and all celebrate his miraculous escape.

SCENE 5—Outside a military fort. The lackluster soldiers are being drilled by their Commandant (*Coro: "Marchemos de frente"*). Argentina is at war with Paraguay, and they are awaiting the brutal General Archiparraguirrigerriberrigorrigurrichea (*sic*) to give them their marching orders. The martinet General arrives (*Coro y Solo: "Viva el general"*) and gets his personal bodyguard of crack troops to show the soldiers how to drill perfectly in the exhilarating *Pasodoble de los Gauchos*. Clyron's party arrive, are promptly arrested as Paraguayan spies, and after a farcical trial scene blithely condemned to death by the General. The kind Commandant takes pity on them, arranging for blanks to be fired by the execution squad. Unlike in *Tosca* the ruse works, and all duly fall down dead except the absent-minded doctor, who has to be pulled down by the others. After the General leaves, the travelers gratefully make their escape.

SCENE 6—The plains, in the rainy season. The party has taken refuge from the floods in the branches of a giant tree. Doctor Mirabel studies Mochila's document more closely, and realizes to his horror that Captain Grant is not in America at all, but Australia! At that moment a bolt of lightning sets the tree on fire, and just as the party is deciding how best to escape they notice a pack of alligators swimming toward them! The alligators begin to savage the tree, and they are left with no alternative but to jump into the water and swim for it.

ACT 3, SCENE 1—Outside a mill in Australia. A group of bandits led by the desperado Jaime, a Catalan forger, celebrate the golden prospects offered by their new-found freedom in the outback (*Coro y Romanza:* "*Ya que ingrata la fortuna*"). Jaime has discovered that the *Scotland* has docked at a nearby port, and has let it be known that he has information which will help Clyron and his friends. Posing as a hard-working colonist, the bandit chief fools them into thinking that he was the Chief Mate of the *Veloz* and knows where Captain Grant is being held by aborigines in the central desert. Clyron suggests they trek inland straight away, taking Jaime as their guide.

SCENE 2—Midnight, at a railway station in a rocky desert. A train arrives, and Jaime descends with the adventurers: all except Mochila, who shouts and waves frantically through a window as the train pulls away and into the distance, toward Melbourne!

SCENE 3—A disreputable hostelry in the outback. Carousing bandits sing a song in praise of brandy, gin and rum (*Coro:* "*En tanto que con gozo*"). Jaime has come on ahead, and orders the innkeeper to hide his horses, leaving the Adventurers stranded. Clyron writes a letter for Jaime to give to the Captain of the *Scotland*, asking him to provide the bearer with whatever he needs. Mochila is reunited with his friends, after a series of hair-raising adventures on the way to Melbourne, which he invites the Doctor to read about in the *Australian Gazette*. Mirabel comes across the description of a bandit who sounds suspiciously like their trusted guide, but Mochila has already acted by bringing along the local police force. Sadly, before they can arrest Jaime, he and his band have raced for the horses and fled with the letter for the *Scotland*.

SCENE 4—A coral-diver's hut on the coast. Doctor Mirabel and Mochila receive news that the *Scotland* has been set upon by pirates and sunk. Learning that Jaime is lurking in the vicinity, Mochila decides to hire the diver's equipment and recover Sir Clyron's case of valuable jewels.

SCENE 5—The wreck of the *Scotland*, at the bottom of the sea. A suavely elegant orchestral *Vals:* "*Al fondo del mar*" accompanies an underwater ballet, in which Jaime and Mochila are seen diving from separate boats down to the wreck to find the jewel case. Jaime finds it first, along with the skeleton of the *Scotland*'s Captain, but in a gripping climax the brave Mochila wrests the jewel case from him just before Jaime is dragged away to his doom by a giant octopus!

ACT 4, SCENE 1—A Maori hut in New Zealand. The adventurers, except for the Doctor, have been caught by Maori cannibals and are to be ritually sacrificed and eaten next morning. Just before dawn, the natives perform their ritual dance round the hut (*Coro:* "*Karateté Ratarabaka*") but in the nick of time Escolastica finds a cunningly concealed trapdoor in the floor, and they are able to slip away just before the disappointed Maoris burst in.

SCENE 2—The sacred volcano, Maunganamú. The adventurers find themselves emerging in the centre of the crater, which naturally causes the volcano to erupt. Our heroes flee in panic.

SCENE 3—A grotto on the seashore. Starving, the party hungrily start consuming mussels in the rock pools. They are amazed to come across Doctor Mirabel, in the warpaint and huge plumes which he used to disguise himself and escape capture. Amazingly, the natives took him for a Chinaman and have made him their chieftain. He now speaks fluent Maori, and has learnt the intricate laws of taboo. The whole party flee in a nearby war-canoe.

SCENE 4—Captain Grant's hut, on a little island off the coast. Captain Grant with his two surviving crew members despairs of ever being found, or seeing his homeland again. The rescuers finally arrive in a canoe, and there are fond greetings between the Captain and his two *sobrinos*—whom he recognizes right away, rather to Mochila's surprise! But Grant is unwilling to leave without reclaiming the *Veloz* treasure, now in the hands of the Maoris. The Doctor offers to help him reclaim it, and all escape the pursuing Maoris in the canoe.

SCENE 5—The Grand Maori Temple. Great Chief Mirabel is leading ritual celebrations and dances. Clyron arrives with Mochila, Captain Grant and his crew, and when the natives start to wave their spears, Mirabel shouts that the White Men are taboo (untouchable) enabling them to walk up to the Sacred Treasure and take it. Mirabel leaves with the rest, and the whole party joyfully heads off to start the long journey back to Spain (*Final:* "*A España ricos ya por fin*").

Jules Verne's early novel *Les Enfants du capitaine Grant* (1867) is the classic "note in a bottle" narrative. It has inspired several more or less faithful film versions including Walt Disney's *The Castaways* (1962) but Miguel Ramos Carrión was quicker off the mark than most with this stage version. He certainly stuck close to the geographical letter of the original novel, but somewhere along the line most of Verne's characters and much of his earnest narrative were jettisoned in favor of a hilarious comedy, a Spanish *Candide* without the philosophy. With no fewer than eighteen mainly exotic locations it certainly provided spectacular entertainment.

This same theatrical extravagance, though ensuring the wild success of the original Madrid production, has mitigated against frequent revival of Carrión's comedy. This is a pity, for *Los sobrinos del capitán Grant* (Captain Grant's Nephews) is graced by one of the most delectable scores in the entire repertoire. Given the fluidity of modern stage technique, it is hard to see why this superb zarzuela is not mounted far more often.

Caballero's music makes the most of the picaresque exoticism. It is elegant, witty and outrageously over the top. There is a catchy ladies' smoking chorus, just as in the topically shocking *Carmen* (1875); not to mention a delirious samba, a stirring Gaucho pasodoble, a splendid heroic opera aria for the Catalan-Aussie bandit, a tongue-in-cheek underwater ballet—and, perhaps best of all for Anglophiles, a bilingual duet in Spanish and Carrión's singular brand of Queen's English:

La viejecita
Zarzuela in one act
(Madrid, Teatro de la Zarzuela, 30th April 1897)

Text: Miguel Echegaray

Principal Characters: Carlos, of the Spanish Hussars (soprano or tenor); Fernando, his friend (tenor); Luisa, his fiancée (soprano); Marquis of Aguilar, her father (actor); Don Manuel, the Marquis' brother (actor); Sir George, an English Officer (baritone).

SCENE 1—The officers' mess of a Spanish artillery barracks, in 1812. After a brief *Preludio* largely based on the later *Minuetto*, the curtain rises to reveal three hussars, Federico, Fernando and Carlos, enjoying several bottles of wine with their fellow officers. They launch into a lively *Brindis:* "*Ya estoy tranquilo . . . Para morir de amor ciego*". Fernando has received a letter from Mexico with news that his rich aunt Doña Teresa de Argelez y Vargas is due to return home to the mother country. As soon as Fernando and Carlos are left alone, the latter confesses to his friend that he is in love with Federico's fiancée Luisa, daughter of the Marquis of Aguilar, who views him as an irresponsible good-for-nothing. That night the Marquis is holding a ball at his palace, and Carlos is determined to use the occasion to make love to his sweetheart.

However, when the officers' invitations arrive, Carlos has been specifically excluded, which makes him the butt of the soldiers' humor (*Coro de la invitación:* "*Pobrecito Carlos . . . En un cerillo se alza un palacio*"). Thoroughly riled, Carlos makes a bet with them: he will gain entry to the party, hug Luisa three times, and fight a duel with Federico. Only Fernando and Sir George, an English captain in the Allied army, take his side against the mocking officers. The wager is sealed with a handshake and all agree to meet at the Marquis' mansion that night.

SCENE 2—The ballroom in the Marquis' mansion. Final preparations for the ball are in train. The Marquis is talking to his brother Don Manuel, a good-humored buffoon, when Luisa comes down. Don Manuel knows that she is not in love with Federico, but his attempts to take her part and speak up for Carlos fall on stony ground when the Marquis refuses to listen to a word he says. Luisa defends Carlos stoutly: agreed, he has exhausted his family fortune in double-quick time, but that is down to his unworldliness and the lack of a good woman by his side. Softened by his daughter's plea the Marquis agrees to reconsider the situation, provided Carlos commits no more acts of idiocy. The civilian guests arrive to the strains of a *Mazurka*, followed by Sir George and a company of young English dragoons (female chorus) who praise Luisa's beauty in an insouciant choral *Chotis: "Como en correcta formación"*.

When the officers arrive without Carlos they understandably think they have won the bet. Then the arrival is announced of Doña Teresa de Argelez, from Mexico. *La viejecita* ("little old lady"—Carlos in disguise) is received with great courtesy by the Marquis and his guests, though the baffled Fernando certainly does not recognize her as his aunt. The old dear sings of her past amorous triumphs in a wistful little song (*Canción de la viejecita: "Al espejo al salir me miré"*) echoed by the entire company. When she strikes up a friendship with Luisa and detaches the girl firmly from the luckless Federico, Fernando at length realizes just who this "aunt" really is.

He asks Carlos to dance, but Don Manuel sweeps the old lady into the centre of the floor to lead a *Minuetto*, during which she makes a lot of clodhopping gaffs which eventually cause the dance to grind to an unseemly halt. *La viejecita* makes another beeline for Luisa. Praising her youthful beauty, she squeezes the girl three times—Sir George meanwhile counting the precise number of hugs out loud. As soon as the officers are left alone Carlos reveals his identity and Federico, furious, challenges him to a fight there and then. Sir George steps between them, but when Don Manuel comes in to see what all the noise is about, he is amazed to find the old lady with saber in hand and shouts to his brother. Carlos quickly pretends to feel faint, and the thoughtful Marquis leaves the frail creature to Luisa's quiet ministrations.

As soon as they are alone, Carlos reveals his identity, causing Luisa to faint in her turn; but he is swiftly forgiven in a touching *Dúo: "¡Pobre viejecita! ¡Qué delicadita!"*. Fernando warns his friend that now he has won the bet he should get out before the Marquis's suspicions are fully aroused, and Carlos leaves to duel with Federico. The Marquis quizzes Fernando on the peculiar habits of his relation; but soon the old lady returns wiping a saber clean, having beaten Federico by drawing first blood. "She" still has enough presence of mind to plead with the Marquis, to such charming effect that he agrees to forgive Carlos if the young man shows willing to settle down and stop playing the fool. Carlos tries to discreetly lose his dress, but is spotted by the enamored Don Manuel, who chases *la viejecita* round the ballroom and up to the gallery. The Marquis asks his daughter why she is so miserable. Luisa tells him that it is because of his refusal to invite Carlos to the ball; and when the contrite young officer appears in full dress Hussar's uniform to beg the Marquis's pardon for past sins, Luisa's father readily forgives him. He must bid them farewell, as the army returns to the front at dawn, but Carlos promises Luisa he will return alive to claim his bride.

The special charm of zarzuela is exemplified by *La viejecita* (The Little Old Lady). Echegaray set his frivolous, romantic farce against the stern backdrop of the late Napoleonic war of Spanish independence, but clearly derived his plot from Brandon Thomas's classic English farce *Charley's Aunt* of 1892. There, too, the central character dresses up as a Rich Old Aunt, partly in order to get his girl and trick her father. Thomas's play is more complicated, and his aging Doña Lucia d'Alvadorez may be "from Brazil, where the nuts come from" rather than Mexico, but her farcical activities are in precisely the same vein as Carlos's in *La viejecita*.

Echegaray's swift, witty and neatly characterized play is successful enough on its own terms, but the abiding delight of *La viejecita* is Caballero's brief score, one of his very best. Much of it had to be dictated due to the composer's encroaching blindness, but he put together a delicious confection of old-fashioned elegance and subtle humor. The suave *Minuetto* and the *Dúo* for Carlos and Luisa are apposite theatrically and personal in musical style. The Old Lady's slow waltz *"Al espejo al salir me miré"* is especially effective, gently touching as well as humorous in context:

It seems the playwright originally intended Carlos for a male performer, but that Caballero tailored it to the talents of the soprano Lucrecia Arana, who later created the role of Pilar in *Gigantes y cabezudos*. Whatever the original circumstances, there is no doubt that this particular "breeches" role is best played these days by a tenor, a solution which makes sense dramatically without doing too much violence to the music. This isn't Shakespeare, and much of the farcical fun and character of *La viejecita* is lost when Carlos "in drag" is in reality a soprano out of it!

El cabo primero (The First Corporal, 1895)
Carlos Arniches and Celso Lucio set their contemporary, one-act *sainete* in an army camp, and this military flavor pervades Caballero's sophisticated and exhilarating score. In essence *El cabo primero* is a diverting little farce of secret nocturnal assignations and mistaken identities; but Caballero nevertheless made space for some expansive lyrical writing, notably the heroine Rosario's atmospheric *Romanza: "Yo quiero un hombre"*.

Chateau-Margaux (1887)
The newly wed Don Manuel has to entertain his rich uncle and aunt; but in her agitation his wife Doña Angelita samples a little too much of the excellent wine provided for their entertainment. All is forgiven when the old couple get a taste of the marvelous liquor themselves. Slight though José Jackson Veyán's one-act zarzuela is, the four musical numbers written for Angelita (soprano) and the comic servant José (tenor) are of equally superior vintage. Doña Angelita's lilting *Vals: "No sé qué siento aquí"* immediately became a deservedly popular hit, and it remains a bulwark of the soprano repertoire.

La Marsellesa (The Marseillaise, 1876)
The action of this heroic, three-act *zarzuela grande* centers on an escapade in the life of Rouget De L'Isle, composer of the famous hymn to liberty, during the French Revolution. The denouement, involving the substitution of victims in the shadow of the guillotine, is highly reminiscent of Dickens' *A Tale of Two Cities*, a novel which the anglophile librettist Miguel Ramos Carrión must surely have known. Caballero's mellifluous, Italianate score includes references to the revolutionary song *"Ça ira"* as well as the "Marseillaise" itself, and a catchy—albeit anachronistic—Spanish *pasodoble*.

10
Joaquín Gaztambide
(1822–70)

Joaquín Romualdo Gaztambide y Garbayo was born in Tudela (Navarra) on 7th February 1822. He studied in his home town, and later in Pamplona where he also played double bass in the theatre orchestra. From 1842 he attended the Madrid Conservatory, studying composition with the leading composer of the day, Ramón Carnicer. Although his pianistic skills led to some solo engagements, he continued to make his living playing double bass, notably at the Teatro de la Cruz where he was promoted to Chorus Master in 1846 with the support of his great friend the comic bass Francisco Salas. He conducted a run of performances featuring Spanish singers and dancers in Paris the following year, visiting London with a similar group ten years later.

In 1849 he became director of music at Madrid's Teatro Español; and although he also wrote piano and orchestral music, including ballets and a symphony, Gaztambide's main energies from that time were devoted to the movement to revive a native operatic tradition. Later that year he produced his first successful zarzuela, the two-act *La mensajera* (The Message Girl). When the Teatro Real opened in 1851 Italian Opera abandoned the Teatro del Circo, and a group of writers and composers including Gaztambide and Salas formed a plan to produce zarzuela at the empty theatre. His *El amanecer* (The Dawn) was swiftly followed by *¡Tribulaciones!* (Tribulations!, both 1851); but he and his four colleagues Barbieri, Oudrid, Hernando and Inzenga went on to compose the much more successful *Por seguir a una mujer* (In Pursuit of a Woman, 1851), a French play adapted into Spanish by Luis de Olona, president of the group and a frequent collaborator. This same play had also been set by the young Verdi, as *Un Giorno di Regno*.

His music for the Teatro del Circo included *El sueño de una noche de verano* (A Midsummer Night's Dream, 1852, based on Shakespeare), as well as the better-known *El valle de Andorra* (The Valley of Andorra, 1852) and *Catalina* (1854). After 1856 he was active at the purpose-built Teatro de la Zarzuela, where *Los magyares* (The Magyars, 1857), *El juramento* (The Oath, 1858) and *Una vieja* (An Old Lady, 1860) proved his most popular successes. His later work included the directorship of the orchestral Sociedad de Conciertos, through which he introduced Wagner to Madrid, and an adventurous trip to Cuba with a zarzuela company in 1868. A major revolt led to their flight to Mexico, where Gaztambide's health and finances declined rapidly. Returning to Spain for an operation, he died in Madrid on 18th March 1870.

Gaztambide's musical and intellectual contribution to the revival of zarzuela was highly significant, but over the last century his own works have almost completely disappeared from the stage. Although the lightweight *Una vieja* had enjoyed the occasional revival, the Madrid production of *El juramento* in 2000 at the Teatro de la Zarzuela provided the opportunity for a broader revaluation of the composer's work. Eminently theatrical, tastefully Italianate in the manner of Donizetti, his absorbing music nevertheless makes use of Spanish dance rhythms and popular songs; and had Gaztambide's career been longer it is very possible he could have developed along the same lines as his great contemporary, Barbieri.

El juramento

Zarzuela in three acts
(Madrid, Teatro de la Zarzuela, 20th December 1858)

Text: Luis de Olona

Principal Characters: Count of Arenal (bass); María, his ward (mezzo-soprano); Baroness of Aguafría, his fiancée (soprano); Carlos, his nephew and heir (tenor); Sebastián, a groom (comic tenor); Marquis de San Esteban, Militia Captain (baritone); Peralta, his second in command (baritone).

ACT 1— 1710 during the reign of Philip V, at the country seat of the Count of Arenal in Galicia. The Count is a bachelor who has brought up María, daughter of his deceased steward, almost as his own daughter. He has also cared for Carlos, his nephew and heir, who is currently recovering from injuries sustained in the war against Austria. The youngsters are in love, but have kept their feelings secret owing to their difference in rank.

After a brief *Preludio*, María and the villagers greet the Count and Carlos back from a game hunt. The old man boasts of his hunting prowess, though the stable groom Sebastián happily mocks his master (*Introducción: "¡Ellos son!"*). After the spoils are distributed, the villagers leave, and Carlos reveals that he has been ordered to return to his regiment. As soon as they are alone, he promises María to return and take her as his wife, in despite of the social stigma. They leave as the Count returns with Sebastián. The old aristocrat has agreed to marry the young and wealthy Baroness of Aguafría, though it emerges they have not yet met. Sebastián offers to marry María, an idea seized on by the old man, who does not want to lose her companionship. Before Sebastián can break the good news to María, they are interrupted by the sound of a carriage overturning.

The Baroness storms in, her sumptuous dress ruined by the accident but otherwise unharmed. The villagers, with María and Sebastián, comment on the richness of her attire and invite her to stay the night while her carriage is repaired. Their lively *Bolero: "Esta señora cruzaba ahora"* leads into a winning *Cavatina* for the Baroness: *"El arroyo, la enramada"*, with coloratura ornaments in Donizettian mode, in which she expresses her preference for sophisticated salon life, over and above the gross inconvenience of the country. She is surprised to learn that this is the estate of her fiancé, and even more surprised when she sees his advanced age. Carlos is much more to her taste, and she tries to prevent the Count's announcement of their engagement. When he finally does come out with the news, Carlos is shocked by the difference in age—and dumbstruck when the Count announces the additional engagement of María and Sebastian. The Count silences his protests; and María, devastated by Carlos's lack of persistence, agrees to marry the groom.

The others leave, and María expresses her sorrow in a touching *Romanza: "¡Ah! Yo me vi!"*. She is joined by the ebullient Marquis de San Esteban, dressed as a Captain of Militia and accompanied by his second-in-command Peralta, regretting that he will soon have to renounce the pleasures of the chase in favor of the uncertain delights of military service (*Salida: "¡Cuál brilla el sol en la verde pradera!"*). The Marquis asks María for hospitality, and the three philosophize on the brevity of life's pleasures in a delicate *Terceto: "Guarde Dios a la niña hermosa"*. The nobleman sees tears in María's eyes, but she will not tell him the cause, going into the manor house to announce his visit. Peralto is sad for his master, but before he can go to drown his sorrows he is interrupted by Sebastián, off to procure a Notary for his immediate marriage; and by the Baroness, who has decided she much prefers the idea of marriage with Carlos to life with his old uncle.

When Carlos begs her to intercede on his behalf with the Count, she tells him he is worthy of something better than María. Before she can suggest herself, the Marquis blunders in and she leaves haughtily. The two men are old friends, and the Marquis is sympathetic when he learns of Carlos's difficulty. He has a plan to make all well—provided Carlos will agree to obey all his instructions without question, and leave the estate immediately. Carlos agrees, and runs off as María comes out of the manor.

When the Marquis tells her Carlos has gone without even saying good-bye she feels humiliated, and asks him to beg her guardian to place her in a convent rather than marry her off to Sebastián. The Marquis agrees, but when the Count reappears with the Baroness and Peralta, amazes everyone by asking for her hand himself. The finale begins as Sebastián returns with the Notary, and the villagers playing rustic instruments (*Final: "Su rara hermosura"*). He is speechless when he hears the news, María falls senseless to the ground, while the villagers continue celebrating the nuptials, though now for María and the Marquis.

ACT 2—A Salon in the Count's manor house, one month later. The Baroness has been unable to leave, because of the proximity of the Austrian army. Sebastián and the villagers whisper gossip about the strange behavior of the newly weds: husband and wife sleep apart and spend little time together (*Introducción y Coro de la murmuración: "Chú, chú, chú"*). María curses her fate in having a husband who cares nothing for her and seems to prefer flirting with the Baroness. The Count storms in, determined to challenge the Marquis to a duel over this bad behavior. To his fury, the apparently errant husband continues to pay court to the Baroness, who in turn mocks the Marquis mercilessly (*Cavatina: "Blandamente murmurando"*) before restating her determination not to marry the old Count.

After they have all left, Carlos returns. He is ignorant of events in his absence, and recalls his former happiness here with María in an elegant, melancholy *Romanza: "Esta es la misma ventana"*. When Peralta tells him of María's marriage to his friend he sees red, only to be calmed by the Marquis himself, who explains his actions. Two months ago he killed a love rival in a duel, and was condemned to death. His General, to avoid disgrace, made him swear an oath that he would die bravely in battle against the Austrians. On his demise, María will inherit both fortune and title, thus enabling her to marry Carlos. In proof of which, he has not touched his wife since the wedding. Carlos, moved, asks to see María, but the Marquis tells him to hide in the garden until he himself has departed for the army that night. He allows Carlos to leave a note for her on the spinet, saying he will meet her later.

Once Carlos has gone, the Marquis tries to avoid meeting María, because he has begun to fall in love with her. She reproaches him with his heartless flirtations, so to soften his wife's mood the Marquis suggests they sit at the piano and sing together (*Dúo: "¡Tan! ¡tan! Niña a tu puerta"* with piano accompaniment). When María discovers the note from Carlos, her nervousness affects her singing. The Marquis, struggling against his jealousy, withdraws to spy on the lovers; but when Carlos appears, María rejects his advances and tells him roundly that she now loves only her husband. Once she has left the room, the Marquis comes out of hiding to bid farewell to his friend before heading off to the Army and his death. As he leaves, he confesses his own growing love for María.

The wounded Carlos reveals all to the Baroness, including the growing attachment between the new married couple. Touched, she makes him ashamed of his anger, encouraging him to behave generously toward his hapless friend and rival. He accepts her advice, and leaves with the intention of saving the Marquis and sacrificing his own life in his place. When they have gone, María rushes in, worried because her husband is preparing for "a long journey to a country from which none returns." She tries to get Peralta to recall him, but instead Sebastián appears with the news that the Marquis has already left. María tells the groom to bring her carriage and drive her after him, and he agrees in the *Dúo Final: "Amor de mi alma"*.

ACT 3—A forest, near the Spanish army camp, late that night. A group of soldiers sing a martial chorus in praise of the forest and leave on patrol (*Introducción y Coro de la diana: "Soldados de la ronda"*). Sebastián and Maria come out of hiding. She is still in the dark about her husband's plans, although Sebastián feels that if he can get Peralta drunk the Sergeant will reveal all. When some officers enter with Carlos and the Marquis, María hides again. Her husband invites them all to dinner in his tent, before the dawn assault on the enemy lines. When they are alone, Carlos tries to persuade his friend to change his mind, and assures him of María's growing love. The Marquis will not hear him, and follows the other officers. Next, the Count appears, having been dragged in pursuit by the Baroness, who is anxious to find María. Carlos takes them both to the Marquis's tent.

After a brief offstage *Brindis* (drinking song) from the soldiers, Peralta and Sebastián appear, roaring drunk on the Marquis's wine. They sing some tipsy couplets together in zapateado rhythm (*Dúo: "O el mundo se menea"*) but Sebastián is unable to elicit any information from him. Dawn is breaking, and María herself decides to try and discover the truth from the Sergeant herself. Before she can try, the Marquis appears with a letter. He asks Peralta to deliver it to María, and stay with her throughout the battle. The drunken Peralta refuses to leave the Captain's side, which touches his master greatly.

Maria comes forward, begging her husband not to die, and confessing her love for him. Before he can reveal his feelings, reveille sounds and he makes to leave, promising to return soon (*Dúo: "Guarde Dios al gentil marido"*). Now Carlos rushes in bearing a Royal Pardon. The Baroness, having taken pity on the newlyweds, has successfully interceded with King Philip on the Marquis's behalf.

He accepts the pardon, but still insists on giving up his wife to his friend. Finally, the Baroness herself arrives with the Count in tow. Between them they manage to convince the Marquis that the most honorable thing is for him to admit defeat, and fall into the arms of his loving young wife. The zarzuela ends with all five expressing their content at this happy conclusion in the *Quinteto Final*, a brief reprise of the *Terceto* from Act 1.

El juramento (The Oath) was one of Gaztambide's finest scores, and an early triumph for the new Teatro de la Zarzuela which had opened its doors two years before. The playwright Luis de Olona was the chief literary figure behind the creation of a truly national Spanish lyric theatre. Paradoxically, he often adapted preexistent material, but though the central character of *El juramento* is taken in part from the Parisian *opéra comique La Rose de Péronne*, Olona's comedy is both original and highly effective. If we can swallow the central device of the Marquis's secret oath, the play exhibits the depth and quality of some of the finest plays of the early romantic movement, notably Lessing's *Minna von Barnhelm*, which it resembles in theme and milieu.

The score has substance as well as charm, especially where its composer leavens his Italianate style with Spanish dance rhythms and a seasoning of harmonic subtlety. As the great early chronicler of zarzuela Antonio Peña y Goñi wrote soon after the premiere, "the lyric melodies, vigorous pacing, and simple clarity of the total effect are typical of Joaquín Gaztambide." Numbers such as the *Bolero* and María's Act 1 *Romanza* breathe a fresh and essentially Spanish air, while the moving *Dúo* at the piano for the hapless husband and wife shows Gaztambide's true instinct for theatrical as well as musical effect. Its sunny simplicity makes for a poignant contrast with the murky cross-currents of the emotional situation:

Catalina (1854)
Luis de Olona's romance of Peter the Great, saved by his beloved Catalina (Catherine I) from a complicated plot to hand him over to his Swedish enemies, inspired Gaztambide's most admired full-length zarzuela. Widely performed outside Spain

during the composer's life, *Catalina* is long overdue for revival; not least for the unusual, witty duet for two tenors *"Mira el vestido nuevo"* and the high quality of its *concertante* movements such as the lovely *terceto nocturno* for Catalina, Pedro (Peter) and the peasant girl Berta.

La conquista de Madrid (The Conquest of Madrid, 1863)
The eleventh-century siege and recapture of Moorish Madrid by Christian forces provides the inspiration for Luis Mariano de Larra's three-act historical drama. Though among Gaztambide's best scores, and staged as far afield as Germany (Coburg, 1878) its revival is unlikely today, not least because of anti-Semitic elements in the plot. The passionate *Romanza* for the imprisoned baritone hero *"Entre los muros de su prisión"* is sometimes encountered in concert.

El valle de Andorra (The Valley of Andorra, 1852)
Luis de Olona took his text from a French libretto originally set by Halévy, while Gaztambide's music draws heavily on the styles and forms of late Rossini and Donizetti. Not surprisingly, there is little distinctively Spanish about the resulting three-act work; and though the score's fresh, light simplicity kept the work in the repertory well into the twentieth century, Gaztambide's later, more personal scores are better bets for modern revival.

Una vieja (An Old Lady, 1860)
Set in Mexico during the 1826 War of Independence, the plot of this short comic opera turns on a false marriage of convenience between an imprisoned, young Spanish officer and a rich old lady. The marriage proves true, the lady youthful (though still rich!). Although based on a French libretto by Scribe, Camprodón's witty one-act zarzuela incorporates nostalgic reminiscences of Spain of which Gaztambide was able to make very good use. The score is among his tightest and most distinctively Spanish, and has been successfully revived in recent years.

11
Gerónimo Giménez
(1854–1923)

Born Jerónimo Jiménez in Seville on 10th October 1854, he began musical training with his father and with Salvador Viniegra in Cádiz. Something of a child prodigy, he joined the first violin section at the Teatro Principal aged twelve, and five years later conducted Pacini's opera *Saffo* in Gibraltar. In 1874 he left Cádiz with a city scholarship to consolidate his technical skills under François Bazin and Ambroise Thomas at the Paris Conservatoire, where he won first prize for harmony and counterpoint. He also carried off the piano prize, for which the runner-up was Claude Debussy. A tour of Italy preceded his inevitable gravitation toward the Spanish capital, where by 1885 he had become conductor at the Teatro Apolo, later moving to the Teatro de la Zarzuela. From around this time he preferred to give his name the less plebeian form (as he conceived it) of Gerónimo Giménez, though both spellings continued to be used.

Aside from a healthy output of zarzuelas, Giménez also managed to write a number of symphonic and chamber works. Many of these were played by the Unión Musical Española and the Sociedad de Conciertos, both of which orchestras he conducted. His best stage works date from relatively early in his career. Among the most notable are *Trafalgar* (1890), *Los voluntarios* (The Volunteers, 1893) and *Los borrachos* (The Drunks, 1899) but his fame largely rests on three works: the twin *sainetes El baile de Luis Alonso* and *La boda de Luis Alonso* (The Dance and The Wedding of Luis Alonso, 1896/7), and his masterpiece *La tempranica* (The Headstrong Girl, 1900).

Perhaps aware of waning powers, he achieved further success after the turn of the century with Miguel Nieto in their witty backstage reworking of *El barbero de Sevilla* (The Barber of Seville, 1901); and with the young Amadeu

Vives, notably in *El húsar de la guardia* (The Hussar Guard, 1904) and *La gatita blanca* (The White Kitten, 1905). Their intriguing *Los viajes de Gulliver* (based on Jonathan Swift's *Gulliver's Travels*, 1910) did not cut much ice. Later solo efforts, such as *Cinematógrafo nacional* (National Cinema, 1907) and *La cortesana de Omán* (The Oman Courtesan, 1920), were cold-shouldered by audiences and critics alike. Giménez's last years were soured by financial problems and ill health as well as the decline in public and professional favor, this last partly down to his own unreasonable behaviour. He was refused a professorial chair at the Madrid Conservatoire, and died virtually penniless in Madrid on 19th February 1923.

The lack of consistency in Giménez's musical output, admittedly partly due to the mediocre quality of many of the libretti that he set, should not be allowed to obscure his technical brilliance and musical sophistication. Many of his orchestral *preludios* are still popular; and *El baile* and *La boda de Luis Alonso* glory in a number of *intermedios* and dances which demonstrate a piquant handling of instrumental color, far in advance of his contemporaries with the exception of Chapí and Bretón. The best collaborations with Vives similarly display both composers at their finest as melodists of taste and wit; but had he written nothing else, Giménez's name would be guaranteed an honorable place through his masterpiece, *La tempranica*.

La tempranica
Zarzuela in one act
(Madrid, Teatro de la Zarzuela, 19th September 1900)

Text: Julian Romea

Principal Characters: María la tempranica, a young gypsy girl (soprano); Grabié, her young brother (soprano); Don Luis, a wealthy landowner (baritone); Mr. James, his English friend (actor); Miguel, a young gypsy (actor).

SCENE 1—The mountain countryside near Granada. After a stirring *Preludio* a group of fashionable young men appears to the sound of hunting horns. They are friends of the wealthy Don Luis, singing the lusty *Coro*: *"La caza ya se esconde"* in praise of the joy of the chase. An Englishman, Mr. James, amuses them with his attempts at Castilian, horribly mangled with English. Like all good tourists he is eager to hear some typical flamenco songs, and Don Luis sends a servant to the nearby farm to look for the gypsy youth Grabié (a "breeches" role) who works for the local blacksmith. When the boy sees Don

Luis, he greets him with surprising familiarity—the whole family loves Don Luis, none more so than his sister María. In spite of Don Luis' attempts to shut him up, Grabié ingenuously goes on explaining how devoted she is to her *"Señorito."* Mr. James suspects a love affair, especially when Don Luis changes the subject and swiftly asks Grabié to sing something. The boy obliges with a cheeky *Zapateado: "La tarántula é un bicho mu malo"* about the wicked ways of the tarantula—or perhaps the dangers of falling in love.

Don Luis is shamed by his friends into telling the truth. Losing his way among the dangerous mountain peaks, he fell and knocked himself unconscious, coming to in the tiny hovel of his rescuers, María's family. The girl, known as La tempranica (headstrong), nursed Luis to full recovery, and truthful to her name fell impulsively in love with him. Luis is evasive about whether he returned her feeling. He certainly left the gypsies as soon as he was able, without even saying good-bye to the girl. María was inconsolable for many weeks, though Grabié tells Luis that she is learning to forget him.

Warned not to tell María of Don Luis's proximity, the boy naturally rushes to let her know. La tempranica instantly appears, demanding to speak to Luis alone. The rest leave, and in the searching *Dúo: "Yo no zé al verte"* he tries to calm her protestations of love, while carefully avoiding the truth—which is that, since leaving her, he has married a beautiful woman of his own class. He warns her repeatedly that love between them is impossible, but she will not accept his word and swears to win him at all costs.

SCENE 2—A gypsy camp in the mountains. Miguel, a serious and hardworking young gypsy, has fallen in love with María and she has agreed to marry him. An intense orchestral *Intermedio* leads into a powerful gypsy *Coro: "A trabajá con faitigas"* lamenting the harsh reality of gypsy life. María remains sunk in melancholy (*"Tempranica me yaman . . . Zuspiroz de mi pecho"*), her mood reflected by the yearning strains of a flamenco song (*"A la nanita nana"*), counterpointed with the joyful nonsense of some of Miguel's friends and La tempranica's own passionate outbursts.

Grabié eventually teases his sister into acceptance of her situation with a little unaccompanied song *"Don . . . don guilindín"*, and the tribe gathers to celebrate the betrothal (*Coro: "¡Ea! ¡Ea! Vayan peniya afuera"*). María appears in her wedding finery, singing proudly of her gypsy life and lover in the intensely beautiful *Romanza: "Sierras de Granada"*. Her song changes course when she sees Don Luis bringing Mr. James along to sample the colorful delights of the gypsy festivities. La tempranica painfully hopes that her true love has come to claim her (*"Ay, amante, amantito . . . Al compás de tus ojos"*); and the tribe, thinking she still sings of Miguel, second her ardent longings by breaking into a joyous *Tango: "Venga un tanguito nuevo"* with prominent castanets. When Grabié, hiding behind a rock, learns the truth—

that Luis is married—María suffers all the torments of hopeless, passionate despair, as the gypsies launch once more into their hedonistic dance.

SCENE 3—The city of Granada. The orchestral *Intermedio* transmutes the gypsy tango into a bland, sophisticated *Vals* which leads us into the brief final scene. María has come to plead with Don Luis, bringing her brother with her. As soon as she catches a glimpse of his wife and baby son, reality breaks her dream apart. Patching up her shredded dignity as best she may, she decides to accept the love of the devoted Miguel and make what she can of her life. The zarzuela ends as she sings of her defiant determination to live on in the fullness of her headstrong, gypsy nature (*Final: "Tempranica me yaman"*).

Giménez wrote many zarzuelas: his detractors would have said too many. At its best, his work has an elegant finish and tuneful verve that disarm criticism, but for sheer intensity this one stands in a class by itself. *La tempranica* may be short, but it covers a surprising amount of musical and dramatic ground. Though the score is undeniably eclectic, the skill with which Giménez marshals his raw material provides an experience of genuine force and originality, and *La tempranica* remains one of the most influential achievements of the zarzuela tradition.

Romea's libretto is innocent of pretension, and very well stocked with the usual selection of picture-postcard vignettes of gypsy life. Giménez's triumph was to turn all this theatrical baggage into potent music drama. María is a fully rounded character, growing in stature as her story unfolds. The gypsy songs and dances, brilliantly done in themselves, illuminate her dark, intractable nature from within rather than simply providing local color. And though she comes in the end to accept second best, Giménez's heroine leaves us with a sense of a woman much closer to tragedy than, say, the hopeless Salud in de Falla's obviously indebted short opera *La vida breve*.

The complex musical patchwork of the gypsy scene is hugely impressive; but there is a wealth of contrasted material elsewhere—the Freischütz-like hunting horns of the opening, the *verismo* passion of the *dúo*, the urbane waltz representing the transition to alien city life at the climax of the action—which works to similar musico-dramatic effect. All these diverse elements are unified by the omnipresence of María La tempranica's own brooding musical "signature":

Tem-pra-ni-ca me ya-man, qui-sá lo se-a, qui-sá lo se-a;

At opposite ends of the scale of Giménez' musical range are Grabié's foot-tapping *Zapateado*, knowing and yet strangely innocent:

Tiempo de Zapateado

La ta - rán - tu - la é un bi - cho mu ma - lo,   no se ma - ta con pie - ra ni pa - lo;

and María's demanding *Romanza* at her betrothal ceremony, a deeply effective fusion of operatic aria and gypsy song:

Torroba's wholesale operatic rewrite, renamed *María la tempranica* (1931) flourished briefly, largely thanks to the talents of Felisa Herrero, Selíca Pérez Carpio and the tenor Delfín Pulido in the expanded role of Miguel. It has curiousity value, but in no way improves on the Giménez original.

El baile de Luis Alonso (Luis Alonso's Dance, 1896)
La boda de Luis Alonso (Luis Alonso's Wedding, 1897)
Although written a year later *La boda* provides a prequel to Giménez's highly successful short farce *El baile*. The plots of these twin *sainetes* revolve around the timeless joke of the rich old man who takes on a lusty young wife. The inevitable amorous complications that ensue are reflected in the sparkling orchestral *Preludios*, *Intermedios* and dances that enliven both scores, full of the colorful "Spanishry" of tambourine, triangle and castanets.

La gatita blanca (The White Kitten, with **Amadeu Vives**, 1905)
Short, brilliant fin-de-siècle *revista*, set in a contemporary Madrid cabaret-restaurant. Manolo and Rosario are a well-brought-up couple engaged to be married, but with amorous interests elsewhere. Through the cunning wiles of Manolo's girlfriend Luisa, a cabaret singer known as La gatita blanca, everything is put to rights. The Offenbach-like score boasts a frenetic *Preludio*, the witty *Habanera el Chocalatito* (Chocolate Habanera); and best known of all, the insouciant, risqué *Cuplés de la gatita blanca* (White Kitten Couplets) for the heroine, Luisa.

El barbero de Sevilla (The Barber of Seville, with **Miguel Nieto**, 1901)
Elena, the heroine of this popular one-act *sainete*, is a promising opera singer; and the fast-paced farcical plot reaches its apogee of confusion after her triumphant debut as Rosina in Rossini's opera in the provincial town of Burgos. Its operatic ambience gave the composers a chance to have fun with pastiche and parody, but the best number is Elena's "rehearsal song," the *Polonesa* (Polonaise): *"Me llaman la primorosa"*, a brilliant display number which remains a deservedly great favorite with Spanish coloratura and lyric sopranos.

12
Jacinto Guerrero
(1895–1951)

Born in Toledo (16th August 1895) to a father who was director of the city's municipal band, Jacinto Guerrero's musical training began early. After his father's death in 1904 he was enrolled as a chorister at Toledo Cathedral, where he studied with Lluis Ferré, who had been impressed with vocal compositions such as a *Salve* in four parts written when Jacinto was only six years old. The writing of a *Hymn to Toledo* won for him a grant to study at the Madrid Conservatory (1914), where he studied violin as well as harmony and composition.

After a brief spell supporting himself as a café violinist, he quickly obtained a post in the orchestra of the Teatro Apolo. As early as 1919 he began writing music for the theatre, climbing rapidly to fame through a succession of three zarzuelas; *La alsaciana* (The Girl from Alsace, 1921), *La montería* (The Hunt, 1922) and *Los gavilanes* (The Sparrowhawks, 1923) in one, two and three acts respectively. A series of highly successful works followed, among which *El huésped del Sevillano* (The Guest at the Sevillano, 1926); *La rosa del azafrán* (The Saffron Flower, 1930) and *La fama del tartanero* (The Wagoner's Reputation, 1931) are especially noteworthy. Guerrero was also active as a Madrid city councillor, and became President of the Sociedad de Autores Españoles in 1948. Madrid went into mourning after his sudden death whilst undergoing an operation on 15th August 1951; and his last zarzuela *El canastillo de fresas* (The Basket of Strawberries, featuring a very young Pilar Lorengar) enjoyed an emotional triumph later that year.

Guerrero also provided music for a great number of *revistas* as well as quantities of film music, but his zarzuelas were and are the mainstay of his reputation. His melodies are memorable, his vocal lines fluent and natural, his construction sound. His orchestration (partly by Jesús García Leoz and others) is clear, straightforward and effective. Guerrero's music may not be distinctively personal or technically sophisticated, but his best works live on through a winning combination of immediacy and elegant simplicity. The Fundación Jacinto y Inocencio Guerrero, founded in memory of the composer and his brother, remains a highly proactive force for the promotion of Spanish music new and old, live and recorded.

Los gavilanes
Zarzuela in three acts
(Madrid, Teatro de la Zarzuela, 7th December 1923)

Text: José Ramos Martín

Principal Characters: Juan, the "Indian" (baritone); Adriana, his former love (soprano); Rosaura, her daughter (soprano); Gustavo, Rosaura's lover (tenor); Clariván, the village mayor (actor); Triquet, Sergeant of Gendarmes (comic tenor).

ACT 1, SCENE 1—The seashore of a Provençal fishing village in 1845. It is dawn, and the fisherfolk are already about their business (*Coro: "Pescador, de tu playa te alejas"*). The fifty-year-old Juan explains how, many years ago, he left the village in search of fortune. Now he returns rich with the silver of Peru, though he never forgot his home, as he recalls in a passionate *Romanza: "Mi aldea"*. Two old fishermen come down to the shore, and when Juan identifies himself they happily spread the news of his return. The villagers had believed him dead, but now all clamor to greet the long-lost "Indian" before he heads off to rest at his brother's home (*Coro y solo: "Pensando en ti noche y día"*). A choral interlude with offstage tenor voice introducing the "Sparrowhawk" motif (*Copla: "Palomita, palomita"*) leads to the next scene.

SCENE 2—The outskirts of the village. The sea is visible in the background. Emma and Nita, Juan's nieces, show off the jewels their uncle has brought them from Peru. Clariván, the lame old Mayor, tells them that he and Juan were very dear friends in their youth: in an exchange of sporting blows, Juan lamed him while Clariván split his friend's skull, and they remained inseparable ever after. Juan's brother Camilo and his wife Renata, luxuriating in splendid if somewhat overblown jewelry, arrive in advance of Triquet, Sergeant of the Gendarmerie and another old sparring partner of Juan. He is soon arguing with Clariván as to which of them was really the

Indian's best friend. When Camilo tells them that his brother intends to spend money improving the town, Mayor Clariván naturally offers to administer the good works. Camilo and Renata go into the house, warning their daughters Emma and Nita that now they are rich, they must leave their fisherman-fiancées.

A pretty village girl, Rosaura, cheers the two girls up in a lively Foxtrot, helped by Triquet (*Cuarteto cómico: "No hay por qué gemir"*). They respond by teasing her about her friendship with a certain Gustavo. She denies that there is anything between them, though her behavior when the young man in question appears leaves that open to question. The villagers burst in, shouting enthusiastically until Juan comes out of the house and greets them with a few well-chosen words in the sweeping *Tango milonga: "El dinero que atesoro"*. Triquet and Clariván compete in a display of friendly ardor, but the Indian pretends not to remember them. He invites everyone to have a drink on him, and after the villagers head off for the inn the Indian tells his old friends why he left so suddenly all those years ago. It was to get wealth enough to marry his sweetheart Adriana. However, her mother swiftly married her off to a rich older man, after which there was no reason for Juan to return. They tell him that Adriana is now a poor widow.

Left alone at last, Juan hears Gustavo in the distance, serenading his love (*Copla: "Soy mozo y enamorado"*). The song saddens him (*"Qué verdad dice la copla"*). A woman's voice is heard, which he seems to recognize: could it be Adriana? It is, and soon they are nostalgically recalling their old feelings in the touching *Dúo: "Dulces recuerdos"*. When she presents her daughter Rosaura, Juan is stirred by the girl's resemblance to the woman he once loved and offers to call on them that evening. Once the women leave, the Indian catches sight of Rosaura slipping away to join Gustavo, and the act ends with the two young lovers singing together by the seashore.

ACT 2—The village square that evening, near Adriana's house. Clariván with the town drummers and Triquet with his trumpet-playing gendarmes compete to outdo one another in celebration of the Indian's return (*Marcha: "Tocad, tamborileros"*). Adriana brings them together with a martial hymn to friendship (*"Amistad, amistad"*), but is moved when the two rivals remind her precisely why Juan trooped off to Peru in the first place. Her proud tears are cut short by her mother, Doña Leontina, who reminds Adriana that only the Indian can save them from destitution. Rosaura arrives home, followed by Gustavo. Adriana has hopes they may marry, Leontina does not. Gustavo gives a rose to his beloved in front of Emma and Nita who quietly admire the graceful compliment of his song, the poised *Romanza de la Flor: "Flor roja"*, before tactfully withdrawing. The boy almost brings himself to declare his love to Rosaura, while she evidently yearns for him just as strongly.

Juan has made his decision and seeks help from Doña Leontina. Clariván, Triquet, Camilo and Renata materialize in time to hear him confess that he wants to marry—with Rosaura (*Solo: "No importa que al amor mío"*). Shocked, the Mayor and the Sergeant beg him to reconsider, and when he refuses each charges the other with the heinous crime of being Juan's best friend. The celebrations for the Return of the Hero turn to dusty recriminations all round, though the dancing continues. Gustavo bursts in and halts them, Adriana confirms that the news is true, and Rosaura breaks down completely. The scandal of the aging man's lechery enrages the villagers, who turn on the defiant Juan as the curtain falls (*Final: "El baile debe terminar"*).

ACT 3, SCENE 1—Adriana's house at night, some days later. Everyone has gathered to celebrate the approaching wedding (*Coro: "Vivan los novios"*) for Juan has taken up all Adriana's debts in order to force the daughter's hand, and Rosaura has bowed to the inevitable. Clariván and Triquet task Juan with his behavior, telling him that the villagers have begun to call him "The Sparrowhawk" for his predatory seizure of such a helpless dove. When they have gone, Adriana confesses to Rosaura that she had loved Juan, but never told him so. Mother and daughter lament together in the moving *Dúo: "No merece ser feliz"* with its moving solo for the older woman (*"Para siempre murió mi ilusión"*). Adriana retires, and Rosaura whispers with Gustavo through the open window. They agree to meet, as the villagers distantly sing the "Sparrowhawk" couplets: *"Palomita, palomita"*.

SCENE 2—The outskirts of the village. The *Final* begins as Gustavo proposes to Rosaura that they elope, and she agrees in a passionate *Dúo: "Rosaura bella"*. Adriana arrives before they can put their plan into action, but Gustavo soon convinces her that it is the right thing to do. "The Sparrowhawk" emerges from the shadows, and surprises them by agreeing heartily with the boy! He has found the courage to renounce Rosaura, and will give her a dowry to marry her beloved Gustavo. Dawn is breaking again and the villagers return to their work: his act of selflessness has won Juan the respect and the gratitude of them all (*Final: "Pescador, de tu playa te alejas"*).

The three-act *Los gavilanes* (The Sparrowhawks) is Guerrero at his most direct. Ramos Martín's libretto is no literary masterpiece, but it does boast a well-constructed and unusually involving storyline not unlike Dürrenmatt's *Der Besuch* (The Visit), and the composer grasped its theatricality with both hands. Beyond that, the poignant subtlety of the protagonists' situations clearly suited the composer's gift for gentle melody and sympathetic, pastel characterization. The orchestral scoring, too, is efficient and even delicate as occasion dictates.

Above all, *Los gavilanes* has a spontaneity which the composer perhaps never quite matched, despite the superior artistic finish of later works such as *La rosa del azafrán*. Number after number hits the spot, the comedy numbers (never Guerrero's greatest strength) being as effective as more obviously stirring numbers like Juan's opening *Romanza* and his *Tango milonga*. Then there is the magically still *Romanza de la Flor* for the tenor; with a high-lying line almost as hard to sustain as Nadir's famous aria in Bizet's *Les Pecheurs de Perles*, Gustavo's *"Flor roja"* is amongst the most perfect pearls in the zarzuela repertoire.

El huésped del Sevillano
Zarzuela in two acts
(Madrid, Teatro Apolo, 3rd December 1926)

Text: Enrique Reoyo and Juan Ignacio Luca de Tena

Principal Characters: Maese Andrés, a Toledo swordsmith (actor); Raquel, his daughter (soprano); Juan Luis, painter to the Royal Court (tenor); Rodrigo, Juan Luis's page (comic tenor); Don Diego, a nobleman (baritone); Constancia, maid at the Sevillano Inn (soprano); A Guest, at the same (actor).

ACT 1—Late afternoon in a small Toledo square, at the beginning of the seventeenth century. In the workshop of Master Andrés Munstein, the town's finest swordsmith, three of his journeymen are tempering swords. A group of girls led by Ginesa are filling their pitchers at a fountain, and their romantic musings merge poetically with the songs of the swordsmiths at their work (*Coro: "En la fuente cristalina"*).

Juan Luis, the Court painter, talks with an army captain and the city Corregidor while waiting for his sword to be returned from polishing. The artist has received an order to paint an Immaculate Virgin for the Royal Oratory, and has come to Toledo in search of a model. He has heard of the rare beauty of a certain Constancia, kitchen maid at the Sevillano Inn; the Corregidor confirms the report but adds that the swordsmith's daughter, Raquel, is no whit her inferior. What's more, he adds in a low voice, her Hebrew origins make her a perfect model for the Virgin. Master Andrés returns Juan Luis's sword, all the more lustrous for his professional attentions. Its owner hails its glory in the popular, martial *Canto a la Espada:* "*Fiel espada triunfadora*" before his companions leave.

The painter's page Rodrigo bewails the misery of his existence to a group of girls. Praying to be saved from a shipwreck, he swore to marry the most ugly woman he met within the year—and now his time is up! Juan Luis, meanwhile, is eager to get a glance of Raquel. He doesn't have long to wait. Painter and page conceal themselves as she leaves the workshop to attend mass at the great Cathedral, and are duly stunned by her classic grace. Raquel sings a folksong in praise of the beauty of Toledo women, and Juan Luis chimes in from his hiding place (*Dúo:* "*Cuando el grave sonar de la campana*").

The artist asks Master Andrés for permission to use his daughter as a model, but as a converted Jew the swordsmith is alarmed when he mentions her Hebraic features and denies the request. At that moment they hear Raquel crying for help; and Juan Luis hurtles to the rescue to find Raquel and the aristocratic Don Diego beset by three citizens. The painter beats off the trio, receiving a wound to the hand in the process. Thanking him for his aid, Don Diego enters his palace.

All, however, was not as it seemed, as Raquel explains once her relieved father has left the scene: the citizens were protecting her from Don Diego's unwelcome attentions, but she is unwilling to worry her father by exposing this powerful libertine for what he is. The young woman and her protector are united in indignation at Don Diego's arrogant behavior, but their mood soon softens and a love scene develops (*Dúo:* "*Insolente, presumido*").

Word has got out about Rodrigo's oath, and the page runs in pursued by a bevy of ugly women. Constancia the kitchen maid is enduring equally pestilential attentions from a group of handsome young men, and the two seek refuge by feigning an assignation with one another (*Pasacalle:* "*No me seas esquivo*"). Frustrated, the ugly women pair off with the handsome men and leave. Constancia tells Rodrigo that she is heading for the swordsmith's to collect a dagger for a charismatic writer who is lodging at the Inn. Master Andrés, who has read several of the man's works, seconds her enthusiasm; and Constancia leaves with the repaired dagger.

Dusk falls and Don Diego slips from his palace with four masked servants (*Solo y coro:* "*Salid, mis fieles criados*"). When Raquel appears they gag her and carry her off to the Inn, despite her father's attempts to intervene. Juan Luis, rushing in too late, promises to rescue her from the kidnappers— even at the cost of his life (*Final:* "*Castellano, toledano*").

ACT 2, SCENE 1—A narrow highway looking down on the city. Juan Luis meets with Rodrigo, who has heard from Constancia that a veiled woman has been carried into the Sevillano Inn and imprisoned in a room there. Ordering the page to verify Raquel's identity, Juan Luis listens pensively to the song of a muleteer, heading into town with some villagers from Lagartera (*Solo y coro: "Para mula de varas"*). The girls have come to sell trinkets, lace and finery to the women of Toledo, and one of them—Teresa—leads them in a vivacious song praising the native wit of their village (*Coro de Lagarteranas: "Corred más que antes que sea noche"*).

SCENE 2—A street in front of the Sevillano Inn. Rodrigo sees Don Diego, disguised as a muleteer, greeting a monk whom he ushers into the Inn. Don Diego tells the innkeeper that he has arranged a dance as a noisy distraction to cover his planned removal of Raquel from the city. Rodrigo manages to purloin one of the monk's habits, and tells Constancia of his master's plot to rescue the abducted woman. She agrees to help, and the pair find time for some flirtatious banter as the "monk" takes the girl's confession, treating it as a sacred charge absolving him from his own marital oath (*Dúo cómico: "Si tu fueras pastora"*).

Don Diego orders Constancia to produce Raquel, and informs the swordsmith's daughter that she will be leaving Toledo that night either by her own will, or by force: the choice is hers. Their dialogue is partially overheard by the writer-guest. He is an ex-soldier who lost an arm at the battle of Lepanto—Miguel de Cervantes, writing a book which he asserts will bring immortal fame to the Inn. Constancia quietly tells Raquel that Juan Luis has a plan to rescue her; and the swordsmith's daughter proudly rejects Don Diego, before singing sadly of her predicament in the touching *Romanza: "La pena me hace llorar"*.

The arranged party gets underway with the arrival of a lively group of youngsters, singing and dancing with Constancia to the rhythm of Don Diego's guitar whilst the disguised nobleman gives orders to his four masked servants (*Coro: "Entren pues, todos los mozos"*). Rodrigo, still in monkish attire, interrupts the music and picks a fight with Don Diego as the revelers scatter. Constancia is able to overhear that Don Diego plans the abduction on the stroke of midnight. She informs Rodrigo, arranging for a small window to be left open. The painter is soon on the scene, and reflects on the beauty of his imprisoned love in the lyrical *Romanza: "Mujer de los negros ojos"*.

He slips into the Inn through the window to protect Raquel. Over an orchestral evocation of the summer night, Cervantes drinks in the cool night air, reflecting in a spoken *Monologo: "Pintura sobre pintura"* on the likely outcome of the story and the "wonderful, strange mixture ... mystics and adventurers and poets and soldiers ... that is Castile and Spain."

Don Diego appears with his masked thugs, but they are held up outside the inn by Constancia, giving Rodrigo time to alert the City Guard. Juan Luis holds him at bay, the Guards arrive and after a short struggle lead Don Diego and his henchmen away. The triumphant painter and Raquel leave to put Master Andrés' mind at rest, and Rodrigo and Constancia plight their troth before the page rushes off after his master. The maid lingers, curious to watch Cervantes working in the serene night air. When she asks what he is writing about, the illustrious Guest tells her that she is to be the protagonist of his next story, *La ilustre fregona* (The Noble Kitchenmaid), and the zarzuela ends with a brief orchestral reminiscence of the theme in praise of the matchless women of Toledo.

El huésped del Sevillano (The Guest at the Sevillano) is Guerrero's most deeply considered work, having taken him six months to write. The composer did not labor in vain. His zarzuela scored an immediate triumph and has been dear to the hearts of Spaniards ever since.

Beneath the twilit, romantic action of *El huésped* lies a deeply felt tribute to the golden age of Castilian Spain and its spiritual home, Toledo. Our sense of watching a tale within a tale is heightened by the fact that we don't meet with the title figure until late in the day. "The Guest" is a writer; none other than Spain's greatest, Cervantes himself; watching, absorbing, commenting on the eternal human drama that unfolds before his and our eyes.

Enrique Reoyo also worked with Guerrero on *La canción del Ebro* (The Song of the Ebro, 1941) and was the writer of the elevated, poetic scenes of *La leyenda del beso* for Soutullo and Vert. Certainly the blank verse he puts into the mouth of Cervantes forms a noble and moving envoi to the action. Juan Ignacio Luca de Tena was perhaps responsible for the comic Rodrigo-Constancia story, a mirror action which provides *El huésped* with the double-plot ambience of classic Renaissance drama.

Given the scrupulous care which Guerrero lavished on his score it's not surprising that this is the composer's most subtly finished and technically flawless work. It is also chock full of memorable tunes; the lively Song of the Girls from Lagartera, the imprisoned Raquel's touching *Romanza*, Juan Luis's Song of the Sword and perhaps above all his brief but beautiful *"Mujer de los negros ojos"* which provides the musical climax of the action before Cervantes' spoken peroration. The *dúos* for hero and heroine display great tenderness and flexibility of mood, and altogether *El huésped del Sevillano* justifies its place among the best loved of Guerrero's works, one of the most popular zarzuelas in the entire repertoire.

La montería
Zarzuela in two acts
(Zaragoza, Teatro Circo, 24th November 1922)

Text: José Ramos Martín

Principal Characters: Duke of Jetkinsson (actor); Sir Edmund, his son (baritone); Pipón, his Master of Hounds (tenor); Ketty, his niece (actor); Marta, Pipón's sister (soprano); Ana, a maid at the Duke's castle (soprano).

ACT 1—A pretty village in rolling English hill country, outside the feudal castle of the Duke of Jetkinsson. After a tuneful *Preludio* preempting many of the zarzuela's most popular themes, we hear Pipón, the Duke's young Master of Hounds, blowing his horn to sound the end of the day's activities. He announces a holiday for all the villagers who took part in the hunt, not the least of whom is Ana, a chambermaid from the castle who is the winsome object of his affections. Pipón frets about the well-being of his sister, Marta, who is greeted enthusiastically by the villagers when she appears. She lightly recalls the amorous attentions she has received from one of the aristocratic hunters, though not without an underlying bitterness (*Coro y canción: "Hermosa aldeana"*).

Marta confesses to the inquisitive Ana that her admirer is none other than the Duke's son, Sir Edmund. Fearing her brother's reaction, she begs her friend to be discreet. Pipón reappears, but has little chance to make headway with Ana before Sir Edmund himself arrives. He laughingly offers to speak up to his father on behalf of the couple, and continues flirting with the dismissive Marta, telling her that he knows all about love's torments (*Cuarteto: "¡Bravo, bien! ... Si en el pecho sentís"*).

Left alone with Marta, Edmund begins to charm her into submission; but he is interrupted by the arrival of four aristocratic ladies—Marquise, Countess, Baroness and Viscountess—who frighten the poor girl off with their withering sarcasm. When they tease Edmund about his imminent wedding with his lovely cousin Ketty ("Katy") the young man claims he is only indulging in a little harmless flirtation; and in a lively ensemble he begs them not to gossip about what they have seen (*Fox-trot: "La murmuración ... ¡Oh baronesa gentil!"*).

The Duke returns from the hunt with Ketty and his other guests. He lectures his son on his sexual delinquency; but although Edmund promises to reform, he makes clear to his friends Edward, Henry and Hugo that he is only marrying this cousin because his father has threatened to disinherit him if he refuses. He has begged Marta to yield her virtue, but she is a girl of principle; and her brother, alerted to the situation by the Duke's words, will guard her honor fiercely. Edmund makes one more attempt, sending a letter to the girl through his six huntsmen (female chorus). Marta refuses their request to take pity on their master, but nevertheless waits for Edmund to reappear (*Marcha de los monteros: "Escucha, bella niña"*). He pours out his heart in the lyrical *Dúo: "No importunéis a la bella . . . Ya la ilusión con que soñé"*. Marta can hold out no longer, and admits that she loves him, too.

Edmund embraces Marta and leaves, but not before her brother Pipón spies what is going on. He swears to be revenged on the philandering heir, and asks Ana to help him. According to village custom, Ana is to be crowned Queen of Justice on the morrow. Her privilege will be to dictate judgments in lovers' quarrels, and those judgments are final. She agrees to use what power she has to save Marta from her fate, and the villagers acclaim their Queen-to-be in the brief *Final: "¡Hurra por nuestra reina!"*.

ACT 2, SCENE 1—The village green, decked out for the holiday fair. The villagers are enjoying the festivities (*Coro: "Alegre día"*). Ana enters in the traditional Queen's costume, handed down from olden times. She mocks such old-fashioned flummery to the strains of a far from outmoded *Tango milonga: "¡Hay que ver mi abuelita!"*, a catchy tune soon taken up by the whistling chorus of villagers.

Upset by the compromising secrecy of her situation, Marta breaks down under Ana's kindly questioning. "The Queen" commands her to forget love and gently leads her out of harm's way. Eduardo, patronizing the fair with his friends, is ruffled by Marta's absence; he goes off to search for her just before Ana rushes back, pursued by the amorous Pipón determined to snatch a rose from the Castle maid—and why not a kiss as well? (*Dúo cómico: "No corras así"*).

Pipón goads the now frantic Edmund further by asking him to deliver a love letter. His real love isn't Ana, he claims, but a lady in the castle—Ketty! After all, if a nobleman can love a village girl, why shouldn't a huntsman love a fine lady? Edmund's response is to tear up the letter, and Pipón in return lets him know that Marta is not to be compromised. The scene ends as Pipón, Ana and the villagers join together in a country dance, decking the maypole with bright ribbons (*Coro: "En el alegre baile"*).

SCENE 2—That night, in a secluded corner of the castle gardens. Marta has agreed to meet Edmund, but Pipón has discovered the plan and advised Ketty what is afoot. Hearing her fiancé and the huntsmen serenading his village sweetheart, she and Pipón hide in the shrubbery. Edmund appears, singing gently to attract Marta's attention (*Serenata: "Esta es la ventana donde mi aldeana"*). The girl arrives, and the huntsmen tactfully withdraw. Edmund swears eternal faith, and though Marta tells him their love is impossible the two sink into each other's arms (*Dúo: "Ven, que amor eterno"*). The supernatural magic of the night is made manifest in a Dance of Fairies among the castle ruins, as the triumphant Edmund sings a passionately warm *Romanza: "Es la noche callada"*.

Coming out of hiding, Pipón shatters the idyll. Edmund flees, and the huntsman tells his sister that the Duke knows all and has sworn to exile his son from the estate forever. Ketty takes pity on the distraught girl; and when she promises to plead with the Duke on her behalf, Marta kisses her rival's hands in gratitude.

SCENE 3—Outside the Castle, next day. The villagers and Ana greet the Duke, who has come to apologize to Pipón for his son's behavior. With the help of Ana and Ketty, the huntsman procures Edmund's pardon, and Marta soon softens the old aristocrat's heart, obtaining his permission to marry Edmund. All praise the Duke's wisdom in the brief *Final: "¡Hurra por nuestra reina!"*.

La montería (The Hunt), like *La Generala*, has an English setting. Unlike Vives' 1912 operetta, where Oxford and Cambridge merely provide a stage for a posse of operetta-Ruritanians to play out their romantic plot, José Ramos Martín's text boasts a cast of real-life, 1920s English aristocrats and peasants. Apparently inspired by an evening spent with Guerrero in Madrid's famous ham and game emporium *Gambrinus*, his slick libretto exploits English snobbery—and hunting pink, with its familiar red jackets, white trousers and black riding boots: a particularly fetching combination, according to contemporary press reports, when worn by the *tiples* (sopranos) who provided the semi-chorus of huntsmen!

The first night of *La montería* on 25th January 1923 at the Teatro de la Zarzuela proved the foundation of the composer's financial fortune. The actual premiere had been two months earlier in Zaragoza, but his operetta's Madrid success franked the critical success of *La alsaciana* (1922) and pointed the way to the richer artistic achievement of *Los gavilanes* later in the year. Strangely, none of these three zarzuelas has a Spanish setting, although there's no specifically English influence audible in Guerrero's score.

Though most of *La montería* is lightweight, generic operetta, its catchy tunes and jazzy harmonic touches were enough to ensure its popularity for many years, even if today it seems somewhat moth-eaten. The most popular number was Ana's *Tango milonga: "Hay que ver"*, with its distinctive whistling chorus; but the best music is nearly all given to the baritone hero Edmundo. His Act 1 *dúo* with Marta contains one really distinguished melody, *"Ya la ilusión con que soñé"*, which could only come from a Spanish zarzuela.

La rosa del azafrán

Zarzuela in two acts
(Madrid, Teatro Calderón, 14th March 1930)

Text: Federico Romero and Guillermo Fernández Shaw

Principal Characters: Sagrario, owner of a La Mancha country estate (soprano); Juan Pedro, a farmhand (baritone); Catalina, a maidservant (soprano); Moniquito, church caretaker (comic tenor); Carracuca, a rich peasant (comic bass); Custodia, the village wise woman (actress); Don Generoso, former owner of the estate (actor).

ACT 1, SCENE 1—The outer courtyard of a rich country house in La Mancha during the 1860s. It is the time of the autumn sowing. Servants, shepherds and farmhands are enjoying a celebration in honor of the Saint's Day of their young mistress, Sagrario, washing the homely feast down with *zurra*—white wine with water and lemon juice—and dancing a *Seguidillas*. The revels are led by Catalina, a pretty serving maid (*Coro y solo: "Aunque soy de la Mancha"*).

The well-to-do peasant Carracuca is anxiously seeking Custodia, the elderly village wise woman. He begs her to save his wife Gertrudis, who has been suffering from hysteric fits which even Moniquito, the young caretaker from the local Hermitage of San Roque, has been unable to cure. Moniquito tries to use his position of authority to win Catalina's favors, but she rejects him scornfully. Don Generoso appears, a previous owner of the estate who lost all his money supporting the Carlist cause in the early years of the century. His misfortunes have turned his brain, and Sagrario has to defend the poor old man from the mockery of the crowd.

A group of farmhands appears looking forward to the next day's sowing, among them Juan Pedro, a young man attached to Catalina. His memorably powerful celebration of the joys of the sower enthuses his audience (*Canción del sembrador: "Cuando siembro voy cantando"*). Moved by the song, Catalina asks her mistress whether Juan Pedro may speak up to ask permission to marry, and Sagrario agrees to receive the lad: on condition that Juan Pedro leaves the house afterward, as it would not be proper for an affianced couple to spend the night under the same roof.

When the farmhand approaches, Sagrario lets him know her decision, though it is obvious that she is attracted to him herself. This proud young woman has never known love, and she asks Juan Pedro to explain this strange feeling to her. With increasing ardor he gives her a lesson in the language of desire (*Dúo: "Ama, lo que usté me pide"*), tactfully omitting to discern her interest when he repeats some key phrases back to her

(*"Manchega, flor y gala de la llanura"*). Juan Pedro dutifully asks Catalina to marry him, but the girl has heard the conversation between him and her mistress, and jealously refuses.

Moniquito and Custodia talk to Don Generoso, who reveals the reason for his distraction: the disappearance of a son he once had by a local girl. When Juan Pedro reappears Sagrario insists that despite Catalina's refusal the young man must still leave next day, and his friends commiserate with his bad luck.

SCENE 2—Later that evening, in the village next to the house. Juan Pedro and some shepherds serenade their sweethearts. Everyone believes the farmhand will address Catalina, but the verses he sings are aimed squarely at the mistress of the house (*Nocturno-ronda: "Como soy, nena mía"*). Meanwhile, in the dark shadows underneath a staircase, the lascivious Moniquito serenades one of the local girls, Carmelo, with a surprisingly risqué multiplication lesson (*Pasacalle de las escaleras: "Dos por dos son cuatro"*).

SCENE 3—Next morning, back in the courtyard. Catalina and the women of the house are peeling the saffron husks, supervised by their mistress. Sagrario sings of the delicacy of the flower, while Catalina and the girls indulge in lively love chatter (*Scena: "De mondar mucha rosa ... La rosa del azafrán es como la maravilla"*).

Sagrario confesses her feelings to the wise Custodia, who tells her that Juan Pedro was a foundling, brought up in the local hospice. A relationship between them is clearly out of the question; and drawing herself up in her pride Sagrario calls the women back to work. As they begin peeling the husks once more, Juan Pedro and some of the men join in the chore (*Final: "Si quieres que te lo diga"*). Working close to Sagrario he makes his own feelings plain, but she gives him the brush-off in no uncertain terms. The workers recognize the impossibility of any bond between rich and poor; and Juan Pedro breaks away, renouncing love as being fragile as the flower of the saffron, before turning his back on the house for good.

ACT 2, SCENE 1—The village square, the following August. Ten months have passed. Catalina tells Custodia that in the light of her ex-fiancé's continued absence, she has decided to settle for Moniquito. Juan Pedro surprisingly turns up to pay his respects to Carracuca, whose wife has died of her fits, and when he has left with old Custodia, Moniquito formally asks for Catalina's hand. Rattled by her former love's reappearance, the girl decides that she can't take on such a dreadful prospect as the caretaker, and their love scene turns into a mutual slanging match (*Dúo cómico y seguidillas: "Pero ven acá. No me vengas con lisonjas"*).

A group of men offer condolences to the bereft Carracuca, who bewails the likely fate of his motherless children. The village women sing the praises of four alternative wives to solve the widower's dilemma, though Moniquito remains skeptical of the women's virtues (*Tanguillo:* "*¡Conformidá! . . . ¡Qué voy a hacer!*").

Juan Pedro runs into Sagrario. Convinced that he has really come back for Catalina, the mistress tries to leave; but when Juan Pedro declares his secret passion for her she is honest enough to admit that she wants him too, imperiously informing him that their difference in social status makes marriage impossible. He leaves heartbroken. Alone, Sagrario expresses her conflicting feelings in the subtle, melancholy *Romanza: "No me duele que se vaya"*.

Juan Pedro asks Custodia whether anything can be done. She proposes to solve his problem (and Don Generoso's madness) by passing him off as the old owner's lost son, and after some internal debate he agrees to the ruse. Catalina is equally in need of Custodia's help to extricate her from the match with Moniquito. The old woman's practical response is to produce Carracuca, similarly in need of a good partner. The young girl and older man are getting on well, until the jealous Moniquito catches them together and chases them away.

SCENE 2—A sunny La Mancha landscape, with flowers, stubble fields and windmills. Offstage voices are heard before Catalina enters with the gleaners, singing in praise of the harvest (*Coro de espigadoras: "Esta mañana, mu tempranica"*). To everyone's joy Don Generoso receives Juan Pedro as his son, and promptly recovers his wits.

SCENE 3—The courtyard of the house. The villagers are enjoying the harvest festival with drink, song and dance. The newly ennobled Juan Pedro, now accepted by Sagrario, leads the lusty *Jota castellana: "Bisturí, Bisturí se quería casar"* in praise of La Mancha and his marriage.

Moniquito weeps over the marriage of Carracuca and Catalina, and moved by his sorrow Juan Pedro decides he must tell Sagrario the truth about Custodia's plot. Quietly, she replies that she already knows, and that it makes no difference whatsoever to her feelings (*Dúo: "Tengo una angustia de muerte"*). The zarzuela concludes with a brief outburst of general content, to the strain of the *Jota: "Bisturí, Bisturí"*.

Although some of Guerrero's later zarzuelas occasionally see the light of day the two act *La rosa del azafrán* (The Saffron Flower) is the last of his works to remain rooted in the repertoire. Romero and Shaw's text is perhaps the finest the composer ever set. As with *Doña Francisquita* and *La villana* for Vives, the famous writing partners sought inspiration from a comedy by Lope de Vega (1562–1635), Spain's greatest dramatist. *El perro del hortelano* (The Gardener's Dog) is concerned, like Lope's better-known *Fuenteovejuna*, with arbitrary social barriers. The librettists retained some of Lope's subtle characterization, but transposed his play from a renaissance court to rural La Mancha in the 1860s. This gave them ample opportunity to trick out the romantic storyline with popular Castilian color, and Juan Pedro's powerfully poetic *Canción del sembrador* (Song of the Sower) is only first among many lyrics of equal beauty.

The composer evidently relished the resulting mélange of realism and romance. The extended music for the star-crossed lovers is as passionately felt as anything in *Los gavilanes*, the big popular scenes as catchy and colorful as those in *El huésped del Sevillano*. Although it does not aim at the direct emotional power of the former, or the orchestral finish of the latter, *La rosa del azafrán* remains Guerrero's most admired score by reason of its deep-rooted subtlety, and sure theatrical intelligence. Many numbers have real musical as well as theatrical substance—the duets, choral scenes and ensembles, Sagrario's *Romanza*, and above all the *Canción del sembrador*:

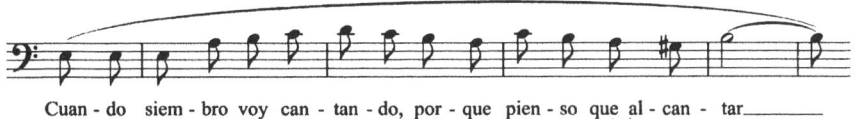

Cuan - do siem - bro voy can - tan - do, por - que pien - so que al - can - tar

La alsaciana (The Girl from Alsace, 1921)
Short though it is, this one-act zarzuela brought Guerrero his first real taste of critical and public approval. Set in an Alsatian village during the Napoleonic wars, the slight plot is a comedy romance with military trappings, not dissimilar to Caballero's *El cabo primero*. The thirty-minute score boasts several catchy martial tunes as well as romantic numbers touching a deeper vein of feeling, notably the heroine, Margot's, lullaby for her child *"Duerme, duerme, corderito"*, and the lyrical waltz melody associated with her devoted Captain, *"Capitán, Capitán, que vas a combatir"*.

El ama (The Lover, 1933)
Highly successful initially, this three-act romantic melodrama is only rarely revived today. The setting is an imaginary Castilian village, and the plot concerns the rivalry between two men for the hand of the saintly Rafaela. Her preferred Clemente has fathered a child by a village girl; when Rafaela discovers the truth she marries the faithful Esteban, and brings about a reconciliation between the reprobate and his wronged woman. The music is robust and assured, two numbers for Clemente (tenor) being specially memorable: his *Tonada Castellana: "Cuando cruzo la llanura"* in praise of the women of Castile; and a guilt-wracked *Romanza: "Mala estrella la mía"*.

El canastillo de fresas (The Basket of Strawberries, 1951)
Guerrero left the orchestration of this two-act sentimental comedy unfinished at his death, and its warm reception later in the year was in part a memorial tribute to its well-loved composer. The plot is a slight affair dealing with love tangles between the local aristocracy and the children of their faithful retainers. The setting is springtime Aranjuez, and much of the music is appropriately light, sunny and relaxed, notably the freshly lyrical *Romanza: "Mi cariño es aroma que se deslíe"* given to the younger and purer of the two heroines, Clara.

La fama del tartanero (The Wagoner's Reputation, 1931)
Three-act dramatic zarzuela, set in the Cádiz region of Andalusia during the Napoleonic wars. Wagoner Juan León's mysterious relations with a beautiful young girl, Blanca, are at the heart of the romantic action. His jealous actions are finally explained by the revelation that she is his long-lost daughter, and his good reputation is restored to him. Guerrero's score is not as consistently inspired as his previous major work, *La rosa del azafrán*; but if his melodic powers were waning, his orchestral palette had widened, as witness the subtly shaded accompaniment to Juan León's highly effective *Romanza: "Mentira, mentira piadosa"*.

Martierra (1928)
Martierra, an imaginary Spanish fishing village, is the scene for a highly convoluted romantic plot in which a fisherman, Américo (tenor), and farmer, José (baritone), are at loggerheads over no fewer than three women. Guerrero's most important three-act work between *El huésped del Sevillano* and *La rosa del azafrán* enjoyed brief popularity but soon fell into oblivion, perhaps because of his tenor's unexpected Peter Grimes-like maritime suicide at the end. The score is strong, notably a fine *Pregón* (Prayer) for Américo: *"Tomillo, hierbabuena"*.

13
Jesús Guridi
(1886–1961)

The Basque Jesús Guridi was born in Vitoria on 25th September 1886. His musical family quickly arranged for him to study at the Madrid Conservatory, and at eighteen he received a bursary from the Count of Zubiria which enabled him to spend two years at the Schola Cantorum in Paris. There he worked under Vincent D'Indy, whose formal, harmonic and orchestral lucidity is apparent in much of his music. He later studied in Brussels and Cologne before returning home to teach organ at the Bilbao Academy of Music, acquiring fame for his skill as an improviser. He also took on the direction of the city's choral society, and taught organ and composition at the newly founded Vizcaya (Biscay) Conservatory.

In 1914 he began teaching organ in Madrid, but not until 1939 did he take up permanent residence in the capital, as Professor of Theory at the Madrid Conservatory and Director of the Ufisa Film Corporation. Various honors came his way, and in 1956 he was finally appointed Director of the Conservatory. Though he died on 7th April 1961 in Madrid, he never lost touch with his regional roots and by the time of his death was revered in his Basque homeland, almost as a National Composer. His son Ignacio wrote: "My father was an upright Basque, filled with the spirit and vitality of his people . . . capturing the sounds of a flowing river, the majesty of a mountain, the rustling of trees, or of a wandering txistu flute."

Guridi's place in Iberian music goes way beyond his influence as an academic. Aside from quantities of film music, his orchestral compositions range from the D'Indyesque *Sinfonía Pirenaica* (Pyrenean Symphony, 1944) and symphonic poem *Una aventura de Don Quijote* (An Adventure of Don Quixote, 1915), through to the internationally known *Diez melodías vascas*

(Ten Basque Melodies, 1941) and a remarkable *Homenaje a Walt Disney* for piano and orchestra (Homage to Walt Disney, 1956). His organ works have been played and recorded throughout Europe. His excellent songs, piano and chamber works have not. His choral works, preeminently the thrilling *Euzko Irudiak* (Basque Scenes, 1922), are highly effective, though lack of familiarity with the Basque language abroad has mitigated against their wider exposure.

His Basque language stage works include the "Symphonic Idyll" *Mirentxu* (1910), the Wagnerian three-act opera *Amaya* (1920) and the zarzuela *Mari-Eli* (1936). Equally important is a sequence of popular Spanish language zarzuelas concerned with Basque country and maritime life. *El caserío* (The Homestead, 1926), to a finely crafted libretto by Romero and Fernández Shaw, is an acknowledged classic; although *La meiga* (The Witch, 1928); *La cautiva* (The Captive, 1931); *La bengala* (The Baton, a comic *sainete*, 1939) and the "popular opera" *Peñamariana* (1944) are not far behind it in quality.

Guridi's language is rooted in the musical forms and rhythms of his homeland. French rather than Spanish composers provided his formal models, and its distinctive nationalist flavor places his music at a further remove from his Iberian contemporaries. His style, notwithstanding some weird echoes of Messiaen's *Turangalîla* in the late Walt Disney *Homenaje*, is generally conservative; and his brilliance as an orchestrator in works like the *Diez melodías* makes it tempting to think of him as the Iberian Respighi. On closer acquaintance, though, his work reveals a quiet depth of feeling all its own, as anyone who has come to know his stage masterpiece *El caserío* will appreciate well enough.

El caserío
Zarzuela in three acts
(Madrid, Teatro de la Zarzuela, 11th November 1926)

Text: Federico Romero & Guillermo Fernández Shaw

Principal Characters: Santi, a country landowner (baritone); Ana Mari, his niece (soprano); José Miguel, his nephew (tenor); Eustacia, his housekeeper (actor); Inosensia, Eustacia's daughter (soprano); Chomin, farm handyman (tenor).

Santi's tragedy was to be secretly in love with a beautiful woman, and never to tell her. When she accepted one of his two brothers, he left the *caserío* (country homestead) in despair, seeking fame and fortune in America. The death of his brothers led to the dilapidation of the *caserío*, but now Santi has returned and restored his home to its former beauty and importance. He has also overseen the bringing-up of his niece and nephew, the cousins Ana Mari and José Miguel. Their uncle's dream is that these two will marry, safeguarding Sasibill's future, although he feels a special affection for his niece, an angelic young woman who is the very image of her mother Marichu, Santi's long-dead sweetheart. José Miguel on the other hand is an arrogant spendthrift, confident of his inheritance, more interested in pursuing his pleasure as a *pelota* player than settling down to his family duty.

ACT 1—The courtyard of Sasibill, Santi's *caserío* close to the picturesque Basque town of Arrigorri. After a pastoral *Preludio* with offstage voices, the returning farmhands look forward to the coming fiesta (*Coro: "Nochesita de estrellas"*). The housekeeper Eustacia dragoons them all back to work, including her stupid daughter Inosensia and the equally brainless young handyman Chomin, who is smitten with Ana Mari. José Miguel, strolling in from one of his customary absences, flirts pleasantly with his cousin, who berates him for upsetting their uncle by leading such a loose existence. José Miguel counters that he wants to enjoy his youth and freedom by playing the field: words that Ana Mari, who is deeply in love with him, least wants to hear (*Dúo: "Buenos días"*). With Eustacia and his cousin well out of the way, José Miguel joins Chomin, Eustacia's husband Manu and the local Alcalde in an all-out assault on the reserved communion wine (*Cuarteto: "Con el trébole"*).

Santi pensively considers this fresh evidence of José Miguel's fecklessness, expressing his deep affection for the *caserío* and love for the lost Marichu in an uplifting *Romanza: "Sasibill mi caserío"*, a nobly beautiful piece mainly in lilting 5/8 zortzico rhythm. He shares his concern with a friend, Don Leoncio the village Curé, who makes a Machiavellian suggestion: Santi should announce his intention to marry. Once José Miguel thinks he will lose his inheritance he will either see the error of his ways and reform, or leave the district for good, clearing the way for Ana Mari to take sole responsibility for the *caserío*. Chomin gets wind of this and tells José Miguel, who storms furiously off the property. In the *Final*, Santi announces his intentions—much to the joy of everyone except Ana Mari, who well understands what this means to her beloved José Miguel.

ACT 2—The town of Arrigori. The fiesta is underway with a lively zortzico dance (*Preludio y Danza*). Pelota players from the town and its rivals cross the stage, singing the popular Basque song *"Pello Joshepe"*. José Miguel has returned to take part in the game, and confides to Ana Mari that he has changed his plan: he will pretend to welcome Santi's idea, and then seduce this fiancée, whoever she might be. The disgusted Ana Mari tells him that all he cares for is money, and leaves him. José Miguel, seriously impressed, wonders what exactly he sees in his cousin (*Romanza: "Yo no sé que veo en Ana Mari"*).

A religious procession passes, to be followed by a vigorous and angular Sword Dance (*Procesión y Espatadantza: "Reina del cielo"*). Ana Mari, fearing for the future of the *caserío* and still furious with José Miguel, offers to marry Santi herself. Deeply moved, Santi neither accepts nor completely rejects her offer, confiding both his gratitude to her and his devotion to her dead mother in the moving *Dúo: "Con alegría inmensa"*.

Some of this is overheard by the desolated Chomin, who wastes no time in getting the news to José Miguel. The young man's confidence is shaken, but he boasts arrogantly of his ability to win back Ana Mari from his uncle: though Chomin still fancies his own chances (*Canción de los Versolaris: "Chiquito de Arrigorri"*). The single-minded Inosensia, however, clearly has her own designs on the handyman. The *Final* begins with a public declaration of the possible betrothal of Santi and his niece. José Miguel now fully understands the depth of his feeling for Ana Mari. After a heartfelt outburst (*"Dime al oído"*) he is rejected by her and leaves, cruelly wounded, as the townsfolk celebrate Santi's wise choice.

ACT 3—The *caserío*, some months later. After a brief, presto *Preludio* the farmhands celebrate the Harvest Home in a lusty chorus (*Coro: "Mientras llueve sin cesar"*). Ana Mari sings a song for them which contains a covert reference to her own unhappiness (*Coro y Relato: "En la cumbre del monte"*). She clearly loves José Miguel still; Santi is also wavering in his resolution. Meanwhile Eustacia takes advantage of the uncertainty by teaching Inosensia how to ensnare Santi herself. She is not so brainless as she looks, and follows her mother's instructions to the letter to seduce … not Santi, but the far from unwilling Chomin into a proposal of marriage (*Dúo Cómico: "Dise mi madre, Chomin"*).

Santi reveals to Ana Mari that he has been keeping back the letters which José Miguel has been sending to her, in order to test the strength of her cousin's feelings and in hope that he will come to claim her in person. Resigned to the failure of his ploy, Santi has decided to marry his niece after all, and Ana Mari sadly accepts the situation—just before José Miguel rushes in to throw himself on his uncle's mercy. He cannot bear to lose the woman he loves, and will renounce his inheritance completely if his uncle will agree to release her. Santi, finally convinced of José Miguel's sincerity, readily agrees to cede Ana Mari to him if she wishes it (*Dúo y Terceto Final: "Yo no sabía"*). The young lovers are finally united, Santi rejoices that the future of his beloved *caserío* is now assured, and all the farmworkers echo his generous blessing on the couple.

El caserío exemplifies one of the paradoxical strengths of the zarzuela tradition: its indifference to musical fashion. Though first heard as late as 1926 the sound world of this *comedia lírica* draws more on Dvorak than on the jazz-influenced twenties. Given that Guridi was inspired just as surely as his Czech precursor by passionate national devotion, this is hardly surprising. *El caserío*, for all its musical conservatism, is a remarkable expression of the Basque spirit and way of life. Its authentic quality was recognized immediately, not least by fellow composer Joaquín Turina (another pupil of D'Indy) who praised Guridi's success in "singing the soul of his homeland without recourse to foxtrots and charlestons." Instead of these, the score relies on distinctive Basque dance rhythms such as the espatadantza (7/4) and zortzico (5/8).

Romero and Shaw provided a text as well-tailored to Guridi's musical style as their *Doña Francisquita* had been for Vives, with a love interest as sensitively balanced as their *Luisa Fernanda* was to be for Torroba. The crucial relationship of *El caserío* is not between the young lovers, but between the aging landowner Santi and his niece, Ana Mari. Santi has something of the gentle, self-sacrificing wisdom of Wagner's Hans Sachs, and an equally fervent belief in his country, its rules and duties as well as its attractions. Little wonder that Guridi responded to the character with music of heartfelt. noble sensitivity:

Santi's musical progress—like that of Ana Mari and her beloved José Miguel—is subtly marked by thematic reminiscence and development, the festivities of town and country are depicted in distinctive melody and quietly assertive orchestral colors. *El caserío* deepens on acquaintance, and a close study reveals the work to be a masterpiece of understated passion, personal and national.

La meiga (The Witch, 1928)
Romero and Shaw's three-act folk-zarzuela is a colorful tribute to the Galician countryside and its customs in the last quarter of the nineteenth century. Young villager Ramón is in love with a girl who seems to share his feelings, but for some reason cannot bring herself to admit them. The limpid *Romanza "Yo te ví pasar"*, in which Ramón sings of his love and increasingly desperate confusion, is the best-known number in Guridi's beautiful score, long overdue for revival.

La condesa de la aguja y el dedal (The Countess of Needle and Thimble, 1950)
This two-act comedy romance of mid-nineteenth century music and manners was one of the composer's last stage works. The plot is set in motion when a beautiful young seamstress, Gloria, is mistaken for a Countess while modeling a dress for a client. The light-hearted farrago of costume balls, military plots, romantic duels and long-lost brothers which follows gives Guridi a chance to write some delightful pastiche ensembles, notably a sparkling comedy *Cuarteto: "¿Qué es eso? ¡Una quemadura!"* over a burnt dress; and in the orchestral *Intermedio*, a fragrantly poetic evocation of old Madrid.

14
Vicente Lleó
(1870–1922)

If Vicente Lleó i Balbastre, born in Valencia on 19th November 1870, is nowadays remembered almost exclusively as the composer of just one zarzuela, that should not blind us to the extent of his popularity during his lifetime. His earliest music experience was as a boy chorister in the Royal College of Corpus Christi in his home city, and by the age of thirteen he had already composed an effective Dixit Dominus for the College services. At seventeen he wrote his first stage work, *De Valencia al Grao* (From Valencia to Grao, 1888) by which time he was studying at the local Conservatory under Salvador Giner.

By the time he left Valencia for Barcelona to pursue his conducting career in 1894, he had already written a considerable number of zarzuelas, as well as founding an organization devoted to performing rights. Two years later came the inevitable move to Madrid, where he combined composition and conducting with editing his political magazine *La Noche*, which lost any money he managed to make by his entrepreneurial activities at the Teatro Eslava and elsewhere. The failure of the magazine at the turn of the century forced Lleó and his partner, the popular actress Juanita Manso, to concentrate on remunerative music making.

Producing zarzuelas and *revista* music by the yard, he had considerable success writing in collaboration with Rafael Gómez Calleja, as well as Caballero and Vives (*Episodios nacionales*, National Narratives, 1908). In 1910 came his great and enduring triumph at the Eslava, *La corte de Faraón* (Pharaoh's Court), a recasting of the biblical story of Joseph and Potiphar's wife to a wittily outrageous libretto by Perrín and Palacios. The scandalous history of this work—not least a lengthy ban under General Franco—has contributed to its huge and enduring popularity.

Several of Lleó's other zarzuelas enjoyed initial success, but nowadays neither the Japanese-inspired *La taza de té* (The Cup of Tea) nor *La república del amor* (Love's Republic, both 1906) are remembered; even the once-triumphant *El método Gorritz* (The Gorritz Method, 1909) is no more than a name. Of his other works, only *El maestro Campanone* (Maestro Campanone, 1903) is still heard. This is not original music, but a recomposition of a minor Italian opera. His Spanish adaptations of Viennese operettas such as Lehár's *Der Graf von Luxemburg* have also survived in the repertoire. The failure of the Teatro Eslava in 1918 led to Lleó's departure for Latin America, and he only returned to Madrid shortly before his death on 28th September 1922.

His last *revista*-zarzuela, *¡Ave César!* (Hail Caesar!, 1922) was first performed three months later in homage to one of the capital's most popular musicians. Nobody would claim that Lleó was a great composer, and of his stage works only one has stood the test of time. *La corte de Faraón* demonstrates his gift for entertaining musical pastiche, never quite directly quoting from its two obvious models, *Aida* and *La Belle Hélène*. Its expansive, fresh tunefulness and alertness to verbal nuance are a living testament to Lleó's theatrical talent.

La corte de Faraón
Zarzuela in one act
(Madrid, Teatro Eslava, 21st January 1910)

Text: Guillermo Perrín and Miguel de Palacios

Principal Characters: The Grand Pharaoh (bass); His Queen (mezzo-soprano); Putifar, his General (baritone); Lotha, a Theban virgin (mezzo-soprano); José, a chaste Israelite (comic tenor); Raquel, an Israelite maiden; Sul, a Babylonian slavegirl (singer).

SCENE 1—The Great Square of Memphis in Egypt. Celebrations are in full swing for the return of General Putifar (Potiphar), fresh from a triumph in the Syrian wars. Pharaoh himself, enthroned with his Queen and attended by his favorite Cupbearer, leads the crowd in their jubilant cries (*Coro: "¡Viva Putifar!"*). The High Priest presents Lotha, a lovely virgin from Thebes, chosen by the Queen herself to become the wife of the General. Putifar enters to pompous trumpet fanfares, but is evidently disconcerted by the offer of a bride, a fact not unconnected with a delicate personal disablement he has suffered in the battle. His wife-to-be is ceremoniously handed over together with her slave, the Israelite Raquel. Everyone leaves to celebrate the wedding inside the Temple.

Ismael, a slave trader, is taking a fetching youth to market. This is José (Joseph), an Israelite sold into slavery by his own family—and yes, it is he of the many-colored coat. Putifar's slaves Selhá and Setí take pity on the boy, purchasing him to work in their master's kitchens. Newlyweds Putifar and Lotha reappear. The General praises his wife's virtue in a noble solo and she replies in kind (*Dúo: "Salve, Lotha"*); but the scene is cut short by Raquel and the two slaves, who present their new purchase. Putifar is so impressed by José's nice manners and appearance that he takes the boy on as his personal valet.

SCENE 2—The Marital Chamber of Putifar's Palace. The ritual celebrations are in progress, Raquel sings and a group of slaves dance (*Solo y Coro: "La luz de la luna"*). José and Raquel then introduce three Theban Widows, who advise Lotha on her wifely duties and bawdily hint at the nuptial delights in store (*Terceto: "Salud a la doncella"*). José disarms his master and tactfully withdraws, leaving the happy couple together. Putifar—understandably, given his lack of marital wherewithal—chooses to entertain his eager wife with a long narration about his military prowess and the virtue of single-breasted army uniforms, much to Lotha's frustration. Before anything more revealing can take place a trumpet announces the dawning day, and the call to arms for Putifar. Buckling on his armor with ill-disguised relief, he hurriedly orders Lotha to amuse herself in his absence by conversing with *"casto José"* (chaste Joseph).

Given an inch, Lotha decides to take a mile. She and Raquel have already had their appetites whetted seeing the boy bathing naked, and her tactile fascination with José's beautiful body rapidly reaches a point beyond which the pure-minded youth is unwilling to go. At the start of their climactic *Dúo: "Yo soy el casto José"* he fends off her attentions as best he can, explaining that he's more used to looking after sheep than women; but in the end resistance is useless and he is forced to run, leaving his mantle in Lotha's hot hands. She cries out, and when Selhá and Setí rush in the General's frustrated wife accuses José of attempting to ravish her, as the dropped mantle conclusively proves.

SCENE 3—Pharaoh's Palace. Pharaoh is in his wife's arms, sleeping off his customary drunken stupor. She is being vaguely entertained by a languid chorus of Babylonian gypsy slaves, one of whom, Sul, leads them in a saucy cabaret song: nobody, it seems, can improve on Babylonian love-making techniques (*Canción: "¡Ay, Ba! . . . ¡Ay Ba!"*). Lotha runs in asking for justice, Selhá and Setí dragging José behind. The Queen hears her version of events, but strangely José's sweet nature (or firm physique) causes Her Majesty to take a more lenient view of the matter. Surely her husband will intervene?

Pharaoh, grumpy at being disturbed, wants nothing to do with the business and stomps off to continue his snooze in the gardens below. The Queen takes charge, and after staging a reconstruction of the supposed violation decides to take José off Lotha's hands and reform him herself. Putifar's wife is not best pleased at this regal justice, and an argument ensues (*Terceto: "Para juzgar"*). José, almost pulled in half by the two tigresses, has no way to save his honor but to dive through a nearby window into the gardens below.

SCENE 4—The Royal Gardens. José lands on top of the Pharaoh, rudely awakening him from a strange dream. Taking advantage of the situation, José offers to interpret the dream for him. The Cupbearer backs him up, providing Pharaoh with evidence that José's reputation as a mage is second to none. José evokes a magic vision for Pharaoh of three beautiful Spanish women dancing a voluptuous Fandango (*Escena y Danza: "Vi entre sueños tres mujeres"*). Charmed, the monarch shows his gratitude by making José his Viceroy, and vows to keep him always by his side.

SCENE 5—The entrance to the Temple of Apis, the Bull God, which looks strangely like a modern Spanish bullring. In a final scene of great brevity but even greater pomp, *"Casto José"* kneels before the Pharaoh and is invested with all the dignity of Viceroy, to the jubilant cries of the crowd prostrating itself before the image of the Sacred Bull.

Vicente Lleó can only be described as a minor composer. Of his hundred or so works, he is remembered for just this one, frivolous little operetta; and yet there are few zarzuelas that have inspired such consistent pleasure and affection as the notorious *La corte de Faraón* (Pharaoh's Court). In large measure this is down to the librettists' shrewd appropriation of subject from the French *opérette Madame Putifar* (1897, with music by Edmond Diet). A blend of biblical pastiche, luscious vaudeville and Art Deco Egyptian chic, *La corte de Faraón* became one of its adapters' most sophisticated and audacious conceptions.

Lotha is a must-play for any stage goddess with half a voice, and *"Casto José"* a gift for any comic actor worth his salt. Indeed, the smuttiness of his double entendres is so obvious that public performance of the work was vetoed by the Franco regime until as late as 1975. Needless to say, the public ban only added to its private appeal.

The music adds spice to the mixture. Grand Triumphal Choruses, sinuous woodwind orientalisms, the slaves' dance, the stylistic distinction between public and private; all these thumb a friendly nose at Verdi's *Aida*. In fact the scope of Lleó's pastiche is much broader. *La Belle Hélène*, *Die Lustige Witwe* and even *Lohengrin* are called in to ring the changes on the basic joke. Yet though Lleó is happy to draw on these models for grand oratory and private impropriety alike, his tunes are all perfectly original, and perfectly seductive.

Most remarkable musically is the extended *Dúo* for Lotha and José, brimming over with memorable tunes, as graphic a musical depiction of frustrated lust as anyone could wish, a quintessentially Spanish mixture of send-up and sympathy. The moral outrage arises from the shocking fact that the send-up is aimed at the ludicrously chaste Joseph, and most of the sympathy reserved for the predatory Mrs. Potiphar. Even more blatant is Sul's *"¡Ay, Ba! . . . ¡Ay Ba!"*, a foolproof teaser which scored a big hit in pre-war Parisian cabarets, and still so effective that it's usually annexed in performance by the singer-actress playing Lotha:

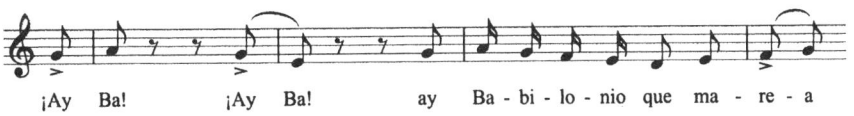

El maestro Campanone (Maestro Campanone, 1905)
A one-act adaptation of Giuseppe Mazza's *La prova di una opera seria* (The Rehearsal of an Opera Seria, 1845), a typical Italian opera of backstage intrigue. Lleó skillfully translated, reorchestrated and condensed his material without destroying the Rossiniesque charm of the original. The highlight of this pleasant score is the scene, reminiscent of Cimarosa's *Il Maestro di Capella*, where the Maestro takes his none too competent orchestra through its paces.

15
Pablo Luna
(1879–1942)

Pablo Luna, born on 21st May 1879 in Alhama de Aragón, began his studies at the School of Music in Zaragoza, where the family moved soon after his birth. He had enough talent as a violinist to find work in a succession of Madrid theatre orchestras, becoming Leader at the Teatro Circo aged twenty-one, at the same time expanding his practical knowledge of chamber music. He had already begun conducting by the time Ruperto Chapí asked him to lead the second violins at the Teatro de la Zarzuela in 1905; and though Luna had produced his first zarzuelas in Zaragoza, work under Chapí enabled him to develop both his musical technique and theatrical instinct. In 1908 came his first Madrid success: *Musetta*, to a libretto by Juan Pascal Frutos, at the Teatro Ideal. Nonetheless, though he continued to work as violinist (and later conductor) at the Teatro de la Zarzuela for some years, many of his greatest successes were premiered away from the capital. This is evidence of a perfectionism unusual at the time, and some quite radical textual and musical revisions often resulted from these out-of-town tryouts.

In 1910 *Molinos de viento* (Windmills) premiered in Seville, and took the whole of Spain by storm. With its foreign setting—Holland—and stylistic debt to Viennese operetta, it set the pattern for many of Luna's most successful works. Equally, it marked a decisive shift in taste away from the realistic comedy and satire of the *sainete madrileño*, toward the blander romance of light opera. A host of long-running triumphs followed, including the Ruritanian *Los cadetes de la Reina* (The Queen's Cadets, 1913), *El niño judío* (The Jewish Boy) and *Los calabreses* (The Calabrians, both 1918).

A particular favorite of many *aficionados* was, and is, *El asombro de Damasco* (The Wonder of Damascus, 1916), which enjoyed the distinction of a run at the Oxford Theatre in London's West End eight years later. This English production incorporated music from *Benamor* (1923), the highly successful sequel which capitalized on the *Thousand and One Nights* setting and musical atmosphere of the earlier work.

After the London venture, Luna turned decisively back to his musical roots in collaborative works such as *La pastorela* (The Pastorale, with Torroba, 1926) and *La chula de Pontevedra* (The Girl from Pontevedra, with Bru, 1928); though his most important work in this later style was written without assistance—*La pícara molinera* (The Teasing Millgirl) produced significantly enough for his theatrical *alma mater*, the Teatro Circo of Zaragoza in 1928. A successful symphonic poem *Una noche en Calatayud* (A Night in Calatayud, 1925) also dates from this "Spanish" period.

With the rise of the talkie Luna turned his talents increasingly toward the new medium, producing among other scores the cinematic musical *Miguelon* (1935), tailored to the talents of the great tenor Miguel Fleta. Theatre work was also interrupted by the Civil War, and his later zarzuelas lack the fire of Luna's best work, though some, such as *Los inseperables* (The Inseparables, 1934) were successful enough. He died in Madrid on 28th January 1942, leaving his last zarzuela *El Pilar de la victoria* (The Temple of Victory) to be completed by Julio Gómez and produced in Luna's beloved Zaragoza, city of the Pilar Basilica itself, two years later.

Luna's output was prodigious, but this should not blind us to the high quality and technical finish of many of his finest scores. Tastes change and, ironically for the composer whose reputation was largely made with zarzuelas in exotic settings and operetta style, Luna now seems at his strongest given solidly Spanish musico-dramatic material. Of all his works perhaps *La pícara molinera* has best stood the test of time, but the melodies of *El asombro de Damasco*, *Molinos de viento* and *El niño judío* are as ravishing now as ever, buoyed up by Pablo Luna's piquant harmonies and luxurious orchestral palette.

El asombro de Damasco
Zarzuela in two acts
(Madrid, Teatro Apolo, 20th September 1916)

Text: Antonio Paso and Joaquín Abati

Principal Characters: Zobeida (soprano); Fahima (soprano); Ben-Ibhen, a Doctor (tenor); The Cadi (comedy singer); Nuredhin, the Grand Vizier (bass or baritone); The Caliph (actor).

ACT 1—The market quarter of Damascus, in the time of Caliph Suliman. There is a brief *Preludio*, representing dawn over Damascus, with a Muezzin-like tenor solo in praise of woman at its heart. The market bustle begins. Fahima, young proprietor of a shop for perfumes and potions, sells her wares to a group of women, while next door old Doctor Ben-Ibhen attends to his patients. Fahima sings of the power of her potions (*Coro y Canción: "Yo he descubierto un perfume"*). Two Dervishes request provisions for a pilgrimage to Mecca, which Fahima teasingly grants, and they retire into her shop. A veiled woman reveals herself to the perfumer as her friend Zobeida, married to a rich Mosul merchant. The distressed woman tells Fahima that her husband has lost his fortune and fallen ill. They are near to ruin, and she has come to Damascus to ask one of her husband's debtors, Doctor Ben-Ibhen, to repay an ancient debt of one thousand gold dinares, money urgently needed to cure his sickness. Unfortunately, no written contract exists to confirm the debt, so Zobeida must rely on Ben-Ibhen's good faith.

Fahima takes Zobeida to meet her medical neighbor. The Doctor unhesitatingly acknowledges his willingness to repay the debt. First, though, he would like to see the face of the woman to whom he must give the money. Zobeida raises her veil, and Ben-Ibhen is astonished by her beauty. To the women's indignation he proposes in a spirited *Terceto cómico: "Ten presente la desgracia"* to deliver up her money that very night, provided she agrees to accept it in his back room by moonlight. He then disappears into his shop chuckling as the two women curse Zobeida's misfortune.

Alí-Mon, the self-important Cadi of Damascus, marches in accompanied by six Guards. He extols his incomparable virtue, good looks and intelligence in a lively entrance song (*Canción comico: "Soy Alí-Mon, soy el Cadi"*) before reading out a proclamation from the Grand Vizier, the Caliph's all-powerful Minister, calling for the capture alive or dead of the bloodthirsty outlaw Ka-Fur who is terrorizing the city. Zobeida, impressed by Alí-Mon's bearing, explains what has happened between her and Ben-Ibhen and calls on the Cadi for justice.

Intrigued, Alí-Mon asks to see the face that has so inflamed the Doctor's passions. Zobeida again reveals herself, and to the same effect. The smitten Cadi makes this "wonder of Damascus" a simple proposal: he will force Ben-Ibhen to hand over the money, on condition she will agree to accept it from Alí-Mon's own hand in his bedroom that night. Stunned by the Cadi's outrageous suggestion, Zobeida withdraws cursing masculine perfidy. Fahima tells her friend that the only truly just man is the noble Grand Vizier himself, who surely will not fail her.

Alí-Mon knocks at Ben-Ibhen's door and sets about berating the Doctor for his conduct toward Omar's wife, when they are distracted by the arrival of a large crowd. As they retire into the shop, the powerful and somewhat sinister Grand Vizier himself is borne in on a luxurious palanquin surrounded by guards and flunkeys. He accepts the reverential acclamations of the crowd with arrogant complaisance (*Coro y solo: "¡Viva, viva Nuredhin!"*). Zobeida seizes her moment, and tearfully begs Nuredhin for justice. The Vizier orders her to be calm, promising in the Caliph's name to redress her wrongs. However, even he cannot resist commanding her to reveal her face, the cause of all the trouble. A third time she lets fall her veil, and Nuredhin himself is smitten with a dark passion to possess her beauty: *"Ah, qué asombro peregrino de donaire y gentileza"* ("Oh, what wonderful, amazing charm and gentleness"). He tells her she is more beautiful than the moon itself, and in a rapturous solo pleads with her to assuage his desire (*Romanza y Dúo: "Esto que pides aquí"*). She refuses, angrily trying to recall him to his sense of duty as she begs desperately for pity.

As the Grand Vizier awaits her answer, the people return with Fahima and an impromptu dance to entertain him begins (*Coro, danza y solo de Fahima: "Baila, baila Musalmana"*). One of the Dervish pilgrims has a plan: Zobeida should invite the Doctor, the Cadi and the Vizier to an intimate banquet that night at Fahima's house on the outskirts of the city. She takes his advice, quietly making the offer to each of the three suitors in turn, unperceived by their rivals. The act ends as the crowd carries the satisfied Grand Vizier away in triumphant anticipation of the delights of the night to come.

ACT 2—Fahima's house. After an orchestral *Intermedio* the curtain rises to reveal a rich banquet in preparation. A group of slaves, led by Mirta and Abriza, are dressing and adorning Zobeida for the approaching night (*Solos: "Por esta noche"*). A sensual Oriental Dance follows, though the accompanying chorus in praise of Zobeida's beauty is very much in the Spanish mode (*Coro y danza: "Sultana de los amores"*).

First to arrive is the Doctor, Ben-Ibhen. Zobeida welcomes him with mocking charm, and the inflamed Ben-Ibhen asks her to dance with him in an expansive duet passionate and comic by turns (*Dúo: "Musalmana apetitosa"*). This culminates in the Doctor's demonstration of a lascivious dance, currently all the rage in Mecca, which turns out to be surprisingly like a Spanish Faruca! Suddenly, and just as the Doctor is about to lose control of his manners, Alí-Mon is announced. The confused Doctor pretends he has been called to attend Zobeida for a sudden, mysterious ailment. Although Alí-Mon believes the story, his bad humor at being cheated of an intimate dinner with Omar's wife is manifest.

Finally the Grand Vizier is announced, but before he can register more than surprise at the undesirable presence of his fellow guests, a slave rushes in hysterically to raise the alarm. She tells them that the house has been surrounded by the notorious Ka-Fur and his gang. Zobeida orders that the terrified suitors be disguised as slaves, so that the outlaws will not seize them for ransom. The three men obey, just as the heavily disguised Ka-Fur enters with his bandits. As they tuck into the banquet they are entertained by comedy couplets about the origins of the Koran, provided by the hostess and one of her "slaves," old Ben Ibhen (*Cuplés: "Allá van los preceptos que ordeno el Corán"*). Ka-Fur makes it clear that he sees through the suitors' disguises, and that he intends to kill them. They grovel for mercy. Ben-Ibhen pleads that he has no objection to joining the outlaw's gang, as he is quite as discredited by the medical profession as Ka-Fur is by the law. Alí-Mon says that he has never put justice before money. Nurhedin outdoes them both, revealing his expertise in extracting money from the people for his own uses, behind the Caliph's back.

Zobeida has been observing Ka-Fur closely, and recognizes the Dervish who gave her such good advice that morning. When he admits as much and removes his disguise, she is amazed to see everyone else fall to their knees. It is the Caliph himself, traveling about his kingdom incognito to find out how his people think and feel about his leadership. This time he has discovered the truth about three hypocritical men. He summarily strips the Doctor, Cadi and Vizier of their goods and titles, delivering their wealth up to Zobeida, the beautiful and virtuous "Wonder of Damascus." The zarzuela ends with another brief *Danza final* from the female slaves, in praise of the Caliph's generosity.

Paso and Abati based *El asombro de Damasco* (The Wonder of Damascus) on a tale from the *Arabian Nights*, though the story of the virtuous woman besieged by importunate and powerful suitors is familiar from many literary traditions. The effective libretto naturally emphasizes the lightweight operetta-comedy possibilities, but *El asombro ...* is not without shafts of satire and deeper passion. The result, curiously, has points of similarity with some of W. S. Gilbert's work for Sullivan, notably *The Mikado*, where a familiar world is equally visible under an exotic surface.

This kinship, aided by the cosmopolitan sophistication of Luna's score, perhaps accounts for the fact that *El asombro de Damasco* was given an unlikely shot at London's lucrative West End theatre market, and on 10th November 1924 it became the first full-length zarzuela to be performed in London, under the title *The First Kiss*. Coincidentally, Gilbert's composer collaborator Sullivan had based his last completed operetta *The Rose of Persia* (1899) on the same original story.

Luna's absorbing score takes full advantage of the *Thousand and One Nights* setting, with triangle, drums and harp adding piquancy to sensual, *alhambrismo* harmonies and colorful woodwind solos. There's plenty of humor, too, notably in the jaunty Persian March of the Cadi's song, tricked out with trumpet, bassoon and saxophone. Later the famous scene for Zobeida and the not unsympathetic Grand Vizier introduces a darker, romantic strand into the tapestry. Memorably accompanied with harp and pizzicato strings, Nurhedin's *Romanza: "Esto que pides aquí"* is the romantic highlight of the score, as effective for a heroic baritone as for the bass intended by Luna:

In truth, Luna's melodic gift is at full power almost throughout *El asombro de Damasco* and several other numbers are scarcely inferior to the *romanza*. One in particular deserves mention: the fine Grieg-like melody in Act 2 given to old Ben-Ibhen as he pleads with the heroine for a dance. This is a moment of generous inspiration, another place where two-dimensional comic operetta is momentarily ousted by something rather deeper:

Molinos de viento
Zarzuela in one act
(Seville, Teatro Cervantes, 2nd December 1910)

Text: Luis Pascual Frutos

Principal Characters: Prince Alberto (baritone); Stok, Commander of his yacht (baritone); Romo, a village youth (tenor); Margarita, a village girl (soprano); Sabina, an aging village maiden (actress).

SCENE 1—The seafront of the Dutch fishing village of Volendan in the early 1900s. The brief *Introducción* depicts a bright summer morning. On the beach are several vessels, including a stranded luxury yacht. Its crew has caused a great deal of trouble by flirting with the local girls, and when these attempt to visit the ship the village boys block their way. (*Coro: "Dejadnos paso franco"*). Stok, the bluff Commander of the yacht, hears out the villagers' grievances. He defuses the tension by telling them about his Captain, Crown Prince of a foreign country on an educational voyage, but a man like any other, thoughtful to rich and poor alike. The villagers are mollified by his explanation (*Canción y coro: "En nombre de mi jefe"*).

Stok has news: the yacht is ready to sail again, and her Captain-Prince, Alberto, has declared a holiday to celebrate the departure. Once he leaves, the villagers are soon at loggerheads again. The men choose young Romo to present an ultimatum to the girls, who in turn select the robust Sabina to answer their threats in kind. They will continue to flirt with the sailors unless their jealous menfolk agree to marry them decently. Romo is enamored of the pert and lovely Margarita, but shyness has prevented him speaking out; and when he calls her over to discuss peace terms, she makes fun of him and walks away. The indignant boys make a pact not to speak to the girls.

Stok reappears with four Lieutenants, all opening love letters from village maidens. In the witty *Quinteto: "Las misivas de diario"* the delight of the four younger men is contrasted with Stok's horror at the passionate outpourings of the superannuated Sabina. She appears and asks the lieutenants to leave Stok behind in the village. They laughingly agree—as does the Prince himself, though he reprimands his officers for upsetting the villagers. Left alone, Alberto is approached by Romo, who tells him of the love he feels for Margarita and asks for advice. How should he declare himself? Alberto, equally enamored of the girl but realizing love between them would be impossible, advises the youth to sing to Margarita. He proceeds to show Romo how to do it in the haunting, latinate *Serenata: "Mis ojos al ver los tuyos"*. Better still, won't the Prince write an eloquent letter for Romo to present to the girl? Alberto agrees.

In a comic *Mímica* (mime scene) over music, four village girls wash clothes while their boyfriends relax in the local brasserie. The four lieutenants arrive, present flowers to the girls and spirit them away, much to the boys' annoyance. Margarita, as much interested in Alberto as he in her, sees the Prince presenting the letter to Romo. She tentatively approaches the youth to discover her fate. At first the pair are too nervous to speak, but eventually Margarita opens the letter (*Dúo: "Tralarara ... Por fin vencí"*). When she reads Alberto's lyrical confession (*"Yo he pasado la vida en un sueño"*) her joy is misinterpreted by Romo as a sign of feeling for him.

Before the mutual mistake can be exposed the village boys intrude; and Romo, anxious not to reveal that he has broken their pact to have nothing to do with the girls, says that the letter is from Alberto. The villagers turn on Margarita, but at this moment Alberto appears to defend her and himself from their anger (*Concertante: "Atrás, miserable"*). When she runs to the Prince, all is made clear to poor Romo. The boy's position is worsened when Alberto firmly declares that the letter was Romo's after all, and the villagers beat him up for his treachery. Left alone, Margarita faints into Alberto's protective arms as the scene ends.

SCENE 2—A flowery Dutch landscape, with prominent windmills. Commander Stok tries to cheer Romo with the news that Alberto has forbidden his crew to lead the girls on any further, and will present dowries to the first five village couples to get engaged. When Romo starts weeping because he will not be among them, the embarrassed Stok leaves to join the holiday and celebrate peace between the villagers. Alberto, swearing that he has acted in good faith, agrees to speak to Margarita on Romo's behalf, and tells the young man to hide himself as the girl appears.

The village girls can be heard in the distance, warning of the perils of love (*Concertante: "En la fuente de cariño"*); but when the moment comes Alberto is unable to lie to Margarita, and they pour out their feelings, fondly recalling the beautiful words of Alberto's letter. To the despair of the hapless Romo, the pair leave as the girls' warning song echoes through the countryside.

SCENE 3—The village, late that night under a full moon. Dawn is near, but Romo cannot tear himself away from Margarita's window. Hearing footsteps, he hides: it is Stok, calling to Alberto that all the villagers are asleep, and it's time to weigh anchor. The Prince jumps down from the girl's window. Assuring Stok that the girl's honor is unsullied, out of respect for her and to keep his word to Romo, Alberto leaves sadly with the Commander (*Dúo: "¡Capitán, capitán! Todo duerme"*).

Margarita emerges from her house and tries to run after him; but Romo, who has heard everything, stops her firmly. There can be no happiness for any of them. They are like the arms of a windmill, blown hither and thither by the winds, eternally pursuing, destined never to come together. As the hapless pair weep, wrapped up in their solitary sadness, the voice of Alberto can be heard in the far distance, still singing of his ideal love (*Final: "Yo he pasado la vida en un sueño"*).

The plot of *Molinos de viento* (Windmills) may initially strike us now as mere flummery, typical of the plethora of sentimental operettas from just about everywhere in Europe during the first decade of the last century. Luis Pascual Frutos's text, with its cod comedy villagers and wooden principals, does little to improve matters, although it does display the twin virtues of simplicity and brevity.

Luna's achievement in making bricks out of this literary straw is all the more praiseworthy. He was not the first *zarzuelero* to try to reinterpret the orchestral sophistication and melodic sweetness of Vienna for Madrid, but his talents were such that he succeeded where others had failed. From fairly unpromising beginnings his score blossoms; and in the through-written *concertante* scenes he develops real musical momentum, defining the drama through skillful use of his wistfully attractive main themes: Alberto's serenade *"Mis ojos al ver los tuyos"*, and the theme of "ideal love" associated with his letter, *"Yo he pasado la vida en un sueño"*.

No one would claim any great depth to *Molinos de viento*, but Luna's richly orchestrated score does succeed in making his characters' painful situations sympathetic and touching. Although Luna was to produce more lively and individual work (his later self would perhaps have made more of the "exotic" Dutch settings on offer) this early score still stands up as perhaps the most perfect mainstream operetta in the Spanish repertoire.

El niño judío
Zarzuela in two acts
(Madrid, Teatro Apolo, 5th February 1911)

Text: Antonio Paso and Enrique García Álvarez

Principal Characters: Samuel, a Madrid bookstall keeper (tenor); Concha, his sweetheart (soprano); Jenaro, her father (comic singer); Manacor, a wandering peddler (baritone); Rebeca, a slave (soprano); Barchilón, an Aleppo Jew (actor); Jamar-Jalea, a Rajah (actor).

ACT 1, SCENE 1—A bookstall near the Madrid Prado, 1900. After a short orchestral *Preludio* built on themes from the later *Canción española* we meet Samuel, the talkative youngster in charge of the stall. He takes more interest in browsing the stock than selling it, at least until his sweetheart Concha turns up. Samuel is anxious to prove himself an ambitious trader with prospects, in order to convince her wealthy father that he will make a desirable fiancé. Concha tells her beloved that his poverty is only incidental to the problem: her father Jenaro has a rooted objection to taking on a Jewish son-in-law. Samuel blithely counters that they only need wait for her father to die in order to become rich and do precisely as they please.

Before Concha can respond to his impeccable logic, Jenaro himself appears with the unwelcome news that Samuel's father has been taken seriously ill and is calling for his son. The young man, mortified at the ill fortune his own quip has foretold, hastens to his father's bedside leaving Concha to mind the stall. Jenaro tells her that the dying man has confessed that Samuel is not his true son. Rather he is the child of a rich Aleppo Jew, Samuel Barchilón; and of Barchilón's wife Esther, whom Samuel's "father" had desperately wanted to marry. In revenge his "father" kidnapped the baby and fled to Spain, bringing up the child as his own. All of which has changed Jenaro's perspective on Samuel's marital ambition. If Samuel turns out to be wealthy after all, the old man will gladly let him marry Concha: indeed it is imperative that the three of them travel to Aleppo immediately and stake the boy's claim.

SCENE 2—The Market Square of Aleppo in Syria, beneath the Citadel. In the opening *Coro* the traders vie to attract the attention of potential purchasers. The traveling peddler Manacor sings of the life of a wandering Jew in a lilting *Romanza: "Qué me importa ser Judío"*, accompanying himself on a harp and echoed by the chorus. Samuel and Concha, watching a group of local pipe-smokers, compare the similarity of Christian and Arab habits in a waltz *Dúo: "Ay, que gusta"*. Barchilón appears, and the traders rush toward him. Seeing some slaves for sale he remarks on the despicable perfidy of these dregs of humanity; one of them, the Spanish-born Rebeca, sings her sad history in a touching *Romanza: "Yo era infanta castellana"* but even this fails to move the old misanthrope. When Manacor innocently tries to interest Barchilón in "jewelry for the wife," he is greeted with a torrent of abuse. Esther had an affair with a great Eastern potentate who was lodging with them in Aleppo, and ran away with him to India years ago. Since then Barchilón has done little but curse the woman and the son she bore.

Exhausted by his rant, Barchilón goes back into his house just before the Spaniards reappear. Jenaro questions Manacor to find out Barchilón's whereabouts. He looks forward with Samuel, Concha and the peddler to the anticipated joyful outcome in a *Cuarteto: "Ay moreno, moreno"*. They are not a little taken aback when Barchilón, instead of embracing his long-lost son, does his best to drown him in the town well before being pulled away, kicking and screaming. Manacor tells them the reason: Samuel is not Barchilón's son at all, but the lovechild of the fabulously wealthy Rajah, Jamar-Jalea. The Spanish party immediately decide to take their dream of untold riches to India, and Manacor prepares to resume his wanderings, gently recalling the melody of his *Romanza: "Beber quisiera yo en ellos"*.

ACT 2, SCENE 1—The Palace of Jamar-Jalea (Gobble-Jelly) in India. The act begins with a short *Interludio*, which leads directly into the *Coro: "Que reine muchos años"*, a peon of praise wishing the Great Rajah a long and blissful life. This leads directly into the famously muscular *Danza india*, in which Jamar-Jalea's warriors and dancing girls cavort in energetic tribute to their Prince. The Spaniards are presented before the Rajah, but Esther has died and he is now under the sway of his second wife, the cruel Jubea. When she accuses them of being imposters the Rajah has no choice but to publicly denounce them. However, as soon as Jubea is off the scene Jamar-Jalea embraces Samuel as his long-lost child. The happy family group look forward to escaping to Spain together, with the help of a liberal supply of gems.

In response to Jamar-Jelea's curiosity about their homeland, Concha sings her flamboyant *Canción española: "De España vengo, soy española"*, the orchestra mimicking Jenaro's guitar accompaniment. The Rajah enjoys the song so much that Jenaro generously offers to give him the guitar, but the party mood is cut short by the unexpected return of Jubea. Furious, she orders the three foreigners to be taken away to the temple and made ready for execution.

SCENE 2—The temple. Samuel and Jenaro try to raise their spirits with ghoulish imaginings of high jinks in the graveyard: after they are dead, their skeletons will be dancing grimly under the light of the moon (*Dúo: "Soy un rayito de luna"*.) Six Brahmin Priests solemnly complete the Hindu death rites, whilst the Spaniards contribute a jaunty version of the Christian Kyrie (*Coro y Concertante: "Salve, salve"*). Jamar-Jalea arrives in the nick of time to annul his wife's cruel decree and free the prisoners—though further revelations await them from the Brahmins. Samuel is not the Rajah's son after all. Esther confessed to the Brahmin before she died that, fearful of Barchilón's jealous fury, she had exchanged her precious lovechild for the illegitimate son of a servant girl before her flight from Aleppo.

The kindly Rajah nevertheless gives them money and jewels to help them escape back to Madrid before bidding them a fond farewell. Samuel's travels have not given him untold wealth, or even a firm identity. But all is far from lost: after what they have been through together, Jenaro consents wholeheartedly to the Jewish Boy's marriage to his faithful Concha. A brief orchestral *Final* provides a triumphant happy-ever-after, with a last reminiscence of Manacor's *Romanza* of the wandering life as the curtain falls.

As the new century got into its stride, the robust comedy of Madrid's *género chico* was seduced by the flimsy, exotic fare that appealed to the jaded palettes of Paris and the other European capitals. When the Viennese operettas of Lehár, for example, started to find favor in Madrid, *zarzueleros* were not slow to tailor their work to the fashion. The most successful exponent of the operetta style in the 1910s and 20s was undoubtedly Pablo Luna, and in *El niño judío* (The Jewish Boy, written with the anonymous and indefinable collaboration of Reveriano Soutullo) his librettists provided him with an unashamed vehicle for highly colored musico-theatrical display.

Luna's score is resilient and varied enough to add substance to their Cook's Tour of a plot. The curried harmonies of the *Danza india*—a number which conveys the weird impression of a herd of elephants dancing a *pasodoble*—offer a delicious pre-echo of the Hollywood Epic style. The mordant graveyard humor of the Act 2 *Dúo* for Samuel and Jenaro is equally prescient: with xylophone suggesting skeletal dancing bones it offers a striking foretaste of that deaths-head rictus which Puccini was to provide for Ping, Pang and Pong in *Turandot*.

The soprano's impressive *Canción española*, a conscious essay in musical "Spanishry" justly popular for its flamboyant combination of strumming orchestral accompaniment and demanding vocal line, remains Luna's best known song. Written as a virtuoso showpiece for the soprano Rosario Leonís, its need for impressive *legato* control on top of the agility to encompass some flirtatious *alhambrismo* turns has understandably appealed to every Spanish diva since:

La pícara molinera
Zarzuela in three acts
(Zaragoza, Teatro Circo, 28th October 1928)

Text: Pilar Monterde, Eulalia Fernández Galván, Angel Torres del Álamo, Antonio Asenjo and Pérez Campos

Principal Characters: Carmona, the mill girl (mezzo-soprano); Juan (tenor); Pintu (baritone); Pepa, a tavernkeeper (soprano); Riverin, her husband (comic tenor); Pondala, her sister (soprano).

ACT 1—Outside a tavern in the picturesque hill country of Asturia. After a short orchestral *Preludio*, the scene opens with a group of villagers taking a much-needed break from work (*Coro: "El mozo que yo más quiero"*). Four card players comment on the bad behavior of the handsome young mill girl, Carmona, whose house is across the way. She is playing off two eligible young men, Pintu and Juan, against one another and enjoying the sense of power. Pintu boasts of his plans to win the girl's heart. He starts a serenade under her window (*Serenata y Coro: "¡Ay, pícara molinera! no sé lo que me hiciste"*) in which the other men join. The tavernkeeper, Pepa, is worried by her sister Pondala's listlessness and asks her husband, the piper Riverin, to find out what is wrong. The couple sing merrily of their own life together (*Dúo: "Lo que pensando estoy"*), while the villagers drink to prime themselves for that evening's fiesta of the Mill (*Coro y solos: "¡Sidra!"*).

Juan, accompanied by his friend the hunchback Cachano, goes to pay court to Carmona, but before he can approach the house Pondala rushes out of the Inn to remind him that he has promised to take her to the fiesta. Passionate recriminations follow, and she pours out her love before Juan can tear himself free; but he remains determined to ask the mill girl to the festivities instead (*Dúo: "Yo rapaza y tú neño"*). Pondala leaves in despair, followed by Riverin who has been watching in secret. Carmona comes out of her house to taunt Juan about his unfaithfulness. He replies that she is the only girl he wants to take to the fiesta. When Carmona tells him that Pintu has the same idea, Juan leaves furiously. His rival appears, only to be teased in his turn. In a sensual *Dúo: "Yo te quiero con locura"* Pintu tells Carmona of the depth of his feeling. The mill girl replies that the man she wants doesn't exist, but that she might be prepared to accept Pintu as the best of a bad bunch.

The village people return, and Carmona responds to their gentle mockery with a challenge: who will get the prettiest girl in the village? (*Coro y solo: "A la mocina mejor"*). Juan comes in all set to take Carmona to the fiesta, with an apposite folksong in which the chorus joins (*Canción y Coro: "La moza que yo adoro, tiene un molino"*). Pintu and Juan clash, and the whole village gathers to witness the ensuing shouting match before the two rivals leave for a fight. Two shots are heard, and to everyone's consternation Pintu reappears, smiling quietly as the curtain falls.

ACT 2, SCENE 1—Later that evening, in the tavern bar. Juan's "accident," which has resulted in a nasty wound to his shoulder, is the talk of the village. The young man is in pain, unable to attend the fiesta. He sings a warmly passionate song of unrequited love and hope for the future, the touching *Romanza: "Paxarin tú que vuelas"*. The heartless Carmona taunts him by suggesting he should go back to his old, dull sweetheart Pondala, and twists the knife with the news that as Pintu is taking her to the fiesta she has almost decided to marry him. His passionate pleas are unavailing and she reasserts her right to please herself, leaving him to curse her heartlessness in their *Dúo: "Juntos nos vimos desde pequeños"*.

SCENE 2—The fiesta. A celebrated orchestral *Intermedio* portrays the carnival atmosphere. Pepa and the women sing a popular Asturian-style song *Las herradas* (*Canción y coro: "Amor mío, vienes tarde"*). Pintu, confident of his own merits and assured of success, defends himself robustly in reply to some ironic comments from the village doctor, Don Pericón: he has as much right to his dreams as anyone (*Duo: "Nada me asusta ni espanta"*). Cold-shouldered and alone, his mood softens in a tender song addressed to his beloved, the *Romanza: "La manzana nació verde"*. His heart was free, but Carmona has changed him. The fiesta is in full swing, and a piper accompanies a lively dance (*Coro y solos: "Vienen aquí la fiesta a celebrar"*); but as it finishes a villager rushes in to call for the doctor—Pintu is dead, killed by a bullet to the brain.

ACT 3—The tavern bar, some days later. The shocked villagers gossip about the murder, and decide that Juan must be responsible (*Coro y solo: "La Pepa tiene un chiquillo"*). Carmona, afraid of being left without a lover, starts making up to Juan again, but he informs her coldly that he is promised to Pondala. The festive mood returns as Juan salutes his faithful bride-to-be, and the villagers celebrate the pairing in joyous song and dance (*Coro final y solo: "No impórtame que me encierren"*). The Doctor asks Juan whether he is responsible for Pintu's death. Juan swears he isn't, and the hunchback Cachano adds quietly that surely "it was the work of providence." Pepa reveals that the man responsible for the shooting was not Pintu but Riverin, insulted by Juan's dishonorable behavior toward his sister-in-law. The culprit has been hiding in the tavern, and plans to escape the hand of justice with the help of his friend the doctor. Carmona weeps wretchedly, but the doctor points out the moral: that the fickle mill girl has only herself to blame for being left without a man, after the way she has treated Juan and the luckless Pintu.

Pablo Luna's last great success, *La pícara molinera* (The Teasing Millgirl) transferred after significant revision to Madrid's Teatro Apolo, where it scored a major triumph. It boasts a large clutch of librettists, but the chief fingers in the verbal pie belonged to Torres del Álamo and Asenjo, who based their treatment on a popular novella of rural love-tangle and tragedy by Alfonso Camín. The strong characters are credibly motivated, and there is a dose of sympathy for everyone, not excepting the rural *femme fatale* of the title.

Of all the great *zarzueleros*, Luna was most inclined to deck out his zarzuelas with the sumptuous exoticism of operetta, and earlier scores such as *El niño judío* owed much of their success to piquant foreign settings and bizarre characters. Though *La pícara molinera* with its folk melodies might appear something of an exception, Luna's opulently upholstered style, wedded to the sweetly sensational verismo plot, brings it closer to Lehár than

Lorca. The music is masterly, a feast of passionate melody, garnished with Asturian flavorings and succulent orchestral writing—not least in the deservedly famous Act 2 *Intermedio* with its stirring cello tune and rhythmically pointed cross-melodies, spiced by pizzicato strings, woodwind and tambourine. It is sad that this thrilling "lollipop" hasn't had the opportunity to make its way outside Spain, for its popularity would be certain:

Benamor (1923)
Based like *El asombro de Damasco* on a Persian fairy-tale, this three-act operetta has a score of comparable quality, though only the fiercely exciting orchestral showpiece *Danza del fuego* (Fire Dance) and the baritone's *Canción Española: "País del sol"* are heard today. The plot turns on a barbaric custom according to which the Sultan's firstborn must be male, the second female, on pain of death. His wife bears two children, Darió and Benamor, born in the wrong order and necessarily brought up as members of the opposite sex—with predictably confusing consequences.

Los cadetes de la Reina (The Queen's Cadets, 1913)
A one-act Ruritanian operetta often coupled in double bills with *Molinos de viento*. Queen Herminia of Tolosa has lost her favorite, and decrees that a replacement will be executed in his memory each month. Carlos, Captain of the Cadets, loves Herminia but is naturally unwilling to put himself in the firing line by admitting it. The intervention of the streetwise courtesan Rosa eventually helps put everything to rights. Luna's music, consciously written in antique courtly style, is tuneful and sweepingly impressive by turns. Carlos's suave *Canción: "Es el pecado más horrible"* and later *Romanza: "Era un pobre capitán"* are among the most celebrated numbers.

La chula de Pontevedra (The Girl from Pontevedra, with **Enrique Bru**, 1928)
This masterly one-act *sainete* came as a surprise from the pen of the sophisticated exponent of operetta-zarzuela. The plot revolves round a clever servant girl from the town of Pontevedra in Galicia, marooned in the Madrid suburbs. Rosiña saves the marriage of her employers at the risk of her own freedom, and eventually chooses a local husband to become "more *madrileñan* than the *madrileños*." Luna's music is varied and attractive, cleverly seasoning the familiar Madrid dance forms with rustic, Galician instrumental flavors including bagpipes.

16
Rafael Millán
(1893–1957)

Born 24th September 1893 in Algeciras near Cádiz, Millán came from a musical family. His first teacher was his father, a military bandsman, and Rafael emerged as a fine violinist, moving to Madrid in 1914 to advance his career. Once established in the orchestra of the Teatro de la Zarzuela under his mentor Pablo Luna, his interest in theatre blossomed; and soon he was conducting and composing stage pieces, the first of which was *El Príncipe Bohemio* (The Bohemian Prince, 1914). He also wrote symphonic, choral and band works, but his forty-three stage works are his most significant legacy.

After 1910, when Luna's own *Molinos de viento* took Spain by storm, operettas (particularly those by the Viennese Franz Lehár) became much more fashionable than *género chico* zarzuelas with a Madrid setting; and many of Millán's early works followed the trend. With *La Dogaresa* (The Doge's Wife, 1920) he emerged as a significant voice in his own right, and his premieres were eagerly awaited from then onward. *El pájaro azul* (The Bluebird, 1921), *Los buscadores de oro* (The Gold Diggers, 1922) and *El dictador* (The Dictator, 1923) franked his fame; the later *La gaviota* (The Seagull, 1924) and *La severa* (The Serious Woman, 1925) augmented it. Millán was particularly popular in Barcelona where he made his home, and where many of his finest works first saw the light of day.

Much of the rest of his life was shrouded in mystery. There were rumors of progressive illness, and in 1938 reports of his death were circulated. The truth was that from 1925 Millán became subject to periods of mental disturbance, and some years later he was permanently hospitalized. The 1928 Madrid revision of *La severa* as *La morería* (The Moorish Quarter, 1928) was mainly undertaken by his fellow-composer Alonso. Touchingly, Millán did enjoy an Indian Summer right at the end of his life, when his mental condition improved sufficiently to allow him to compose one last stage work, *El tesoro de Golconda* (The Golconda Treasure, 1952) for his beloved Barcelona. He died in Madrid on 8th March 1957.

Millán gained the swift approval of Madrid's critics by reason of his orchestral imagination, and its influence on the work of his less precocious contemporaries is patent. Although his music may lack Sorozábal's individual, contemporary flavor, Millán's best scores are nevertheless of absorbing musical interest. The melodies of *El pájaro azul* or *El dictador* may not be so instantly hummable as Luna's or Serrano's, but these zarzuelas have a symphonic strength and integrity which makes their comparative neglect a pity. Only the melodrama *La Dogaresa*, with its glamorous Venetian settings, is much encountered today.

La Dogaresa
Zarzuela in two acts
(Barcelona, Teatro Tívoli, 17th September 1920)

Text: Antonio López Monís

Principal Characters: Paolo, a Venetian gondolier (tenor); Marietta, his fiancée (soprano); Marco, a fencing master (comic tenor); Rosina, Marco's wife (mezzo-soprano); Zabulón, a moneylender (bass); Doge of Venice (bass); Miccone, his jester (baritone).

ACT 1—A Venetian marketplace in the time of the Mediaeval Doges. The traders cry their wares to the crowd in a lively *Coro: "Venid aquí, venecianos a comprar"*. The fencing master Marco offers his services to anyone anxious to protect himself in these dangerous times; an old sorceress offers fortune-selling; and the old Jewish moneylender Zabulón plies his trade among the crowd (*Solos y coro: "El que quiere saber"*).

Some female admirers wonder what has happened to the handsome gondolier Paolo, who has not been seen for over a week. The sorceress predicts his imminent doom through the conjunction of a woman, a powerful man and a traitor; and the women mull over the hot city gossip: that Paolo's beloved Marietta has attracted the eye of the elderly Doge. The gondolier has gone to ground to escape their ruler's vindictive ire. Marco silences the gossip and the market folk drift away, mystified by the fencing master's atypical mood. His wife Rosina is even more baffled by his strange behavior, and determines to get to the bottom of it. Marietta comes out of her house, deeply anxious about Paolo but hopeful the danger may pass, as she tells Marco in her barcarolle *Romanza: "Ya muerto está, mi amor en flor"*. A masked man approaches through the shadows, and she leaves before the stranger reveals himself as Paolo. Marco tells him the worst: that the Doge wants to marry Marietta, and kidnap the gondolier himself. Paolo sings of the confidence born of love in a *Romanza: "Pondré en la empresa mi fe y mi honor"* in powerful bolero rhythm. Rosina, who has been watching unseen, believes she can hatch a plot to save Marietta, and the three leave to plan the details.

The Doge's jester Miccone visits Zabulón, revealed as the informer behind the plot to kidnap Paolo. Zabulón is in it for the money, while Miccone is motivated by desire for Marietta, with whom he too is secretly in love. The Jew finds this highly amusing, and in their *Dúo: "Inspiras risa así ... Si una mujer nos enamora"* the pair express their very different attitudes to amorous passion. They do agree on the need to find a confidential page who can be infiltrated into the palace to watch the Doge's future wife and lead them to the missing Paolo. Rosina, who has overheard, suggests to Zabulón that she would be the ideal candidate; and in a vivacious Viennese-style *Duetto Cómico: "No es posible lo que pretendes"* she convinces him by some heavy flirtation to give her the job. Rosina leaves with the moneylender, as Marco and Paolo reappear, wondering what she is plotting.

The *Final* begins as a group of Court Ladies and Gentlemen approach Marietta's house to greet the Doge's chosen wife (*Coro: "El tambor con su son expresa"*). Rosina restrains Paolo when Miccone formally asks Marietta to accompany them to the palace. She accepts the Doge's command with dignity, and when presented with flowers sings of her happiness; although the song's tender melancholy contradicts her words (*Canción y concertante: "Las flores de mil colores"*). The "Doge's wife" is carried into the palace, with her "page" and the courtiers, leaving Paolo alone to swear that he will rescue Marietta, even at the cost of his own life.

ACT 2, SCENE 1—The atrium of the Doge's Palace, adjoining the Grand Canal. The Doge and his chosen bride are acclaimed by the courtiers (*Coro y solos: "Grande fiesta hoy"*). Miccone entertains them with a tale about a cruel lord who loved a shepherdess and jealously murdered a young lad for daring to love her too—though, of course, not a word of it is true! (*Cuento y tarantela: "Un conde fue"*). His daring story concludes with a mocking, boisterous tarantella (*"Pastorcilla, pastorcilla"*) dear to many Spanish baritones.

Watched by the "page" Rosina, the Doge attempts to persuade Marietta to accept his hand. Her silent denial enrages the ruler, who gives her until next day to make up her mind and sweeps out. Rosina reveals her true identity to Marietta, and outlines her plan: the sound of a serenade from the adjoining canal will be their signal for flight. All the more urgently, since her own disguise has been penetrated by four genuine pages. In a delicious quintet, the four teasingly ask their companion to spend a night with them, but she manages to put them off until next morning (*Quinteto: "Callad, amigos míos"*).

Marco whispers from a boat on the canal for Rosina to unlock the gate, which she manages to do despite the suspicions of the lurking Miccone. Paolo appears in his own gondola with a group of mandolinists, who provide cover with a lilting *Barcarola: "Ya duerme Venecia tranquila"* as the gondolier enters the palace. The lovers sing of their happiness at being reunited (*Dúo: "Tu voz resonaba"*). Marietta and Paolo enter the gondola, but before they can escape the Doge breaks in, led by Miccone and the Pages, and the palace guards detain the fugitives.

SCENE 2—An anteroom to the infamous Council of Ten. Zabulón and the sympathetic Captain of the Guard await Paolo's certain sentence of death. They are joined by Rosina and her friend, Cordalia: although there is little to be done for Paolo, perhaps some diversion might be arranged at the moment the condemned man appears on the Bridge of Sighs to receive the formal Viaticum before proceeding to execution. The ten judges leave the courtroom in their masks and red robes, and Rosina is amazed when the last of them raises his visor and is revealed as Marco!

Miccone watches the judges depart; and when Marietta with one last, desperate effort begs him to save her beloved, the jester's heart melts. In the intense, brooding *Dúo: "Miccone ... Tras de esa puerta un hombre"* he swears to save Paolo, whatever the cost. There is a cry from Rosina: Paolo's sentence is confirmed by Marco, and with one kiss Miccone quietly leaves Marietta with her friends. An orchestral *Intermedio* recalling the *Dúo* for Miccone and Zabulón *"Si una mujer nos enamora"* leads to the final scene.

SCENE 3—The Bridge of Sighs, at first light. Led by the Captain of the Guard, Paolo begins his sad progress over the bridge toward the gibbet, watched from the palace balcony by Miccone, and from the canal bank by Marietta and the crowd. Paolo sings farewell to the world in a brief, heartfelt *Romanza: "Ven a mí, muerte querida"* as he waits for the formal arrival by black gondola of the Viaticum.

As the bell tolls, the boat—rowed by Marco—approaches, and Miccone disappears. To everyone's surprise the Viaticum is landed, not at the Bridge, but by the Palace. All is made clear when Miccone reappears: the last rites are needed for the Doge in his death agonies, struck down by the jester's hand (*Final: "Venecianos: El Dux acaba de ser herido"*). Paolo is freed to embrace Marietta, and as day breaks, the assassin Miccone gives himself up into the Captain's charge.

Next to his mentor Luna, Rafael Millán is the most important purveyor of large-scale operetta-zarzuelas. With *La Dogaresa* (The Doge's Wife) López Monís, the real-life Conte de López Muñoz, offered him a spectacular libretto of Verdian flavor, drawing on *Rigoletto* for the rounded central character of a cruel but lovelorn court jester, and on *I Due Foscari* for the melodrama of Venetian intrigue. The story has echoes, too, of Offenbach's *Le Pont des Soupirs* (1861), which also features the Council of Ten. The prevailing romantic gloom is effectively relieved by lighter elements, such as the machinations of the streetwise "comedy couple" Marco and Rosina, both characters squarely within the native, Spanish tradition.

Millán's atmospheric score for this typical tragi-comic mixture draws on Venetian barcarolle rhythms, and maintains a high quality throughout. The beautifully scored *Dúo* for Marietta and Miccone, with its important *concertante* parts for solo strings, breathes a heavily Spanish melancholy. The baritone's narrative song *"Un conde fue"* with its breathless tarantella conclusion is a flight of musical daring which matches Miccone's dangerous stage gambit.

El dictador (The Dictator, 1923)
A good libretto by the leading writing team of the day, Romero and Shaw; an attractive Imperial Russian setting; a stellar cast; and, not least, Millán's powerful score account for the initial triumph of this three-act work, which clearly influenced Sorozábal's later *Katiuska*. That it is rarely revived today is partly down to the difficulty of the central role of Boris Daneff, tailored to the gifts of the great baritone Emilio Sagi-Barba. His Letter Song (*Canción de la carta: "Mi carta, mujer de mis amores"*) remains one of the most impressive *romanzas* in the repertoire.

El pájaro azul (The Bluebird, 1921)
The Bluebird is a Portuguese patriot, Esteban, fighting against the attempted annexation of his country by Spain during the reign of Philip II (1580). The preposterous romantic action at least allowed Millán space to produce his strongest score, rich in contrasted Castilian and Portuguese folk elements; quite aside from this, the love music is the best he ever wrote. Lucinda and Esteban's extended, moonlit *Dúo: "La luz de la luna ... En la noche clara"* is especially fine, its sheer beauty a match for any such duet in the Spanish repertoire.

17
Federico Moreno Torroba
(1891–1982)

The career of Moreno Torroba, with that of his equally long-lived contemporary Sorozábal, embodies the latest flowering of the zarzuela. Born in Madrid on 3rd March 1891, the son of a well-known Madrid organist, he became an outstanding pupil of the pedagogic master of musical nationalism Felipe Pedrell. Torroba divided his talents between composing, conducting and impresario work, writing a great deal of symphonic and instrumental music. His major contribution to the concert hall is the series of fine works for guitar (with and without orchestra) written for Andrés Segovia; these include the popular *Sonatina*, *Concierto ibérico* and *Concierto flamenco*.

As a conductor-impresario he was at one time managing no fewer than three stage companies, giving important productions of works by Sorozábal, Guridi and Guerrero in addition to his own. His touring company brought the zarzuela tradition to international audiences, not least in the United States and Spanish Central America, throughout the 1930s and 40s. The fine singers who worked with Torroba included Plácido Domingo Sr. and Pepita Embil, encouraged by his success to form an offshoot company in Mexico, where their son the great tenor was brought up. Torroba later held academic posts, becoming president of the Sociedad General de Autores de España (SGAE) in 1975, and dying in Madrid on 12th September 1982 in his ninety-second year.

He first zarzuela appeared as early as 1920, but it was the success of *La mesonera de Tordesillas* (The Hostess of Tordesillas, 1925) which encouraged Torroba to devote himself to the genre. *La pastorela* (The Pastorale, 1926, with Pablo Luna) and *La marchenera* (The Girl from Marchena, 1928) augmented his fame; and among the plethora of successful zarzuelas from the pre-Civil War period the three-act *Luisa Fernanda* (1932) and *La chulapona* (The Chick, 1934) stand out as masterpieces. His operas include *La Virgen de Mayo* (1925), and the late *El poeta* (1980) in which Plácido Domingo himself sang the title role.

After the Civil War Torroba and Joaquín Rodrigo were able to develop their musical creed of *casticismo* (authenticity), collaborating together in *El duende azul* (The Blue Ghost, 1946). For Torroba, this authenticity came from the power of a tried and tested tradition, the "popular nationalism" of Spanish folk music which informs the world of Rodrigo's famous *Concierto de Aranjuez*. Torroba never quite had the luck—or time—to develop his own music in accordance with the theory, and his post-war zarzuela-operettas from *Monte Carmelo* (1939) through to *Rosaura* (1965) are considerably less "authentic" in tone than the two *zarzuelas grandes* on which his reputation now rests. These great stage works remain priceless jewels of the tradition in which he believed so strongly, and for which he worked so hard.

La chulapona
Lyric Comedy in three acts
(Madrid, Teatro Calderón, 31st March 1934)

Text: Federico Romero and Guillermo Fernández Shaw

Principal Characters: Manuela, La chulapona (mezzo-soprano); Rosario (soprano); Venustiana (contralto); José María (tenor); Señor Antonio (actor); Epifanio, Manuela's father (actor); Juan de Dios, her brother (baritone); El chalina (comic tenor).

ACT 1—Manuela's laundry in the Cava district of Old Madrid, 1893. After an orchestral *Introducción* the curtain rises to reveal the laundry girls, led by the pretty Rosario, singing a song from Caballero's *El dúo de la africana* as they iron away (*Coro y solo: "No cantes más la africana"*). The witty El chalina (cravat) appears at the door, and soon the girls are dancing an impromptu *Mazurka: "Las chicas de Madrí"* to the tune of his *organillo*, or barrel organ.

El chalina flirts with Rosario and is gently teased by her and another girl, Emilia, for his pains. Manuela's indigent father Don Epifanio rushes into the laundry. His drinking has put him in debt to Rosario's moneylending mother, Venustiana, who is in furious pursuit. The old man just has time to hide behind a rack of petticoats; and the moneylender, swiftly charmed by El chalina's compliments, departs temporarily mollified. Don

Epifanio emerges, and after thanking Rosario effusively for not giving him away, hurries out.

The room lights up as the popular Manuela La chulapona (chick) appears, and in her *Chotis: "Creí que no venía"* she laughs about the compliments she received from passersby in the street. She loves her Madrid life, as she makes clear in the *Pasacalle: "Como soy chulapona"* which follows. Emilia's father, the widowed café proprietor Señor Antonio, flirts with La chulapona; but although she respects this older man, Manuela dotes on her boyfriend José María. When he turns up, the couple enjoy some sweet talk—soured by asides from Rosario who is profoundly jealous of Manuela and wants José María for herself (*Terceto: "¿Se puede pasar, paloma?"*).

Once he is gone Rosario insinuates that Manuela's man may not be as faithful as he seems. Manuela, cursing the girl's gossip, has little time to act on her suspicions before her ne'er-do-well brother Juan de Dios sneaks in, begging for money. Before she can deal with him another imbroglio breaks out: Venustiana has got two policemen to arrest Don Epifanio, much to the amusement of the gathering crowd (*Escena: "¡Mecachis! ¡Qué voces!"*). La chulapona is forced to pawn her beautifully embroidered Manila shawl to Venustiana to gain her father's release, and the crowd dissolves.

Manuela goes down the street to check up on her boyfriend; and when her male relatives saunter off too, Rosario is left alone in the laundry. José María returns looking for Manuela, and Rosario takes the opportunity to pour out her own love, eventually bursting into tears. The soft-hearted José María takes the pretty girl in his arms (*Dúo-habanera: "Ese pañuelito blanco"*). The returning Manuela senses that she has interrupted something and proudly dismisses her guilty lover, telling him she does not care if he marries Rosario instead.

ACT 2, SCENE 1—A small square in the Morería district. An orchestral *Introducción* portrays the cheerful masses strolling toward the bullring. They are pestered by Juan de Dios, posing as a blind beggar to wangle a few pesetas for his entrance to the *corrida*. He sings a popular Cuban-style guajira to the crowd (*Escena y guajira: "¡Válgame San Pedro! . . . En la Habana hay una casa"*). Don Epifanio recognizes him, and finally gets hold of his son's guitar to sell for drink.

José María is buttonholed by Señor Antonio, who discovers to his surprise that the young man is now engaged to Rosario—mainly because Manuela is too proud to take him back and he too stubborn to beg her pardon. The generous café owner gives José María advice to help regain the girl's love, while El chalina flirts heavily with old Venustiana and plays a lively tune for the crowd on his *organillo* (*Pasacalle: "Vamos, que es tarde . . . Dejaría de ser madrileño"*).

La chulapona appears in her Sunday best, and is greeted by the admiring Señor Antonio. They approach the moneylender's to reclaim Manuela's Manila shawl, only to run into José María with Rosario and her mother setting off for the bullfight. Worse, Rosario is brazenly wearing the garment. To José María's shame, Manuela gives Rosario a piece of her mind for stealing her clothes as well as her man, before paying off the debt and proudly reclaiming her shawl (*Chotis-habanera: "Dígale usté a la Rosario"*).

SCENE 2—La plaza de la Cebada, in front of Señor Antonio's Café de Naranjeros. A delicate orchestral *Nocturno* evokes the warmth of the Madrid night. A flamenco singer can be heard inside the café. Juan de Dios, who has been drinking with friends in the café, runs into Rosario, out looking for José María. He has been missing for a week but nothing has been heard of him. She leaves sadly just as Epifanio strolls in, impressing a country farmer with his urban sophistication. Failing to extort money from the booby, the old reprobate goes into the café with his tail between his legs.

José María, unable to make up his mind between the two women, has come to drown his sorrows. He asks Juan de Dios whether his sister is inside, and the well-meaning wastrel advises him to beg Manuela's pardon and make it up. The flamenco song is heard inside once more, as José María ponders his dilemma in the evocative *Romanza: "Tienes razón, amigo"*. Plucking up his courage, he enters the café.

SCENE 3—Inside the café. A troupe of singers and dancers entertain the locals in a series of lively flamenco numbers—bulerías, tanguillo, petenera and zapateado (*Escena: "Si me dices que me quieres"*). Epifanio and his son are drinking noisily with a host of colorful characters including El chalina. Manuela comes in with a wedding present for Antonio's daughter Emilia, who is shortly to be married, and goes upstairs to see her friend. Venustiana comes in for a drink—much to the discomfiture of Epifanio, who still owes her money and coerces Antonio into bailing him out. Manuela comes down and spots José María, but before she can leave Señor Antonio sits them down at a table together. Watched by the hushed crowd the couple are soon reconciled, much to Antonio's secret disappointment (*Terceto-habanera: "Déjeme, Señor Antonio"*).

ACT 3—The leafy Viveros de la Villa. An orchestral *Intermedio* introduces the final act. Manuela is about to be married to José María, and a photographer tries to line up the vivacious wedding party for a posed shot (*Introducción: "¡Ande, señor retratista"*). Everyone is there, except for Venustiana; the old moneylender has surprised everyone by eloping with El chalina, the organ-grinder! The group breaks up to dance a catchy *Chotis: "¡Ay, madrileña chulapa!"*, after which Antonio makes a slightly stiff speech offering to buy everyone a meal. Rosario manages a quiet word with José María. She begs him to return to her, and when he refuses alleges that she is pregnant with his child. The shaken José María reassures the concerned Antonio that he is still going ahead with the marriage to Manuela.

Don Epifanio once more importunes La chulapona for money, and she sadly regrets never having had a father she could rely on for support. One by one the laundry girls offer Manuela the customary good-luck kiss; and when the penitent Rosario approaches her she cannot refuse to listen. In a moving *Dúo: "No es que te quiera besar"* Rosario admits that she wanted to take José María away from Manuela out of an envy she no longer feels (*"Confieso que le quise por envidia"*). Now she is pregnant by him, and a lost woman. Kissing Manuela tenderly, she leaves.

Recalling once again her own hapless childhood, the generous Manuela will not hear of the unborn child being brought up without a father. In the *Final* spoken over music, she dismisses the stunned José María, who departs after Rosario. Then to Antonio's delight Manuela calmly tells the café owner that she will marry him after all. He hurries off to tell his daughter and friends the good news; but once alone, the heartbroken Manuela concedes that in the long, sleepless nights ahead, she will think only of José María.

For many, the lyric comedy *La chulapona* (The Chick) is the quintessential Madrid zarzuela. It is certainly a fabulous compendium of the dances, sounds and popular scenes of that lost Golden Age of the 1890s which it evokes so strongly. Yet beyond the barrel organs, café-bar castanets and guitars, what distinguishes *La chulapona* from several other nostalgic "retro" zarzuelas of the pre-Civil War years?

Romero and Shaw packed their highly theatrical libretto with a host of situations familiar from the *género chico* classics of Chueca, Chapí and Torregrosa (whose *La fiesta de San Antón* is notably similar in general outline) without inducing any sense of *déjà vu*. At the centre of their colorful web of characters is the inevitable love triangle; yet all three luckless lovers are sympathetically drawn, not least La chulapona Manuela herself. Many find her self-sacrifice tragic; but the librettists ensure a conclusion very far from downbeat, by providing a hint that she may be better off with the steady Señor Antonio after all.

As with *Luisa Fernanda*, Torroba provided a score of unusual length. Indeed some punctilious commentators have preferred to define the pair as *operones* (half-operas) rather than zarzuelas. The music has had its detractors, mainly on the grounds that *La chulapona* doesn't have the melodic inspiration of *Luisa Fernanda*. While there may be a grain of truth in this, such was inevitable in an ensemble work with room for only one solo *Romanza*—José María's *"Tienes razón, amigo"*, which lacks nothing in quality. The final *Dúo* for the two women is equally distinguished, as is the orchestral *Nocturno*;

but elsewhere the score is more notable for smiling energy and operetta-lightness of touch than for emotional depth.

As those fortunate enough to see the Teatro de la Zarzuela's 1988 production or its subsequent revivals can readily testify, any such doubts are blown away in the theatre, where *La chulapona*'s dazzling mixture of popular song, catchy dance and orchestral wizardry has enthralled audiences at home and abroad. Indeed, its ecstatic reception at the 1995 Edinburgh Festival exploded the received idea that Madrid zarzuela was somehow too provincial to travel, in one, joyous blast.

Luisa Fernanda
Lyric Comedy in three acts
(Madrid, Teatro Calderón, 26th March 1932)

Text: Federico Romero and Guillermo Fernández Shaw

Principal Characters: Luisa Fernanda (soprano); Duchess Carolina (soprano); Javier Moreno, an army colonel (tenor); Vidal Hernando, a country landowner (baritone); Luis Nogales, a revolutionary (actor); Aníbal (actor); Mariana (mezzo-soprano).

ACT 1—Outside a tavern in San Javier Square, Madrid. It is 1868, and the regime of Queen Isabel II is under threat from the revolutionary republican movement. After the orchestral *Introducción* we meet the innkeeper Mariana, chatting in the sun with her lodgers (*Escena: "Mi madre me criaba"*). These include a seamstress, Rosita, the republican Don Luís Nogales and his enthusiastic young supporter Aníbal. A wandering Savoyard singer performs a sad story about a girl and an unfaithful soldier (*Habanera: "Marchaba a ser soldado"*) to entertain the loungers.

The elderly former palace clerk Don Florito Fernández and his daughter Luisa join the group. Luisa's fiancé Javier Moreno has recently been made a Colonel, and despite the fact that he is not paying Luisa his accustomed attentions, the girl leaves to pray for him. Jeromo, a servant of the monarchist Duchess Carolina whose house is just across the square, warns Mariana about Nogales' dangerous activities. Javier comes looking for Luisa, and is thoroughly scolded by Mariana for his nonchalant attitude. He admits his ambition and impatience with the quiet life of Madrid (*Romanza: "De este apacible rincón de Madrid"*).

Overseen by the Duchess from her balcony, Aníbal tries to talk Javier into joining the revolutionary movement and introduces him to Nogales. The men leave and Luisa returns. Mariana strongly advises her to forget Javier and think about marrying a rich Estremaduran landowner, Vidal Hernando, who has come to Madrid to look for a wife. Mariana introduces him, and though the young woman takes to Vidal she warns the landowner that she is deeply in love with another man and leaves politely (*Dúo: "En mi tierra extremeña"*).

When Aníbal tells him that his rival Javier is joining the revolutionaries, Vidal has no hesitation in declaring himself a staunch monarchist: the landowner will fight to win Luisa from the soldier. Javier returns, looking for Luisa, but the alluring Duchess Carolina takes the opportunity to further her acquaintance with the handsome soldier (*Dúo: "Caballero del alto plumero"*).

Under her seductive influence, and much to the astonishment of Aníbal, Nogales and Vidal, Javier's political allegiance takes another about turn. As Luisa Fernanda returns just in time to see Javier sauntering away with the Duchess Carolina on his arm, Vidal promptly declares himself a revolutionary and proposes to her. Hurt and confused, Luisa faints into his arms as the act ends (*Final: "Abrasado en la llama"*).

ACT 2, SCENE 1—The Paseo de la Florida, near the "Goya" hermitage church of San Antonio. After an impressive orchestral *Introducción* a group of singers significantly repeat the Savoyard's *Habanera*. Mariana and the seamstress Rosita have been persuaded by Carolina to organize a charity collection outside the hermitage, next to a drinks stall run by the taverner Bizco Porras. Street vendors and musicians mingle with the crowd, and young men chat with a group of elegant ladies carrying parasols. These *sombrilleros* are visiting the church to ask St. Anthony to send them lovers, and Javier and Carolina join them in the elegantly witty Parasol Mazurka (*Mazurka de los sombrillas: "A San Antonio"*).

Their flirtation is watched by Mariana; and when Luisa and her tired father arrive the innkeeper swiftly puts them in the picture. Luisa unconcernedly explains that she has come here to meet Vidal, and taking Mariana off for a stroll leaves Don Florito in charge of the collection table with Rosita. Aníbal shares some bad news with Bizco and Nogales about a bungled republican attack, but Bizco is more concerned at the lad's failure to deliver some lemons promised for the stall. Carolina takes over at the table, soon to be joined by Vidal. She offers him a substantial sum to join the monarchist movement, but he refuses, quoting the fable of the village idiot who believed he was a swallow: Vidal at least has no intention of flying above his station (*Dúo: "Para comprar a un hombre"*).

Luisa returns, apologizing to Vidal for being late, and when Vidal assures her that he will remain a republican for her sake Luisa, irritated by Javier's arrogant possessiveness, tells the soldier that she prefers the landowner after all (*Terceto: "¡Cuanto tiempo sin verte, Luisa Fernanda!"*). Carolina, finding the charity table hasn't had much luck, proposes to add to the proceeds by auctioning herself off as a dance partner (*Escena: "Señoras y caballeros"*). Vidal easily outbids the jealous Javier, but insultingly passes on his prize dance to the soldier, who quietly confirms his determination to fight his rich rival.

SCENE 2—The Calle de Toledo at dawn. The rebels are gathering. Bizco and a *churros*-seller discuss the troubled situation. Nogales makes an impassioned speech to his rag-bag of an army, which goes off in good heart to fight and die in the name of liberty.

SCENE 3—The courtyard of Bizco's tavern. Waiting anxiously for news of the fighting, Mariana tells the rosary with Luisa and some neighbors. The wounded Aníbal staggers in and reports how bravely Vidal has fought, but the Estremaduran disclaims heroic status: he merely fought for love of Luisa (*Romanza: "Luche la fe por el triunfo"*).

When Don Florito tells them that Javier is leading a counterattack for the monarchists, Luisa herself defies Carolina with surprising revolutionary fervor. The attack fails, and Javier is led in a prisoner by Nogales. The crowd bays for his death as the *Final: "¡Muera el prisionero!"* begins. Luisa steps in and bravely defends him, just before the courtyard is invaded by Vidal and the republicans in flight from a fresh troop of hussars. The soldiers free Javier and announce the defeat of the insurgents. Vidal, admitting defeat on all fronts, is content to be arrested as chief rabble-rouser by Javier, but Nogales steps in and claims that honor for himself. The troops take Nogales away, Javier and Carolina embrace and leave together, and Luisa promises to marry the wounded but ecstatic Vidal.

ACT 3—Vidal's country estate *La Frondosa*, at Piedras Albas in Estremadura. The revolution has finally succeeded. Carolina has been exiled to Portugal, while Javier has disappeared, reported missing after the battle of Alcolea in which Queen Isabel II lost her throne. Mariana, Luisa and her father have joined Vidal to prepare for the wedding.

A group of *vareadores* (harvesters) appears (*Coro: "Si por el rido"*); and in his justly celebrated *Romanza: "¡En una dehesa de la Extremadura!"* Vidal praises his lovely sweetheart. Aníbal rushes in, announcing that he has found Javier in Portugal and has brought him back. Vidal had sent the boy there to fetch a wedding dress for Luisa, but in his excitement Aníbal has foolishly forgotten to fetch it—a bad omen.

Javier, wounded and broken, has asked Aníbal to persuade Luisa Fernanda to meet him once more before the marriage. Luisa agrees, and in the moving, melancholy *Dúo: "¡Cállate, corazón!"* she admits to Javier that she still loves him, but must stand by her promise to Vidal. Javier wanders away, as Luisa insists to Vidal that she will go through with the wedding. The guests, led by Aníbal, gather to dance and enjoy themselves (*Final: "El Cerandero se ha muerto"*), but when Javier returns in despair to plead with Luisa once more, Vidal realizes that Luisa will never love him. Despite her guilty objections he releases his fiancée from her promise and generously encourages her to leave with Javier. Telling the harvesters to get on with their work, Vidal is left alone to grieve, with only the memory of his lost *morena* (dark beauty) to comfort him.

Luisa Fernanda is in many ways the last great romantic zarzuela. It owes something to the earlier masters of the *zarzuela grande* and *género chico*, more to the example of Vives' recent *Doña Francisquita*, but the range and scale of its emotions surpasses any of Torroba's models. Musically *Luisa Fernanda* embodies its composer's ideals of *casticismo*, and Torroba's music certainly offers colorful Spanish charm as well as fair helpings of graceful Viennesse musical comedy and Italian operatic *verismo*. His musical personality may not be specially individual, but Torroba's score is full of character, his melodies consistently strong and his theatrical instinct unfaltering.

Romero and Shaw produced the librettos for many of the most important zarzuelas written between the First World War and the Spanish Civil War. The action of *Luisa Fernanda* may be complicated, but flows most naturally. Its characters move easily between elegant comedy of manners and revolutionary politics; between the sophistication of Madrid and the simplicity of the Spanish countryside; between romantic high spirits and near-tragic melancholy. Torroba's masterpiece owes some of its success (more than 10,000 performances at the last count and still rising) to their adept handling of the period setting; and not a little to their spirited dialogue and the passionate speeches of Nogales and Aníbal in praise of liberty.

Torroba's score is organized along operatic lines, with *arioso* conversations leading into many of the *Romanzas* and *Dúos*. These are all of the highest quality, and the refrain of Vidal's waltz-song in the final act (*"¡Ay, mi morena, morena clara!"*) has acquired almost mythic popularity:

Torroba's handling of the orchestra is masterly throughout: the *Introducción* to Act 2, with its haunting reminiscence of the Savoyard's *Habanera*, carries the drama forward as surely as any music in Spanish opera. The evergreen *Mazurka de los sombrillas*, with its lilting refrain, seductive rhythms and delicious "triple click" from the orchestral percussion as the ladies raise their parasols—to shield themselves from the inviting glances of their young beaux as much as from the sun—exemplifies the composer's priceless ability to refashion something memorable and fresh from tried and tested operetta conventions:

La caramba (1942)
La caramba was the soubriquet of a famous folk singer of the late eighteenth century, and Torroba's three-act zarzuela tells the story of her rise from rural obscurity, "immoral" life style in Madrid and final conversion to the service of Christ. The music is an effective mixture of lyric *Romanzas* and colorful folk scenes, though an effectively scored orchestral storm sequence is probably the highlight.

Maravilla (1941)
The contemporary plot centers on Manuela, an opera diva known as *La Maravilla* (The Marvel) and the love life of her daughter Emilia, forced to choose between a rich industrialist and a talented but indigent baritone from Madrid's Teatro Real, named Rafael. Believing Emilia has rejected him Rafael sings the showstopping *Romanza: "Amor vida de mi vida"*, which remains one of the most affecting and well-loved songs in the Spanish baritone repertoire.

La marchenera (The Girl from Marchena, 1928)
Set in the revolutionary turmoil of 1840s Andalucia, the plot of Torroba's first major success is a complex web of elopements, duels and secret intrigues in the mould of Alonso's *La calesera*. Torroba's three-act score is not as characterful as the best of his later work, but is notable for some atmospheric orchestral writing as well as the quality of its solo numbers, of which the best known is the *Petenera: "Tres horas antes del día"* (a popular love song of the region) sung by the aristocratic soprano heroine Valentina.

María Manuela (1957)

Torroba's last major three-act zarzuela is centered on Madrid's Royal Tapestry Works in the 1920s, and concerns the life and loves of its artisan workers. Like the heroine of Sorozábal's *La del manojo de rosas*, María Manuela initially rejects her most appropriate suitor when she discovers him to be a rich boy in disguise. Torroba's score is an exercise in soft-centered nostalgia, which despite undoubted charm cannot be said to scale the heights of his finest pre-Civil War works.

Monte Carmelo (1939)

Granada in the mid-nineteenth century provides the backdrop for this aristocratic lyric comedy, the first major zarzuela to be premiered in Madrid after the Civil War. Romero and Shaw's elegant libretto sidesteps any charge of frivolity through the self-denying religiosity of its central character, the Count of Monte Carmelo, the very element which works against its revival today. A pity, for the score (Torroba's own personal favorite) is among his most varied and lively. The ensembles, notably the *Terceto: "¡Guarda, guarda, Leonarda!"*, and the glittering, nocturnal orchestral *Intermedio*, are outstanding.

18
Manuel Penella
(1880–1939)

Born in Valencia on 31st July 1880, son of the director of the city conservatory Manuel Penella Raga, young Manuel began composition studies there under Salvador Giner, presiding spirit of the city's vibrant musical life. Penella showed at least equal promise as a violinist, and had it not been for an accident to his left hand would perhaps have chosen to become a concert virtuoso rather than a composer. After graduation, he worked locally as a church organist, but soon succumbed to the lure of theatre, producing the first of over eighty stage works with the zarzuela *La fiesta del pueblo* (The Village Fiesta, 1894). A compulsive traveler, he spent much of his working life with zarzuela and opera companies in Latin America, Cuba, the United States, and Mexico; even serving as director of a military band in Quito, Ecuador.

His first notable success, the *revista Las musas latinas* (The Latin Muses, 1912) was typical in that its first performance was outside Madrid, in this case Valencia. *Revistas*, zarzuelas, operettas and operas flowed in a steady stream. Penella's best-known work is *El gato montés* (The Wildcat, 1916), a popular opera in red-blooded Spanish verismo style, the well-muscled pasodoble from which is still invariably played in the *corrida*. Its popularity extended to New York, where the composer conducted a sold-out run of ten weeks at the Park Theatre in 1920, and this strong if brash score has been lovingly revived and lavishly recorded by Plácido Domingo in recent years.

Penella's most lasting musical legacy is *Don Gil de Alcalá* (1932), tastefully scored for string orchestra, a delectable work which transcends its apparent limitation as a pastiche of eighteenth century musical manners. He planned to settle in Barcelona, where later works such as *El hermano lobo* (Brother Wolf, 1933) and the opera *La malquerida* (The Hateful Woman,

1935) achieved some success without matching the musical quality of *Don Gil*. Soon enough he left Spain for another extended tour, and it was while supervising the music for a film of *Don Gil* that Penella died suddenly in Cuernavaca, Mexico, on 24th January 1939.

One result of his compulsive globe-trotting was that Penella's name became better known in the Americas than those of his more eminent Spanish contemporaries. Viewed by some as a solitary, even austere figure, as a *zarzuelero* he certainly stands apart in one respect: from *El gato montés* onward he wrote his own libretti. A musical chameleon, his best work has a freshness and energy which is strongly effective; and in *Don Gil de Alcalá* at least, he produced a subtle and individual jewel.

Don Gil de Alcalá
Comic Opera in three acts
(Barcelona, Teatro Novedades, 27th October 1932)

Text: the composer

Principal Characters: Niña Estrella, a mulatto girl (soprano); Maya, her maid (mezzo-soprano); Don Gil de Alcalá (tenor); Carrasquilla, his Sergeant (bass); Chamaco, a servant (tenor); Don Diego (baritone); The Governor (bass); Father Confessor (bass).

ACT 1, SCENE 1—Vera Cruz, Mexico, toward the end of the eighteenth century. The cloister of a Convent School for Young Ladies. A lively *Preludio* in the style of a classical overture precedes the action. A group of college girls are praying to the Virgin (*Introducción: "Maria Inmaculada, protégenos"*). The Abbess asks Chamaco, the college servant, why he and the girls are crying: it is because Niña ("Child") Estrella, a mulatto orphan raised by the Governor, is leaving the college that day. The Father Confessor informs the Abbess that the Governor will be arriving shortly with Don Diego, an aging grandee with whom Estrella is to be married. A bell rings, and the pupils, released from their devotions, run in playfully. Estrella is in no mood to join their games. Though she must suffer in silence she does not love Don Diego, devoted as she is to the handsome young soldier, Don Gil de Alcalá, whom she met years before when she was a child in Yucatan (*Solo y coro: "Un capitán español"*). The bell sounds again, and the girls bid her farewell before running back to their lessons. Left alone, Niña Estrella prays fervently to a little cross given her by her mother, asking the dead woman to change her sad destiny or let her die (*Plegaria: "Bendita Cruz"*).

Her maid Maya hurries in. She has brought a secret letter from Don Gil, in which the young soldier vows to marry Estrella, even if he has to resort to trickery (*Dúo: "Mi adorara Niña Estrella"*). Chamaco tells the Abbess that the Governor and Don Diego are on their way, having been ambushed by a group of bandits; luckily the attack was repulsed by a brave Captain and his Sergeant. The Governor arrives with Don Diego, whose feathers have been ruffled by the incident. Their rescuers turn out to be none other than Don Gil and his Sergeant Carrasquilla, and the Governor thanks the soldier, promising him a substantial reward (*Solo: "A este bravo capitan"*). Don Gil is introduced to Niña Estrella, and relates the details of the incident, aided by Carrasquilla and his comic amplifications.

Don Diego and the Governor withdraw for discussions with the Abbess, and the Sergeant tactfully leaves the young couple together. Don Gil pours out his love, and tells Estrella not to fear the outcome (*Romanza: "No temas no, confía en mí"*). He admits that the ambush was a set-up to bring them together, and convinces her that the end justifies the means. The delighted Chamaco announces that he has been taken on as Niña Estrella's servant, and eventually the whole party sets off to fond farewells from the Abbess, Father Confessor and the bereft girls.

SCENE 2—A reception room in the Governor's Palace. A party is being held for Don Gil, and the Governor introduces him and the Sergeant to the assembled company (*Concertante: "¡Señoras y caballeros!"*). Don Diego asks Niña Estrella to dance, but Don Gil intervenes: as guest of honor he has the privilege of the first dance. The Governor asks the girl to choose, but the rival claimants play a round of cards to decide the victor. Their game—best of three rounds at Faro—takes place to a delicious *pizzicato* orchestral accompaniment. Don Gil wins, and leads Niña Estrella in a *Pavane*.

The guests remark on Don Diego's jealous discomfiture, which is augmented when Don Gil takes the middle voice in a Madrigal the trio sing together (*Madrigal: "Tos ojos son dos rayos de sol"*). The Governor announces that he will ask the Viceroy to present Don Gil with the Great Cross of New Spain next day; and the act ends with Carrasquilla leading the whole party in a brilliant toast to the delights of Spanish Sherry (*Brindis: "¡Jerez! este es el vinillo de la tierra mía"*).

ACT 2—A formal garden of the Governor's Palace. After the short *Preludio* (a gracious minuet) Don Gil and Carrasquilla are discovered at their ease. Though Don Gil is feeling guilty about his false pretensions of heroism, the Sergeant convinces him to grasp their good fortune (*Dúo: "¡Ah! de audaces la fortuna"*). Chamaco, neatly dressed in gubernatorial livery, serves them chocolate before they depart for polite converse with Niña Estrella. The servant has fallen for Maya, and declares his love to the far from unwilling maid as they sing a catchy *Dúo: "¡Ay, zúmbale!"*, in the swinging waltz rhythm of a native jarabe.

Niña Estrella runs into the garden with a group of ladies. She sings a light, agile song comparing love to the careless flight of the butterfly (*Canción: "Como una mariposa que va de flor en flor"*). The Governor enters with the Father Confessor, who brings disturbing reports of Estrella's devotion to Don Gil; and when her guardian asks the girl if the rumors are true, she candidly admits it. The Governor threatens that she must make up her mind to marry Don Diego and storms off. Don Gil finds Estrella in tears, but when she tells him they cannot marry, he reassures her passionately that love can overcome all obstacles (*Dúo y Romanza: "¡Mi Don Gil! . . . Juntos, bien mío"*).

Don Diego demands a private interview with Estrella. When Don Gil withdraws, his rival tells the girl the truth about his background. Don Gil is no better than an adventurer, the illegitimate son of an unknown father without name or fortune, and unworthy of her attention. Why not respond to his own deeply felt love instead? (*Dúo: "El capitán, que con torpe afán"*). Estrella infuriates him by taking the news on the chin, and haughtily leaves him. The affronted Don Diego vows to have vengeance at any price (*Romanza: "Cuando se tiene una espada"*).

Chamaco and Maya hurry in with a crowd of Ladies and Gentlemen to prepare for the arrival of the Viceroy, come to present the medals to the heroes. The couple fill in the courtiers on the gossip concerning Don Gil and Estrella (*Dúo y coro: "Yo no sé nada"*). The Governor and his party greet the Viceroy. He is predictably charmed by Estrella, and agrees enthusiastically when the Governor asks whether he would like to hear her sing. Accompanied by Maya she obliges with the lush, sensual *Dúo Habanera: "Todas las mañanitas"*.

The ceremony is interrupted by Don Diego, claiming Don Gil is nothing but a lying imposter. He produces a group of bandits, who identify his rival as the man who paid them to hold up the Governor's party the previous day. Carrasquilla denies the charge on the quibbling grounds that he never actually paid them for their work; although, he adds threateningly, tomorrow he will. Don Gil freely confesses his crime, pleading that he acted out of an insane love; but the Viceroy sentences him to leave tomorrow to fight the Zaceteca Indian uprising, an almost certain death. Estrella's sadness, Don Diego's satisfaction and the indignation of the rulers counterpoints the young man's shame in the *Concertante Final: "Humiliado y deshonrado"*.

ACT 3, SCENE 1—A sitting room in the Palace. In the brief *Dúo: "No llores más, mi niña"* Maya consoles the weeping Estrella for her lover's disgrace and departure. Don Gil comes to apologize, and bids his beloved farewell in another tender *Romanza: "Mitzilán, no llores más"*. As they depart, Chamaco sneaks in to steal some of the Governor's wine. Hearing his master approaching with the Father Confessor, he has no alternative but to hide quickly in the drinks cabinet, from which cover he overhears the Governor's confession concerning a deeply regretted affair he had with a washerwoman as a young man in Madrid. He lost touch with the son he fathered, and knows nothing of his destiny (*Dúo: "Yo me acuso de que he tenido... Fue en Madrid"*). When the coast is clear Chamaco emerges, inspired with a daring plan to help Don Gil which he runs past the girls: Don Gil must pretend he is the Governor's illegitimate son! He fetches the Captain and Carrasquilla, and in a deftly syncopated *Quinteto: "Con este ardid"* Don Gil agrees to hazard all on his story.

SCENE 2—A large salon in the Palace. After an orchestral version of the earlier *Habanera*, the Viceroy and the Father Confessor are discovered enjoying a game of chess, watched by the Governor's party and Estrella. Don Diego fondly believes that now Don Gil is out of the way his marital path will be smoothed (*Concertante: "¡Jaque al Rey!"*). Don Gil and Carrasquilla come to bid farewell; and in the course of his effusive apology, Don Gil manages to slip in some affecting details of his childhood by the Manzanares River in Madrid, which miraculously coincide with everything the Governor told his Father Confessor. Deeply moved, the Governor remits the young soldier's punishment and embraces him as his long-lost son. Much to everyone's joy—excepting the indignant Don Diego—he offers Estrella's hand in marriage to his new son. The pair rejoice in the fulfillment of their love, and all join in admiration of the fortunate Don Gil de Alcalá (*Final: "Un capitán español"*).

Zarzuela, lyric opera, comic operetta, pastiche, call it what you will; *Don Gil de Alcalá* is not like anything else in the Spanish repertoire. Its three acts and aristocratic milieu bring to mind the early *zarzuelas grandes* of the 1850s and 60s. It is through-written without dialogue, mainly in the witty style of eighteenth century Italian comic opera, but shot through with romantic passages reminiscent of Puccini's *Manon Lescaut*. It is delicately scored for a string chamber orchestra with harp, reminiscent of nineteenth century Mexican salon bands. It is structured round an eclectic mixture of dance movements, from the polite European minuet to the steamy American *habanera*.

The influences on Penella's libretto are similarly varied. They range from Lope de Vega (whose *El perro del hortelano* is the source of the trick to solve the hero's dilemma, as in Guerrero's *La rosa del azafrán* from two years earlier) to Cuban novels and *Los intereses creados* (1907) by the great Spanish dramatist, Jacinto Benavente (1866–1954). Penella's work is elegant and economical, his characters credible and entertaining. At the centre are the mulatto Niña Estrella and illegitimate Don Gil, two characters on the edge of society both of whom invite our sympathetic interest.

Perhaps "Neo-classical Creole" is the best sound-byte to describe Penella's mixture: but whatever it is, it certainly works. His score is light as a souffle but rescued from insipidity by the romantic fervor of the lovers' music and the injection of hot-blooded native forms such as the jacabe and habanera. Nothing outstays its welcome.

The scoring, in complete contrast to the coarse effects of his better-known opera *El gato montés*, is delicate throughout. The purely orchestral movements, not least the card game with its *pizzicato* accompaniment and the exquisite Pavane, are among the highlights, though all give place to the luxuriant, subtropical *Habanera-Dúo*. A poignant blend of melancholy and sunshine, it encapsulates much of the appeal of zarzuela; and if Penella had written nothing else, this one number would have ensured his immortality:

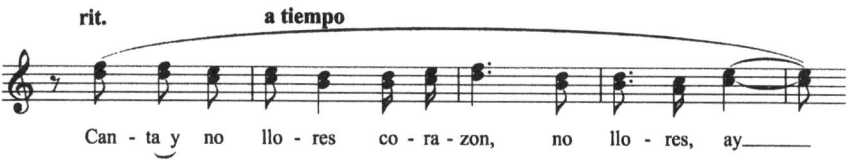

El gato montés (The Wildcat, 1916)
Penella's three-act *ópera española* is his best-known work, written in popular *verismo* style and successful in New York as well as Latin America and Spain. The story is a tragic love triangle, with young bullfighter Rafael and the bandit known as "Wildcat" vying for the favors of the beautiful Solea. Though by no means as consistent as *Don Gil de Alcalá*, the musical highlights are stirring. Aside from the ubiquitous *Pasodoble* and related *Dúo* for Rafael and Solea, the bullfighter's prayer before his death in the ring *"Señó, q'e no me farte er való"* is the most memorable.

Las musas latinas (The Latin Muses, 1912)
This one-act *revista* to a book by Manuel Moncayo was Penella's first big success, at home and abroad. Three drunks argue the relative merits of Italian, French and Spanish wine, and in succeeding tableaux the Latin Muses celebrate their three nations. The Italian scene finishes with a lively tarantella; the French respond with some sexy *couplets* and a fragrant waltz; the Spaniards cap that with a suite of dances culminating in a classic seguidillas, before the three muses return to Parnassus in a grand vinicultural apotheosis. Penella's apt music is irresistible throughout.

19
José Serrano
(1870–1941)

Born in Sueca, Valencia, on 14th October 1873, Serrano was the son of the town's band conductor. In 1889 he left for Valencia itself, spending two years in the Conservatoire studying with Salvador Giner, who later also taught Manuel Penella. In 1892 he took a scholarship to Madrid, only to return home a year later disillusioned with the capital artistically as well as economically. Five years later came a turning point. He took on the job of amanuensis for the nearly blind Caballero, working on the orchestration of *Gigantes y cabezudos* and familiarizing his name with the musical establishment.

In 1900 he got his chance and took it, when he was offered the libretto of *El motete* (The Motet) by the famous Álvarez Quintero brothers. The work was a decided success, in a straightforward new style to suit the new century. From then on he was never short of commissions, taking his place among the most prolific *zarzueleros* of the day. He also wrote songs and vocal works including the celebrated *Himno a Valencia* (1909), some film music, and an unfinished opera *La venta de los gatos* (The Thieves' Inn, 1943). He died in Madrid on 8th March 1941.

A considerable number of Serrano's fifty or so zarzuelas have retained their place in public affection. The exotic tragedy *Moros y cristianos* (Moors and Christians, 1905); *El pollo Tejada* (That Tejada Fellow, 1906) and *El amigo Melquíades* (Friend Melquíades, 1914), both written with "Quinito" Valverde; *La alegría del batallón* (The Joy of the Battalion, 1909); and *Los de Aragón* (People of Aragon, 1927) are all in the one-act *sainete* tradition. Some of them, such as *La reina mora* (The Moorish Queen, 1903) and *Alma de Dios* (Good-hearted, 1907) contain only a few musical numbers, tenuously tied to the action.

Not all his works have Spanish settings. The masterly *La canción del olvido* (The Song of Forgetting, 1916) with its ubiquitous *"Soldado de Nápoli"*; and *Las hilanderas* (The Spinners, 1927) are two of a group of Italian romances. Some later zarzuelas such as *Los Claveles* (The Carnations, 1929) and *La dolorosa* (1930), his last and best-loved score, are more ambitious in musical scope. *Golondrina de Madrid* (Madrid Wanderer), a lighter work on which he was working at the time of his death, proved a failure when finally produced in San Sebastián in 1944.

His musical personality is robust rather than specially distinctive, though he often taps a rich vein of melodic inspiration. He fully recognized his own limited technical ability, keeping his harmonies and orchestrations uncomplicated; his strongest suits are a sound theatrical intuition and an unfailing power to touch the heart. He certainly steered the mood of *género chico* zarzuela away from the sophisticated urban wit of Chapí and Bretón towards a simpler, popular theatre of the emotions. In this sense, Serrano was the true heir of Chueca, albeit with a substantial transfusion of red blood from Puccini and his *verismo* contemporaries.

Alma de Dios
Sainete in one act
(Madrid, Teatro Cómico, 17th December 1907)

Text: Carlos Arniches and Enrique García Álvarez

Principal Characters: Mathías (comedy singer); Ezequiela, his good-hearted wife (actress); Agustín, her nephew (actor); Eloísa, Agustín's fiancée (actress); Irene, Eloísa's friend (actress); Adrian, Irene's fiancé (actor).

SCENE 1—A run-down tenement in a poor quarter of Madrid. Timid Signor Matías has been left in charge of domestic duties by his "dragon" of a wife, Ezequiela. As he desperately tries to rock the baby to sleep while simultaneously keeping the stove burning with the aid of an inadequate little bellows, his friend Saturiano comes in. Having lost his job, he offers to help Matías with the chores on condition that there's a free meal at the end of it. They soon get bored with domestic duties, and pass the time of day by chatting up a pretty young neighbor through the window. Before things can get interesting, Ezequiela appears, delighted to be able to bawl them out for their hopeless idleness.

When supper appears, so does Eloísa, fiancée of Ezequiela's nephew Agustín, looking pale as death. The young couple's happiness is threatened by rumors that Eloísa has secretly had a baby. The facts are very different. Eloísa, left an orphan when very young, had been brought up in her uncle's house with her cousin Irene. Irene took a lover, and when the worst happened the two girls agreed to pretend that Eloísa was the mother—for the very sensible reason that Irene was about to marry a wealthy old man, Señor Adrián. Agustín threatens to break off the engagement unless Eloísa proves her innocence. Surely, all she needs to do is point to the baptismal record at the church of San Lorenzo to reveal the true mother. Eloísa is loathe to bring shame on the good people who brought her up, but when Ezequiela learns that the suspicious Adrián is also on the case, she takes matters into her own hands and marches Matías off to San Lorenzo to establish Eloísa's innocence.

SCENE 2—The Vestry of San Lorenzo. The choirmaster, Don Ramon, is attempting to take a practice, with farcical results. His treble, Carrascosita, has a breaking voice; and when Ramon calls for the organ and a barrel-organ starts up instead, he gives up and calls the whole thing off until the morning, much to Carrascosita's delight (*Escena: "Gracias agimus tibi"*). Choir and organist depart, leaving the Sacristan, Signor Orencio, to work in peace—for one moment. Señor Adrián arrives with his friend Pelegrin, Irene and her mother Marcelina. The nervous Irene makes an excuse to leave with her mother just before Ezequiela hurries in with Matías, Eloísa and Agustín. When Orencio eventually gets round to producing the baptismal record, he announces to general surprise that the mother is Eloísa after all. Adrián leaves well satisfied, and Agustín throws over Eloísa in disgust. Ezequiela is the only one who still believes in the girl's innocence, and the scene ends as she marches Mathías off again in tireless pursuit of evidence.

SCENE 3—The street, that night. Bellows in hand, Matías is selling roast chestnuts, hoping to overhear some clue as to the whereabouts of the baby. He flirts with a young *chulapa*, Balbina, singing her a dubious but jolly song about the uses of his little bellows (*Seguidillas: "Hoy me han dicho dos niñas"*). Adrián is still not completely convinced his wife is innocent; certainly, Irene is still behaving strangely, and Matías overhears her in tearful conversation with her mother about the need to keep up the lie. Ezequiela gets Matías to follow them, but finding out about his flirtatious behavior from the ingenuous Balbina, she sails swiftly off in renewed pursuit of her husband.

SCENE 4—A gypsy camp outside the city. One of the women, María Carmen, sings a lively *Farruca*, and the other gypsies improvise a lively dance. (*Escena y danza: "La Farruca"*). A troop of Hungarian beggars and vagabonds makes an appearance, and one of their number leads them in the famous Song of Hungary (*Canción Húngara: "Canta mendigo errante"*), a mixture of homesick nostalgia and praise of beggarly freedom. Matías and

Ezquierda hide, with Agustín and Eloísa in tow. They catch Irene and her mother visiting the child, which is being cared for by another gypsy, Seña Rosa. Further deception is pointless, and Irene asks Eloísa's pardon, which is swiftly forthcoming. Agustín is relieved and the lovers are happy again. The same cannot be said for Adrián. Coming in to find the child in his wife's arms he bitterly denounces Irene, accusing her of the mockery of marrying an old man for his money. Cursing his fortune, he leaves, while the rest of them—even Matías—plead with Ezequiela to talk some sense into him. She good-heartedly agrees, and the *sainete* ends with "the dragon" charging off on another errand of mercy: this time without her Matías, relieved to be left to his own devices at last, and dancing as the curtain falls to the strains of his little *Seguidillas*.

Alma de Dios ("Good-hearted" Ezequiela) is the most enduring of Serrano's earlier works. Arniches and Álvarez delivered a fast-paced, lower-class urban farce squarely in the tradition of Chueca. Here, grinding poverty and family strife rub shoulders with gypsy romance, vaudeville routines, and of course the Troubles of Young Love. Its gritty realism and tentative conclusion suggest that Álvarez rather than the sunnier Arniches may have provided the guiding hand for the libretto. Their *sainete* remains a perennial favorite, and the 1941 film version by Ignacio F. Iquino became a Spanish classic.

There are just five musical numbers, none of which has much to do with the action: indeed only one of the main characters, the likeable Matías, has anything to sing at all. Nonetheless, the amusing choir practice and the gypsy scene (culminating in the stirring, hypnotic *Canción Húngara*) have ensured *Alma de Dios* several complete recordings and a secure place in the repertory.

La canción del olvido
Zarzuela in one act
(Valencia, Teatro Lírico, 17th November 1916)

Text: Federico Romero and Guillermo Fernández Shaw

Principal Characters: Rosina (soprano); Captain Leonello (baritone); Sergeant Lombardi (tenor); Toribio (actor).

SCENE 1—The action takes place in Sorrentinos, a fictitious city in the Kingdom of Naples, 1799. A square in the town, to one side the Goose Inn, to the other the palace of the courtesan Flora Goldoni. It is dusk. After a delicate *Preludio* the curtain rises. The middle-aged Sainati is loitering in hope of a glance from the famous courtesan, but the Innkeeper tells him he has too many rivals: if he wants a chance, he should first get rid of his wife! Sainati slinks away, as a poor Roman musician, Toribio Clarinetti, parks himself outside The Goose with his harp. He has been paid to serenade the guests, and demands a meal from the Innkeeper, who asks him about a mysterious young woman who is lodging there. The stranger is Rosina, a rich and beautiful Roman Princess who owns the nearby Marinelli Palace, but who is lodging at The Goose in pursuit of a plan to attract one Captain Leonello, with whom she has fallen in love. The Captain is as yet oblivious of her existence; and her maid Casilda warns the Princess that, given Leonello's reputation as a Don Juan, things had better stay that way. Nonetheless, Rosina remains determined to pursue him.

The Captain arrives at The Goose with two friends to enjoy a bottle of wine. Rosina overhears from her window as he coolly recounts the story of his first meeting with the beautiful courtesan who lives opposite, and his confident plans to enjoy her (*Canción: "Junto al puente de la Peña"*). When the Innkeeper tells him that one of the lady guests has been asking about him, he replies that she can have him when he's done with La Goldoni—perhaps even for a couple of days! All this only makes Rosina desire him the more. Leonello tells his friends that he has commissioned his company Sergeant, Lombardi, to provide musicians to sing a serenade while he recites Petrarch sonnets to win La Goldoni's favors. When he spots the courtesan on her balcony he orders Toribio to sing a song— any song. The harpist chooses a Roman favorite, the *Canción del olvido* (Song of Forgetting) and launches into the introduction; but as he opens his mouth to sing, another voice—Rosina's—takes up the melody. Leonello and his friends are captivated by the sound of the beautiful, mysterious singer (*Canción del Olvido: "Marinela"*).

Leonello swiftly comes to his cynical senses: "Just like a woman. Another one in love with the moon!" Sergeant Lombardi reports that no musicians are to be had, but that the soldiers themselves have volunteered to stand in. His friends leave with Lombardi, and Leonello goes into the shadows to write a passionate love letter to La Goldoni. Rosina has her own plan, for which she needs Toribio's help. In return for 3,000 guilders he is to play Rosina's putative husband "The Prince of Ferratta" and pretend to be in love with the courtesan. After a little comical priming he is just about fit to play his part, though he jibs at the idea of the Princess acting as his page. Another 500 remove that objection and Toribio, chuckling over his luck, goes into The Goose with Rosina. As Leonello finishes his letter he hears once again the voice of the mysterious lady in her Song of Forgetting. The sheets of the love letter fall to the ground: Leonello stands transfixed as the curtain falls.

SCENE 2—A nearby street. On one side is the Goldoni, and on the other the Marinelli Palace. A group of musicians approach (*Coro: "Ya la ronda llega aquí"*), one of whom addresses a serenade to La Goldoni (*Serenata: "Hermosa napolitana"*). Toribio is reveling in his princely role, and gets ready to sing his own serenade to Flora. Leonello takes the absurd musician for a rival and offers to fight him. Baffled by Toribio's verbal gymnastics he departs; though "The Prince" runs off in the opposite direction, leaving his "page" to perform the serenade to mandolin accompaniment (*Canción: "Canta el trovador"*).

Flora Goldoni opens her window and asks the page for whom he is singing such a lovely song. Rosina's gracious rhetoric on behalf of her master charms Flora into agreeing to receive the Prince; and after some further priming on polite behavior Toribio enters the palace, just before the soldiers finally march in with Lombardi, strumming their mandolins and declaiming their robust idea of a serenade (*Coro y solo: "Soldado de Nápoles"*) before strutting back to barracks.

Leonello swaggers in confidently, only for the page to tell him that his master is already with Flora, and that Leonello has missed his chance. The Captain threatens to run the Prince through, but the page mocks his lack of subtlety. "How little you know of love," he laughs. "Use your wits, not brute force." Impressed in spite of himself, Leonello offers the lad 500 guilders for some advice. Well then, says Rosina, why not enjoy himself with the Prince's wife? That will be the perfect revenge, and make Flora jealous into the bargain. The Marinelli Palace is just over the way—but how will he get in? The page tells the Captain to arrive punctually at ten o'clock, sing a serenade, and leave the rest to him. Leonello leaves to ready himself, a second before Toribio gets thrown out ignominiously by La Goldoni. Rosina calms him down, and listens quietly as the seductive sound of the serenade is borne in on the evening breeze (*Voz interno: "Hermosa napolitana"*).

SCENE 3—A chamber in the Marinelli Palace, with a door leading directly into the garden. Rosina prays to the Virgin to bless the night's plan (*Dúo: "Virgen y madre"*). Hearing Leonello's serenade from the garden, she retires to her couch and feigns sleep. He turns the lock and enters. The sight of the sleeping woman strikes him like a thunderbolt, and the cynical womanizer melts before Rosina's defenseless loveliness (*"¡Oh, mujer! Bella flor"*). How could he stain her honor? She wakes, and challenges him to reveal his motives for breaking in on a sleeping woman. Discovering him to be the infamous Captain Leonello she refuses to believe his protestations of love (*"Ese amor que sentís"*), but gives him at least a glimmer of hope by agreeing to meet him in town next day. As he leaves Rosina cunningly repeats her 'Song of Forgetfulness', which the stricken Captain hears as he creeps away across the garden, marveling at the coincidence of hearing the fateful song again.

SCENE 4—The Princess's garden by night, two weeks later. A subtly scored *Intermedio* suggests the passage of time before the curtain rises. Toribio, still disguised as Rosina's princely husband, is giving a large party and telling risqué stories to the guests. Two weeks have effected a huge difference in Leonello, no longer interested in anyone except the Princess, and well prepared to defend her against his friends' snide remarks. She has told him she loves him but will not compromise her honor, so he must suffer nobly. Wouldn't it be better to finish the business by killing her silly old husband in a duel? Having planted this idea, his friends leave to enjoy the regatta the Princess has provided for their amusement.

Toribio is horrified when Leonello offers to fight a duel on the spot; but before matters can come to a head Rosina appears to mock her Captain's *machismo* posturings, laughing that only in suffering can he find true love. He protests that his days as a Don Juan are over, and in despair challenges her to deny the one thing she has said to keep his hope alive: that she would never forget his love. At last she softens, and falls into his arms (*Dúo final: "Pero, capitán"*). To Leonello's confusion, in rush the guests with Toribio and the Captain's friends. Rosina's plot is swiftly explained, and the loyal Toribio is rewarded with the post of Major Domo. Everything has been a charade—except of course for Rosina's true love for Leonello, and his for her.

Remarkably, *La canción del olvido* was the first collaboration between Federico Romero and Guillermo Fernández Shaw. Their success, like that of the piece they concocted for the well-established Serrano, was huge, instant and lasting. Indeed, the superior quality of their craftsmanship is the most immediately striking feature of this miniature Neapolitan romance, even today. *La canción* has a Napoleonic setting, but its ambience is more reminiscent of Italian renaissance comedy: a tale from Boccaccio, say, or even *All's Well That Ends Well*. The crucial acting role of Toribio is certainly a character of Shakespearean cut, the verse for the lovers is lapidary, and the heroine Rosina is drawn with care, insight and sympathy. The plot may seem trivial in the telling, but in Romero and Shaw's hands this frothy soufflé takes on the timeless quality of classic comedy.

Serrano's score is as polished as the libretto, which isn't to say that it lacks feeling. Quite the reverse. As ever, Serrano responded to a nocturnal, Italian setting to produce top-drawer work. The set-piece songs and choruses of the first two scenes would surely have been reason enough to make this score a success, but in the extended duet which comprises the whole of the third scene Serrano managed an integration of music and drama that he never surpassed. The themes of the Song of Forgetting itself and Leonello's *"Mujer, primorosa clavellina"* are deployed to great theatrical effort; the Soldiers' Chorus is if anything more popular than either; and who could forget the delicate tone-painting of the *Preludio*, or the piquant scoring of the *Intermedio* before the last scene? Composer and librettists succeeded brilliantly in their work; and the result is a great romantic zarzuela, unpretentious but richly durable, the Apotheosis of the Serenade.

Los Claveles
Sainete in one act
(Madrid, Teatro Fontalba, 6th April 1929)

Text: Luis Fernández de Sevilla and Anselmo Cuadrado Carreño

Principal Characters: Rosa, overseer of "Los Claveles" (soprano); Jacinta, another worker (soprano); Goro, her fiancé (comic tenor); Remedios, Goro's mother (actress); Everisto, his father (actor); Bienvenido, Jacinta's uncle (actor); Fernando, cashier (tenor).

SCENE 1—The shop floor of the Madrid perfume factory "Los Claveles" (The Carnations). The workers, including Jacinta, Paca and their overseer Rosa, gossip as they sit labeling bottles and parceling cakes of soap. Goro, the junior accounts clerk in love with Jacinta, rubs out figures to give himself an excuse to spend longer with the working girls (*Escena: "Anímate, Irene, que el negocio es bueno"*).

It's the lunch break; and as the girls prepare to head off into town Jacinta and Paca tease Rosa about her apparent interest in the new cashier, Fernando, a man every bit as proud as herself. Rosa vehemently dismisses the suggestion, greeting the young man with pointed contempt as he appears on the shop floor and vowing to prove her point by humiliating him in some way. Fernando privately asks the janitor, Goro's mother Señá Remedios, to direct any young lady visitor he may have through to his office. When Remedios hints that Rosa ought to be quick and make a move for him, she's rewarded by a taste of the young woman's sharp tongue before the overseer hurries off after the other girls.

When Remedios hears from Braulio, Goro's boss, that her son is making a lot of mistakes, she questions the young man about the cause of his slackness. Jacinta's uncle Bienvenido arrives with his niece's lunch, disturbing this inquisition. He spices his compliments to Remedios with witty classical allusions but his real motive is more sinister: reminding the janitor about the supposed infidelity of her husband Evaristo, he tempts her to move out and live with him instead. Their conversation is interrupted by Evaristo's arrival;

and when Remedios retires into her janitor's booth her husband, who works in a butcher's shop, passes a parcel of liver over to the other man. The duplicitous Bienvenido is simultaneously seducing the wife, blackmailing the husband for another supposed indiscretion many years ago, and demanding kidneys rather than mere liver for tomorrow's lunch into the bargain!

The men leave, and Jacinta sneaks back to meet Goro. They sing a *Dueto Cómico: "Goro del alma, ven junto a mí"* full of flirtatious banter, before being interrupted by Evaristo. When he hears that they are engaged he flies into a mysterious passion and forbids them to have anything more to do with one another. Remedios, hearing the commotion, takes the side of the youngsters and sends them all about their business, though Evaristo remains strangely implacable. Fernando comes in to find Jacinta still in tears. He comforts her and promises to intercede on her behalf. In return she warns the grateful cashier of Rosa's intention to bring him down a peg or two. He vows to take care that the boot will be on the other foot.

The girls return, and Rosa launches into a blistering verbal attack on Fernando. The workers and office staff—including the venerable manager of the business, Don Facundo—listen spellbound to the exchange (*Dúo y scena: "Tenga muy buenas tardes"*). Fernando's sincere admiration for Rosa's beauty is answered with scorn, especially when his young lady friend calls for him. Turning at the door the cashier gently reproves Rosa, intimating that pride may come before a fall (*"Cuando un hombre de bien"*); but she laughs in his face, and he leaves amid the mocking sound of the workers' laughter. Rosa, strangely unappeased, swears to get back at him, and as the factory bell rings everyone settles back to work.

SCENE 2—Outside a bar in the downtown Plaza de la Cruz Verde, afternoon. Braulio and a friend try to get a drink and some tapas, but the waiter of the hopeless local bar has nothing to offer them. They depart in high dudgeon as an unusually nervous Rosa comes in with Paca. She has finally agreed to Fernando's repeated pleas to meet with her after work; and though she tells her friend that she only means to take the opportunity to mock him again, it's obvious to the younger girl that Rosa puts great store by his arrival. Paca warns Rosa that Fernando has been seen around with another woman and goes off home, leaving Rosa to a series of bad-tempered exchanges with the useless bartender as she waits with increasing impatience.

Remedios and Goro enter the plaza. The youngster is shell-shocked from an interview with his father, and refuses to explain his conviction that marriage with Jacinta is impossible. His mother, now in a bad mood herself, tells Rosa that she saw Fernando getting into a taxi with another woman. "His sister," says Rosa, but Remedios spitefully informs her that it was a waitress from a fashionable restaurant. After a further exchange of taunts between the two women, Remedios and Goro leave Rosa alone. She reveals her complex unhappiness in the great *Romanza: "¿Qué te importa que no venga?"*. The depth of her feeling makes her angry with herself, and she faces up to the fact that she cares for Fernando much more than she likes to admit. When she sees him arriving, she prepares to give him a piece of her mind. But he is with the other girl and doesn't even look at her. Cursing her fate (*"¡Maldito sea mi sino!"*) Rosa leaves in floods of tears.

Bienvenido comes along with Remedios and the despairing Goro in tow. Once he has packed off her son, he again presses Remedios to live with him: in return for which he promises to smooth the way for Goro's marriage with Jacinta. Goro runs back in turmoil, having seen Jacinta coming their way. His badly feigned indifference makes the girl cry, and when Evaristo appears Remedios threatens to leave her husband there and then, unless he gives way over his son's marriage. Evaristo appeals to Bienvenido for help, but that worthy's advice is simple: "rent a room."

Once the older men have gone Goro tells the women that his father has confessed the truth: Jacinta is his own daughter, and therefore Goro's half sister! Remedios counters this on the spur of the moment by declaring that Evaristo may indeed be Jacinta's father, but that Goro's real father is now living in Barcelona! The young pair, for the moment, are relieved and happy at the news. An orchestral *Intermedio*, based on themes from the first *Final*, leads to the last scene.

SCENE 3—Outside the "Goya Church" of San Antonio de Florida. Goro is enjoying a picnic with Jacinta, while his mother is apparently succumbing to Bienvenido's unctuous flattery, although privately she still doubts his sincerity. Fernando appears with a note from Rosa, who has finally agreed to meet him. He sings of the fickle affections of women in a deceptively light *Romanza: "¡Mujeres!"*.

The numbed Evaristo tells Fernando about the marital mess he has got himself into. The alleged recent affair is a fiction, but his wife will not believe it. Fernando agrees to help, and Evaristo leaves to fetch his wife and son. Before they return Rosa arrives with Paca, who tactfully leaves her friend alone with the cashier. In the passionate *Dúo: "¿Por qué vuelve la cara?"* they admit their love, only for Fernando to spoil the moment by blurting out that he is married. Rosa rushes into the church, weeping, leaving Fernando smiling quietly.

Evaristo returns with Remedios, Goro, Jacinta and Bienvenido. At last the truth emerges: Evaristo is not Jacinta's father at all, though Bienvendio has been using the rumor to get free lunches out of the poor man. Remedios is free to admit that Goro really is Evaristo's son after all; and Bienvenido, shown up as a lecherous liar and cheat, takes to his heels. Remedios and Evaristo are happily reunited, and Goro can finally look forward to marriage with his beloved Jacinta. Finally, Fernando admits to Rosa that he has been getting back at her for mocking his marital pretensions. They forgive one another, and all is set to end happily as the curtain falls to a few bars from Rosa's *Romanza*.

By 1929 the long operetta-style zarzuela and short *revista* between them had come to dominate Madrid's theatrical life. So when Sevilla and Carreño prefaced their one-act *sainete madrileño* with a dedication to the city itself, their words sounded as a nostalgic tribute to the lost Golden Age of the 1890s. Surprisingly, *Los Claveles* proved much more than a throwback to the old, urban *genéro chico*. Its contemporary setting, language, and ordinary working characters provided a template for a new style which was only broken with the outbreak of the Civil War.

Other major composers were quick to take up the "retro" fashion, but *Los Claveles* has been particularly associated with *La del manojo de rosas* (1934, Sorozábal) and *Me llaman la presumida* (1936, Alonso)—both to texts by Carreño, working with Francisco Ramos de Castro—as the first part of an unofficial Madrid Trilogy of classic mid-twentieth century zarzuelas.

Los Claveles survives, of course, because it inspired some of Serrano's best music. The aging composer's instinct for theatrical novelty was as strong as ever, though the popular jazz influences paraded by Sorozábal and Alonso have no place in his score. Serrano's six numbers in direct, melodic style had no need to bend to fashion. He takes his working lovers and their tangled emotions seriously; and in his sympathetic hands farcical figures, in particular the woman embittered by the understandable feeling that she is better than everyone else around her, become living and breathing human beings. There is surely no more intensely felt *Romanza* in the repertoire than Rosa's "*¿Qué te importa que no venga?*" with the lost pathos of its opening phrase:

¿Qué te im-por-ta que no ven-ga?__ me a-con-se-ja el pen-sa-mien-to.__

The contrast between this and Fernando's light but bitter dismissal of women ("*¡Mujeres!*") is superbly judged. The three *dúos* are on a comparable level, and altogether *Los Claveles* remains one of the most moving and theatrically subtle creations in the entire repertoire.

La dolorosa
Zarzuela in two acts
Madrid, Teatro Reina Victoria, 24th October 1930

Text: Juan José Lorente

Principal Characters: Brother Rafael (tenor); The Prior (baritone); Dolores (mezzo-soprano); Perico, a lay worker (comic tenor); Nicasia, his girlfriend (soprano); José, Perico's father (actor); Juana, his mother (actress); Bienvenido, Nicasia's father (actor).

ACT 1—Outside a Carthusian convent near Zaragoza. Brother Rafael, a young artist who recently entered the novitiate, is trying to teach the none-too-bright lay worker Perico the technique of perspective, without much success. Laughing, he sends the lad off to fetch water to clean their brushes. Rafael is working on a major portrait of the Virgin Dolorosa, which has caused controversy in the monastery by its direct, sensual appeal. One of the brothers, Lucas, has complained to the Prior about the painting, and the pair approach to ask Rafael to explain his work. In a passionate *Relato: "La roca fría del Calvario"* he describes the scene: the Virgin walks slowly up the road toward Calvary, catches her first sight of the cross where her son is dying, and cries out, heartbroken and inconsolable. The Prior quietly doubts Rafael's religious vocation, while the more forthright Brother Lucas believes him to be inspired by the devil.

Left alone, Rafael compares La Dolorosa's suffering to his own. Every time he tries to depict the Virgin's face, she turns into a lost love whom he cannot forget for a moment. Perico distracts him once again from his gloomy thoughts, and he goes into the monastery to fetch pencils and paper to continue with the drawing lesson. The lad is soon distracted by the attentions of his girlfriend Nicasia. They dream about what they'll wear for their wedding in a delicate *Dúo Comico: "Ya verás cuando me ponga"* which comes to an end when, after a dance, Perico tries to snatch a kiss and is roundly slapped for his pains.

Their canoodling is cut short by the appearance of Nicasia's stern father Bienvenido. Perico's father José stands up for the youngsters, and the two men settle down for a drink and smoke to discuss dowry arrangements, with predictably drunken consequences. They stagger off, but before Perico can gather his thoughts Rafael comes back with pencils for the drawing lesson. José returns, fussing anxiously. His wife Juana has discovered a woman fainting in the road, hungry, worn out from a journey—and carrying a baby boy in her arms. Rafael runs into the convent to fetch medicine, and Juana brings the woman in. She is

Dolores, whose lover has abandoned her and their baby son in favor of a rich wife. She is reduced to traipsing the roads, in search of charity.

Returning with first aid, Rafael is pierced by the sight of the fallen Dolores, who is indeed his old, unfaithful love. Gathering himself together, he generously tells her not to lose hope and helps her into Juana's house. The monk stands rooted to the spot as he hears Dolores sing a simple lullaby to her baby boy (*Nana: "Duerme, mi tesoro"*). Perico tells his scandalized mother that he has recognized the woman's face: she is the Virgin Dolorosa of Rafael's picture. The two enter the house, leaving Rafael to brood over his description of the Virgin's endless walk to Calvary (*"Camina, camina, llorosa"*) as the curtain falls.

ACT 2, SCENE 1—Outside the Monastery garden. Perico and Nicasia are snatching some time together. The baby boy has been ill, which reduces the couple's high spirits temporarily, something a kiss soon puts to rights. Dolores thanks Juana for her kindness, and promises to leave as soon as she and the boy are strong enough, although the kind-hearted woman won't hear of it. José comes in, fumbling with some flowers for the fiesta procession of the Virgin of the Farms next morning, and goes in search of his wife to arrange them. Rafael cannot rest. Despite his prayers he is tormented by his love for Dolores, and feels he is heading for the abyss.

As he goes to enter the garden, Dolores appears (*Dúo: "¡Rafael! . . . Ten piedad, Señor, para la infeliz"*). Wracked with guilt, she is determined to set off on the road once again. Rafael tries to convince Dolores to let him confront the child's father and force the man to repair the damage he has done; but Dolores wants nothing more to do with the faithless coward, except to curse his name (*"Maldito el cobarde"*). She weeps, and the pair reflect on their ruined love which can never be restored (*"Alma mía, nunca más has de volver"*) before going their separate ways.

SCENE 2—The Prior's cell, at first light. The Prior meditates on Rafael's state of mind, which his intuition warns him is shadowed by earthly feeling. In a gravely beautiful *Romanza: "Me da mucho que pensar . . . El amor"* he meditates on the powerful poison of love, which infects everything it touches. Through his window he hears the village celebrations of the festival, still in full swing. A *rondalla* band plays, and a young man is distantly heard singing a dawn serenade to his beloved (*Alborada: "Clavellina de la huerta"*). The Prior sadly shuts his window on all this "pagan happiness," and leads the monks into the chapel to celebrate matins.

The guilt-wracked Rafael breaks away from the procession and enters the Prior's cell for confession, but he is unable to concentrate. Even here a vision of Dolores cradling her baby son disturbs his meditations (*Solo: "La vida con sus encantos"*). The Prior discovers Rafael, and in a powerful *Dúo:*

"La mujer que fue mi vida" listens patiently as the young monk pours out his heart. The Prior tries to be stern, but is wise enough to understand that it will be better for Rafael to follow his destiny with Dolores outside the monastery walls, rather than torture himself within them—a sacrifice which God would not desire. He tells Rafael to follow the dictates of his conscience. Whatever he decides will have the Prior's blessing: the monastery gates will be left open for Rafael to make his way without guilt or hindrance. Rafael kisses his hands in gratitude and leaves the Prior to his sad reflections.

SCENE 3—Outside the monastery gates, next morning. Perico and Nicasia banter and flirt happily, until the voice of his mother brings them back to a sense of reality. They scamper off happily to find a good vantage point to watch the fiesta procession. Juana asks Dolores to stay, but privately she has determined to leave with her child. Rafael departs from the Monastery wearing an ordinary suit, and quietly bids farewell to the cloister that has offered him refuge (*Romanza: "Dejo tu sombra, santa mansión"*). Dolores comes out of Juana's house, weeping, but Rafael convinces her that their destiny is to walk onward together to face whatever life holds in store. With growing confidence, arm in arm, the pair watch the procession starting forth from the monastery gates as the curtain falls (*"Alma mia, tu ilusión vuelve a nacer"*).

La Dolorosa's combination of *verismo* passion, monkish solemnity and robust local color makes for one of the composer's strongest, if not subtlest works. Lorente's libretto is tightly constructed, and thin though they are the comedy scenes at least complement the main concern, Rafael's internal struggle between renunciation and acceptance of the world and its travails.

The painter turned guilt-ridden monk, religious mystic and passionate lover, inspired a stream of red-blooded melody that makes Serrano's last zarzuela his most insistently memorable. Rafael's *Relato* (Narration) is among the most powerfully effective of all tenor *romanzas*:

The figure of the wise Prior inspired music of similar quality, and for the scene in his cell Serrano contrived an unbroken sequence of discrete movements—Prior's solo, distant chorus and *Alborada*, Rafael's solo and culminating *Dúo*—which generate an impressive theatrical momentum. Set against this, and the melancholy passion of her *Dúo* with Rafael, Dolores' simple, little *Nana* (Lullaby) to her baby son is all the more touching.

La alegría del batallón (The Joy of the Battalion, 1909)
This light-hearted one-act zarzuela centers on a group of soldiers billeted in Valencia. The Andalusian Rafael, homesick and missing his girlfriend, steals a cross from a church to get money. He is condemned to be shot, only to be saved by his quick-thinking friend Sergeant Cascales, who manages to pass it off as a miracle. The highlight of Serrano's delightful score belongs to the girlfriend, Dolores; her *Canción: "A una gitana presiosa"* has been memorably sung by many great Spanish singers, notably Conchita Supervía in a classic 1932 recording.

Los de Aragón (People of Aragon, 1927)
Gloria left her native Zaragoza to pursue a singing career, leaving her fiancé Agustín and breaking her mother's heart into the bargain. Her return and eventual reconciliation with Agustín forms the meat of this admirable one act sentimental drama. Serrano deploys Gloria's hauntingly nostalgic *Romanza: "Palomica Aragonesa"* at various key points of the drama, counterpointed with Agustín's confident paean to his people *"Los de Aragon"*. Both these fine songs, for soprano and tenor respectively, are deservedly popular recital standards.

El amigo Melquíades (Friend Melquíades, with **"Quinito" Valverde**, 1914)
A classic Madrid *sainete* by leading playwright Carlos Arniches, notable more for its spicy dialogue and realistic plot than for its brief musical score. The good-hearted Melquíades brings about an honest marriage and reveals a rich lecher in his true colors during the course of a dance which he has organized. The composers put together a lively and enjoyable score harking back to Chueca, which incorporates some genuine Madrid street songs.

Las hilanderas (The Spinners, 1927)
Tuscany under Spanish rule is the scene for a complicated one-act romantic drama, mainly light in tone. It is not without some darker shadows, including an impressive musical invocation to the Devil (*"¡Satan! ¡Satan!"*) sung by the mock-magician Farello and two Spanish Captains, both intent on using supernatural aid to gain the objects of their affection. Serrano's score uses a recurring barcarolle *leitmotif* to poetic effect. The title refers to an undignified disguise the two Captains are forced to assume in consequence of their amorous machinations.

El mal de amores (Love's Sickness, 1905)
La mala sombra (The Bad Influence, 1906)
Two high-quality, farcical *sainetes* in contrasted Andalusian settings by the Álvarez Quintero brothers, notable alike for fast, wise-cracking dialogue. The first takes place in the countryside, the second in the city of Seville. Serrano's total contribution only runs to half an hour's music, but is of high standard. The gypsy music and lovers' *Dúo: "Aquí me tienes, Carola"* in *El mal de amores* are outstanding; the follow-up has a *Dueto Cómico: "Ven aquí clavellina"* which is a sharply amusing parody of those self-same gypsy songs.

✓ **Moros y cristianos** (Moors and Christians, 1905)
Despite an infamously bad libretto disowned by the writers before the premiere, this one-act tragedy enjoys popularity for Serrano's glorious score, especially the gorgeously sensual love *Dúo: "Cesaen mis pesares"* for Amparo and her illicit lover Daniel. He is to play the Christian King in the annual village reenactment of the struggle of the Valencians against the Moors. Unfortunately Amparo's husband is cast as the Moorish King, which enables him to strangle the luckless Daniel for real at the climax of the drama.

✓ **La reina mora** (The Moorish Queen, 1903)
One-act *sainete* set in Seville. The mysterious dark gypsy of the title, Coral, is pursued by various admirers. Her secret is that she has moved into town to be close to her beloved Esteban, incarcerated in the city jail. Serrano's moody, atmospheric score culminates in an intense *Dúo: "A las rajas de la cárse"* for the faithful couple when Coral visits the prison.

20
Pablo Sorozábal
(1897–1988)

Sorozábal's artisan family moved from the Basque countryside to San Sebastián a few years before Pablo's birth on 18th September 1897. He was something of a child prodigy on piano and violin, earning his living in cinemas, cafés and fairgrounds, and playing with the San Sebastián Casino Orchestra under the influential Fernández Arbós. In 1919 he moved to the capital, joining the Madrid Symphony Orchestra which performed his *Capricho español* (1920). His distinctive musical personality was forged by study in Leipzig; and in Berlin, where he preferred Friedrich Koch as composition teacher to Schöenberg, whose theories he disliked. It was in Germany that he made his conducting debut, and the rostrum remained the focal point of his working life.

His later concert works include the choral *Suite vasca* (Basque Suite, 1924); *Dos Apuntes* (Two Sketches) and *Symphonic Variations on a Basque Theme* (both 1928); the suite *Victoriana* (1951); and the Funeral March *Gernika* for chorus and orchestra (1966). Two short but powerful compositions for chorus and orchestra, *Maite* (Our Lady, from a 1940 film) and *¡Ay tierra vasca!* (Ah, Basque Lands!) retain their place in the hearts of his countrymen.

Katiuska (1931) was his amazingly assured stage debut. The twenty or so works which followed combine lyric fire and inimitably pungent orchestration with a highly individual sense of theatre. Best-loved are the classic *madrileño* comedy *La del manojo de rosas* (The Girl with the Roses, 1934) and the "nautical romance" set on the Atlantic Coast *La tabernera del puerto* (The Port Tavernkeeper, 1936).

Sorozábal's liberal sympathies left him somewhat isolated after the Civil War, and many of his later zarzuelas from the ambitious, allegorical *Black, el payaso* (Black, the Clown, 1942) to *Entre Sevilla y Triana* (From Seville to

Triana, 1950) were first seen in less prestigious Madrid theatres or outside the capital altogether. His tenure as conductor of the Madrid Symphony Orchestra ended abruptly in 1952 when he was refused permission to conduct Shostakovich's "Leningrad" Symphony; and though his musical comedy *Las de Caín* (Caín's Daughters) was premiered at the Teatro de la Zarzuela in 1958, the opera *Juan José* still awaits production after rehearsals were suspended there in 1979. With his death in Madrid on 26th December 1988 the last chapter in the creative history of the romantic zarzuela came to an end.

Sorozábal remains the most controversial of the great zarzuela composers, adored by many *aficionados* while leaving others cold. Thanks to his German training, symphonic use of *leitmotif* and no-nonsense style his music stands apart from that of his contemporaries. It may exhibit a range of influences from Debussy and Puccini through to Kálmán, Gershwin and the Hollywood musical, but the fusion of these disparate musical elements makes for highly characterful results. The sweet-sour romanticism and almost shocking pugnacity of his best work can justly be compared to Kurt Weill's in Germany, though Sorozábal's theatrical vitality and acerbic bite are second to none.

Black, el payaso
Operetta in a prologue and three acts
(Barcelona, Teatro Coliseum, 21st April 1942)

Text: Francisco Serrano Anguita

Principal Characters: Black, a clown (baritone); White, his stage partner (bass); Princess Sofía (soprano); Catalina, her sister (soprano); Marat, a French journalist (comic tenor); Carlos Dupont, a pianist (tenor).

PROLOGUE—A stage with its proscenium boxes at a Paris theatre. During the brusque orchestral *Preludio* a playbill announces "Sensational attraction—BLACK and WHITE—The most serious clowns in the world." The curtain rises and they begin their act, a quicksilver mixture of romantic melody, bitter jests and jazz songs (*Dúo: "Ilustre concurrencia"*). Princess Sofía appears in one of the stage boxes together with her aides the Countess of Saratov and Baron Orsava. All three are exiles from the turbulent state of Orsonia. Catching sight of the party, Black freezes, silently gazing at the Princess. After a whispered word between them White announces that Black is going to play *Las melodías de la estepa* ("Song of the Steppes") rather than the promised Futuristic Overture. Black moves toward Sofía's box playing a gypsy tune, putting down his violin to sing the haunting song (*"Princesita de sueños de oro"*). Sofía angrily demands the man be silenced, before fainting into the arms of her companions. The ensuing uproar leads to the abandonment of the mysterious performance as the curtain falls.

ACT 1—A salon in the Princess's Paris mansion, next evening. Sofía is still indisposed, but her forthright younger sister Catalina gives an interview in her stead to a magazine gossip writer, Marat, come to ferret out the scandal of the night before. She explains that the song brought Sofía's homeland so powerfully to mind that it caused her to faint. Catalina's increasingly flirtatious banter with the attractive young Frenchman culminates in a jazzy *Dueto cómico: "¡Dos besos míos!"* before Marat retires, well satisfied with his scoop for *Le Journal*.

Sofía nervously explains her behavior to the Baron. The "Song of the Steppes" was composed for her by her fiancé Grand Duke Daniel, heir to the throne of Orsonia, and could have been known only to the two of them. She never met Daniel, who was reported killed during the uprising which led to their flight to Paris, but it seems that Black must be the Grand Duke in disguise. Sofía is giving an audience to the clowns this very evening, to establish the truth; and she sings of her awakened feelings in a delicate *Romanza: "Yo, que jamás había sentido"*, which incorporates the fateful Song itself.

The clowns are announced, and the Baron soon steers the voluble White away for a drink, leaving Black alone. He muses on a portrait of Sofía, who soon joins him; and in the expansive *Dúo: "Para mi Príncipe, rendidamente"* the Princess tries to force the enamored clown to confess to his "real" identity. Although Black resists, he is too much in love to hold out for long, and assents to being called Daniel, after which they passionately confess their mutual love.

The returning White is amused to hear his stage partner answering to the title of Grand Duke of Orsonia, and narrates the invented story of their flight and metamorphosis into common clowns (*Canción: "Aunque todos nos daban por muertos"*). He enigmatically warns Sofía to put her conclusions on hold now she can return to Orsovia, where the revolutionaries have been defeated. Marat and Catalina confirm White's news, and the act ends as Sofía's entire staff of chambermaids, cooks, chauffeurs and grooms rush in, joining their mistress and her beloved "Daniel" in mass determination to set off at once for Orsonia and reclaim their rightful places (*Final: "Sofía, ¿qué ocurre?"*).

ACT 2—King Daniel's Cabinet Room in the Royal Palace of Orsonia. Courtiers and military officers gather to greet their Queen-to-be (*Coro: "Para ofrecer a nuestra Soberana"*). Black modestly deflects the compliments offered to him and his Prime Minister, the Marques de Tarnevitz—White—and blanches at the thought of the wildly complicated nuptial ceremonials that will have to be observed once Catalina has tracked down the old fifteenth century Chronicle (*"El Cronikón"*) of court etiquette. Left alone, Black reflects on how love has had the magic power to turn a clown into a king (*Romanza: "Hacer de un mísero payaso"*).

White, clown at heart despite his fancy uniform, joins Black to transact some diplomatic business. A servant announces that the Royal Forester Zinenko has come to pay his respects, and he is granted an audience together with a French virtuoso pianist called Carlos Dupont. Black retires to prepare for the meeting. No sooner has he gone than Catalina breezes in with her friend Marat, come from Paris to cover the Royal Wedding. She has found *El Cronikón*, and together with the Baron and the Countess they picture the sumptuous pleasures in store during the ceremonial festivities in an irresistible *Cuarteto: "¡Ya se encontro!"* before rushing off to prepare their finery, nearly knocking Zinenko and Dupont over in their haste. The old forester is full of sentimental memories of the King as a young boy: he even taught him to sing a harvest folksong. Black receives the visitors courteously, but Zinenko, hurt that Daniel does not seem to remember him or the song, leaves sadly.

Left alone with Black, the pianist Dupont surprises the King by exhibiting an unusually detailed knowledge of the royal art collection, and goes on to reveal a secret door by manipulating the wall panels. At last he declares openly that he is the true King Daniel of Orsonia. In a *Dúo: "¡Daniel Estebanoff!"* Dupont tells his story. Deeply in love with a commoner, but pressed by the Emperor to accept a political alliance with Sofia, he made up his mind to marry his true love and assume a new identity. Now he and his wife have two children, and he has returned only to satisfy his curiosity about the clown who has usurped his throne.

Black in turn reveals his true identity. He is the son of the engraver who made the plate on which the Song of the Steppes was privately inscribed for Sofia. His love for the Princess has led him to impersonate Daniel and take the throne. Dupont withdraws as she approaches, courteously offering to play the piano in the court concert that evening, though Sofia laughs at the flowery manners of the departing artist—much to Black's chagrin. Despite her attempts to reassure him he remains tormented by doubts that the Princess loves him not for himself, but for his rank (*Dúo: "¡Ah, Daniel! ¡Ay, qué gracia Daniel!"*).

ACT 3—The Cabinet Room late that night. In the adjoining Salon a party is in full swing, as we gather from the *Intermedio*, a punchy orchestral version of the *Cronikón* quartet. Dupont, resting in the Cabinet after his concert, hears Zinenko's tale of rejection. To hearten the old man Dupont sings the folksong that Zinenko remembers so fondly, the exhilarating *Czardas: "Deja la guadaña, segador"* which Dupont claims the King has taught him.

When Black and Sofía come in from the party Zinenko, after dancing a few steps of the czardas with Dupont, leaves with the pianist. The Princess finds it suspicious that Dupont knew and played the Song of the Steppes, and as soon as they are alone together Black guiltily confesses everything, including the identity of the mysterious pianist. The appalled Sofía vows never to speak to him again and leaves in tears. Black tells White they must take to the open road immediately to resume their old careers, and his partner greets this latest turn in Fortune's Wheel with humorous equanimity.

While Black changes out of his royal finery, White puts a phone call through to Military Headquarters. He has received intelligence of an imminent coup, and requests that a detachment of Cossacks be sent to the palace (*Final: "Al habla . . . ¿Jefatura?"*). Black enters in peasant dress, but before the two clowns can leave they hear the singing of the approaching insurgents. When a frightened Sofía appears with Dupont, Black triggers the panel mechanism and decisively orders them to hide in the secret room just before the rabble arrive baying for the King's blood. They pull back the curtains, only to find the two clowns in full motley. Black and White reproduce some of their droll routines from the Paris show, and in spite of the furious urgings of their leader the rebels laugh uproariously and demand more, lingering just long enough for White's Cossacks to come to the rescue. The rebels disperse, and Sofía and Dupont emerge from their hiding place.

Having saved the life of the woman he loves, Black is ready to depart. Dupont, however, orders him to stay and continue as King, for if ever anyone proved he was worthy of a crown, Black has done so tonight. Sofía adds her plea, telling him that it is not Daniel that she loves, but Black the clown. To everyone's relief Black concedes; and hearing the joyful shouts of the crowd outside, goes out onto the balcony to greet his people as the curtain falls.

Black, el payaso (Black, the Clown), adapted from a story by the journalist Francisco Serrano Anguita, is perhaps Sorozábal's most wide-ranging work, an ingenious allegory of art and nationalist politics. The time and place of its premiere—1942 Barcelona—are significant. As a confirmed liberal, Sorozábal's sympathies had been with the losing side in the cataclysmic Civil War, and unlike some of his fellow composers he remained *persona non grata* with the Franco government for many years.

Although its three-act structure and Ruritanian plot align *Black, el payaso* with the old *zarzuela grande* of Barbieri's epoch, the contemporary allusions are striking. Sofia's recollections of the Orosovian Civil War in her *Romanza* are perhaps the most pointed: *"Destrozó mi país la tragedia cruel"* ("The cruel tragedy shattered my country"). The hero is a performing artist embroiled in political intrigue, to the point where he has to masquerade as a King. The real King has adopted a new identity—as a concert pianist! Black turns out to be a good ruler, halting an uprising through his clowning skills, and is acclaimed the monarch by right when all is done. The Ruritanian setting and fantastic characters evidently sugared the pill sufficiently to make it palatable to the authorities. If the satirical edge of *Black, el payaso* is less abrasive today, its vision of the artist triumphant was clearly close to the composer's heart.

Sorozábal called *Black, el payaso* an operetta, and its Central European flavor makes this very appropriate. It is altogether a dizzying score, spiced with clever orchestral touches, *sprechgesang* and austere modernist harmonies, Broadway jazz, brutal marches, and a fair helping of Latin sweetness for good measure. Spanish dance rhythms are out. Instead we have a strong gypsy element, a show-stopping czardas, and an irresistible comedy quartet in the style of a Hungarian *Marche Militaire* with klesmer overtones. The hauntingly beautiful Song of the Steppes is in Sorozábal's special vein of poignant tenderness:

Don Manolito
Sainete in two acts
(Madrid, Teatro Reina Victoria, 24th April 1943)

Text: Luis Fernández de Sevilla and Anselmo Cuadrado Carreño

Principal Characters: Don Manolito (baritone); Don Jorge (bass); Margot, his niece (soprano); Guillermo, an athletic young man (bass); Leocadia (soprano); Nica (comic tenor); Doña Candida, his aunt (actress); Emilio (tenor).

ACT 1, SCENE 1—A chalet at a skiing resort in the Sierras north of Madrid. Don Manolito and his old friend Don Jorge are playing poker with two young acquaintances, Nica and Emilio. Seeing some youngsters heading off for the ski-slopes (*Coro: "Juventud que escalaste"*) the two older men mock themselves for having one foot in the grave. When they are left alone, Jorge proposes marriage to fellow confirmed bachelor Manolito—with his niece Margot. His friend laughs off the suggestion, partly because he enjoys the freedom of the single life, and partly because he considers the difference in age too great. Their conversation is disturbed first by Nica's affluent, sporty aunt-protectress Doña Candida in pursuit of her simple-minded nephew, convinced he will be trapped into an unsuitable relationship; and again when the impecunious Emilio smooth talks Leocadia, the young daughter of his tailor, into extending his credit.

Margot, having conveniently hurt her leg in a slight skiing accident, makes an impressive entrance in the arms of Guillermo, a brutally handsome young athlete. In a voluptuous *Habanera: "Yo hubiese querido"* the plausible Emilio tenders his solicitude, but she only has eyes for Guillermo. Unfortunately, he thinks of nothing but athletic pursuits, though he does sincerely value Margot as a friend (*Solo: "Dicen que el amor"*). Humiliated, she storms off—oddly without assistance from anybody—leaving Guillermo to his dreams of sporting glory. Don Manolito encourages him to follow the obviously smitten girl, but the older man's romantic visions of marital bliss (*Romanza: "En la vida de casado"*) go right over his head. Don Jorge has sounded Margot out, and soon finds a pretext to leave her alone with his old friend. Poor Manolito is too abashed to say anything except stress his advanced age, but Margot cuts him short: if her uncle insists she must marry Don Manolito, she will obey. Don Manolito promises that he will never marry her against her will (*Dúo: "No sé por qué lloro"*).

SCENE 2—The snow-covered garden in front of the chalet. Doña Candida has caught up with Nica, who plainly prefers the much more attractive prospect of a chat with Leocadia. The old amazon, however, carries him bodily away from the danger zone. Leocadia discovers Emilio's duplicitous nature from Margot, and curtly informs him that he'll have to pay his debts to her father after all. Don Jorge, misunderstanding the nature of Manolito's promise to his niece, leaves the couple alone together again. When the sad Margot confesses her passion for Guillermo, Don Manolito reassures her: she will be married to Guillermo within six months, he will see to that himself. Pretending indifference, Manolito tells Margot of a secret passion of his own, and recites some verses which he has dedicated to his beloved (*Romanza: "Dile"*). Margot, deeply moved, wishes she had chosen somebody who could write so beautifully to her.

SCENE 3—Inside the chalet. Emilio confides his dire financial straights to Nica: if he cannot marry the rich Leocadia, with her country estate in Malaga, he must set his cap at Margot. Nica agrees to tell Leocadia that Emilio has gone off in despair to Madrid, in the hope she will leave in guilty pursuit. When it comes to it Nica rather fancies her for himself, but Leocadia soon disabuses him of Emilio's tall stories about country estates, and laughs at him for dreaming (*Dúo cómico: "Sueña"*). Doña Candida swoops to carry the weak-willed Nica away again; and Leocadia, genuinely upset, goes in pursuit of Emilio after all.

As soon as the coast is clear Emilio makes another attempt to charm Margot. Don Manolito gets rid of the young adventurer by telling him that he is engaged to Margot himself, so when the older man urges Guillermo to court his devoted girl, the athlete is stupefied—until Don Manolito offers to coach him in appropriate sweet talk. Margot, swiftly divining the source of her beloved's new-found eloquence, begins to discern the depth of Manolito's feeling for her; while Jorge, blissfully believing his plan has worked, announces his niece's engagement with Don Manolito, to the utter bafflement of Guillermo and the joy—real or feigned—of everyone else (*Final: "Margot: yo te quiero"*).

ACT 2, SCENE 1—The public gardens of the resort the following spring, with the snow-capped peaks of the Sierras in the distance. Emilio and a group of youngsters amuse themselves with a spirited choral *Ensalada Madrileña*, a medley of popular songs from the capital. Don Jorge chides Don Manolito for not getting on with the marriage. He is worried by Margot's attentions to the opaque Guillermo, who spends all his time listening to soccer commentaries down the telephone, and by the predatory Emilio. Manolito overacts the jealous anger he really feels (*Romanza: "Es tu pecho ingrato"*), and Jorge has to restrain him from starting a fight as Guillermo arrives with Margot in tow. The athlete is over the moon, as his soccer team Maravillas has just won. Showing more animation than he ever has over Margot, he describes the superb passing maneuver that led to the winning goal (*Canción: "¡Alirón!"*).

Margot herself, disillusioned with the macho Guillermo and his sporting obsessions, sadly laments the waste of her affections in the exquisite *Romanza: "Una rosa en su tallo"*. Piqued beyond endurance, she confirms to the ever-hopeful Emilio that Don Manolito really is her fiancé; and tensions rise when Doña Candida finally disabuses the enraged Jorge of his belief in Margot's devotion to Manolito, and Leocadia admits she has fallen in love with the appallingly cynical Emilio. Margot confides her own bitterness to Manolito. Despite his good offices, she cannot marry such a thoughtless hulk as Guillermo (*Dúo: "No te dejes llevar del enojo"*). As the voices of the youngsters echo from the distance (*Coro: "El amor no es sólo un niño"*) Don Manolito wisely refuses to accept her offer to marry him on the rebound, and reflects on the folly of all this loving. Who, Margot asks him slyly, is really the fool?

SCENE 2—A pine wood near the chalet. Don Jorge gives his thoughtful old friend an antique bracelet to present as a formal betrothal token to Margot. When she and Guillermo enter arm in arm, Don Manolito naturally believes that they are reconciled, especially when Margot tells him that she has made up her mind. Almost in tears he generously offers his congratulations; only giving way to his intense loneliness when they leave to speak with her uncle (*Romanza: "Pulserita de pedida"*). The young couple return and Manolito hands the betrothal bracelet to Guillermo. She stops him gently: "No, not him! You—only my fiancé may place this bracelet on my arm." At last Don Manolito understands; and the reconciled Leocadia and Emilio, together with Doña Candida and Nica, arrive just in time to see him blissfully embracing his young fiancée for the very first time. Everyone joins in the joyous *Final: "Porque lo quiso tu tío"*.

Though mountains, snow and ski-sports provide a refreshingly novel backdrop to *Don Manolito*, most genial of all Sorozábal's works, it remains at heart a throwback to the classic *sainete madrileño*. Carreño and de Sevilla, the team responsible for Serrano's *Los Claveles* in the heady days before the Civil War, produced a lively piece of tongue-in-cheek romantic nostalgia where the older man finally gets the girl.

To a remarkable degree Sorozábal succeeds in having his cake and eating it, gently mocking the timeworn conventions of the genre whilst indulging himself gloriously in its honest sentiment. His music is luscious, witty and ingeniously scored, and the hit numbers from *Don Manolito* were amongst the last zarzuela songs to achieve mass popularity. Among a clutch of succulent, absorbing *Romanzas* and *Dúos*, Guillermo's bravura piece describing a memorable goal in a soccer match stands out as an unexpected (and hugely entertaining) patter song for the bass singer.

Katiuska
Zarzuela in two acts
(Barcelona, Teatro Victoria, 27th January 1931)

Text: Emilio González del Castillo and Manuel Marti Alonso

Principal Characters: Katiuska (soprano); Pedro Stakoff, Soviet Commissar (baritone); Bruno Brunovich (bass); Olga (soprano); Prince Sergio (tenor).

ACT 1—An inn deep in the Ukraine, soon after the Bolshevik revolution. Groups of dispossessed farmworkers troop in from the countryside (*Coro: "Todo es camino"*). The royalist innkeeper Boni promises to aid them and listens to their harrowing stories about the Red Army, a detachment of which has burned the castle of Prince Sergio, former ruler of the region.

Pedro Stakoff, the Soviet Commissar newly arrived from Kiev, arrives at the snug little inn without identifying himself. Despite his revolutionary fervor, he yearns for the peace of a quiet home and the love of a good woman (*Romanza: "Calor de nido"*). He announces that the Prince and other condemned nobles have escaped and taken refuge in the area. Boni and his fiancée Olga recall happier times with ex-colonel Bruno Brunovich of the Kazan Cossacks, in the energetic March *Terceto: "El cosaco en su brioso corcel"*.

The Catalan stocking salesman to the Czar, Amadeo Pich, seeks refuge at the Inn; as does Prince Sergio accompanied by a young girl, Katiuska. Everyone greets him joyfully and Bruno offers him refuge, but since he has a price on his head the Prince selflessly asks only that Katiuska be cared for (*Coro y Romanza: "Es el príncipe . . . es delicada flor"*).

Katiuska recounts her own sad story in a touching song (*Romanza: "Vivía sola"*). The Red hordes devastated her house and killed her grandmother, leaving no choice but flight. As he leaves the Prince gives Bruno funds to take care of Katiuska, but in reality the corrupt ex-colonel is more interested in simply pocketing the money. Just as everyone is settling down for the night (*Concertante: "Ya anocheció, ya no debéis partir"*) a troop of Red Army soldiers arrive looking for drink. Katiuska, believing the Prince has been captured, comes out of hiding and the soldiers pounce on her.

At that moment Pedro arrives. He defends the girl, threatening the soldiers, and eventually persuades them to leave by appealing to their patriotism in his vigorous *Canción: "La mujer rusa"*. Though Katiuska begs Pedro to let her take care of a flesh wound he has received in the shoulder, he insists on going outside to make sure everything is safe. The farmers discuss the opportunity to get away, but eventually settle down again for the night. Bruno plots to abscond with Boni's fiancée Olga and the Prince's money, and Pich offers to join in the plan. Soon afterward Pedro Stakoff reappears to thank Katiuska for helping him, only to vanish again when he hears shooting. The girl prays for his safety, but hearing another burst of firing she is left in fear and dismay as the act ends (*Final: "El reloj las diez ya dio"*).

ACT 2—Olga and Boni's aunt Tatiana serve food; and in an attempt to salve everyone's fears Ivan, an itinerant old accordionist, accompanies Olga and the farmers in a yearning lament over their homeland (*Canción y coro: "Ucraniano mi amor"*). Ivan appears to know Katiuska and tells the innkeeper's wife that he will return to reveal his reasons the following day. Katiuska, who cannot sleep, sings a song in praise of the beautiful Ukrainian night (*Romanza: "Noche hermosa"*), after which the lecherous Bruno and Pich lead a jazzy Boston Waltz in praise of Russian women, ironically countered by their dance partners Olga and Tatiana (*Cuarteto: "Rusita, rusa divina"*).

At midnight Pedro reappears with his soldiers, bringing in the captured Prince. They lock him up in one of the bedrooms and set a guard. Katiuska remonstrates with Pedro, who stoutly defends his actions and Bolshevik ideals. Left alone together they finally admit their love (*Dúo: "Somos dos barcas"*), but when Katiuska asks Pedro to save the life of the Prince and flee with them the Commissar sets his face against such treason, and Katiuska breaks down in tears.

A soldier tells Pedro that there is a suspicious concentration of armed men in the forest. Bruno, Olga and Amadeo Pich decide this is the moment to make a move and head for jazzy Paris (*Terceto cómico: "A París me voy"*). Before they can get away Pedro and the soldiers return, once more having captured Ivan—revealed as a nobleman in disguise—with his insurgent followers.

Katiuska dimly recognizes the old man and recalls memories of her childhood. Ivan reveals to Katiuska her full name: Princess Katiuska Ivanova, his daughter. The soldiers want to order the arrest of all the aristocrats but Pedro prevents them, maintaining that they are not aristocrats at all and extending a safe-conduct to the lot of them.

At this crucial moment the Chief Commissar for the Ukraine appears on the scene with reinforcements. Pedro is accused of treason and arrested. However, when he discovers exactly what has happened the Commissar declares that the Prince, Ivan and the rest of the nobles are condemned, while Katiuska can choose between exile as a Princess and marriage with Pedro Stakoff. As the curtain falls she makes her choice. Pedro and Katiuska rush into one another's arms, vowing never again to separate (*Final: "Esta mujer, tuya nunca ha de ser"*).

Katiuska was Sorozábal's first stage work, but demonstrates all its composer's major strengths. The contemporary Russian theme, as in Millán's *El dictador* (1923), and near-tragic denouement caused almost as much of a stir as the fact that it took as its hero a Red Commissar torn between love and his Bolshevik duties. The political scales are pretty evenly balanced between nostalgic sympathy for the old, paternalistic certitudes, and respect for the youthful idealism of the new order: though in truth all of this functions primarily as a backdrop for the brooding, intense emotions of the romantic plot.

The piquant Ukrainian folk-palette of the scoring with *bandurrias* masquerading as balalaikas; the jazzy songs for the decadent, aristocratic hangers-on; above all, the melodic inspiration of its romantic numbers made this entertaining work an instant classic in the operetta-zarzuela style. What fewer commentators noticed was the brilliance of the musical architecture. Sorozábal's transformations of original Russian folk material gives his work a symphonic tautness and economy. The ubiquitous "Song of the Volga Boatmen" turns up in various guises; for example, in the rocking string accompaniment to the Prince's lovely *Romanza: "Es delicada flor"*:

and later as the melody of Katiuska's radiant nocturne *"Noche Hermosa"*. By these means, the composer produced a work that is musically even more impressive than the sum of its parts.

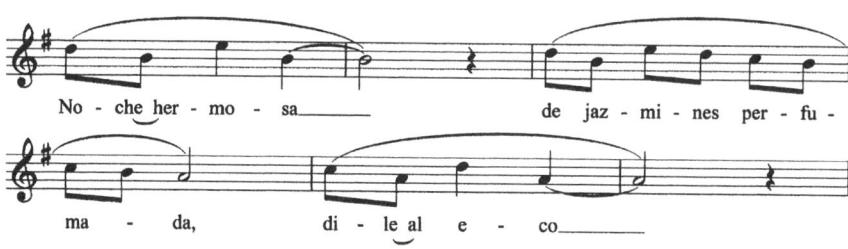

La del manojo de rosas
Zarzuela in two acts
(Madrid, Teatro Fuencarral, 13th November 1934)

Text: Francisco Ramos de Castro and Anselmo Cuadrado Carreño

Principal Characters: Ascensión, a florist (soprano); Joaquín, a mechanic (baritone); Capó, a mechanic (comic tenor); Clarita, a manicurist (soprano); Espasa, a waiter (actor); Ricardo, a pilot (tenor).

ACT 1, SCENE 1—A small plaza in a well-heeled neighborhood of Madrid with a bar, florist shop and garage. After a brief *Preludio* the curtain rises on the waiter, Espasa, wiping tables and passing the time of day with Don Daniel, the well-born man fallen on hard times who owns the florist's (*Escena: "Ya está aquí el pelmazo"*). In front of the garage the mechanic Joaquín is inflating a tire, assisted by Capó who manages to avoid most of the hard work. Don Daniel's daughter Ascensión carries some bouquets of roses into the shop, though not before everyone has admired her good looks and wondered who the lucky man will be (*Entrada: "Dice la gente del barrio"*).

Espasa, who has intellectual pretensions, spouts about the pretty *florista* in a convoluted, pseudo-sophisticated manner. Clarita, the manicurist at the "Feminine Athenaeum," passes through, full of the feminist jargon of her clients. Next, the dashing young pilot Ricardo appears and asks Don Daniel for Ascensión's hand in marriage. The father agrees to consult his daughter, promising to lend the elated Ricardo his support. When Don Daniel raises the matter Ascensión tells him she is determined to marry a man of her own class, and her cowardly father escapes with embarrassment. No sooner has he gone than Joaquín comes across to pay court to her. She mocks him, too, but he gives as good as he gets and there soon develops an understanding between them (*Dúo: "Hace tiempo que vengo al taller"*).

Ricardo comes to speak to the florist, but Joaquín intercepts him. They needle one another, coolly at first, but the atmosphere becomes increasingly heated before they leave (*Dúo: "¿Quién es usté?"*). Don Pedro enters in search of a drink. He is a well-to-do scrap metal merchant desperately in need of increased military spending to raise prices. Like Espasa he has pretensions to verbal dexterity, and their conversation is dazzlingly unintelligible. Clarita comes back and Capó takes the opportunity to tell her that he is crazy about her; the girl teases him, saying she too has come to improve her mind with Espasa. Capó tells her he thinks the waiter is a fool, but when Clarita speaks to Espasa about some feminist theories she has heard down at the Athenaeum the waiter takes the chance to utter a mouthful of high-flown phrases that impress even Capó, who envies his rival's cultural credentials.

Ascensión goes to deliver some flowers to an important rich client, with Joaquín accompanying her. Ricardo wants to follow them; but Don Pedro, leaving the bar with Espasa, delays him with another salvo of verbal bilge which lets the pilot know that Joaquín is his son—hot news to everybody in the plaza!

SCENE 2—The entrance hall of a smart modern apartment. Ascensión has brought two large bunches of roses for the mistress of the house, Doña Mariana. She advises her to marry a good man like her own husband, Don Pedro—who sneaks through, drunk, while the two women are speaking. Her smartly dressed son Joaquín is as surprised to find Ascensión in the hall as she is to see him. He tries to hide behind his hat as he makes his escape but to no avail. The florist, though poor, is proud; as she returns to the Plaza she sings of her crushing disappointment in discovering that Joaquín is a rich boy who is playing around with her (*Romanza: "No corté mas que una rosa"*).

SCENE 3—The Plaza. Espasa tries to worm out the cause of Ascención's depression, but the florist takes advantage of the incursion of a snooty English tourist to avoid his probings. Capó wants to thrash Espasa for sneaking off with Clarita to a spiritualist meeting but the girl sweet-talks him back into a good humor in the jazzy *Dúo Cómico: "Tienes que ser docíl"*. The waiter stuns Capó with his erudite language, and Clarita fixes another date with the victorious Espasa. When Joaquín comes in Ascensión bursts into tears and refuses to listen to his explanations. Ricardo comes out of the shop and re-enters the lists. Ascensión tells him that a spoilt rich boy masquerading as a worker has tried to have his way with her for a lark. The others take sides with their favorite "girl with the roses," and Joaquín retreats crestfallen (*Final: "Ascensión ¿qué es lo que quieres?"*).

ACT 2, SCENE 1—The plaza, some months later. After a pasodoble *Intermedio* based on the lovers' earlier *Dúo* we find Clarita, now in charge of the florist's, tying some bouquets. Capó, at last accepted as her fiancé, surprises her with a kiss. There have been changes, too, in the bar; for Espasa, now a bus driver, comes to buy a bunch of roses for his boss's wife. He lets loose one of his rodomontades, but Capó outpoints him with a volley of verbal flourishes culled from a dictionary of gypsy flamenco. Espasa retreats into the bar while Clara and the triumphant Capó sing and dance a stirring *Farruca: "Chinochilla de mi charniqué"* to more nonsensical gypsy-talk.

Ascensión and Don Daniel enter fashionably dressed, having won a long legal battle and recovered their money and social position. Clara intuits that Ascensión does not seem entirely enamored of her fiancé Ricardo, and when the pilot appears, the ex-florist taunts him with brusque, bitter coldness, telling him to come back for her later. Ricardo leaves, fuming.

Doña Mariana follows Joaquín into the square. Her son has come to beg the garage owner to take him back on, but hearing Don Pedro and Espasa coming out of the bar, Mariana scuttles away. The net is closing in on Pedro, who has been threatened with arrest for debt and now needs nothing less than a quick war to rescue his scrap business. Ascensión and Clara leave the shop and run straight into Joaquín, coming out of the garage brandishing a monkey wrench. Ascensión laughs bitterly in the belief that he is at his tricks again posing as a worker. Joaquín tells her coldly that now he has to work to keep himself and his parents alive. Ascensión is overwhelmed with remorse; and though Ricardo takes her away, Joaquín can see that she still wants him and sings his confident *Romanza: "No: no me importa . . . Madrileña bonita"*. Another *Intermedio*, an orchestral repeat of the *Farruca*, leads to the next scene.

SCENE 2—A ramshackle tenement. Ascensión, wearing her old flower-seller's dress, comes in with a bunch of roses. She asks a seedy neighbor to direct her to Doña Mariana's door. Both women weep for Doña Mariana's poverty and unhappiness, and when Joaquín comes in his mother tactfully withdraws. Joaquín and Ascensión nostalgically recall the happiness they have lost for ever. It is evident they still care deeply for one another (*Dúo habanera: "¡Qué tiempos aquellos!"*).

SCENE 3—Back in the plaza. Capó idly watches Clarita cleaning the shop windows. Times are hard, and the girl berates the mechanic for getting thrown out of his job. Espasa comes in with a bandaged head. His bus has crashed, and he too is out of a job. He has come to meet with Ricardo, hoping his experiences in the travel business have made him suitable for employment in aviation. Ascensión comes in looking for Joaquín, but they tell her he has not been seen at the garage for eight days. Seeing Ricardo coming she hides in the shop and begs Clarita to tell the pilot that she cannot go through with marrying him. Conversely, Ricardo pleads with Espasa to say the same to his "girl with the roses."

When the two messengers finally deliver their news Ascensión and Ricardo, hurt and confused, shout angrily at one another before declaring a truce: they will be friends, but thankfully never married (*Dúo: "¿Es que tú te has creído?"*). The pilot leaves, and Joaquín arrives, having passed his examinations for a career as an engineer. Ascensión and he forgive one another and leave together as Clarita, Capó, Espasa and the rest wish them good luck in a toast with beer from the bar (*Dúo y Final: "En este calle hace tiempo"*).

La del manojo de rosas (The Girl with the Roses) was the second of a trio of memorable zarzuelas written by Sorozábal in the early 1930s. The title and Ascensión's *leitmotif* recall another strong-minded heroine, Chapí's *La revoltosa*, being a quotation from the famous *dúo* in which Felipe describes his Mari-Pepa dressed for the verbena (*p. 63*). Sorozábal also quotes Caballero's *El señor Joaquín* (*p. 100*) at the first mention of his own hero. This self-consciousness of its place in the *sainete* tradition places *La del manojo de rosas* between *Los Claveles* and *Me llaman la presumida* as the central panel in another triptych, in which Carreño and company painted a vivid picture of Madrid with its diverse cultural, social and political passions in the years immediately preceding the Civil War. Their comedy characters—notably the verbally incontinent waiter Espasa and the sinister scrap-metal merchant Don Pedro—possess Jonsonian satiric gusto; and like the Jacobean playwright, they glance nostalgically backward as well as forward to the horrors to come.

The libretto, dry, wise-cracking and tightly focused, proved perfectly suited to Sorozábal's gifts. The result is masterly, the best integrated and most economical score he ever wrote. Every number succeeds perfectly, from the emotional, yearning *Preludio* through the brilliant jazz-dance numbers for the "comedy couple" to the more muted *Romanzas* for Ascensión and Joaquín. Their two *Dúos* lie at the heart of the work. The first is an thrilling pasodoble of verbal sparring, the second an incomparable essay in that tender, wistful melancholy which so often characterizes the world of zarzuela:

La tabernera del puerto
Zarzuela in three acts
(Barcelona, Teatro Tívoli, 10th May 1936)

Text: Federico Romero and Guillermo Fernández Shaw

Principal Characters: Juan de Eguía, a pirate (baritone); Marola, a tavern keeper (soprano); Leandro, a fisherman (tenor); Simpson, an English fisherman (bass); Abel, an orphan boy (soprano).

ACT 1—The harbor of an imaginary fishing port in northern Spain, with a tavern and a café. It is dawn, and sailors can be heard singing a love song out to sea (*Coro: "Eres blanca y hermosa como tu madre"*). Some others enter the tavern while the fisherman Verdier sits down outside the café, calling for the proprietor Ripalda to serve his coffee. The orphan boy Abel produces an accordion and plays for Verdier, declaiming his love for the young *tabernera* (tavern keeper) Marola in spoken words and song (*"En la taberna del puerto"*). This doesn't go down well with two of the local wives, who are suspicious of this pretty girl. The fishermen head out to sea, praying to the Virgin for a safe return (*Coro: "¡Salve, Señora!"*). Ripalda tells Verdier about the mysterious girl. She arrived in town two months ago, set up in business by a dangerous pirate, Juan de Eguía, who everyone assumes is Marola's lover despite their difference in age. Verdier, surprised, says he knows Eguía, and sends Abel to fetch him.

The old skipper Chinchorro asks Leandro, a handsome young fisherman who is spending a lot of time in Marola's tavern, to set sail with him, but the lad seems less than willing. When Leandro leaves to work on his boat the old salt heads for the tavern to see this pretty girl for himself. Juan de Eguía greets Verdier in the company of Simpson, a drink-sodden old English sailor who scrapes a living by acting as an interpreter for foreigners. Verdier is worried about speaking out, but Juan reduces the tension with a lush *Habanera: "¡Qué días aquellos de la juventud!"* in which he invites the other two to recall the good times they had together in their youth. To Ripalda's surprise all three enter the café, and Chinchorro's drunken old wife, Antigua, tries to wheedle him out of some gin while nominally selling sardines to his customers. He pushes her away toward the tavern, where she thinks she sees her husband flirting with Marola. She drags her old man out by the ear, and they indulge in some colorful mutual insults before going off arm in arm on their inebriated way (*Duo Cómico: "¡Ven aquí, camastón!"*).

When Marola comes out of the tavern Eguía orders her to help them all in a shady plan, by convincing her young admirer "simply to go out for a little sail."

She dares not contradict him, but leaves in tears. Leandro himself, gathering from the drunken Simpson that his love for Marola is common knowledge, realizes it is time to act. When Marola comes out to serve him, he pours out his feelings; though she warns him to have nothing to do with her but go back to sea (*Dúo: "Marinero, vete a la mar"*). He leaves, and Marola is still in a daze when young Abel starts spouting love verses at her, too. She laughingly tells him he's still only a boy and sends him off toward the café.

A group of local women led by Antigua surround the *tabernera*, accusing her of sending their men crazy with lust. Marola gives as good as she gets: if they weren't such drunken sluts they wouldn't have such difficulty keeping their husbands sweet (*Final: "¡Aquí está la culpable!"*). Things take a nasty turn when Eguía comes in, knocks Marola to the floor and pushes her back into the tavern. He asks the women whether this is good enough for them, and they shamefacedly withdraw. Abel offers to fight the bully but Eguía dismisses him with imperious good humor, settling down to smoke his pipe and listen to Leandro singing in his boat.

ACT 2—Inside the tavern later that day. The sailors' noisy *Coro: "Eres blanca y hermosa"* prompts Simpson to ask Marola for a proper song to shut them up. Eguía orders her to obey, accompanying on guitar as she sings a gentle romantic legend about an old musician, his magic flute, and how he charmed the birds— which she herself imitates in her *Romanza: "En un país de fábula"*. Everyone applauds, and Eguía responds with a cheerful number in praise of women and their innumerable charms (*Canción: "La mujer, de los quince a los veinte"*). Later he goes off to find some cutlery for Ripalda, who pretends he has a sudden influx of customers: in reality he's smitten with Marola, like all the rest.

Chinchorro and Simpson worry that despite Eguía's obvious optimism about his plan the customs officers are on to them. Abel reveals to the shocked company how the pirate has mistreated Marola. Appalled, the sailors go, led by Chinchorro shouting "Death to Eguía!" and leaving the drunken Simpson alone apart from four sleeping Black marines from an American cruiser. As they doze fitfully, he exhorts them to wake up to the realization of their exploitation by their white masters in his muscular *Tango: "Despierta, negro"*. One of their white officers appears at the window, and the marines march off like automata as soon as he blows his whistle.

Leandro appears just in time to dissuade Simpson from following them to cause trouble. In gratitude the Englishman tells him that Eguía is using Marola as bait to get Leandro to smuggle in a shipment of cocaine. He warns the youngster that if things go wrong it will mean jail, and leaves the sailor confused and unhappy. In his famous *Romanza: "¡No puede ser!"* Leandro wonders whether Marola can really be so duplicitous. No, he decides; she is unhappy, but would never lie to him. When she comes into the bar, he tells her he will do anything to win her, no matter how criminal. Horrified, Marola is about to confess that she loves him; but they are interrupted by Antigua, and as soon as Marola goes to sort out the empty bottles the old woman takes the opportunity to thank Leandro for falling in love with the *tabernera*: now all married couples can live in peace again.

When she also tells him how Eguía beat the girl in front of the women, he has to be restrained from going straight out to drown his rival by Marola herself, now forced to reveal her true story. Over an orchestral accompaniment, she tells him that Eguía is in reality her father (*Relato: "Yo soy de un puerto"*). Leandro pledges to forgive her father and keep Marola's secret, and they swear their love for one another. The lovers plan to collect the cocaine together, before simply throwing it in the sea.

Ripalda, looking for another pretext to chat up Marola, returns the cutlery he borrowed earlier. Abel is hanging around too, and the two join the girl in a good-humored *Terceto: "Marola resuena en el oído"*. After they leave, Marola begs her father not to involve Leandro in the business, but Eguía pleads with her to give him this last chance to get rich. The fact that she loves Leandro makes him the most suitable courier for the cocaine. She is appalled at her father's cynicism (*Final: "¡Padre, deja que te bese!"*).

The sailors try to dissuade Leandro from getting involved with a villain who beats his woman, but he awkwardly argues that Abel was making it all up. When Abel proves him wrong he finally agrees to talk to Eguía alone, and the sailors leave to avoid witnessing the inevitable fight. The ensuing negotiation, however, centers on Leandro's price for fetching a package in his boat and bringing it back that night. If he wants the woman, he can take her. Leandro shakes hands with Eguía on the deal, Marola unhappily fetches drinks, and the rest of the sailors reappear cautiously, surprised to find the deadly rivals smiling together and sharing a bottle. Abel bursts into tears, and Marola comforts him as the curtain falls.

ACT 3, SCENE 1—That night. Leandro and Marola are alone at sea in an open boat. In their *Dúo: "Por el ancho mar"* they take comfort in the power of their love. Suddenly a wind whips up from the northwest: the dreaded *Galerna*. Leandro makes for safety as the storm breaks above their heads, and the scene ends with a triumphant orchestral statement of the love theme, hinting at their salvation with the dawning day. An *Intermedio*, an orchestral repeat of the *Dúo Cómico* from Act 1, leads into the final scene.

SCENE 2—Outside the tavern. The door is barred, and Abel disconsolately repeats his little accordion song *"En la taberna del puerto"* to the waiting sailors. Chinchorro and his crew believe that Leandro and Marola must be at the bottom of the sea. Ripalda is fairly happy that the competition seems to be scuppered, until Antigua announces that she has found a new dive selling all kinds of cheap drinks. Before the sailors can set off, Eguía appears looking haggard. He thinks he sees Marola's ghost and collapses, asking forgiveness and explaining that she was his daughter. The men and women are moved to pity by his powerful disburdening of guilt and grief (*Solo: "No te acerques"*).

Simpson hobbles in, announcing that Marolo and Leandro are alive but have been arrested by the customs officers with the cocaine still in their possession. Everyone calls upon Eguía to take the guilt upon himself, and as the young couple are brought on in handcuffs he embraces them both, confessing his crime and asking the soldiers to arrest him instead (*Final: "Yo sólo fui culpable"*). He is taken away, leaving Marola distraught in Leandro's arms. Simpson asks Ripalda to cook him a stew: otherwise he'll start believing there is a God. Young Abel sadly kisses his accordion, and as the two lovers shut the tavern door behind them, quietly throws it into the harbor.

Toward the end of his long life, Pablo Sorozábal said he was a man who lived with three women: a Russian princess, a Madrid flower girl, and a tavern keeper from the north coast. If *Katiuska* and *La del manojo de rosas* made Sorozábal's reputation, this third addition to the harem *La tabernera del puerto* (The Port Tavernkeeper) made his fortune. Leading librettists Romero and Shaw, working with Sorozábal for the first time in a full-length zarzuela, provided a well-constructed "nautical romance" in three acts, set in his beloved Basque country and rich in seedy characters, strong situations and spectacular stage effects. It is the most conventionally operatic of Sorozábal's zarzuelas, and the most generally admired.

The libretto was originally offered to Jesús Guridi, who was already working on a similar theme. His *Mari-Eli* was eclipsed by Sorozábal's Marola, but the younger composer pays tribute to his fellow Basque in his descriptive sea music, which leans heavily on Guridi's atmospheric *Euzko Irudiak*. There are also hints of *La Mer* and *Tristan und Isolde*; but if this isn't Sorozábal's most sharply personal score, there can be few zarzuelas so generously tuneful. In particular, the sequence of show-stopping numbers in Act 2 for the four principals is rightly famous, Simpson's cavernous, throbbing tango topped by that most popular of all tenor *Romanzas*—Leandro's *"No puede ser"*, made famous worldwide by Plácido Domingo's inclusion of it in the "Three Tenors" concerts:

Adios a la bohemia (Farewell to the Bohemian Life, 1933)
Sorozábal accurately called his forty-five-minute vignette an *ópera chica*. Although it is through-written its scope and subject matter—1900 Madrid with its bars, artists and men about town—ally it to *género chico* zarzuela. Pío Baroja was one of the most vivid writers of the post-Galdós generation, and Sorozábal responded to his sketch of a final parting between a painter and prostitute with music that is terse, brutal and poignantly romantic by turns. The *Prólogo*, delivered by an artistic beggar, is a conscious counterthrust to the famous prologue of Leoncavallo's *Pagliacci*, asking us to remember that what we are about to see is not make-believe, but all too real.

Los burladores (The Tricksters, 1948)
Sorozábal's three-act version of the Don Juan story is unusual, in so far as it ends with both Don Juan and his servant (here called Baratillo) happily married. There are Mozartian allusions in the libretto, notably Baratillo's list of his master's conquests to mirror Leporello's "Catalogue" Aria, but the music is undiluted Sorozábal. The most original scene is a *melodram* for the drunken Corregidor of Madrid; the musical highlight is Don Juan's lyrical *"Queda flotando en esta estancia"*, perhaps the most poised baritone *Romanza* the composer penned.

Las de Caín (Caín's Daughters, with **Pablo Sorozábal** *hijo*, 1958)
Musical comedy in three acts, and the composer's last zarzuela. Sorozábal and his son adapted the libretto from a preexisting play by the Álvarez Quintero brothers which presents a lively picture of fashionable turn-of-the-century Madrid. The plot concerns the attempts of the harassed Don Segismundo Caín to marry off his five troublesome daughters, and the score is more consistently sweet-toothed than the composer's earlier work. The waltzing *Concertante: "Mamá ... hija mía"* and pasodoble *Dúo: "Canta la creación"* are especially effective.

La eterna canción (The Eternal Song, 1945)
An ambitious two-act *sainete*, centered on the lives and loves of a family of poor musicians working in a Madrid café-bar. *"La eterna canción"* is the latest song by composer Don Aníbal, and its melody acts as a *leitmotif* yoking the disparate elements of the score together. Although not so consistently inspired as Sorozábal's pre-Civil War work, the zarzuela still contains much that is memorable. Among the gems are a jazzy *Pasodoble-Dúo*; the steamy *Danzon Cubano* sung in the café-bar, with its floating counter-melody for strings; and the Straussian orchestral *Amanecer* introducing the final scene, a miniature tone poem evoking dawn over modern Madrid.

21
Reveriano Soutullo and Juan Vert

Reveriano Soutullo (1880–1932)

Reveriano Soutullo Otero was born in Punteáreas, Galicia on 11th July 1880. His father was director of the local Municipal Band of Arena, and Soutullo senior gave his son a thorough musical grounding—by the age of sixteen the youngster was competent enough to become cornet soloist for the 37th Murcia Infantry Regiment. Here he received further harmony lessons from the bandmaster, Cetina, before moving on to the Madrid Conservatory. Starting part time in 1900 Soutullo eventually won first prizes for harmony and composition, and after graduating in 1906 he took up scholarships to study in Italy, France with Ravel and Saint-Saëns, Switzerland and Germany before returning to Madrid to make his way as a composer: a promising prospect, as his compositions (over one hundred in all forms by then) had attracted the favorable notice of Ruperto Chapí.

He soon began to make his mark with collaborative zarzuelas such as *La paloma del barrio* (The Local Girl, 1911) with Lorenzo Andreu, 1911; and *Amores de aldea* (Village Loves, 1915) with Pablo Luna, with whom he also collaborated anonymously on *El niño judío* (The Jewish Boy, 1918). In 1919 he began the famous musical partnership with Juan Vert, which continued until the latter's death in 1931. Soutullo did not long survive his younger collaborator, dying after a car crash in Vigo on 29th October 1932. Aside from the works with Vert, he wrote the symphonic suite *Vigo* (1911) marked by fastidious orchestral craftsmanship and Gallic shifts of harmony; and the tuneful pasodoble *Puenteáreas*, in honor of his home town but popular throughout Galicia and the whole of Spain.

Juan Vert (1890–1931)

Juan Vert Carbonell was born in Carcagente in Valencia, 22nd April 1890. As soon as he was old enough he entered the Conservatory in Valencia, studying harmony and composition with Emilio Vega. His progress was sure, and in 1911 he made the move to Madrid to continue studies at the Conservatory (still with Vega) in hopes of a lucrative musical career. In this he was assisted by a wealthy guitar manufacturer, Andrés Marín Simón, who helped pay his way through the difficult postgraduate years. He finally graduated with first prizes in harmony and composition in 1916, marrying Simon's sister-in-law María Ortega, and settling down to life and work in the capital.

His first two solo efforts, the one-act comedy *Las vírgenes paganas* (The Pagan Virgins, 1917) and *El Versalles madrileño* (The Madrid Versailles, 1918), enjoyed some success; and in 1919 he began the musical collaboration with Reveriano Soutullo which until his death. Vert's demise after a cardiac arrest, on 16th February 1931, shocked the capital. He was at the height of his fame, and one of the undoubted leaders of the young generation of *zarzueleros*.

Soutullo and Vert

El capricho de una Reina (A Queen's Caprice, 1919) was their first joint work, but like their first major success, *Guitarras y bandurrias* (Guitars and Bandurrias, 1920) it is now almost completely forgotten. Not so *La leyenda del beso* (The Prophecy of the Kiss, 1924), nor *La del soto del Parral* (The Lady of the House in the Parral, 1927), both of which maintain their hold on the repertoire.

Other popular successes, such as *Encarna, la misterio* (The Mysterious Encarna, 1925) and the revue *Las maravillosas* (Wonderful Women, 1928) have dimmed with time, but their final theatre triumph together, *El último romántico* (The Last Romantic, 1927) is still held in great affection for its gently lilting, Viennese-style melodies and easy charm.

It is difficult to say whether Vert or Soutullo was most largely responsible for the varied strengths of their work together. Well-defined in musical atmosphere, rich in melodic succulence, sophisticated in harmonic and orchestral resource—all three of their major zarzuelas, perhaps preeminently the genuinely realistic *La del soto del Parral*, seem guaranteed a place in the hearts of zarzuela *aficionados* for many years to come.

La leyenda del beso
Zarzuela in two acts
(Madrid, Teatro Apolo, 18th January 1924)

Text: Enrique Reoyo, Antonio Paso Díaz and Silva Aramburu

Principal Characters: Count Mario (baritone); Gorón, his friend (comic tenor); Amapola, a gypsy girl (soprano); Iván, a gypsy (tenor); Ulita, an old gypsy wise woman (actress).

ACT 1—The park of an ancient Castilian castle. An heraldic *Preludio* contrasts aristocratic hunting horns with melancholy romance, as Iván and his tribe sing a gypsy song, complete with tambourines, of love and loss (*Canto:* "*Cantando amarguras*").

The horns resound, and the youthful Lord of the Manor Count Mario appears with fashionable friends of both sexes. They extol the joys of the chase in a jolly *Coro y Canción:* "*¡Que viva Mario!... Tras de la jauría*". Mario must shortly be married, and his friends tease him because this will mean giving up pursuit of one animal at least—beautiful women. Gorón, a waggish Lothario from Madrid, comes in wearing a straw hat which he has taken as a trophy from Simeona, the pretty but naïve fiancée of the brutish Cristóbal. This well-muscled keeper has followed his rival's scent with some fearsome hunting dogs but soon retreats, baffled by Gorón's sophisticated banter.

The gentry settle down to a champagne lunch, during which Gorón continues to boast of his conquests. Simeona's father, the old keeper Juan, tells Mario that a tribe of gypsies has asked permission to camp in the castle grounds for a few days. The young Count receives Iván with a group of gypsies who sing in praise of their wandering life (*Canto:* "*Caminar sin fin*"); and after a short dance, the beautiful Amapola steps forward to finish the song ("*Mi canción quiere fingir*") with the rest of the tribe.

Their chief Alesko formally asks permission for a two-day stay. Mario grants it willingly, provided the gypsies agree to entertain his friends with a gypsy zambra dance before they leave. He is evidently attracted to Amapola, and detains her when the others leave to be fed and watered inside the castle. She meets his compliments with fatalistic gloom and when Iván disturbs them Mario leaves, fascinated by the mystery. The young gypsy himself is obsessed with Amapola, but she makes it clear she does not want him in their proudly matched *Dúo:* "*Amor mi raza sabe conquistar*".

Alesko and Ulita, an old gypsy wise woman, thank Mario for his hospitality before returning to their camp with Iván and Amapola. The simple Simeona runs in, pursued both by the jealous dog-handler and her father, Juan, who attempts to make peace and drags Cristóbal off. Gorón takes advantage of his absence with a further assault on the girl's not unyielding virtue, before Cristóbal returns in pursuit. Simeona runs off, and Gorón again succeeds in pulling the wool over the baffled keeper's eyes.

Mario's friends Alfonso and Ernesto come in search of Gorón to join in a merry jape. The three "serenade" their female friends Ketty, Margot and Charito with a noisy ringing of bells (*Pasodoble: "Seguidme, troveros"*). The love-smitten Mario teaches them how to do it properly in a graciously civilized *Serenata: "Oye, hermosa prisionera"*.

The ladies join the party, and are enjoying some good-humored mockery of Mario's sudden infatuation when a loud scream disturbs them. Hurrying to the spot they find Amapola cornered by a wild boar. Mario returns with the terrified gypsy in his arms. Moved by his declaration of love, she almost allows him to kiss her; but at the last moment she fends him off, telling the confused Count that the touch of her lips will be fatal to him (*Dúo: "¡Gran dios! ... Oye, gitana"*).

Old Ulima emerges from the gloom to explain Amapola's behavior. The girl's mother, a *femme fatale* whose life was ruined by her beauty, returned to her tribe to die. With her last breath the woman prophesied a terrible fate for her young daughter—whoever kisses Amapola's lips will die. The wise woman vanishes with Amapola, leaving Mario to swear that he will take that kiss, though it may cost him his life.

ACT 2, SCENE 1—The gypsy camp. In their *Canción: "Quien trabaja cantando"* the Romanies, led by Gurko, praise their wandering life as they prepare for the zambra: though Iván moodily sharpens a knife (*"Hecho de un rayo de luna"*). He is determined to settle accounts with Mario, although Aleko and Ulita do their best to make him see reason. Gorón strolls in for some amorous byplay with an inviting gypsy, Coral. Some of her friends join the pair as the Madrid man-about-town attempts to teach the gypsies to dance in the Paris fashion. The result is the lively and unexpected Gypsy Foxtrot (*Fox: "Qué vaivén tiene el fox"*).

Mario and his friends settle down for the festivities. After a formal invitation from Aleko, Amapola steps forward to read Mario's fortune. She foretells that his love will be his sorrow, and warns him to avoid it. Aleko takes the gentry off to look at some gypsy trinkets; and after another incursion from Cristóbal and his dogs on the scent of Simeona, Mario is able to speak to Amapola alone. He persuades her to meet him by the castle steps that evening, though she warns him once again that she must leave on the morrow.

Cristóbal drags Simeona in. She is determined to go for a cool bathe in the river, whatever he says. All he can do is conceal himself in the bushes to make sure that nobody else joins her. Gorón has bought himself a bearskin in the camp, with the idea of frightening Simeona out of the water and into the woods. The resulting spectacle as "the bear" chases the nearly naked Simeona out of the water, pursued by Cristóbal and his dogs, gives Mario and his friends much amusement as they settle down to watch the zambra, a spectacular sequence of dark, rhythmic song and dance, performed by Amapola, Coral and the other gypsy girls (*Zambra: "Tiene el son de mi cantar . . . Niña qie no tiene amores"*).

Mario proposes a toast to Amapola's dark eyes, but Iván jealously dashes the glass from his hand. Alesko and Ulita ask the Count's pardon, and the scene ends with the gypsies taking up their song and dance (*Brindis: "¡Oh, licor! que das la vida"*). The famous *Intermedio*, with its inexorable tread and dark evocation of fatal passion, leads to the last scene.

SCENE 2—The castle steps, by moonlight. Mario waits anxiously for Amapola, and nothing the chastened Gorón and his friends can offer in the way of entertainment can tempt him back inside. Amapola comes to him, and at the ardent climax of their *Dúo: "¿Vendrás, mujer? Mi corazón te aguarda"* they kiss.

Iván is swiftly on the scene, but before he can knife his rival Ulita interposes: he must let the Prophecy of the Kiss do its work, not his knife. The old woman implores Amapola to depart with them, and called by the spirit of her mother the girl goes quickly, leaving Mario to brood on the fatal prophecy. His friends find him too late: Amapola's kiss and departure has indeed killed all his hopes, and left him nothing but despair.

The libretto of *La leyenda del beso* (The Prophecy of the Kiss), an attempt to cross the gypsy tragedy of *La tempranica* with the gentrified hunt comedy of *La montería*, is not its strong suit. The elevated tone of the encounters between Count Mario and his gypsy love, Amapola, is undermined by a bevy of sentimentally well-bred Romanies and a coarse comedy subplot which would not be out of place in a fifth-rate Jacobean tragedy. The anticipated bloody conclusion is sidestepped in favor of an implausibly damp squib, as the "prophecy" proves true only in a metaphorical sense.

This threadbare farrago is almost completely redeemed by Soutullo and Vert's strong score. At first glance, much of it may seem like Poor Man's Puccini—indeed, the Act 1 *dúo* for Mario and Amapola quotes *Madama Butterfly* almost verbatim—but their potent evocation of the gypsy tribe is more original, and as melodically rich as anything the partnership wrote. The oft-played *Intermedio*, a strong if unsubtle piece of musical Spanishry, is only the best-known number in a score which is full of life and power.

The Act 2 *Zambra* is a thrilling set piece, with the unlikely Gypsy Foxtrot not far behind. The duets for the fatal Amapola with Mario have great charm, but perhaps the finest number is her intensely melancholy confrontation with the luckless Iván. The clash of indifference with passion always seemed to bring out the best in Spanish composers, and Soutullo and Vert were no exception. Two of the most memorable gypsy themes recur as *leitmotifs* to bind their score together: Iván's *"Caminar sin fin"*; and his related *"Amor mi raza sabe conquistar"*, which almost comes to stand for the fateful prophecy itself.

La del soto del Parral
Zarzuela in two acts
(Madrid, Teatro de la Latina, 26th October 1927)

Text: Luis Fernández de Sevilla and Anselmo Cuadrado Carreño

Principal Characters: Germán, a farmer (baritone); Aurora, his wife (soprano); Miguel, a landowner (tenor); Damián (comic tenor); Catalina (soprano); Tío Prudencio, an old village poet (actor); Tío Sabino (tenor or baritone).

ACT 1 —The edge of a country village near Segovia, one Sunday morning in September, mid-nineteenth century. The scene is dominated by a handsome farmhouse shaded by impressive trees, El soto del Parral (The arbor in the Parral). Past events are crucial to the events of the zarzuela. The tenant farmer Germán once saved the life of Miguel, son and heir of the old squire, and the two young men became fast friends. Miguel inherited the property, and respected a clause in the old man's will enabling Germán and his wife Aurora to work toward buying their farm and house outright. Miguel has now fallen in love with Angelita, a mysterious girl who lives locally, while a mysterious unease has clouded the happiness of Germán and his wife.

It is a day of fiesta. After a brief orchestral *Preludio* evoking the bright morning sunshine, the curtain rises on a group of farm workers praising the beauty of the Segovian land, as they walk to a hermitage to pay their respects. (*Coro: "Voz de la Campana"*). We hear the distant voice of Germán blessing his luck in having such a farm, and such a wife as Aurora (*Solo: "No hay en tierras de Segovia"*). A group of local lads make fun of Bruno the village idiot, and beat him with a stick (*Coro: "No hay un tonto"*, often cut in performance) before Germán concludes his morning song of praise.

Damián, a lazy young farmhand, is intent on having a snooze under the trees; but the village elder and local quack Tío Sabino ("wise uncle") berates him for his illness—idleness—and sends him about his business. Catalina, young housemaid at the farm and Damián's intended bride, directs a volley of insulting banter at her departing lover, and Sabino tells her that this "illness" may make it unwise for Damián to marry. A rustic would-be poet, old Tío Prudencio ("prudent uncle"), tries to read some doggerel entitled "Of Love and Of Jealousy"; but his recital is cut short by the mistress of the house, Aurora, who enters in no good temper, and orders all of them back to work to prepare for the fiesta celebrations.

Prudencio sits under a tree to compose his poem; and when Germán comes in singing he punctures the farmer's good mood, warning that happiness never lasts. When Aurora comes out of the house to speak to her husband she interprets his preoccupied air as loss of affection, and though he tries to laugh it off he is silent when she accuses him of keeping some secret from her. Left alone, Germán hears the sound of singing from across the fields, and in a famous *romanza* he contrasts his troubled situation with the carefree happiness of the farmhands: how he yearns for a return to the blissful earlier times with his beloved wife (*Romanza: "Los cantos alegres . . . Ya mis horas felices"*).

Miguel comes to the farmhouse, looking for his darling Angelita. Germán and Aurora greet him warmly but the farmer becomes uneasy when talk turns to the saintly nature of Miguel's late father, welcoming the distraction when Prudencio offers to read his latest poetic effusion, a poem about beauty. Prudencio congratulates Miguel on his coming marriage, Germán pointedly sends him about his business, and the three friends enter the house. Damián sneaks in for a doze under the trees, but Catalina spies him and the pair hurl high-spirited banter at one another before launching into an affectionate, sparring duet (*Dúo cómico: "Que soy la más linda"*). After discussing their mutual lack of qualifications for marriage—Damián's attitude to work is matched by Catalina's dubious talents as a cook—they happily go about their business.

Germán uneasily broaches the subject of Angelita to Miguel, warning his friend not to contemplate marriage with the girl, as she is unworthy. Miguel, offended by his friend's lack of support, demands proof of such assertions and leaves to question Angelita. As Germán sadly goes back into the house, the workers return from the fields. The lads court the girls in the graceful and expansive *Coro: "Al fin de la faena"* (often known as *Ronda de los enamoradas*, or Lovers' Round). Prudencio argues with Sabino, claiming that Angelita has a long-standing liaison with Germán, who married Aurora out of convenience, an accusation Sabino dismisses as idle gossip.

Aurora has overheard. Though Sabino assures her the rumors are nonsense, she tells him that true or not, the pride of *"la del soto del Parral"* (the lady of the house) will not be mocked. Once alone she breaks down, unable to rid her mind of her husband's infidelity (*Solo: "Mintió su cariño"*). When the furious Miguel storms in, having come to the same conclusions and determined to fight Germán, the broken-hearted Aurora loyally bars the door (*Dúo: "Quiero la infamia"*). Sabino drags Miguel away, and the act ends as Aurora tells her husband that she knows all about his infidelity. Angrily he orders her back into the house, and sets off to talk to Angelita himself.

ACT 2, SCENE 1—A room inside the farmhouse, three days later. In the afternoon sunshine Catalina is embroidering her trousseau and keeping Damián at bay, as they are to be married the very next day; though Sabino frightens the young man by taking his pulse and telling him he has a terrible illness, the only cure for which is work. A group of eager young girls approach the quack for advice on how to make themselves more attractive to the men, and Sabino treats them with a flirtatious laying on of hands (*Coro de la consulta: "¿A la consulta se puede entrar?"*). Aurora is out of her mind, as Germán has been away for three days, but Sabino again assures her of her husband's good faith. She calms down, though her composure is severely tested when Miguel informs her that Germán has been seen sneaking out of Angelita's house. If this turns out to be true, Aurora vows that she will leave her beloved farmhouse, never to return.

[In his *Romanza: "Fuerza que me vence"* Miguel sings of his pride in the Segovian landscape, contrasted with his own bitter plight. This was cut before the premiere, to be recycled in the later *El último romántico* as *"Bella enamorada"*, but is sometimes reinstated today.] Damián tries to hint to the squire about wedding presents, but Miguel is too distracted to pay him much attention and leaves. Prudencio is delighted with all this new material for his tragic love poem, though when Catalina comes in the young couple mock him mercilessly until he is goaded into paying them back with a flight of verbal rodomontade.

All is quiet when Germán finally returns to the farmhouse. He tells Sabino what has happened, and at last we learn the truth. Germán and Sabino alone know Angelita's secret. For years she was the mistress of the old landowner, who confessed all on his deathbed and made them vow never to reveal the truth. Germán's loyalty is clear, and he has tried—so far without success—to persuade Angelita to leave the district without revealing her past to Miguel. Sabino praises his honorable behavior, and leaves husband and wife together. Germán's passionate avowal of love, however much the evidence might seem to conspire against him, renews Aurora's faith; and in a warm duet she agrees to believe and trust him fully once again (*Dúo: "Ten pena de mis dolores"*).

The interfering Prudencio has come to give Germán a message: Angelita wants to meet him next day at a cabin in the glen. At first Germán indignantly refuses, but then has an idea: he will meet Angelita, and asks Prudencio to spy on them to gain material for his romantic poem. Miguel comes back to pick a quarrel, still believing he has been shamefully betrayed. Aurora and Sabino intervene, but Germán responds to Miguel's taunts and the scene ends with the two men agreeing to meet and fight it out (*Final: "¿Qué buscas?"*).

SCENE 2—The road through a glen near the farmhouse, next day. Sabino and Prudencio are still arguing about the affair, and even Sabino is shaken when Prudencio tells him about the assignation at the cabin, which he has naturally let slip to Miguel. Sabino spies the bridal party coming down the road after the ceremony at the hermitage, and orders Prudencio to keep quiet. Damián and Catalina, together with Aurora, the village people and some musicians, burst onto the scene in all their wedding finery. Damián encourages everyone to dance, and Aurora leads them all in a celebratory song praising the rich Segovian land (*Canto: "En la cumbre nace el agua"*).

"As a matter of conscience," Prudencio tells Aurora about Germán's assignation. It seems Aurora's faith in her husband is to be shattered once and for all, until the brokenhearted Miguel appears and assures her that Germán is as honorable, loving and true to his wife as any man living. He knows all, having overheard the farmer's heated conversation with Angelita in the cabin, at the end of which she has agreed to leave the district for the peace of the whole village. When Germán reappears he is swiftly reconciled to both wife and friend. Harmony is fully restored, and as the curtain falls the dance begins again for the folk of the "arbor in the Parral."

Of the zarzuelas written together by Soutullo and Vert, *La del soto del Parral* (The Lady of the House in the Parral) is the most frequently performed. Carreño and Sevilla's Parral is as close as Spanish theatre gets to the realistic rural society of Mascagni's *Cavalleria Rusticana*. Such genuine realism is markedly different from *verismo*, the world of Leoncavallo's opera *Pagliacci*, *Las golondrinas* or Luna's *La pícara molinera*, which present sensational melodrama in a popular setting. The drama of *La del soto del Parral* is markedly unsensational to the point of self-denial. How many writers would have kept the shady Angelina, mainspring of the plot, offstage throughout? The central characters are a well-matched husband and wife, and the nearest approach to bad behavior is the curiosity of the local poetaster, old Tío Prudencio, desperate for some real-life romance to inspire his latest doggerel epic.

The two composers produced a score consistently strong on melody, color and atmosphere. The choral and orchestral numbers paint an attractive picture of the Segovian countryside and its people, and Aurora's duets with her husband and Miguel bring unusual operatic situations to vivid life. Best-known of all is Germán's *Romanza: "Ya mis horas felices"*, justifiably popular in gala concerts around the world. This is that operatic rarity, a love song from a husband to his faithful wife, and Soutullo and Vert made the most of the opportunity with a powerful display of passionate lyricism and formal subtlety:

El último romántico (The Last Romantic, 1927)
Soutullo and Vert came close to the sweet-toothed, sentimental world of Viennese operetta in this two-act zarzuela, their last major triumph before the latter's death. The love of Madrid aristocrats Enrique (tenor) and Aurora (mezzo-soprano) is shattered by time and revolutionary chance, but fifteen years later they meet again and are able to find happiness together. The score has lightweight charm. Its most memorable "hit" number, Enrique's graceful *Romanza: "Bella enamorada"*, was ironically cut from *La del soto del Parral* for holding up the action, but found its place here with a brand new, very neatly turned, text.

22
Tomás López Torregrosa
(1868–1913)

Born in Alicante on 24th September 1868, Torregrosa trained at the Madrid Conservatory where his composition tutor was Chapí, a sure sign that great things were expected of the young student. On graduation he was immediately appointed as a conductor at the Teatro Apolo, where he rapidly established himself as a leading composer of incidental music and short *género chico* zarzuelas, sometimes in collaboration with other composers, notably "Quinito" Valverde.

His first notable success was *La banda de trompetas* (The Trumpet Band, 1896) to a text by Carlos Arniches. *El pobre diablo* (Poor Devil, 1897) written with "Quinito" to a text by Celso Lucio, is a modern *revista* where Madrid's Seven Deadly Sins are bad enough to shock even the devil—shades of Ben Jonson's *The Devil is an Ass*. *El primer reserva* (The First Exception, 1897, also with "Quinito") was a prelude to the appearance of his best works, *El santo de la Isidra* (Isidra's Saint) and *La fiesta de San Antón* (The Fiesta of Saint Anthony, both 1898 to texts by Arniches), which well deserve their place among the best-loved one-act *sainetes* and have often formed a double bill together.

Of his later works only the short *El pobre Valbuena* (Poor Valbuena, 1904, again with "Quinito") proved as popular. This too had Carlos Arniches as librettist, together with Enrique García Álvarez, and its musical content is slight. Torregrosa continued to compose *sainetes* (as well as operetta-style pieces and revues) until his regrettably early death in Madrid on 23rd June 1913, without ever quite scaling the heights many of his contemporaries had expected. Certainly none of his more ambitious pieces, despite such resonant titles as *La muerte de Agripina* (The Death of Agrippina, 1902) achieved anything like the success of the 1898 pair, both of which are full of fresh melody and strong situation. Torregrosa's own personality is elusive, though perhaps he might be described as the sentimentalist's Chueca. A century on his reputation has certainly declined, but the two popular *sainetes* are sure to keep Torregrosa's name alive for some time to come.

La fiesta de San Antón
Sainete in one act
(Madrid, Teatro Apolo, 25th November 1898)

Text: Carlos Arniches

Principal Characters: Antonio, a saddler (tenor); Regina (soprano); Felipa (mezzo-soprano); Eusebio (actor); Genara, his wife (actress); Señor Ramón (actor).

SCENE 1—A downtown Madrid street. Antonio Olmedo, a handsome saddler and great favorite with the girls, is dismounting from his horse outside his house. Assorted locals are enjoying a drink and watching the world go by ... a fortune teller with his birds, some bargaining at a fruit stall ... a pot boy brings drinks and the Falstaffian Señor Ramón complains to Antonio about short measure (*Escena: "Paco, dile el chico"*).

Antonio treats his companions to drinks and cigars; but when he has left, one of them, the pessimistic Eusebio, talks critically to a jolly fellow known as El Pintao (blotchy-faced) about the handsome saddler. It is rumored that Antonio has been two-timing his faithful girlfriend Regina—the only woman in Eusebio's eyes who can really make him happy—with an icily handsome barmaid called Felipa. El Pintao speaks up for Antonio, emphasizing his essential decency. The pair listen in the shadows when Antonio returns with Señor Ramón. He asks the cynical old man for advice on what to tell Regina, now he no longer wants her. Left alone, he admits that his feelings aren't quite so clear-cut, and curses his uncertainty before heading off into the bar after Ramón.

Eusebio's wife Genara comes in with her husband's lunch. She tells him and El Pintao of a distressing encounter she has witnessed between Regina and Felipa with her calculating mother Leoncia. After physically separating the women she advised Regina to have it out with Antonio and Felipa next day; but in the cold light of day Genara feels that this could lead to serious trouble.

Eusebio unwillingly agrees to reason with Antonio; but the saddler refuses to hear Eusebio's faltering objections and goes into his house. Genara spies Felipa and her mother coming and sees red, but Eusebio drags her away before she can do any more damage. Felipa tells her mother and Ramón that she doesn't really care one way or the other about the well-heeled Antonio, but might as well have him as not. When the saddler joins them, Leoncia and the duplicitous Ramón (who sees Antonio as an easy touch) leave the lovers alone. Felipa wants Antonio to meet her in her bar the following day, the fiesta of Saint Anthony, in order to let Regina know exactly how things stand. He equivocates, but ends up agreeing to her request (*Dúo: "¿Qué es lo que te pasa?"*).

Regina appears. Eusebio advises her to accept the situation, but she remains determined to speak with Antonio. In a scene of operatic intensity, Regina prepares to face the worst (*Escena: "¡Ay, que me encuentro más triste!"*). She hears Antonio strumming his guitar and singing a *Soleares* to entertain his new friends, but though the song is like a dagger in her heart she stays firm in her resolve. A housemaid alerts the inmates to her presence and silence reigns for a moment. Then Felipa comes outside and the inevitable heated exchanges which follow attract a crowd into the street. Regina cries out to Antonio, who tells her firmly that he no longer loves her. The crowd melts away leaving Regina lonely, with the renewed sound of Antonio's guitar song inside the house ringing in her ears.

SCENE 2—A Madrid street the following day. In a verbal interlude two low-life characters, El Tulipa and El Mangas, discuss the news. Can it really be true that Felipa has hooked the wealthy saddler? Yes, because the indigent Señor Ramón has confirmed it and could do well by setting up the match. They hurry to the bar to see for themselves.

SCENE 3—Felipa's bar. To the sounds of a honky-tonk pianola, the customers led by the riotous Señor Ramón and Leoncia are celebrating the fiesta. Tulipa and Mangas arrive, but Ramón warns them to stay away until Antonio has committed himself. The saddler arrives and buys drinks all round, but before he can toast Felipa the crowd parts and Regina interposes. The two women fight like tigresses until Eusebio and Genara manage to separate them, while the despairing Antonio takes to his horse and gallops off.

There is a sudden commotion: the horse has thrown its rider, and soon Antonio is carried back apparently more dead than alive. After an apothecary administers first aid and affirms that his injuries are slight, Antonio opens his eyes. He realizes that he cannot bear to lose Regina, and wishes Felipa good luck and good-bye. She coldly turns her back and goes into the bar with her wrangling mother and Señor Ramón, as Regina cradles her repentant lover. The delighted Eusebio and Genara look on happily, and beg the audience to pardon the faults of the play as the curtain falls.

La fiesta de San Antón (The Fiesta of Saint Anthony) is the darker of the two 1898 collaborations between writer and composer, much more strongly focused on the seamy side of Madrid life and loves than *El santo de la Isidra*. Arniches' characters are strongly drawn, his dialogue fluid and amusing. The sentimentally implausible conclusion, in which a concussion brings the hero back to his moral senses, is its only real blemish. Torregrosa's music only covers the first of the three scenes, but his four numbers are of high quality. The galloping rhythms which bind the *Preludio*, itself based on the main theme of the flamboyant *Dúo* for Felipa and Antonio, make clever allusion to the hero's trade and horsy nemesis. The street scene which follows is a lively example of that typical *género chico* mixture of spoken dialogue and song.

Most remarkable is the highly operatic scene centered on Regina which closes Torregrosa's contribution. The inspired, major key string melody which accompanies her expression of sadness is never sung by the soprano, who instead provides an *arioso* accompaniment to the primary orchestral material, in a rarely beautiful Spanish example of a technique associated with Puccini. The intensity is if anything enhanced by the intrusive offstage *Soleares* with its *punteado* (strumming) guitar accompaniment. Although what follows is more conventional, the scene remains Torregrosa's finest achievement, one of the most striking in Spanish stage music of its epoch:

El santo de la Isidra
Sainete in one act
(Madrid, Teatro Apolo, 19th February 1898)

Text: Carlos Arniches

Principal Characters: Matías (bass); Isidra, his daughter (soprano); Ignatia, his wife (actress); Epifanio, Isidra's suitor (baritone); Venancio, a baker (tenor); Eulogio, a cobbler (actor).

SCENE 1—A small plaza in a poor neighborhood of Madrid, at the end of the nineteenth century. A brief *Preludio* culminating in the street cry of a flower seller leads directly into the action. Two lovers, Cirila and Secundino, are enjoying some amorous banter under the eye of the local cobbler, Eulogio. He hears them make a date to dance that evening at the fiesta of Saint Isidro at the Pradera, the town meadow on the bank of the Manzanares river. When they leave, Eulogio gives the news to the bashful Pérez, who would like to accompany Cirila there himself.

Eulalio observes a fight brewing inside the nearby tavern between Señor Matías and Epifanio, an arrogant thug engaged to the old man's daughter Isidra, very clearly without any goodwill from the family (*Dúo:* "*¡Toma, granuja!*"). Epifanio eventually leaves with his friend El Rosca (wheedler), boasting that he will dance with Isidra next day at the Pradera, come what might. Isidra calms her father down, but Eulogio senses that the girl herself is tiring of her lover's belligerent behavior. The cobbler feels that she would be better suited to the baker Venancio, a hard-working, steady man who secretly loves her deeply; and he determines to sound out her mother Ignatia on the matter.

Ignatia is quickly convinced of the benefits of his matchmaking plan, especially when Eulogio observes that her daughter is not badly disposed toward Venancio. The cobbler engineers a "chance" meeting between Isidra and the baker, who plucks up courage to approach the girl. In a gentle *Dúo: "Anda, y desembucha"* he proves too shy to speak his mind directly, eventually deciding to buy a bunch of carnations to speak for him.

The course of true love is interrupted by Epifanio's return with El Rosca. The thug issues a threat to Venancio, warning him to steer clear of his property. The normally gentle baker is about to go for his throat when Isidra and Eulogio intervene; Epifanio goes into the tavern, sneering at his fiancée as well as the baker. A crowd gathers, led by Isidra, ready to stroll down to the Pradera (*Final: "Alegre es la mañana"*). The girl refuses to confirm that she will dance with Epifanio, despite his hectoring, and Matías adds that she may dance with whomsoever she pleases. When Isidra announces that she would even prefer to dance with Venancio, the supremely self-assured Epifanio merely goes back into the tavern with a threatening laugh.

SCENE 2—The Toledo Bridge leading to the Pradera. Secundino is searching for Cirila in the crowd. She turns up with her baby sister in tow, much to his annoyance; but eventually they set off for the fiesta, pursued by the jealous Pérez and his military friend Torrija.

SCENE 3—The fair on the Pradera. Barkers hawk their wares, and the crowd exuberantly enjoys the entertainments on offer (*Coro: "Con tres ó cuatro orquestas"*). Secundino has arrived with Cirila and the child; but thanks to some military distractions from Torrija, Pérez manages to disappear into the crowd with Cirila, leaving Secundino cursing his luck—and holding the baby!

Isidra arrives with her parents and their friends. They consider the various treats on offer, until to mass delight an *organillo* (barrel organ) starts up, and the dance begins. Epifanio turns up in truculent mood with El Rosca, but when he demands a dance Isidra turns him down point-blank, nor will anyone else consent to dance with the overconfident braggart.

Venancio and Eulogio saunter in, and to her father's surprise Isidra has no hesitation in agreeing to dance with the baker. It's now Venancio's turn to taunt Epifanio, who despite his threats is too cowardly to respond and becomes the butt of general humor. Goaded into a jealous frenzy the thug produces a razor, but he is quickly bested by Venancio and leaves crestfallen with his weasel-like friend. The *sainete* ends as all unite in praise of the happy young couple, who lead the interrupted dance with redoubled zest.

Of the twin *sainetes* from 1898 that keep Torregrosa's name alive today, this is the earlier and more high-spirited. The title *El santo de la Isidra*—literally Isidra's Saint, the wise cobbler Eulalio who behaves like a sort of *madrileño* Hans Sachs—also plays on the name of the Saint whose festival occasions the action of Arniches' sentimental sketch. Saint Isidro (d. 15th May 1172) is Madrid's patron, a farmer who consecrated his life to work in the city and whose tomb lies in the great Church dedicated in his name, close to the Plaza Mayor.

The composer's twenty-minute contribution is gracious and lively by turns, with both moods present in the short *Preludio* which sets the musical tone precisely. Torregrosa is at his most distinctive in portraying delicately nuanced sentiment, and the *Dúo* between Isidra and her hesitant lover is the highspot of his genial score.

El pobre Valbuena (Poor Valbuena, with **"Quinito" Valverde**, 1904)
Carlos Arniches and Enrique García Álvarez wrote this typically farcical one-act *sainete* of low-life Madrid, very popular in its time but little seen nowadays. The roguish Valbuena pretends to suffer from a fainting sickness, which he uses as a means to extricate himself from tricky situations, amorous and financial. The Japanese Polka and *Habanera del pompóm*, guying the rhythm of the popular dance, are the best-known pieces in the very brief score.

23
José María Usandizaga
(1887–1915)

Born 31st March 1887 in San Sebastián, chief city of the Basque country, José María Usandizaga Soraluce was the first son of the resident Uruguayan Consul. As a nine-year-old he composed his first piece, a waltz, and showed such enthusiasm for music that his parents agreed to let him study at the local conservatory. By the time he left for Paris in 1901 to complete his training at the Schola Cantorum, he was already recognized as an extraordinary and precocious talent. In Paris he studied (as would Jesús Guridi) with Vincent D'Indy, extending his stay until 1906 to work with Paul Dukas.

Many of his orchestral, choral and chamber works date from the Paris years. The orchestral *Suite in A*, *Dans la Mer*, and *Obertura Sinfónica* reflect his teacher's belief in rigorous formal concision; though the fine String Quartet Op. 31 has greater amplitude and expressive scope. Usandizaga's music after his return to San Sebastián shows increasing harmonic daring, and in works such as the *Rhapsody on 3 Basque Popular Songs* and the Fantastic Dance *Hassan y Melihah* (1912), with its oriental marketplace and lively circus ambience, a distinct personality is clearly emerging. His health was never strong, and perhaps sensing that time was short, he set about the writing of the three stage works which were to occupy him exclusively until his death from consumption on 6th October 1915, at the age of twenty eight.

The first of these, the Basque pastoral folk-opera *Mendi Mendiyan*, was performed in Bilbao in 1910 and attracted favorable attention from many critics and composers for its youthful, fresh directness. The last was the unfinished *La llama* (The Flame), completed by his brother Ramón and premiered in its final three-act form in San Sebastián early in 1918. Although admired for its musical consistency, *La llama*—unsurprisingly given the circumstances of its composition—was generally held not to pack the emotional punch of the central work of Usandizaga's stage trilogy.

This was the lyric drama in three acts *Las golondrinas* (The Wanderers), written at white heat between late September and mid-December of 1913 and performed in Madrid a few weeks later. Its sensational success saw the young composer hailed as the most exciting musical hero Spain had known for many years. How far knowledge of his fragile state of health contributed to the wave of enthusiasm is impossible to say, but there is more than enough in *Las golondrinas* musically to account for it. No wonder the sense of loss attending his death the following year was greater than any Spanish music had previously felt, at least since the equally premature demise of Arriaga nearly a hundred years before. Still, *Las golondrinas* is far more than a work of mere promise. It is a mature achievement, with a unique place as the only *verismo* tragedy in the zarzuela repertoire.

Las golondrinas
Lyric drama in three acts
(Madrid, Teatro Price, 5th February 1914)

Text: Gregorio and María Lejarraga de Martínez Sierra

Principal Characters: Roberto, a theatrical manager (baritone); Lina, his daughter (soprano); Cecilia, an actress (mezzo-soprano); Puck, an actor (baritone); Juanito and Boby, actors (actors).

ACT 1—A temporary dressing cabin in the square of a small town in Castile. After the stirring *Preludio*, we meet the touring theatre troupe engaged to provide a show for the local fiesta. The leader of the company, Roberto, is a hardened drinker who has known better days. With him are his young daughter Lina, a promising singer-dancer; two bright hopefuls, Juanito and Boby; the beautiful leading lady Cecilia; and Puck, talented mainspring of the operation (*Escena: "Aquí tiene usted la peluca"*).

Puck is involved with Cecilia, but she is ambitious, sickened by the continual wandering from town to town and yearning for the wealth and fame her beauty deserves. Lina, herself hopelessly in love with the handsome Puck, sees which way the wind is blowing when Cecilia tells her a little of her unhappiness (*Dúo: "Camino sempre"*). Puck's love is no compensation for this living from hand to mouth. Not for her the noble life of the road of which Puck sings so passionately (*Romanza: "Caminar, caminar"*). His passion merely irritates Cecilia whose frustration boils over into withering scorn; and Puck, goaded past breaking point, hits her and rushes away in self-disgust (*Dúo: "Fuego de paja en el viento"*). Young Lina meanwhile sings with quiet melancholy of her own unrequited love, hoping that time may change Puck's feelings (*Romanza: "Me diches che ya no mi quieres"*).

The townfolk crowd in, ready to enjoy themselves at the show (*Coro: "Noche clara de San Juan"*). Lina, seeing Cecilia heading off with her suitcase, tries in vain to stop her from leaving them in the lurch. The older woman tells Lina that she must have the money, fame and comforts which are now denied her, and the girl's plea that she is breaking Puck's heart falls on deaf ears (*Escena: "No lo sé, voy un busca de algo"*). Cecilia leaves. Lina, blaming herself and knowing she will have to break the news to Puck, who is out front starting his pitch for the show, consoles herself with the thought that perhaps after all things will turn out for the best.

ACT 2—A theatre in a large city, the following spring. The combined talents of Puck, Lina and the two young comedians have attracted the interests of a powerful impresario. Now they are about to make their debut at his theatre in the capital as the "Family Sanders", with a new *Pantomima* or dance-piece put together by Boby and based on the well-known characters and story of the Italian *commedia dell'arte*, Columbina-Lina, Harlequin-Puck, and Pulchinello. Lina takes heart, hoping that she and Puck can put old memories behind them and make a new start (*Romanza: "En viejas memorias"*).

Meanwhile Juanito, who is to play Pulchinello, has his own problems, being pestered beyond endurance by Puck's dresser Leonor and the whole of the admiring female chorus (*Canción y Coro: "Juanito, Juanito, Juanito"*). Lina confesses to Leonor that she loves Puck; but when the kindly dresser tells her that she is sure the feeling is reciprocated, Lina admits that deep down she knows he can feel no more than a brotherly love for her. Puck comes in with Juanito: all is ready for the stage show.

Their *Pantomima*, a substantial orchestral number incorporating mime action and a Serenade for Harlequin (*"Columbina, Columbina bella"*) is a huge success. Another artist had been watching their triumphant performance: Cecilia, now herself wildly successful as La Bella Nelly. With her powerful protector Count Stein in tow, she tells the impresario she wishes to join his company, an offer he cannot refuse. Puck and especially Lina are rapturously applauded, and things are looking up even for Roberto, who is regaining some of his old self-respect as nominal leader of the troupe (*Coro y escena final: "¡Que Linda es Columbina!"*). When he discovers Cecilia in the crowd, Puck moves toward her. The Count sweeps her away, and when Lina tries to stop Puck from following he shakes her off violently and leaves.

ACT 3, SCENE 1—Lina's dressing room. In spite of their triumph and his affection for the faithful and increasingly famous Lina, Puck is remote and distant from her (*Dúo: "¡Oh, Puck!, Por tí mi corazón"*). A familiar laugh echoes from the dressing room, and Puck's instant distraction at the sound of his old love fills Lina with terrible foreboding. The unexpected return of Cecilia has divided the "Family Sanders." Although Roberto is all for it, Lina is adamant La Bella Nelly must not join the company, especially when Cecilia insolently tells her she will reclaim Puck whenever she wants. Then Puck reappears and Lina, understanding that her situation is hopeless, leaves him alone with her rival. Cecilia spitefully goes along with his passionate avowals, pretending to feelings she does not have. They slip away together (*Dúo: "Cecilia ... ¡Habla!"*), after which a vibrant *Intermedio* recaps many of the work's major melodies.

SCENE 2—The same. Lina returns to her dressing room, and when a clearly distraught Puck materializes and stammers out a final farewell, she demands to know what has happened. Puck decides to speak out (*Dúo: "¡Adios! ... Me fui con ella"*). He tells her that when he took Cecilia into the wings and tried to kiss her, she laughed in his face (*Solo: "¡Se reía!"*) and told him she loved another man. Mad with jealous rage, Puck has strangled her. Lina is horrified, but still clings to her beloved when the police rush in with the full company to arrest him. Boby accuses Puck of Cecilia's murder, and he confesses. Before they are finally torn apart Puck asks for and receives Lina's forgiveness (*Final: "Estrella de mí camino"*). Heartbroken, she collapses into her father's arms as the curtain falls.

Las golondrinas (The Wanderers) holds a unique place in the history of zarzuela. It is a no-holds barred *verismo* tragedy in three acts, comparatively unleavened by comic relief. To some extent its composer's early demise has glamorized the reputation of his work. Certainly the Martínez Sierras' libretto, based on their own play *Saltimbanquis* (Mountebanks) is pretty squarely indebted to Leoncavallo's *Pagliacci*, though their three main characters are more three-dimensional creations than Canio, Nedda and the rest. The original zarzuela version with spoken dialogue is now neglected in favor of the through-written operatic version made by Usandizaga's brother in 1929. Ramón did his work sensitively enough, so very little of the original score (and less of its impact) is lost in the transition.

Usandizaga's score certainly avails itself of contemporary musical manners, specifically through some sophisticated post-*Tristan* harmonic twists, and his melodic inspiration is uneven. Yet there is a single-mindedness about this music, a focus of energy which makes it not quite like anything else in the repertoire. The great majority of zarzuelas, including some of the very finest, sound at least twenty or so years behind the musical fashion of their time, but that cannot be said of *Los golondrinas*. There is a modernity about it which hasn't quite faded, and the best of Usandizaga's music remains haunting and tender to a special degree.

His individual, harmonic subtlety is far in advance of his Italian models; his characterization is clear and strong; his use of binding motifs gives the work a symphonic strength; his notably large orchestra is handled with conspicuous imaginative power, especially in the *Pantomima*. Above all, there is enough high-quality melodic material in *Las golondrinas* to lend the Martínez Sierras' strong melodrama an emotional force rare in opera of this, or any other period.

La llama (The Flame, 1918)
Completed by the composer's brother Ramón, Usandizaga's last work is a setting of the three-act oriental fantasy by Gregorio and María Lejarraga de Martínez Sierra, the husband and wife team responsible for *Las golondrinas*. Although the libretto is flimsy orientalism, the best pages of the score have a new, sensual radiance; and the composer's symphonic structures are perhaps even more taut than in the earlier work. The heroine Tamar's delicate *Romanza*, her *Dúo* with her lover Prince Adrian and an Albéniz-like song for The Water Spirit are highlights of Usandizaga's underappreciated swansong.

24
Amadeu Vives
(1871–1932)

Born at Collbató, near Montserrat, on 18th November 1871, Amadeu Vives was an early pupil of Felipe Pedrell, the father figure of twentieth century Spanish music who taught such diverse figures as Albéniz, de Falla and Roberto Gerhard. While studying in Barcelona Vives helped found the influential Orféo Catalá (1891), a key element in Catalunya's musical renaissance. Madrid soon beckoned, and he divided the rest of his life between the two cities. Before turning to the zarzuelas on which his reputation rests, he gained popularity with a series of deeply felt choral songs, notably *L'emigrant* (The Emigrant, 1894), which became a rallying cry for Catalan exiles around the globe.

Over a hundred stage works followed the ambitious four-act opera *Artús* (King Arthur, 1897, based on Tennyson's *Idylls of the King*) mounted in Barcelona. His first zarzuela, the one-act *La primera del barrio* (First Lady of the Neighborhood) was produced at the Teatro de la Zarzuela in Madrid a year later. A host of first nights followed; but despite some critical esteem, particularly for *Don Lucas del Cigarral* (1899) and *La balada de la luz* (The Song of Light, 1900), his real breakthrough came with the one-act *Bohemios* (Bohemians) in 1904, boldly based on the same literary source as Puccini's masterpiece. Two one-act zarzuelas written soon after with Gerónimo Giménez are still heard: *El húsar de la guardia* (The Hussar Guard, 1904) and *La gatita blanca* (The White Kitten, 1905), though other once-popular collaborative works such as *Los viajes de Gulliver* (Gulliver's Travels, 1911) have faded.

Not so the operetta *La Generala* (The General's Wife, 1912); the through-sung pastoral opera *Maruxa* (1914); and *La villana* (The Yeoman's Wife, 1927). His last works, the two-act zarzuelas *Los flamencos* (The Gypsies, 1928) and *Noche de verbena* (Fiesta Night, 1929) have not proved so durable; and the lyric comedy *Talismán* (The Talisman, 1932) was only respectfully received after his death. *Doña Francisquita* (1923) is without doubt the best known and loved of all his works, one of the few zarzuelas which has established a secure reputation outside the Spanish-speaking world. With its easy lyricism and colorful evocation of nineteenth century Madrid, not to mention its fluent vocal and choral writing, it certainly encapsulates Vives' sweetly potent charm. His orchestral and harmonic succulence allies him closer to mainstream European operetta than many of his contemporaries, but the Iberian spirit which informs his best work makes him for many the essential twentieth century *zarzuelero*.

Having said which, his talents extended beyond stage music. He wrote at least one successful "straight" play, though his dream was to become an established orchestral and symphonic composer. Isaac Albéniz once said that if Vives had wanted to compose Spanish music with a universal accent, he could undoubtedly have become an international figure. Perhaps he simply lacked the confidence to try. His book *Sofía* (1923) paints the revealing self-portrait of a neurotic artist, suffering from a bout of infantile paralysis which left him with a practically useless right arm, never entirely satisfied with being "merely" the leading *zarzuelero* of the day. Be that as it may, by the time of his death on 1st December 1932 he was a revered figure—a parliamentary session was postponed for members to attend his funeral—and his music remains dear to many Spaniards today.

Bohemios

Zarzuela in one act
Madrid, Teatro de la Zarzuela, 24th March 1904

Text: Guillermo Perrín and Miguel de Palacios

Principal Characters: Roberto, a composer (tenor); Victor, a writer (baritone); Cossette, their neighbor (soprano); Marcelo, her father (tenor); Pelagia, a housekeeper (mezzo-soprano); Girard (baritone); a Bohemian (baritone).

SCENE 1—Paris, 1840. An artist's garret, through which the snowy rooftops of the city are visible. The young composer Roberto Randel is at the piano, working on a fragment of a romantic opera which he is writing with his friend Victor (*Romanza y Dúo: "Mudos testigos de mis amores"*). The librettist joins his friend at the piano, but they are soon disturbed by the voice of their neighbor's daughter

Cossette outside in the street (*Canción: "La mariposa, de rosa en rosa"*). Roberto complains that she is always singing his songs out loud, which stops him working. Victor tells him not to mind too much, as she has a pleasant voice and is exceedingly pretty. Marcelo, Cossette's father, joins them. He asks to borrow Roberto's coat—the only one they have between them—so he can accompany his daughter in the open audition that evening at the Opéra-Comique. If Cossette is successful it will put the whole family on a sounder financial footing. All three leave for the Bola de Oro Café, hoping to wangle a meal without paying, and leaving their key with the caretaker Pelagia.

Cossette puts her head round the door to check that Roberto is out and joins Pelagia, who has stayed to tidy up (*Dúo: "La niña de ojos azules"*). The older woman teases her: why be so backward in coming forward? Cossette responds by admitting that though she does indeed yearn for Roberto, she must put her musical ambitions first. After that, there will be time for love (*Romanza: "Si es amor el sentir"*). While Pelagia goes to fetch wood for the stove, Cossette purloins Roberto's score, intending to sing it at the audition that evening. Another neighbor, Girard, who is forever promising to help everyone, appears. True to form he says he will help her clinch the job that evening, and the two of them place an invitation for Roberto on the keyboard. After they depart, two shopgirls, Juana and Cecilia, leave a badly-spelled note for Roberto asking him to dine with them at their friend Mimi's. When he returns he discovers both notes, deciding to have dinner with Mimi before going on to the Opéra-Comique.

SCENE 2—A square in the Quartier Latin, close to the Bola de Oro and a dancehall. Couples are heading for the dance, and the sound of a delicate waltz drifts through the night air. Victor emerges from the café having been unable to get free food out of the landlord. He tries to flirt with Cossette, who has come to look for her father in the restaurant before going off to sing, but she ignores him (*Escena: "La noche misteriosa"*). Temporarily dashed, he lurks in the background when a party of his friends bursts in. Led by a solo baritone, they sing the intense *Coro de Bohemios: "En la luz del sol que enciende"* in praise of passion and the bohemian way of life. Victor sees the two shopgirls heading for the dance and tries his luck with them, but the well-heeled Girard whisks them off for drinks in the café. Finally Victor admits defeat, and meeting Marcelo goes off with him to get a meal.

Coming out of the restaurant Cossette nearly runs into Roberto, in high spirits after his dinner with Mimi. She hides to avoid him, but becomes furious when she sees him chatting up the shopgirls when they reappear from the café (*Cuarteto: "¡Qué alegre es el cielo!"*). Taking her courage in both hands she calls to him, and he immediately diverts his attention to the pretty newcomer. The two girls depart making pert curtseys to their successful rival and a romantic scene ensues (*Dúo: "¿Por qué vuestros labios?"*). When Roberto asks for her name

Cossette tells him, but she is torn between accepting his amorous overtures and thoughts of her career. He leaves her, and the scene ends with Cossette, Girard and Marcelo heading off for the Opéra-Comique together with the still unfed Victor. An impassioned *Intermedio* leads into the last scene.

SCENE 3—A lavish party in the artists' salon of the Opéra-Comique. Girard is telling Victor that his libretto is too good for Roberto: it should be sent to someone important like Auber, whom he says he knows. Victor heads off to buttonhole the famous composer. Girard reassures Cossette and Marcelo that all will be well, and then tells Roberto that his music is too good for Victor's text: he should be setting someone of the quality of his good friend, Scribe. Roberto goes off to find the famous librettist. Having both been mercilessly snubbed, the young collaborators are furious to discover that Girard has been lying to them. Girard tries to save face by introducing them to one another, and leaves hastily to prepare Cossette for her appearance. Marcelo tells her that she needn't be nervous, as her own father is going to accompany her.

Girard, pretending to be Cossette's rich patron, prepares the audience for the appearance of the young singer (*Escena: "Ven, linda Cossette"*). Marcelo sits down at the piano but says he is too nervous to read from the score, and Cossette asks Roberto to accompany her. When he sees his own music on the stand the young composer understands everything. He gladly accepts, and Roberto and Cossette perform the song from the new opera (*Dúo: "Por fin llegaste"*) to the enraptured audience. The zarzuela ends in a romantic glow, as fame and fortune beckon to all the young bohemians—even the penniless librettist Victor.

Based like the operas of Puccini (1896) and Leoncavallo (1897) on Henri Murger's *Scènes de la Vie de Bohème*, *Bohemios* belongs despite its Parisian setting to the tradition of the short, one-act *género chico*. The librettists, who always wrote in collaboration, were to triumph a few years later with the outrageous Aida-parody of *La corte de Faraón* (Pharaoh's Court) for Lleó. This was the first of many gentler texts they provided for Vives, and it proved his greatest success to date. *Bohemios* is a romantic vignette which does not attempt to emulate the scope of Puccini's masterpiece, but its air of youthful sweetness and high spirits have ensured its lasting popularity.

French rather than Italian influences are apparent on the score, which nevertheless shows Vives' growing individuality. His technique owed more to French opera than to *opérette*, and the most immediately impressive feature of *Bohemios* is its composer's ability to build more complex units than was usual in *género chico* zarzuela. Lovely *romanzas* and *dúos* there are, but they emerge from an orchestral rather than a spoken dialogue. Vives is never less than suavely tuneful, closer to Massenet than Chapí or Chueca; but in at least two numbers—the famous *Coro de bohemios* and *Intermedio*—Parisian elegance gives way to a brooding vitality which is very distinctively Spanish in feeling.

The operatic breadth of the musical scenes tempted Vives to sanction a through-written version of *Bohemios* patched together in 1920 by Conrado del Campo for Madrid's grand opera house, the Teatro Real. This merely diluted the delicate charm of the original and has not displaced it.

Doña Francisquita
Zarzuela in three acts
(Madrid, Teatro Apolo, 7th October 1923)

Text: Federico Romero and Guillermo Fernández Shaw

Principal Characters: Encarnación, known as Francisquita (soprano); Doña Francisca, her mother (mezzo-soprano); Aurora La Beltrana, an actress (mezzo-soprano); Fernando Soler (tenor); Cardona, his friend (comic tenor); Don Matías, Fernando's father (bass).

ACT 1—A plaza in mid-nineteenth century Madrid, on carnival eve. The brief *Preludio* paints a vivid picture of the lively street scene. A tinker and a peddler are crying their wares (*Escena: "¡El lañador!"*); while two students, the would-be poet Fernando Soler and his friend Cardona, talk of the former's love for Aurora la Beltrana, a popular actress who only requites him by mocking his inexperience. While this is going on Francisquita and her mother Francisca come out of the church with some friends. The young girl is in love with Fernando despite his obvious preference for the actress, who goes into a refreshment stall owned by her accepted beau, Lorenzo Pérez. Dropping her handkerchief to attract Fernando's attention Francisquita takes the opportunity to engage him in flirtatious conversation (*"Señorita ... Caballero"*). Cardona praises Francisquita's beauty, but his hints fall on deaf ears. The two women finally go back into their house, and the cries of the street sellers are heard once again.

Cardona tries to make his poetic friend understand that the dropped handkerchief was a sign, and when Fernando hears Francisquita singing inside her house he begins to take the hint (*Terceto: "Peno por un hombre, madre"*). After the students go into the church to order flowers for the wedding of a friend, Doña Francisca berates her daughter for vulgar behavior. They receive a visit from Don Matías, Fernando's father. He has come to court not the mother, as both initially hope, but the daughter. Francisquita plays along and pretends to accept his proposal, solely in order to make Fernando jealous. La Beltrana reappears with her friend Irene, and orders the jealous Lorenzo to find her a carriage to take her to the carnival. Much to Cardona's irritation she continues to mock Fernando, who gives as good as he gets in the *Cuarteto: "Allí la tienes"*, before she retreats to the refreshment stall.

Cardona stops the angry Fernando following them, and dismisses Aurora as an empty-headed flirt—a comment overheard by Matías, who believes they are discussing Francisquita and gives his son a good dressing down. Cardona and Fernando hear the wedding party of their friends coming toward the church accompanied by a *rondalla* of *bandurrias* and guitars (*Coro: "Cuando un hombre se quiere casar"*); and the two students lead the crowd of well-wishers in a joyful, sweeping song encapsulating the youthful spirit of Madrid (*Canción de la Juventud: "Canto alegre de la juventud"*).

When Don Matías reveals his successful proposal, Cardona convinces Fernando to flirt with his prospective "mother-in-law" in order to aggravate Aurora. When Francisquita reappears Fernando puts his ruse into operation (*Escena: "Ese es mi nombre"*). She sings the witty, sensual Song of the Nightingale about a triangular love affair involving a nightingale, a rose and a bee (*Canción del ruiseñor: "Era una rosa que en un jardín"*) and Fernando finally understands how desirable she is.

Francisquita's mother calls, and when she leaves the poet's thoughts return to Aurora, who still has power over his heart. A group of musicians, arrived for the Carnival, sing a lusty street song; and the actress provokes Fernando's jealousy once more by singing of her own pride in being a simple Madrid girl (*Pasacalle: "Me ha dicho mi marido . . . Soy madrileña"*). The act ends as the wedding party emerge from the church, watched by Fernando and the secretly confident Francisquita. The acclamations of the crowd mingle with Aurora's blessings, as she leaves in her carriage and wishes the happy couple a long life (*Final: "¡Vivan los novios!"*).

ACT 2—An esplanade alongside the Madrid Canal. Aurora's singing inside a nearby tavern attracts the praise of various listeners outside (*Escena: "Cunado te digo que vengas"*). La Confradía de la Bulla, the Brotherhood of Noise, appear amid the merry throng and perform their ebullient street act (*Terceto: "Con el tiroliroli"*).

Cardona appears disguised as a pretty woman. After fending off several male admirers he regrets thinking up such an idiotic ploy to get close to the girls without attracting suspicion. Don Matías and Doña Francisca bring Fernando along to meet his future "mother-in-law," which only feeds his growing passion for Francisquita. The girl provokes Fernando into declaring his love, continuing to tease him by reminding him of his passion for Aurora in their extended *Dúo: "¡Le van a oír!"*. When Matías returns to pay court, the young man is stricken with horror at the idea that his new love would marry his father to become "Doña Francisquita." He sings of being torn between the two women in an exquisite, poetic *Romanza: "Por el humo se sabe donde está el fuego"*.

"Señorita" Cardona reappears, and successfully provokes Aurora by pretending to be Fernando's sweetheart. Much to the jealous actress' chagrin, Fernando tells Aurora that she no longer has any power over him in their feisty *Dúo: "¡Escúchame!"*. When Don Matías formally introduces his son to his prospective "mother-in-law" (*Quinteto: "Bella estrella de la tarde . . . ¡Ay, Madrid de mi alma!"*) both he and the girl's mother are alarmed by the young couple's excessive intimacy. Cardona encourages his friend to persist, and when Francisquita pretends to faint into Fernando's arms Don Matías is apoplectic with rage.

Carnival revelers arrive and an impromptu dance is arranged (*Coro: "Los que quieran patatas"*). Aurora enrages Lorenzo by trying to push Fernando into dancing a *Mazurka* with her. Francisquita artfully provokes him into accepting, but Matías jealously intervenes and asks La Beltrana to dance with him instead. This in turn provokes Lorenzo to fight, but the older man easily defeats him and graciously defuses the situation (*Solo: "Pero ¿qué te has creído, jovenzuelo?"*) before leading Aurora in the dance. Francisquita is finally free to dance with Fernando and the act ends as the *Mazurka* merges into the festive carnival scene.

ACT 3, SCENE 1—A Madrid street, later that evening. Distant sounds of night revelry are heard as the night watchman does his rounds (*Preludio: "¡Ave María Purísima!"*). The warm sensuality of the night envelops six pairs of girls and boys gathered lazily in the lamplight to make love (*Coro de Románticos: "¿Dónde va, dónde va la alegría?"*). Francisquita continues to provoke her elderly suitor's jealousy, and when Doña Francisca tells Don Matías that her daughter wants to go out to the *Baile de Cuchilleros* (Cutler's Dance) he grumpily decides to stay at home. Francisquita convinces her mother that Fernando really prefers older women, and flatters Francisca into accompanying her.

Cardona informs the moody Aurora that Fernando has gone to the dance with Francisquita. She tells him to get lost, and takes out her fury on the hapless Lorenzo. Convinced that Aurora is now in love with Fernando, Lorenzo goes to Don Matías' house to challenge his son to a duel, thus provoking Don Matías to visit the dance after all to find out precisely what is going on.

SCENE 2—The patio of the dance house. The voice of the night watchman is heard once more. Aurora is by now more or less resigned to the inevitable, and happily sings the cheeky *Bolero: "Marubú"* with Cardona before everyone breaks into a wild, flamboyant *Fandango*. When the actress, seeing Fernando is now obsessed with Francisquita, flounces off, Cardona explains the true state of affairs to the spiteful Lorenzo, who in turn informs Don Matías. Aurora adds fuel to the fire by passing on the rumors about his son and the ludicrously flirtatious Doña Francisca. When she appears to ask for Fernando's hand in marriage, the baffled father indignantly replies that she's old enough to be his mother. Cardona tactfully points out that Matías could equally well level the same reproach against himself; and when Francisquita and Fernando gently ask his pardon together in their *Dúo: "Yo no fui sincera"* Don Matías melts and gives the couple his blessing. He invites everyone to the wedding, and all celebrate the happy outcome with a brief reprise of the *Canción de la Juventud*, the hymn to the eternally youthful spirit of Madrid.

With its nineteenth century Madrid setting, its roots in classical Spanish drama—in this case Lope de Vega's comedy *La discreta enamorada*, The Ingenious Lover—and its festive nocturnal amours, *Doña Francisquita* provides at once a retrospective on the romantic zarzuela tradition and its crowning glory. The work was immediately recognized not only as Vives' masterpiece, but as the greatest full-length zarzuela of its era. In no small part this is down to the brilliance of Romero and Shaw's fast-moving libretto, which renders the complicated emotional twists and turns of Lope's plot crystal clear, while giving full rein to their composer's ability to produce through-written scenes of operatic quality.

As in opera, it is the music which defines and drives the drama and characters of *Doña Francisquita*, a factor which has made this the most frequently recorded of any Spanish theatre work, and her most consistently successful export to the operatic world. As in the earlier *Bohemios*, Vives has lyrical *romanzas* and *dúos* rubbing shoulders with ensembles, choruses, street music and popular songs, but now the level of structural integration is much higher. Everywhere, his cultivated harmonic and orchestral palette is cunningly deployed—not least in the sensual, opulently nocturnal *Coro de Románticos*:

Yet set pieces such as the clamorous wedding scene from the first act, and this virile *Fandango* from the last, come across with a direct power as thrilling as anything in zarzuela:

(Orchestra)

Trumpets + Trombones

Above all Vives' characters, though rooted in *commedia* archetypes, display real individuality and subtlety in their amorous machinations. Francisquita's *Canción del ruiseñor* is far more than simply the finest coloratura display piece in the repertoire. It combines wit and sinewy, seductive melody in a potent brew which brings the girl fully to life:

E - ra u - na ro - sa que en un jar - dín lan - gui - de - cí - a de cas - to a - mor

Aurora's quicksilver personality and emotional force are brilliantly portrayed in her *Dúo: "¡Escúchame!"* with the correspondingly callow Fernando. He himself can be felt growing to maturity through his encounters with Francisquita, a process which culminates in the glowing, lyric outpouring of "*Por el humo se sabe donde está el fuego*", perhaps the supreme tenor *Romanza* in the zarzuela tradition. Altogether it is no exaggeration to say that in *Doña Francisquita* Vives created one of the most enduring works in twentieth century music theatre, one whose quality is at length being recognized the world over.

La Generala
Operetta in two acts
Madrid, Gran Teatro, 14th June 1912

Text: Guillermo Perrín and Miguel de Palacios

Principal Characters: King Cirilo (comic tenor); Prince Pío, his son (tenor); King Clodomiro (bass); Princess Olga, his daughter (soprano); General Tocateca (actor); Berta Tocateca, his wife (soprano).

ACT 1—A large castle near Oxford, England. King Cirilo II of Molavia has been overthrown in an uprising and has sought refuge in Oxford, England, together with Queen Eva and their son and heir, Prince Pío. After an orchestral introduction full of regal pomp the courtiers hail their displaced monarch with martial enthusiasm (*Introducción y Marcha Militar: "Para presentarse a su Majestad"*). Given the dire economic straits in which the triumphant revolutionaries have left the Royal Family, the King's only object is to marry the Prince off to a rich heiress; who must, however, be of royal blood. Pío, entering fresh from a game of tennis with some companions, announces his willingness to put his romantic ardor at the service of his father (*Salida del Príncipe: "Os invito, amigos míos . . . Era yo en la corte"*).

After weighing up various possibilities, Cirilo's choice falls on Princess Olga, daughter of his great friend King Clodomiro of Espartanopia. But a difficulty immediately arises: in order to visit his would-be fiancée, Pío needs money to buy the necessary clothes and pay for the journey, and that money is not to be had. At this critical juncture the Adjutant to the King, the Duke of Sisa (petty theft) remembers that General Tocateca, Venezuelan Ambassador to the old court of Molavia and an immensely rich man, has just bought himself a castle in nearby Cambridge. Even as they get down to discussing the pros and the cons of asking Tocateca for a loan (in a lively *Cuarteto Cómico*) the General's deputy makes a fortuitous appearance, requesting an audience with King Cirilo for his superior, who is in Oxford on business.

Needless to say the King receives General Tocateca immediately, investing him and his wife Berta with full diplomatic honors as well as such refreshment as the precarious royal economic situation allows. Berta entertains the courtiers in return with a dashing song about a Harlequin marionette, the *Canción del Arlequín: "Es un muñeco el Arlequín"*, which puts her husband into such a good mood that he unhesitatingly agrees to loan the money to Cirilo.

In the course of the conversation, King Cirilo finds out that Clodomiro has been invited by Tocateca to spend time as a house guest in his Cambridge castle. Taking advantage of this happy chance Cirilo wangles an invitation for himself and his son, to give Pío the opportunity to make his mark with Princess Olga. But an unexpected complication is on the horizon: as soon as he sets eyes on Berta, Pío recognizes her as the first object of his adolescent love, the famous *chanteuse* who starred at the *Olimpia* in Paris. In a wistful duet notable both for bizarre verbal double entendres and elegant lyricism (*Dúo: "Mi dulce sueño de adolescente"*) she warms to him as he recalls the charms of their past: perhaps his pure, youthful feeling for the singer may be transmuted into a less platonic passion for La Generala (General's wife). Pío is flattered by Berta's attention, and assents in principle to her amorous overtures. The courtiers return and hail the General and his wife, as everyone looks forward to reviving the royal fortunes in the expansive *Final Concertante*.

ACT 2—The garden of Tocateca's Cambridge castle, a few weeks later. Following an orchestral *Introducción* based on the *Canción del Arlequín*, we find a colorful flower festival in progress. In her *Canción de las flores* (Song of the Flowers) Princess Olga sings of her happiness at the suggested marriage with Pío. On the other hand Cirilo, Eva and Sisa are full of foreboding about the Prince's growing indifference to the proposed marriage, as witness his cool politesse in their strangely formal *Dúo: "¿Te agradan las flores?"*.

Tocateca asks his wife to sing once again, and she obliges with an exotic *Canción escocesa* (Scottish Song) to harp accompaniment, which is followed by an infectious *Giga Militar* (Military Gigue). The general quizzes his wife about Pío's apparent lack of interest in marriage, but she feigns surprise. La Generala finds herself talking alone with Olga, and soon realizes that the Princess is sincerely in love with Pío and hurt by his coldness. She reflects on the contrast between this true devotion and her own frivolity in treating the Prince as an amusing diversion, a plaything. Consequently, there is only one logical decision to make: rather than create selfish difficulties, she must retire from the fray and leave the field clear for the young Princess. Her first step is to disillusion Pío about the strength of her own feelings. To that end Berta arranges a secret assignation with the Prince in the garden at nightfall, firmly intending that he will discover Olga there in her place.

Their conversation gives rise to unforeseen complications. Kings Cirilo and Clodomiro have overheard Berta's whisperings and in a witty *Terceto Comico: "Señora, Señora"* they question her actions. Misunderstanding La Generala's strategy they decide she is merely a cheap adventurer, and head straight off to Tocateca to expose his wife's behavior. The old men agree to hide in the garden at the appointed hour, and so put a spoke in the adulterous wheel.

Nightfall is represented by an orchestral *Nocturno*, and soon the denouement comes about. Berta meets with Pío, but swiftly disappears; and when the General emerges to expose his wife's infidelity he only discovers the Prince and Olga in the act of affectionately declaring their mutual love (*Escena Concertante: "Llego la hora"*). In a sweet *Dúo: "¡Que bella noche!"* the young couple express their joy; and the operetta ends with relief and reconciliation all round—not to mention Berta's wistful contentment at the budding happiness of the two young Royals—in the short, martial *Coro Final*.

Written two years after the mold-breaking success of Luna's *Molinos de viento*, *La Generala* (The General's Wife) is in all essentials a fluffy Spanish operetta, evoking Ruritanian amours in an exotic setting, in this case Edwardian England. Its two librettists, who had previously provided the composer with *Bohemios*, were notorious for work of uneven quality. This time, however, the customary *madrileño* cynicism about their work proved out of place. Loquacious though it is, their text crackles with wit and energy.

Vives provided a score of considerable if not entirely consistent charm, verve and élan. *La Generala* was the first of the composer's full-length works to demonstrate his superior melodic and orchestral gifts; and although there is nothing specially Spanish about them, the witty comic ensembles at least pick up where nineteenth century *zarzuelas grandes* such as Chapí's *El rey que rabió* left off. Otherwise Berta's lively *Canción del Arlequín* would not be out of place in a French *opéra-comique*, and the lilting romantic highlights of *La Generala* could be slipped into a Viennese operetta of the period without exciting undue alarm.

Maruxa
Lyric eclogue in two acts
(Madrid, Teatro de la Zarzuela, 28th May 1914)

Text: Luis Pascual Frutos

Principal Characters: Maruxa, a shepherdess (soprano); Pablo, a shepherd (baritone); Rosa, a landowner (soprano); Antonio, her cousin (tenor); Rufo, her overseer (bass).

ACT 1—A meadow on the Galician plain. It is dawn, and the shepherdess Maruxa cradles her pet lamb, Linda, as she sings of her feelings for Pablo, a handsome shepherd (*Romanza: "Mírate en el espejo"*). Pablo joins her, and they sing happily of their love and future wedding (*Dúo: "Con la aurora salió la zagaliña"*).

When Rufo, overseer and majordomo combined to the townfolk who now own the land, berates them for kissing when they ought to be working, the two shepherds mock him gently and make off together across the meadow. Rufo bewails his impossible situation: he is expected to sort out all the problems of the tenancy without getting any thanks at all. Still, he's determined not to take notice of the indignities he must put up with (*Coplas: "Golondrón"*).

Bored with city life, the young proprietor Rosa arrives with her callow, doting cousin Antonio in tow. She has no time for his amours, preferring the thought of an affair with Maruxa's shepherd, whom she is determined to take for herself. In a powerful, sweeping *Dúo: "Rufo, amigo"* Rosa orders Rufo to fetch Pablo, but before the uneasy overseer has finished arguing with her Pablo himself appears with his flock. Rosa loses little time in probing him about his love life, artfully offering to stand in for Maruxa so he can demonstrate his ardor. At the climax of their *Dúo: "Por nombre me pondré Maruxa"* the confused shepherd eventually allows her to kiss him passionately; but Rufo, who has been secretly watching, stumbles out of the undergrowth at the crucial moment, allowing Pablo to beat a hasty retreat.

Rosa orders Rufo to fetch Maruxa; and when the shepherdess appears, deeply distressed at the loss of her straying lamb, Rosa and Antonio are swift to offer her comfort (*Cuarteto: "Ay, por dios señorita"*). The sympathetic Rosa even offers Maruxa the post of personal maid; overcome with gratitude the shepherdess agrees and the three of them leave for Rosa's mansion. A few seconds later Pablo appears, having rescued Linda the lamb from a steep cliff. Rufo has to tell him that Maruxa has decamped with Rosa, leaving Pablo in doubt and sadness.

ACT 2, SCENE 1—Outside Rosa's mansion, above the plain. After a rousing orchestral *Preludio*, we find Rufo grumbling as he waters the plants and flowers. When quite sure he is alone, he tries to decipher a letter he has brought from Pablo to the girl. Maruxa herself comes in with Antonio and Rosa, who loses no time in extracting Pablo's letter from the suspicious overseer. Antonio reads the letter out, adding his own sophisticated gloss on Pablo's simple but heartfelt words. Pablo wants to meet his shepherdess that evening; and when Maruxa, who cannot read, asks her mistress to reply on her behalf, Rosa silently changes the suggested time with the intention of meeting the shepherd herself (*Cuarteto de la carta: "¿Cumpliste mis instrucciones?"*—Letter Quartet). She sends Rufo off to deliver the reply; but before he can leave, Antonio waylays him, changing the hour yet again so he himself can meet with Maruxa.

A group of shepherds and shepherdesses come to celebrate the return of the Lady of the Manor with song and dance (*Coro y Danza: "Aunqu'a tua porta me poñan"*). As they are leaving, a thunderstorm blows up which provides an impressive *Intermedio* preceding the last scene.

SCENE 2—Later that evening. The storm has passed. Rufo, exasperated by the gentry's behavior, returns with Pablo, leading him to an arbor where he can secretly wait for Maruxa. When Rufo has gone to fetch his beloved, Pablo sings of his unswerving love for the shepherdess in a *Romanza Nocturnal: "Aquí n'este sitio"* of touching nobility, couched in Galician dialect. Rufo brings the two lovers together, before they sing of their joy at being reunited (*Terceto: "Allí tienes a tu Pablo"*). As they leave, Antonio and Rosa appear in the shadows, both disguised in shepherd costume. They clasp one another under the impression that they are embracing Maruxa and Pablo respectively, but at that moment the real shepherd-lovers are heard descending the hill in the moonlight. The deceitful cousins realize they have lost their prey. Antonio is ashamed, but Rosa reacts with petulant tears of rage as the true lovers make their way back to the innocent happiness of the plain.

Together with *Doña Francisquita* and *Bohemios*, *Maruxa* remains one of Vives' most celebrated works. Much academic ink has been spilled as to whether *Maruxa* should be classified as opera or zarzuela. It is through-sung, certainly, but its lightness of tone belies any suggestion of operatic weight. Vives himself called it a Lyric Eclogue, which is as good a definition as any of his amorous, rural idyll.

In contrasting the purity of simple countryfolk with the unscrupulous immorality of urban sophisticates, Maruxa offers a contemporary gloss on the pastoral tradition of which Handel's *Acis and Galatea* is the classic musical expression. Like Handel's shepherd-lovers, Maruxa and Pablo face a powerful external threat, though their Lady of the Manor is a more sophisticated antagonist than the ugly, brutal giant Polyphemus. Indeed Rosa's intrigues, together with the tribulations of her put-upon overseer, Rufo, lend a certain spice to Frutos' otherwise stilted and mawkish libretto.

There is a pervasive ease about Vives' score which has not been to all tastes. Certainly, the harmonic palette is intentionally bland, there is the odd suspicion of rhythmic inertia, and the characters' musical language (except for the endearing Rufo's) is more or less interchangeable. Far more important is the fact that Vives' melodic inspiration is at full tide, his orchestration sensual, his theatricality unerring. This is remarkable considering the haste with which the score was put together. Two of the most famous numbers were last-minute additions. Rufo's song was shoehorned in from an unpublished *Sardana*, "Sant Pol":

Andante

Gon, go - lon - drón, go - lon - dri - na que a mí

The sweeping Act 2 *Preludio* with its famously difficult writing for orchestral cellos was actually written the very morning of the opening. This circumstance recalls another notorious last-minute musical dramatist, the not-dissimilar English composer Arthur Sullivan, some of whose works Vives adapted for production in Madrid and whose scores share the uplifting sweetness of the Catalan *maestro*.

La villana

Zarzuela in three acts
(Madrid, Teatro de la Zarzuela, 11th October 1927)

Text: Federico Romero and Guillermo Fernández Shaw

Principal Characters: Peribáñez, a Castilian yeoman (baritone); Casilda, his wife (soprano); Don Fadrique, the Commander of Ocaña (tenor); David, a Jewish merchant (bass); Olmedo, a farmhand (comic tenor).

ACT 1—Early fifteenth century Castile. A farm courtyard, one late summer afternoon. The foreman Miguel Ángel, his young wife Juana Antonia and the farmhands enthuse over the imminent nuptials of their rich master Peribáñez and the beautiful Casilda (*Dúo y coro: "Mi amo Peribáñez"*). When they hear a distant group of reapers hailing the yeoman's approach (*Coro: "Trébole de la soltera"*) Miguel Ángel, his wife and eight of the workers perform a brief, formal dance in honor of the marriage.

The bridegroom arrives accompanied by the local *curé*, his fellow farmers and their wives. He offers wine to his guests, lauding the wonderful vintage his land produces in a warm *Romanza: "Tengo un majuelo de tres verdores"*. He receives homage from the peasants, in particular the clever Olmedo, who sings a *Coplas: "Segador: Este anochecido case a desposar"* in praise of the harvesters. A lively procession of women leads the bride to her husband (*Coro: "Ya suenan los campanillos"*). Casilda sings of her joy, and the pair meet with gentle affection before setting forth toward the nearby hermitage to solemnize their vows, accompanied by their well-wishers (*Solo y Dúo: "Jamás soñe ... Ni la parva de trigo blanca"*).

Miguel Ángel discusses Peribáñez's fine qualities, though Olmedo is more inclined to flirt with his wife. Roque and Blasa, an older married couple working in the farmhouse, report on the joyous scenes inside the church itself, and soon the newlyweds reappear (*Coro y solos: "Nostrama ya se ha casado"*). Their happiness is clouded by an unlucky accident: the Commander of the nearby town of Ocaña, Don Fadrique, has fallen from his horse when it was gored by a bull. The nobleman is carried into the courtyard and Peribáñez hurries in to make his house ready, leaving the wounded man in the charge of Casilda. In the poised, lyrical *Dúo: "¡Caballero ben portado, por tus hechos alabado!"* she addresses the Commander with polite solicitude. When he comes round, Don Fabrique praises Casilda's aristocratic beauty, and is surprised by the admission that she is merely the wife of a yeoman farmer.

Peribáñez returns, and the Commander, his equanimity restored, announces that in recognition of his hospitality he will formally elevate Peribáñez to the gentry as a *caballero*, or knight. Peribáñez is delighted at the turn of fortune and does not suspect what might lie behind it (*Dúo: "Señor, feliz me heciste"*). Don Fadrique departs, and the farmhands leave the couple alone together to exchange intimate loving vows (*Dúo: "Ven Casilda conmigo"*). They go into the farmhouse; and Olmedo, come to tempt Juana Antonia, is surprised to see the Commander returning. Don Fadrique is open in his admiration of Casilda, and despite Olmedo's well-meant warnings he addresses a *Serenata: "Tus ojos me miraron"*, full of courtly grace, to the fair yeoman's wife.

ACT 2, SCENE 1—The kitchen of Peribáñez's farmhouse. The doors are barred for the night and the workers are enjoying their evening meal. In the course of a poetic *Preludio: "Villanos y lugareños"* we hear the voice of the Crier: Peribáñez has been made a captain by the Commander of Ocaña, and will soon lead a conscripted farmer's army against the Moors of Jerez. Miguel Ángel and his friends have heard the news, and congratulate Peribáñez on his fortune. Casilda takes tender leave of her loving husband in a heartfelt *Romanza: "La capa de paño pardo"*.

Despite the lateness of the hour, there is a knock on the door. It is an old Jewish merchant from Toledo, David, who requests hospitality. He brings a pearl of wondrous beauty (*Canción: "Allá, en la judería toledana"*) which he is determined to present to Casilda without payment, a fact which arouses the suspicion of Olmedo and his friend Chaparro. When Peribáñez leaves after a further brief farewell from his wife (*Dúo y coro: "Me guarda la sombra"*), Roque and Blasa press their suspicion that David is in the pay of Don Fadrique in a lively *Terceto: "Cayó en el ardid"*. When the Jew has retired for the night, Casilda appears briefly to ask Blasa what the disturbance was about, before retiring upstairs to her own chamber. On Blasa's advice she bolts her door.

The Commander arrives, dressed as a farmhand. Despite Roque's pleas he determines to speak with Casilda, but finding the door bolted he calls out to her. Casilda comes to her window, watched by Olmedo and Chaparro; in a poetic dialogue she resists all pleas and courtly blandishments with polite but firm clarity. The laborers praise her honest virtue in the face of Fadrique's pressure.

SCENE 2—Next day, outside an inn on the Toledo-Ocaña road. Miguel Ángel and the other young conscripts are served drinks by the innkeeper, Quintanilla. Old David is subjected to the insults of the farmers for his obsequious manners; and when Peribáñez appears on the scene he gets his own back by taunting the Captain about his wife's affair with the Commander. In a powerful *Dúo: "¡Malvado! . . . ¡Calma tus iras!"* the Jew gives as good as he gets, and though Peribáñez stands up for his wife staunchly, by the end he is sufficiently rattled to ride home and find out the truth.

SCENE 3—Peribáñez's threshing barn. Olmedo, who has skillfully avoided conscription, sings a *Copla: "A la fuente de la Zarza"* to amuse the overseer and three boys. He plans to use Miguel Ángel's absence to assault the virtue of Juana Antonia, but her continual mockery puts paid to his hopes. Peribáñez, preoccupied with his thoughts (*Recitado: "Con qué diversa alegría"*) hears Olmedo singing in the distance about the Commander's amorous exploit in another verse of his *Copla: "La mujer de Peribáñez"*. Casilda's joyful greeting and honest relation of the event swiftly reassures him, and their conversation becomes a passionate declaration of renewed love (*Dúo: "Poder saborear"*).

The conscripted farmers march in, hailed by their womenfolk and praised by Don Fadrique. The Commander formally declares Peribáñez a *caballero*; and the new gentleman deftly puts his wife under Don Fadrique's protection during his absence, in a subtle appeal to the nobleman's sense of honor. The act ends with Peribáñez's determination to return as soon as possible, Casilda's fear for her husband, and Don Fadrique's abashed weakness in the face of his growing obsession (*Concertante Final: "Por el tono de su voz"*).

ACT 3, SCENE 1—The Farm Courtyard, by night. Juana Antonia rejects Olmedo's advances once more. At last accepting her loyalty to the absent Miguel Ángel, he determines to join his fellows in the fight against the Moors.

In an extended scene, Casilda pines for her husband and prays to an image of the Virgin that he may return home safely (*Romanza: "Se fué"*). Rising from her knees she catches sight of Don Fadrique, come once more to assault her virtue, this time by force if necessary. In the intense and passionate *Dúo: "¿Por qué os asusta mi presencia?"* she again resists his demands, but when she finally goes inside and bolts her door, the passionate nobleman can no longer contain himself and jumps in through her window (*Romanza: "¡Ah, villana orgulosa!"*). Peribáñez hurries in and discovers the Commandant's cape outside the window. Hearing Casilda's pleas for help, he unsheathes his sword and calmly follows the nobleman into the house (*Final: "¡De nuevo mis pasos!"*).

SCENE 2—The square outside Toledo Cathedral. A brilliant, festive *Preludio* depicts the pageantry as groups of knights and ladies arrive to process into the Cathedral with the King, admired by the awestruck populace (*Preludio y coro: "Vengo de despedida"*). The King and his courtiers enter the Cathedral to the acclaim of the crowd, which includes the returned Olmedo, Miguel Ángel and his Juana Antonia. Before the people can disperse, the Crier announces the shocking news that the Commander of Ocaña has been murdered, and that the King is offering a thousand escudos for the capture of his killer. Olemedo and the others, knowing the truth, fear for Peribáñez; and as the King comes out of the Cathedral, the Captain steps forward, yields up his sword and confesses to the crime. In an eloquent *Monologo: "Señor, aunque villano"* Peribáñez staunchly defends his action in the name of law and morality. Casilda adds her plea for mercy; and amid scenes of mass enthusiasm the King returns Peribáñez's sword, grants pardon to the noble yeoman, and resumes his royal progress.

La villana (The Yeoman's Wife) is its composer's most ambitious stage work. Romero and Shaw created a fine libretto closely based on Lope de Vega's classic *Peribáñez y el Comendador de Ocaña*, capturing the essence of the tragicomedy's multi-layered debate on caste, fidelity and honor but leaving plenty of room for musical expansion. Such was the scope and quality of Vives' response that the librettists felt the work would succeed better as through-written opera. The composer determined to stick to his ideal of a three-act zarzuela with spoken dialogue, and the results are problematic. *La villana* is a long score of considerable complexity, needing world-class opera singers to make its effect; yet those same singers must also be able to cope with substantial passages of blank verse dialogue, all of which makes ideal performance difficult to envisage.

The absorbing quality of the music is not in doubt, though the score does not have the consistently fresh inspiration of its predecessor *Doña Francisquita*. Although Vives does not attempt to create a consistent mediaeval ambience, there are hints of older Spanish music about his score. Romantic nationalism is definitely at work in the heraldic pageantry of the thrilling *Preludio* to the last scene, which parallels the operatic statements of the Czech Smetana in the previous century. Don Fadrique's *Serenata*, with its major-minor shifts and antique harmonies, is reminiscent of the neo-renaissance work Manuel de Falla produced during the 1920s. Both composers owed their knowledge of this distant musical heritage to their teacher Pedrell:

La villana ultimately stands or falls by the beauty of its lyric inspiration. The *dúos* for the three principal characters, especially those for husband and wife, maintain a marvelous standard; and Casilda's extended solo scene "*Se fué*" at the beginning of Act 3 (inspired by Desdemona's similar *scena* in Verdi's *Otello*) has a sensitive Mahlerian delicacy unmatched elsewhere in Vives' work. Perhaps Mahler is called to mind by the orchestration, notable for unexpected imaginative touches, such as the use Vives makes of the ethereal sound of the glockenspiel at crucial moments. If *La villana* is ultimately too top-heavy to be accounted a complete artistic success, *zarzueleros* can ill afford to overlook a score and text of such ambition and quality.

Balada de Carnaval (Carnival Ballad, 1919)
As with *Maruxa*, the lighter style of Vives' later through-written one-act opera links it to the zarzuela repertoire. The story, set in 1830 Nuremberg at Carnival time, is a droll, romantic version of *Pygmalion*. The magician and watchmaker Zacarías attempts to magically animate a female doll to cure the melancholia of his ailing son, but his scheming nephew Frantz substitutes a real woman with dramatic results. Rare revivals have shown the score to be as lyrically distinguished, varied and theatrically effective as Vives' better-known works.

Don Lucas del Cigarral (1899)
A three-act zarzuela which was the making of Vives' critical reputation, *Don Lucas del Cigarral* is a well-constructed dramatization of a renaissance classic, *Entre bobos anda el juego* (The Fool's Game) by Francisco de Rojas. The plot is the tried and tested story of the rich old man who wants to marry a young wife, with predictable consequences. The most esteemed number is the bravura *Dúo: "Por Dios, don Pedro, bajad la voz"* between Doña Isabel and her young lover Don Pedro; and although not everything is mature Vives, his score has a fresh and robust construction which impressed his contemporaries.

Los flamencos (The Gypsies, 1928)
Vives himself described this late, two-act zarzuela as "a facile work, popular in style, as a *sainete* should be. A thing without pretensions." The libretto, by Romero and Shaw, is a light romantic *madrileño* comedy; and Vives' score made it a great popular success, though it has rarely been seen since his death. Outstanding numbers include two *dúos* for sparring tenor and soprano lovers, including the witty *"Mala mujer"*; and an outrageously original *Intermedio* combining an orchestral evocation of flamenco dance with a Charleston played on a pianola!

El húsar de la guardia (The Hussar Guard, with **Gerónimo Giménez**, 1904)
A one-act collaboration in light operetta style, written just after *Bohemios*. During Bonaparte's first exile a Lieutenant of Hussars is warned that he is about to be arrested for his Napoleonic sympathies. His brave sister Mathilde impersonates him, thus enabling his escape and setting off a train of farcical events which end with Napoleon's triumphant return to Paris. The music is lively and insouciant, with appropriate military trappings: the outstanding number is the witty orchestral *Intermedio*, an exercise in elegant scoring, especially for the wind instruments.

Juegos malabares (Juggling Games, 1910)
Miguel Echegaray enjoyed great success with this one-act circus drama, largely thanks to Vives' contribution. Tonino the Juggler loves Marietta the tightrope walker; while singer Julia and strong man Jorge fight to save her decrepit father, the clown Guillermo, from getting the sack for being unfunny. Both women are pursued by the lecherous circus manager, who is finally deflated by Tonino's threat of "juggling games" with knives. Of the excellent handful of musical numbers, the best known is a coloratura showstopper, Julia's Song of the Little Bird (*Canción del pajarito: "Yo soy un artista"*) with its circus brashness and subtly spiced Spanish inflections.

25
Nineteenth Century

Isaac Albéniz (1860–1909)
One of the greatest Spanish composers, whose stage works are finally beginning to attract the attention they deserve. His operas, mainly written to English libretti by the wealthy Lord Latymer, Francis Burdett Money-Coutts, have real musical distinction if little sense of the theatre. They include *Henry Clifford* (1895); the magnificent Arthurian *Merlin* (c. 1898); and *Pepita Jiménez* (1897), based on the novel by Juan Valera. In 1964 Pablo Sorozábal translated the text into Spanish, reworking the plot and Albéniz's original material comprehensively; but although the result was a theatrical and musical triumph, his adaptation has not achieved a place in the operatic repertoire. Albéniz himself was ambiguous about zarzuela, not least when the most substantial of his three to reach the stage, *San Antonio de la Florida* (1894), had the ill fortune to be premiered in Madrid at the same time as Bretón's *La verbena de la Paloma* and failed. It was produced in Brussels in 1903, and adapted by Sorozábal with some success in 1953.

Gabriel Balart (1824–93)
The leading Catalan composer of his generation, Balart trained in Barcelona and Paris. He devoted much of his creative life to the production of Italian operas and Spanish zarzuelas, before succeeding Engelbert Humperdinck as professor of harmony and composition at the Liceu in his home city and abandoning the stage. His Spanish-language zarzuelas, notable for their immaculate Italianate grace, include *Amor y arte* (Love and Art, 1862); *Los diamantes negros* (The Black Diamonds, 1863); and, a curiosity, *El tulipán de los mares* (The Sea Tulip, 1871) which uses the same plot as Mozart's *Die Zauberflöte*.

Guillermo Cereceda (1844–1919)

Toledo-born Cereceda is remembered for just one of his many zarzuelas, *Pepe-Hillo* (1870), which concerns the life and career of the famous bullfighter painted by Goya who had already appeared as a minor character in Barbieri's *Pan y toros*. Otherwise, Cereceda is remembered as a domineering personality and influential impresario, who was particularly active in bringing European operettas including Suppé's *Boccaccio* to Madrid in the last decades of the century.

Salvador Giner (1832–1911)

Valencian composer-teacher, whose pupils as professor of composition at the city's conservatory included Vicente Lleó, Manuel Penella and José Serrano. His operas and zarzuelas were esteemed in the Madrid of their time but have not been revived since. The latter include ¿*Con quién caso a mi mujer?* (Who has married my wife?, 1875), *El rayo de sol* (The Ray of Sunshine, 1883) and *Los mendigos* (The Beggars, 1896). In his later years he wrote several zarzuelas in Valencian dialect, but these did not succeed.

Enrique Granados (1867–1916)

Among the most celebrated of Spanish composers for his piano and vocal music, his best-known stage work is an adaptation of the piano suite *Goyescas* into a poetic evocation of the Madrid of Goya's day. This was performed at New York's Metropolitan Opera in 1916, and it was on his return from America that Granados and his wife were drowned when the ship on which they were returning to Spain, the *Sussex*, was sunk in the English Channel by a German torpedo. His earlier opera, *María del Carmen* (1898) is stylistically akin to *género chico* zarzuela, and enjoyed a great success in its time; and two of his later theatrical collaborations with the Catalan poet Apel·les Mestres, *Picarol* (1901) and *Follet* (1903), are written in a popular style which would lend interest to their revival today.

Rafael Hernando (1822–88)

Madrid-born Hernando studied under notable composers Baltasar Saldoni and Ramón Carnicer before removing to Paris for lessons with the great tenor and song composer Manuel García. He worked successfully in the French capital until the Revolution of 1848 forced him to return to Spain. Once reestablished in Madrid, he became a leading light in the group of young composers working to revive the native tradition, producing the successful two-act zarzuela *Colegialas y soldados* (Schoolgirls and Soldiers,

1849). He took over the direction of the Teatro de Variedades later that year, swiftly writing the influential two-act *El duende* (The Ghost, 1849) and the collaborative *Por seguir a una mujer* (In Pursuit of a Wife, 1851) with Barbieri, Oudrid, Inzenga and Gaztambide. His later successes included *El novio pasado por agua* (The Bridegroom in Water, 1852) and *Don Simplicio Bobadilla* (1853, with Barbieri, Gaztambide and Inzenga); but he was gradually eclipsed by his colleagues, and when his zarzuela *El tambor* (The Drum, 1860) enjoyed only a brief *succès d'estime* he retired from active stage composition. None of his works have survived into the modern repertoire, though he remains an important figure in the artistic development of the romantic zarzuela.

José Inzenga (1828–91)

Another important figurehead, Inzenga's career mirrors Rafael Hernando's. Madrid-born son of an Italian singing master and a noted operatic soprano, he left for Paris at an early age where he came under the eye of the composer Auber. This friendship led to his appointment before the age of twenty to the post of Chorus Master of the Opéra Comique, but the 1848 Revolution cut short his Parisian career. Starting afresh in Madrid, he became a staunch advocate for vernacular music theatre, writing his first zarzuela *El campamento* (The Encampment) to a text by Luis de Olona in 1851 and becoming a regular collaborator with Barbieri, Oudrid, Gaztambide and Hernando in a series of works including *Por seguir a una mujer* (In Pursuit of a Wife, 1851) and *El secreto de la reina* (The Queen's Secret, 1852). Less productive than his colleagues, his finest hour came in 1862 with *¡Si yo fuera rey!*, a success he was unable to repeat, although his last zarzuela *A casarse tocan* (Let's Try Marriage, 1877) survived in the repertoire for several seasons. Late in his life Inzenga published a significant collection of popular Spanish songs (1888), but his reputation nowadays hangs by the thin thread of his one great success.

¡Si yo fuera rey! (If I were King, 1862)
An adaptation of a French libretto famously set by Auber as *Si J'etais Roi!*, Inzenga's three-act *zarzuela grande* became even more popular in Spain and the Hispanic world. The plot, translated to eighteenth century Florence, revolves round a trick played on the poor fisherman Genaro by a group of noblemen, who convince him that he is their King. Inzenga's score is gracefully Italianate, with strongly direct melodic inspiration. The best known number is Genaro's fetchingly melancholic *Romanza: "Por el mar de la esperanza"* in barcarolle rhythm, but much else is of similar quality in a score overdue for modern revival.

Sebastián Iradier (1809–65)

After work in Madrid, Paris (as singing teacher to the Empress Eugénie) and Cuba, he ended his career as professor of singing at the Madrid Conservatory, writing at least one zarzuela with Oudrid, *La pradera del canal* (The Canal Meadow, 1847). Principally known in his lifetime for songs such as *La Paloma* (The Dove) and Cuban-style habaneras, his chief claim to fame was to compose *El arreglito* (The Compromise) which Bizet used as the *Habañera* (sic) in *Carmen*, apparently under the impression that it was a genuine folk-song.

Miguel Marqués (1843–1918)

Born in Palma de Mallorca, Marqués was the son of the town's chocolate maker. After 1859 family finance enabled him to study in Paris, and in 1863 he was admitted to the orchestra of the Théâtre Lyrique, commencing serious compositional studies with Hector Berlioz. His training was cut short by a call-up for Mallorcan military service, but from 1866 he was able to study composition at the Madrid Conservatory with Arrieta while playing in the orchestra of the Teatro de la Zarzuela. His numerous and highly esteemed orchestral compositions include five substantial symphonies (1869–80), as well as the once-popular light classic *Primera lágrima* (First Tear). Symphonic composition gradually took a back seat as his theatrical reputation developed.

His first zarzuela *Justos por pecadores* (Justice for Sinners) dates from 1872, but his first and best sustained success came in 1878 with the *zarzuela grande El anillo de hierro*. Later three-act works include the critically esteemed *El reloj de Lucerna*, and he took up the new *género chico* style appropriately with *El plato del día* (The Dish of the Day, 1889) and in *El monaguillo* (1891) which is still occasionally revived. He continued to write, but faded from the public eye, dying a forgotten figure back in the town of his birth. Marqués' theatre work was championed by the great critic Antonio Peña y Goñi, and he was celebrated in his heyday as the most powerful composer of the *zarzuela grande*. The unusual breadth and depth of his formal training is evident from his harmonic and instrumental sophistication; and though his muse may sing with a strong French or Italian accent, his symphonies and several of the stage works may prove well worth reviving.

El anillo de hierro (The Ring of Iron, 1878)
This three-act melodrama set on the coast of Norway remains the composer's best-known work, not least because substantial highlights are available on a classic CD with Teresa Berganza. The iron ring is a keepsake given to her fisherman lover Rodolfo by Margarita, a Count's daughter. Her cruel, aristocratic suitor convinces the fisherman that she has been untrue, but in the nick of time his villainy is revealed, Rudolfo

turns out to be the long-long son of a nobleman, and the young couple are able to marry. The highlights of Marqués' intense score is the heroine's second *Romanza*, the melancholy, Italianate *"Lágrimas mías"* with its rich writing for strings.

El monaguillo (The Novice, 1891)
An amusing one-act *género chico* farce set mainly in a convent school, where the boy Colás is deputizing for his sister Antonia as a novice, to give her the opportunity to marry a cavalry officer and avoid becoming a nun. Marqués' brief score reveals command of a light musical style quite different from his weighty *zarzuelas grandes*, and the results are delightful and highly theatrical. The undoubted highlight is a catchy mazurka for "the novice" and a chorus of young lady boarders (*Canto del monaguillo: "Yo amaba a una muchacha"*).

El reloj de Lucerna (The Lucerne Clock, 1884)
Based on events in Switzerland after the death of William Tell, the three-act, melodramatic *zarzuela grande El reloj de Lucerna* is of operatic scope and intensity. Marqués' most ambitious work, it triumphed not only in Spain, but in Hispanic America. Even though the score is shadowed by Wagner's *Lohengrin* as surely as by Rossini's *Guillaume Tell*, it is full of fine things. The Overture and substantial third act *Preludio*, with its unexpected chromatic modulations, are especially impressive; and a revival is long overdue.

Miguel Nieto (1844–1915)

The son of a bandmaster, Nieto wrote his first zarzuela at the age of fifteen and enjoyed a long and lucrative career in Madrid. His greatest solo efforts were the unpretentious *El gorro frigio* (The Phrygian Cap, 1888) and *El gaitero* (The Piper, 1896). The amusing farce *El barbero de Sevilla* (The Barber of Seville, 1901) written in collaboration with Gerónimo Giménez (q.v.) is still very often encountered. Of many other works successful in their day, perhaps *Cuadros disolventes* (Dissolving Scenes, 1896) is best remembered for the ubiquitous *Chotis: "Con una falda de percal planchá"*, still popular throughout Spain in many arrangements.

Cristóbal Oudrid (1825–77)

One of the more flamboyant figures involved in the resuscitation of zarzuela during the middle years of the century, Oudrid's father was of Estremaduran gypsy stock, and Cristóbal was largely self-taught. In 1842 he arrived in Madrid, earning his living as a pianist and having his first, short zarzuela-style musical entertainments performed in 1847. Over the next few years he actively promoted zarzuela at the Teatro Circo and the new Teatro de la Zarzuela, writing in collaboration with Barbieri, Gaztambide, Hernando and Inzenga as well as alone. His most successful works included *Estebanillo* (1855); *El postillón de la Rioja* (1856); and *El molinero de Subiza* (The Miller of Subiza, 1870).

Conducting gradually took up more of his time and attention; and after the failure of his magnum opus *Ildara* (1874) he largely gave up composing in favor of the podium. His work is now almost forgotten, though the *Jota* taken from his incidental music for Lombia's play *El sitio de Zaragoza* (The Siege of Zaragoza) remains a staple of the wind band repertoire. What remains is the memory of a provocative, bohemian personality who cared more for pragmatic music making than theory or technique—a choice which may account for the fact that his once-popular body of work has sunk almost without trace.

El postillón de la Rioja (The Postillion from Rioja, 1856)
A light comedy of aristocratic amours in the French style, where farcical complications stem from disguises and mistaken identities—not least that of the hero, Feliz, a nobleman disguised as the eponymous postillion. Despite the titular coincidence, Oudrid's two-act zarzuela has few points of similarity with Adam's well-known comic opera *Le postillon de Lonjumeau* (1836). The music, including the once-popular *Jota: "A la orilla del Ebro niña te vi"*, is uncomplicated, tuneful and direct, much less in debt to Italian models than the music of Oudrid's more sophisticated contemporaries.

Agustín Pérez Soriano (1846–1907)

A leading light of Zaragoza's music scene who wrote chamber and symphonic works as well as zarzuelas, Pérez Soriano is now remembered for just one song from one work: Perico's *Jota: "Suena guitarrico mío"* from his one-act *sainete El guitarrico* (The Little Guitarist, 1900). The composer was a noted musicologist, and his famous *Jota* has all the freshness of the Aragonese folksongs and dances he loved to collect.

José Rogel (1829–1901)

Chief composer for Francisco Arderius, whose *Bufos madrileños* provided the competition which helped steer zarzuela away from the *zarzuela grande* toward the one-act, *género chico* style prevalent in the latter years of the century, Rogel wrote and adapted huge quantities of music for the actor-impresario in the 1860s. He was instrumental in introducing Offenbach's operettas such as *La Belle Hélène* to Madrid, and his own music owes much to the parodistic Parisian style. His most influential single work was the zarzuela *El joven Telémaco* (Young Telemachus, 1866) but Rogel is remembered for historical rather than musical reasons.

Emilio Serrano (1850–1939)

A highly influential teacher and academic who succeeded Arrieta as composition professor at the Madrid Conservatory in 1894. His works included a symphony, overtures and tone poems as well as operas including *Doña Juana la Loca* (Crazy Doña Juana, 1890) and zarzuelas. Late in his life he helped the young Alonso with the instrumentation of *La bejarana* (1924), and his encouragement to younger musicians and composers remains strong in Spanish musical consciousness.

Joaquín Valverde (1846–1910)

Born in the Estremaduran capital of Badajoz, Valverde studied composition at the Madrid Conservatory under Emilio Arrieta, winning first prize in 1870 and thereafter conducting theatre orchestras in the capital. His forgotten orchestral works include two symphonies, but the majority of his works were theatrical collaborations. The long list of his theatrical partners includes Fernández Caballero, Chapí, José Rogel, Bretón and Torregrosa.

His friendship with Federico Chueca dates from 1872, and their first work together was *El sobrino del difunto* (The Deceased's Cousin) three years later. The epoch-making *La canción de la Lola* (Lola's Song, 1880) was followed by a long stream of works, of which *La Gran Vía* (1886), *Cádiz* (1886) and *El año pasado por agua* (The Year Under Water, 1889) are among the most important. Indeed, for the March from *Cádiz* both composers were awarded the Military Grand Cross.

After breaking with Chueca he enjoyed several solo successes, notably *La baraja francesa* (French Cards, 1890) to a libretto by Sinesio Delgado, but these soon faded from view. In any case, he continued to write *sainetes* with other composers, notably his son "Quinito," of which *La noche de San Juan* (Saint John's Night, 1894) was perhaps the most successful.

Valverde was the collaborative musician par excellence, and though it is impossible to speak categorically about the extent of his work with Chueca, it is generally accepted that his main contribution was some orchestral and harmonic polish. The paradoxical fact of his being one of the very few zarzuela composers to acquire a reputation outside Spain is down to one work alone: *La Gran Vía*, the great *revista* which he wrote with his friend Federico Chueca, and which brought their names to popular notice in Paris, Vienna, New York and London.

Joaquín ("Quinito") Valverde Sanjuán (1875–1918)

Son of Joaquín Valverde, Joaquín Junior (known as "Quinito") studied under his father and at the Madrid Conservatory, writing his first zarzuela *Con las de Caín* (With Cain's Children, 1890) when only fifteen, to a libretto later set by Sorozábal. This was the first of over two hundred *género chico* zarzuelas and *revistas* in which he had a hand. A few of these were solo efforts. Others he created with his father; but the best of them, beginning with *Los puritanos* (The Puritans) in 1894 were written with Torregrosa. *El pobre diablo* (Poor Devil, 1897), *El primer reserva* (The First Exception, 1897) and the short *El pobre Valbuena* (Poor Valbuena, 1904) were amongst their successes. With Ramón Estellés he wrote some popular works including *La marcha de Cádiz* (The March from Cadiz, 1896); and of his several collaborations with the young Serrano, *El pollo Tejada* (That Tejada Fellow, 1906) and *El amigo Melquíades* (Friend Melquíades, 1914) are still occasionally heard.

His career blossomed when he moved to Paris after the death of his father in 1910. Success followed both there and on Broadway in revues and pastiches such as *L'Amour en Espagne* (Paris, 1909), *The Land of Joy* (New York, 1917) and the less successful *A Night in Spain* (New York, 1917). He died aged forty three only eight years after his father whilst on tour in Mexico City. Just as natural a collaborator as Valverde Senior, his contributions are equally hard to isolate; and strangely like his father, his fame has been larger—at least compared to that of his contemporaries—outside his native Spain. His only well-known unaided work is the song *Clavelitos* (Carnations, 1909), a lively vignette popular with sopranos and their audiences the world over. It reveals a deft hand without any strongly personal style.

26
Twentieth Century

Tomás Barrera Saavedra (1870–1938)

A pupil of Chapí in Madrid, who produced a series of effective, lightweight zarzuelas just after the turn of the century, alone and in partnership with "Quinito" Valverde, José Serrano and others of his generation. His solo works include *El código penal* (The Penal Code, 1901); *La silla de manos* (The Sedan Chair, 1905); and *La mujer de cartón* (The Cardboard Lady, 1908). His oeuvre is pretty much forgotten, except for the haunting *Romanza: "Granadinas"* from *Emigrantes* (1905, with Rafael Calleja), made famous by Tito Schipa, Miguel Fleta and many later tenors.

Rafael Gómez Calleja (1874–1938)

Burgos-born Calleja studied composition at the Madrid Conservatory with Arrieta before embarking on a stellar career as orchestral conductor and composer. His zarzuela company successfully toured Spain, Portugal and Latin America, performing many of his works written alone or in collaboration. Amazingly, these number more than 300 titles, among the most famous of which were *El iluso Cañizares* (Deluded Cañizares, with Quinito Valverde, 1905); *El banco del Retiro* (The Bench in the Retiro Park, 1908); and *La estrella de Oriente* (Star of the East, 1915). His greatest critical triumph was probably *Las bribonas* (The Rascals, 1908) but even this is unfamiliar nowadays.

Fernando Díaz Giles (1887–1960)

For many years the Sevillian Díaz Giles combined a musical career with life as an army officer based in Toledo, where he wrote the *Himno de la Academia de Infantería* (Infantry Academy Anthem, 1911) which is still performed on ceremonial army occasions. Music for silent films and concert pieces, including a dashing *Danza Siberiana* (Siberian Dance) written just after the Russian Revolution of 1917, formed the bulk of his output before 1923, the year he resigned his commission.

A brilliant pianist and musician of taste and discrimination, albeit without any special individuality, Díaz Giles went on to create a series of attractive zarzuelas, preceded by the opera *Rocío* (1926). His finest works include *El romeral* (1929); *El renegado* (The Renegade, 1931) following the career of Juan Valdés; *El cantante enmascarado* (The Masked Singer, 1934); and *El divo* (The Singer, 1944). Songs from these are still occasionally heard in recital, but his only zarzuela to hold the stage nowadays is the much-loved *El cantar del arriero* (1930), which admirably exhibits his generous melodic gift.

El cantar del arriero (The Song of the Muleteer, 1930)
A two-act zarzuela set in and around a rural inn. The sensational plot culminates in an attempted kidnapping and rape by the brutal but attractive muleteer Lorenzo. He is deflected at the eleventh hour by the fortunate revelation that the girl, Mariblanca, is in fact his own daughter, and the work ends happily all round. The score is skillful and robust if not specially subtle; the highlights are the baritone Lorenzo's lusty entrance number (*Canción: "Soy arriero"*) and his surprisingly delicate *Romanza: "Sólo una boca que se pueda besar"*, a love song ironically addressed to his own daughter.

El romeral (The Rosemary Field, with **Emilio Acevedo**, 1929)
The story of this two-act romantic zarzuela revolves around the familiar situation of the virtuous wife, Carmela, groundlessly suspected of infidelity. The picturesque customs of the small village in which the action takes place add color to proceedings, but the main musical impact comes from the graceful lyricism of the romantic *dúos* and solo *romanzas*, of which Carmela's *"¡Que triste Cruz de Mayo!"* is an outstanding example.

Juan Dotras Vila (1900–78)

One of the last generation of creative *zarzueleros*, Dotras Vila's prolific output enjoyed considerable success in its day but has not endured the test of time. A brilliant pianist, his first great compositional success was the *revista Kosmópolis* (1928), though the majority of his stage works were written after the Civil War. They include *Romanza húngara* (Gypsy Romance, 1937); the operetta *El caballero del amor* (The Knight of Love, 1939); and perhaps least forgotten nowadays, the sentimentally retrospective *Aquella canción antigua* (That Old Song, 1952).

Manuel de Falla (1876–1946)

One of the acknowledged twentieth century masters, Spain's greatest composer had some bruising early encounters with the robustly commercial zarzuela world, and expressed negative feelings about the genre ever after. Around the turn of the century he did some anonymous orchestrations for Chueca, and wrote five zarzuelas—three in collaboration with Amadeu Vives, a fellow pupil of Pedrell—of which only *Los amores de la Inés* (1902) reached the stage. Nonetheless the influence of zarzuela, specifically Giménez' masterpiece *La tempranica*, on his early opera *La vida breve* (Short Life, 1913) is patent.

Los amores de la Inés (The Amours of Inés, 1902)
Falla's zarzuela to a text by Emilio Dugi is a modest, farcical *género chico sainete* with a Madrid setting. There is a lively *Preludio*, a gentler *Intermedio* and four vocal numbers. Most notable is a *Dúo* for soprano and tenor in the alternating 3/4 and 6/8 meter that was to become a trademark of the mature composer; but otherwise little suggests Falla's transcendent talent.

Jesús García Leoz (1904–53)

Best known for his music to over eighty films including such Spanish classics as *Balarrasa* and *Bienvenido Mr. Marshall*, Leoz worked as an orchestrator for Jacinto Guerrero before writing one masterly, prize-winning zarzuela *La Duquesa del candil* (1949) of his own. He was at work on another, *La alegre alcaldesa* (The Merry Mayor's Wife), as well as an opera *Barataria*; and his early death was a considerable blow to the future of Spanish musical theatre.

La Duquesa del candil (The Duchess of the Oil-lamp, 1949)
A three act *zarzuela grande* in an aristocratic, eighteenth century milieu, *La duquesa del candil* is much more than an exercise in operetta-nostalgia. The closed forms and courtly, antique harmonies give Leoz's score a paradoxically modern, neoclassical ambience; and the fine quality of his lyrical inspiration is equaled by his structural grasp. Amid many attractive vocal numbers, the tenor *Romanza: "Paloma de mis madriles"* stands out for the quicksilver elegance of its emotional shifts.

José Padilla (1889–1960)

Trained in his home town of Almería, at the Madrid Conservatory and in Italy, Padilla rapidly became immersed in Madrid theatre life, and the first of his large output of zarzuelas was *La mala hembra* (Wicked Woman, 1906), a one-act *sainete* to a libretto by Ventura de la Vega, grandson of the well-known playwright of the same name, who was to be a regular collaborator in his early years. A string of one-act *sainetes* and *revistas* followed, among which *Juan Miguel* (1909), *Los viejos verdes* (The Old Boys, with "Quinito" Valverde, 1909), and *Luzbel* (1917, with Miguel Nieto) stand out.

He later spent much time in Paris, where he wrote the scores for two *opérettes*, as well as the many popular songs which were incorporated in revues at the Moulin Rouge and elsewhere. These songs, which include *El relicario* (The Reliquary), *La violetera* (The Violet Seller) and the pasodoble *Valencia*, brought him international celebrity and keep his memory green today. Despite his success abroad, Padilla continued to write for the Spanish stage. Many of his best-known songs were in fact adapted from zarzuela numbers: *Valencia* comes straight from the enjoyable *La bien amada* (The Well-beloved, 1924) which enjoyed a notable success in Barcelona. Perhaps the best received of his later works was *La hechichera en Palacio* (The Palace Witch, 1950).

Many people who would claim never to have heard of Padilla will certainly know his tunes, the best of which retain their freshness despite years of hackneyed maltreatment at the hands of tea-room quartets and suburban dance orchestras. The graceful, sun-drenched, lilting *El relicario*, for example, obstinately refuses to lie down and die. *La violetera* was appropriated by Charlie Chaplin for his film *City Lights*. The jaunty *Valencia* has even become a sort of unofficial national anthem. His skill as a sweet melodist and orchestrator is to communicate a delightful air of relaxed enjoyment, and although his complete zarzuelas are unlikely to regain a foothold in the repertoire, the songs will be with us for many years to come.

Manuel López Quiroga (1899–1988)

Perhaps the most famous exponent of the *copla*, Madrid's answer to the Paris *chanson*, of which his best known are *A la lima y al limón* (The Lime and the Lemon) and *Ojos verdes* (Green Eyes). His musical comedies such as *Maria de la O* (1935, not to be confused with Lecuona's Cuban zarzuela) and *La reina fea* (The Fairy Queen, 1941) provided a platform for many of these; most of his handful of zarzuelas were written early in life, a notable exception being the tuneful one-act *La Marquesa chulapa* (The City-girl Marquesa, 1949).

Joaquín Rodrigo (1902–99)

Spain's most celebrated composer from the last half of the century is known the world over for one work: his justifiably ubiquitous *Concierto de Aranjuez* for guitar and orchestra. The blind Rodrigo was closely associated with Federico Moreno Torroba in their determination to reestablish *casticismo* (authenticity) in Spanish music, and together they wrote the operetta *El duende azul* (The Blue Ghost, 1946). Eighteen years later Rodrigo's *El hijo fingido* was finally mounted at the Teatro de la Zarzuela to critical acclaim, and it has been successfully revived in Madrid since.

El hijo fingido (The False Son, 1964)
Rodrigo's lyric zarzuela in a prologue and two acts is based on a pair of Lope de Vega's lighter aristocratic comedies, and maintains the seventeenth century setting of the originals. It was written in the mid-1950s, during his most fertile musical period. The style is his personal fusion of witty, tasteful neoclassical form and quintessentially Spanish romantic content. One piquant number follows another; and if the sum is less than the parts, there is no gainsaying the quality of Rodrigo's score. The Act 2 *Preludio*, an extended series of variations for harp and orchestra on the folksong *Guárdame las vacas* (Watching the Cows), is perhaps the most delectable highlight.

María Rodrigo (1888–1967)

A fine pianist and composer who studied under Emilio Serrano at the Madrid Conservatory, and later in Munich. She left Madrid after the Civil War to live in Puerto Rico, and disappeared from public view during the 1950s. Her music, in a variety of forms, exhibited an individual, poetic delicacy and was well received critically. The best of her theatre pieces were written before 1920, and none have been revived in recent years; they included the operetta-zarzuelas *Diana cazadora* (Diana the Huntress, 1915) and *Las hazañas de un pícaro* (Exploits of a Crook, 1920).

Jesús Romo (1906–95)

A prolific composer for stage and screen, his first zarzuela was *La bien ganada* (The Woman Well Won, 1934). Many others followed, notably *El mesón del Pato Rojo* (Red Duck Inn, 1938); *Los cachorros* (The Cubs, 1945); *Un día de primavera* (A Spring Day, 1947); and perhaps his most absorbing work *El gaitero de Gijón* (The Piper of Gijón, 1953). Romo's easy, fluent style was very popular in its day, but has not worn well.

Ernesto Rosillo (1893–1968)

A highly talented pupil of composer Conrado del Campo at the Madrid Conservatory, Rosillo's career as a *zarzuelero* got off to a fine start with *La serranilla* (The Eclogue, 1919) for which Romero and Shaw provided the libretto. The trio followed up with *Las delicias de Capua* (The Delights of Capua) the following year, and their operetta *Luna de mayo* (May Moon,

1934) stands out from the many stage works Rosillo wrote during the prewar years—though the freshly tuneful *revista La granjera de Arlés* (The Farmgirl from Arles, 1923) is equally deserving of revival. After the war, he turned to popular jazz-operettas such as *La rubia del Far West* (The Blonde of the Far West) and *¿Qué sabes tú?* (What Do You Know?, both 1943) continuing to write until at least 1965. It has been said that Rosillo was hampered by a lack of personal ambition; all the more frustrating, given his musical wit, strikingly individual melodic gift and refined instrumental imagination.

Juan Tellería (1895–1948)

Basque composer who studied under the very young Usandizaga in San Sebastián, with Conrado del Campo in Madrid, and after 1928 in Paris. Most of his short working life thereafter was spent as an academic at the Madrid Conservatory; but he did score a signal success with his zarzuela *El joven piloto* (The Young Pilot, 1934) which remained in the active repertoire for many years after the Civil War. Its longevity was partly due to official gratitude for the now notorious Falangist Anthem *Cara al sol* (Face to the Sun) which Tellería penned at the time of the Civil War. A second major zarzuela *Las viejas ricas* (The Rich Old Ladies) mounted the year before his death did not enjoy the same good fortune.

27
Catalan Sarsuela

In the middle of the nineteenth century Barcelona's writers and musicians were not far behind their Madrid colleagues in their desire to bring a vernacular music theatre to birth. Although a number of worthy native operas were created (not least the great teacher Felipe Pedrell's Wagnerian trilogy *Els Pirineus*, The Pyrenees) Catalan *sarsuela* did not enjoy the same healthy growth as its *madrileño* sibling; and despite the fact that many of the greatest Iberian composers and musicians over the next 100 years were Catalan speakers *sarsuela* always took second place in popularity to the Spanish form. Nevertheless, a number of composers produced native language works which courted comparison with the best that Madrid could offer.

Josep Anselm Clavé (1824–74)

An autodidact whose involvement in the renaissance of Catalan nationalism went far beyond his compositional work, Clavé underwent deportation and imprisonment on several occasions before the declaration of the first republic in 1873 made him a national as well as regional hero. His most significant *sarsuela*-style works, *L'aplec del Remei* (The Remedy Applied, 1858) and the politically controversial *L'art de la Bruixeria* (The Witch's Art, 1867) were the first significant attempt to create a modern lyric theatre in the Catalan language.

Urbà Fando (1855–1911)

Barcelona's most popular composer during the great days of the Madrid *sainete* in the last years of the nineteenth century, Fando wrote several successful kindred *sarsuelas* to librettos by Conrad Colomer. His palmy days were the three years 1894–1896, during which he produced many of his best works, including *L'illa tranquil·la* (The Tranquil Isle) and *El príncep del Congo* (Prince of the Congo, both 1894); the brief, farcical *Lo somni de la Ignocència* (Sleep of the Innocent, 1895); and *Veralet, pare i fill, del comerç de Barcelona* (Veralet, Father and Son, of the Barcelona Business, 1896).

Nicolau Manent (1827–87)

Born at Mahón in the Balearics and spending most of his working life in Barcelona, Manent's substantial musical work in all fields, sacred and secular, is now largely forgotten. His Catalan stage works, which included *El pou de la veritat* (The Well of Truth, 1875) and *El cant de la Marsellesa* (The Marseillaise, 1877) were overshadowed by his major Spanish-language triumph at Madrid's Teatro de la Zarzuela: the musical version of Zorrilla's great comedy *Don Juan Tenorio* prepared by Manent in partnership with the author in 1877. This, too, awaits a modern revival.

Rafael Martínez Valls (1887–1946)

Though originally a Valencian, and a medical student, Martínez Valls eventually took his place among the most important Barcelona-based composers. He is the only Catalan musician whose *sarsuelas* are regularly accorded a niche in the repertoire's pantheon. He wrote substantial amounts of orchestral and chamber music, sacred motets and masses, but it is largely for his stage work that he is remembered today.

The political fervor of the 1920s was conducive to music theatre of a nationalistic bent; and with *Cançó d'Amor i de Guerra* (1926) Martínez Valls scored a huge success. The work became a focal point for a new-style romantic sarsuela with room for political as well as social messages; and his later Catalan works such as the almost equally famous *La Legió d'Honor*, *L'Àliga Roja* (The Red Eagle) and *La Ventera del Ansó* (The Innkeeper of Ansó, all 1930) cemented his fame and influence. He also wrote Spanish zarzuelas, but these did not succeed so well; and perhaps inevitably his work was largely eclipsed after the Civil War. His musical technique was sound, his melodic gift direct and strongly theatrical; these qualities have enabled his greatest *sarsuela* to weather the storms of political fortune.

Cançó d'Amor i de Guerra (Song of Love and War, 1926)
The action of this two-act *sarsuela* takes place in the Vallespir, the Catalan region of France, in 1793. Eloi is a simple blacksmith who wants nothing to do with the revolutionary ferment around him, but finally becomes a Republican captain to win

the freedom of Francina, the woman he loves. Víctor Mori and Lluis Capdevila's dramatic libretto makes express points about the necessity for political action, and the musical score powerfully underlines the romantic and political turmoil of the plot. In particular, the leading role of Eloi has become a showcase for great tenors from Emilio Vendrell to José Carreras. Highlights include his Song of the Blacksmith (*Cançó del Forjador: "Forjador, bon forjador"*); the intoxicating Farandole Ballet which closes the first act; and Eloi's uplifting evocation to the Pyrenees mountains *"Pireneu, les blanques comes"* from the last scene.

La Legió d'Honor (The Legion of Honor, 1930)
The Foreign Legion are billeted in a Normandy village during the last months of World War I. The amours of Catalan volunteer Marcel and black regimental trumpeter Trabuc form the backbone of the plot: after saving his beloved Carlota from the clutches of a villainous officer Marcel has to volunteer for a heroic death mission. After the war he returns, having lost his left arm but gaining the girl—and the medal of the Legion of Honor. The musical highlights include a remarkable chorus in which hungry soldiers rhythmically bang their spoons against metal plates (anticipating Zimmermann's opera *Die Soldaten*!). Marcel's Catalan origin allows him a fine *Sardana: "Ja la cobla toca al lluny"*, and his noble *Romança: "Tot s'ha acabat er mi"* provides a fine climax to a consistently high-voltage score.

Enric Morera (1865–1942)

One of the most proactively influential of Catalan composers for much of his life, Morera spent a considerable number of years in Argentina, and the sunny simplicity of his lyric style owes something to his experiences there. The main thrust of his work was devoted to the development of Catalan opera and *sarsuela*. His opera *Tassarba* (1916) has been successfully revived; but like the best of his *sarsuelas La Santa Espina* (The Holy Thorn, 1907, source of a still-popular *Sardana*); *Don Joan de Serrallonga* (1922); and *Baixant de la Font del Gat* (1925) its memory is honored more in the breach than the observance.

Baixant de la Font del Gat (Down at Cat Fountain, 1925)
Morera reworked a spoken tragicomedy into a one-act musical drama, very much in the style of the *sainete madrileño*. The plot, set in tumultuous 1840 Barcelona, follows the consequences of a spitefully slanderous ballad sung by the jealous Teresina about her innocent friend Marieta. Morera's music is clear, facile and unfailingly popular in style; the *Sardana: "Visca l'alegria"* and tenor *Romança: "No puc esser feliç"* are memorably so.

Don Joan de Serrallonga (1922)
A full-length tragedy recounting the adventures and sorry end of a famous Catalan highwayman, acclaimed at the time of its premiere as Morera's most masterly popular stage work, and a genuine breakthrough in the history of Catalan *sarsuela*.

The unpretentious music shines with the composer's customary lyric distinction: the attractive *Romança: "Jo vull morir amb ell"* sung by El Fadrí de Sau (The Lad from Sau) is an outstandingly beautiful piece of writing for tenor voice.

Francesc D'Assís Rosselló I Sintes (1828–98)

Rosselló founded the first symphony orchestra and choral society in his home town of Ciutadella de Menorca in the Balearic Islands. His compositions include many sacred works, including a tuneful three-part Mass with orchestra (1884). Rosselló's popular three-act *sarsuela Foc i Fum* (Fire and Smoke, 1885) has an old-fashioned charm far removed from Madrid's *sainetes* of the time; though thoroughly Donizettian in mode, it does employ a traditional Menorcan town band and rustic pipe and tabor music.

Eduardo Toldrá (1895–1962)

One of the most distinguished of twentieth century Iberian composers, Toldrá's output contains masterful works in almost every genre and form. His songs, orchestral and chamber music are well known at least in Spain; as is his chamber opera *El giravolt de Maig* (The May Somersault, 1928) dedicated to Amadeu Vives and written in a lucid, popular poetic style which has clear debts to the *género chico* tradition.

28
Cuban Zarzuela

Most Hispanic countries developed their own zarzuela-like traditions. Peru's dates back to 1701, with Torrejón's version of *La púrpura de la rosa*; Mexico and the Philippines can boast strong, native lyric theatre movements; Argentina produced Astor Piazzolla, whose tango-opera with spoken narrations *María de Buenos Aires* (1967) is zarzuela by any other name; some *aficionados* would even claim Leonard Bernstein's *West Side Story* (1957) is *zarzuela americana*. His Voltaire operetta *Candide* (1956) is certainly from the same stable as Caballero's even zanier global tour, *Los sobrinos del capitán Grant*.

One nation stands out. Cuba's enthusiasm for musical theatre dates back to the late eighteenth century, and after 1850 La Habana (Havana) was often the first foreign port of call for Madrid's newest sensations. Gaztambide and Caballero spent time there; and gradually after independence (1892) native writers and composers modified the *zarzuela grande* form to suit their own tastes, using strong, even lurid story lines and incorporating the melodies and rhythms of the island's rich Afro-Spanish heritage. The mid-1920s witnessed an explosion of popular enthusiasm for zarzuela, and Lecuona and Roig turned the trade wind with colorful dramas which have become a cherished part of the mainstream Madrid repertoire.

Ernesto Lecuona (1896–1963)

Cuba's best-known composer was given a solid musical grounding at the Cuban National Conservatory, under Joaquín Nin and others. He began his remarkable series of *Danzas Cubanas* (Cuban Dances) for piano at the age of fifteen, and his amazing facility as the pianist of Lecuona's Cuban Boys made him well known in America and Europe, where he attracted the enthusiastic attention of Ravel.

Lecuona's reputation centers on piano works such as the *Suite Andalucía* (1929), which incorporates the brooding *Malagueña* from ten years earlier; and on his popular songs, such as the ubiquitous *Siboney* (1927).

As an entrepreneur Lecuona inaugurated a musical theatre company which mounted zarzuelas by several Cuban composers. His own *Niña Rita* (Child Rita, 1927), written in collaboration with Eliseo Grenet (1893–1950), proved a breakthrough; and the brief, brilliant flowering of the Cuban zarzuela dates from its premiere. Of the long list of mainly two-act works which followed, *El cafetal* (1929), *María la O* (1930) and *Rosa la China* (1932) are the most celebrated; but several others, such as *El batey* (The Sugar Factory, 1929) and *Lola Cruz* (1923, rev. 1935) were almost equally famous in their day. His last substantial zarzuela was *La plaza de la catedral* (The Cathedral Square, 1944).

The secret of Lecuona's success was to yoke the romantic sweetness of European operetta to the powerful motor rhythms of Afro-Spanish American folk music, in melodramatic plots of often brutal bloodiness. Compared with his piano music, the results may seem eclectic and crudely populist; but they are undeniably exotic, intense and memorably full of life.

El cafetal (The Coffee Plantation, 1929)
Two worlds cross in *El cafetal*: the suavity of mid-nineteenth century Havana's colonial masters, and the raw, vibrant emotion of the Negro slaves. Two rich young lovers have their amours disturbed by the obsessive plantation slave Lázaro, who is eventually shot in cold blood by his white rival. The fact that Lázaro is already married to the sympathetic slave girl África balances the moral fulcrum of a gripping and serious work. Lecuona's score is his tightest and most consistent, an intoxicating cocktail of sophisticated sentimental melody, percussive native song and dance, tangos and guajiras. Lázaro's passionate *Romanza: "Triste es ser esclavo"* is its *leitmotif*, and África's *Canción: "Africana soy"* is equally memorable.

María la O (1930)
1800 Havana is the setting for Lecuona's most widely traveled two-act zarzuela. A two-timing aristocrat and a poor white, José Innocente, vie for the favors of María la O, a beautiful mulatto. At the sensational climax of the action the jealous José is about to stab his rival when María interposes with the revelation that she is carrying the rich man's child. Lecuona's score, more diffuse than *El cafetal*, is generously full of good things; not least a breathtaking choral-orchestral version of his famous piano piece, the voodoo-tinged *Danza Lucumi*, and the heroine's famous, melancholic *Romanza: "María la O"*.

Rosa la China (Native Rosa, 1932)
This two act modern melodrama takes place in Havana at carnival time. Unhappy Rosa wishes to leave an exploitative husband for the young and ardent José. The husband threatens to kill the lover, but Rosa turns his own knife against him, and

though the guilty pair try to cover up the crime Rosa is arrested and taken to prison. Lecuona's score is felt by some commentators to be too formulaic and lacking in spontaneity. His music is in the same lively, technicolor vein as his earlier triumphs, and numbers such as the choral *Conga: "Va a pasar la conga"* over the Puente de la Lisa bridge have infectious verve.

Rodrigo Prats (1909–80)

Prats commenced musical training under his father Jaime, director of the Cuban Jazz Band, before joining Roig's Havana Symphony Orchestra as a violinist. Later he founded a successful chamber orchestra, becoming an effective conductor as well as composing hit songs (not least the favorite *"Una rosa de Francia"*) before graduating to zarzuela. His vocal writing is more complex than Lecuona's, with a high level of musical sophistication. Prats' stage works include *María Belén Chacón* (1932), *El mayoral* (The Overseer, 1933) and the much-esteemed *Soledad* (1932); but apart from *Amalia Baptista* (1936) his best known work today is the popular *Misa Cubana*.

Amalia Baptista (1936)
Like *Cecilia Valdés* and *María la O*, Prats' popular zarzuela centers on the mulatto girl as tragic victim of Cuban society, lost in limbo between slave and master race. Prats was technically a more finished composer than his older colleagues; and many consider *Amalia Baptista* at least worthy to stand beside those earlier works musically, though perhaps it does not pack their theatrical punch.

Gonzalo Roig (1890–1970)

Starting professional work aged seventeen as a silent cinema pianist, he wrote his first songs the same year and in 1911 produced his most popular, the Creole *Bolero: "Quiéreme mucho"*. By 1922 he was established enough to found (with Lecuona and others) the Havana Symphony Orchestra, a major spur to modern Cuban symphonic composition. Becoming an internationally celebrated band conductor, he worked regularly with the U.S. Forces, and his original pieces and arrangements for wind band are still widely played.

His many zarzuelas, which include *La hija del sol* (Daughter of the Sun, 1933), *El cimarrón* (The Runaway Slave, 1936), and *La Habana de noche* (Havana by Night, 1936) are notable for the range and quality of their popular songs and dances—habanera, guajira, conga, danzón, guaracha and the rest. Roig's finest hour was the first night of his *Cecilia Valdés*, written in a month and a day during early 1932, and still the most universally admired and frequently performed of all Cuban zarzuelas.

Cecilia Valdés (1932)
Adapted from a nineteenth century Cuban novel by Cirilo Villaverde which remains influential today, *Cecilia Valdés* is a sensational melodrama of tragic resonance. A beautiful *mulata* who unwittingly has a love affair with her aristocratic half-brother Leonardo, Cecilia bears his child. Her clarinetist Negro admirer stabs Leonardo as he emerges from his marriage to a rich heiress; and Cecilia retires into a convent, where she recognizes her dying mother who entered the cloister in shame eighteen years before. Roig's score is the classic Cuban mixture of sentimental operetta-romance and wild, percussive song and dance, including a riotous wind band *Contradanza*. The most memorable character is the crazy old Black woman, Dolores Santa Cruz, whose prayer-like *Tango-Conga: "Po, po, po"* is as extraordinary in conception as execution.

29
Writers

Much has been written about the composers of zarzuela, very much less about the merits of the writers who put their plays at the musicians' service. Yet the text is the main vehicle for the comedy, the satire, the drama, the characters and their feelings at every period of the zarzuela. In many cases, at least half of the running time will be "straight" theatre without music. These texts vary from brilliant to anodyne or worse, but the finest writers created a body of high quality work which sets the Spanish lyric theatre on a higher pedestal than others.

Carlos Arniches (1866–1943)

Arniches became the most prestigious writer of one-act *sainetes* in the first decade of the twentieth century, although his background was far removed from the Madrid literary coffee houses and *tertulias* that bred so many of the capital's celebrated stage writers. He left home in Alicante aged fourteen for a post in a Barcelona bank, later working in a sewing machine factory. A benevolent maiden aunt covered the costs of a mutual move to Madrid in 1885, though she soon retired to Valencia and left him to his own financial devices. Penury forced him to move back to Barcelona, but one clever idea—a Rhyming Alphabet based on incidents from the life of Alfonso XII, dedicated to his young son and heir Alfonso XIII—won the heart of the Queen, who ordered its use in all Spanish schools. Arniches returned to Madrid, this time for good.

Arniches' scripts were in great demand, and altogether he had a hand in over two hundred stage pieces. For Chapí he penned many works alone or un-aided including *El puñao de rosas* (1902); for Caballero he wrote the spruce *El cabo primero* (1895, with Celso Lucio); for Chueca, *Los descamisados* (The Ragamuffins, 1893) and *El coche correo* (The Mail Coach, 1896), both with José López Silva. Of his many *sainetes* for Torregrosa *El santo de la Isidra* and *La fiesta de San Antón* (both 1898) retain their popularity; as does *El pobre Valbuena* (1904) with music by Torregrosa and "Quinito" Valverde, and lyrics by Enrique García Álvarez. Arniches and García Álvarez also enjoyed great success writing *sainetes* for the young Serrano such as *El pollo Tejada* (1906) and the gritty, fast-paced *Alma de Dios* (1907). *La alegría del batallón* (1909) was written for the same composer with Félix Quintana. Alone, he wrote *El amigo Melquíades* (1914) for Serrano and "Quinito" Valverde.

All these are one-act *sainetes* with or without music, full of *costumbrismo* (popular life and customs) and written in the effortlessly fresh, buoyant style which was his trademark. His spoken dialogue (other writers often wrote the sung lyrics) is fluent but far from vapid, sparkling with keen wit. His texts have a moral framework which allays any suspicion of frivolity; though it has been truthfully observed that it is not so much what an Arniches character does which is important, but what he or she says. His heyday was the period between 1916 and 1921, when he was a nationally known and loved figure. Arniches moved to Argentina at the onset of the Civil War, but returned to die in his beloved Madrid.

Francisco Camprodón (1816–70)

Camprodón was one of the leading spirits in the revival of native theatre, and he worked with most of the influential composers of the day. Like all his fellow playwrights at the dawn of Spanish nationalism, he felt his way tentatively, first translating comedies from the French. His best-known work for Barbieri was *Los diamantes de la corona* (from a French original, 1854); and only after he had acquired confidence in his technique did he risk the creation of fully original texts. With Gaztambide his many successes included the one-act gem *Una vieja* (1860); he collaborated with Arrieta on the original zarzuela version of *Marina* (1855), adapted after his death by Miguel Ramos Carrión into the opera still popular today. A genial, generous man much mourned at his death, the best of Camprodón's plays and libretti demonstrate a clarity which was a model for later writers.

Anselmo Cuadrado Carreño (1896–1952) and Luis Fernández de Sevilla (1888–1974)

Carreño was among the most prolific *zarzueleros* of his day. The few libretti he wrote unaided have not remained in the repertoire, and many of his best remembered theatre pieces were put together in collaboration with de Sevilla. One of their first works together was *La vaquerita* (The Cowgirl, for Rosillo, 1924). Many successes followed, including the evergreen *La del soto del Parral*

(Soutullo and Vert, 1927) and *La cautiva* (Guridi, 1931). Their epochal *Los Claveles* (Serrano, 1929) stands somewhat apart. This was the first of an unofficial *madrileño* trilogy which make up a colorful picture of the capital in the frantic years before the Spanish Civil War, though Carreño went on to bring out the other two—*La del manojo de rosas* (Sorozábal, 1934) and *Me llaman la presumida* (Alonso, 1935)—with another popular comic writer, Francisco Ramos de Castro (1890–1963). Of the later collaborations with de Sevilla *Don Manolito* (Sorozábal, 1943) stands out as perhaps the last perfect flowering of the *sainete madrileño* tradition.

It is difficult to speak with certainty, but Carreño is not credited with the lion's share of the writing with de Sevilla, or for that matter with Ramos de Castro. His most significant contribution would seem to lie in his bold and even innovative theatrical imagination. For example, Ascención's *Romanza* in *La del manojo de rosas* serves effectively as a bridge between two distinct scenes, starting in one location and ending in another. Although this is now a commonplace of the musical theatre, Carreño seems to be the first writer to have attempted the trick. At all events, many of the robust libretti he wrote with de Sevilla and Ramos de Castro have stood the test of time admirably.

Miguel Ramos Carrión (1845–1915)

Miguel Ramos Carrión initially embarked on a military career. Finding a soldier's life far from his taste, he simulated profound deafness and was discharged as "quite useless." After this happy release he worked as a newspaper editor and journalist, novelist, poet and prolific theatrical writer. So successful were his most popular plays that they were translated into French (a reversal of the usual literary trade of the time) and many other languages, including English.

His first lyric work was for Arderius' *Los bufos madrileños*, nursery of the emerging *chico* style. There he met Arrieta, who later asked Carrión to write texts for the operatic expansion of *Marina* (1871). This he did with the graceful fluency of Camprodón's original, a model for many of his later, original three-act works. Carrión wrote for many leading composers of the day but two regular "clients" stand out. For Caballero he wrote a group of zarzuelas including the egregiously tongue-in-cheek spectacular *Los sobrinos del capitán Grant* (1877). For Chapí he provided involving *zarzuela grande* plots including the maritime melodrama *La tempestad* (1882), the supernatural thriller *La bruja* (1887, with Vital Aza) and the operetta-comedy *El rey que rabió* (1891, again with Aza).

Ramos Carrión's output was phenomenal. He moved easily between *zarzuela grande* and the realistic *chico* style, writing about thirty *revistas* and comedy *sainetes*.

His longer works were very much in the poetic, Italianate style, prized by Madrid's literary lions; while for Chueca, in *El chaleco blanco* (1890) and *Agua, azucarillos y aguardiente* (1897), he provided a pungent realism, sharp satire and broad comedy in *sainetes* that were a match for anyone. Carrión's work may be uneven, his structures sometimes ramshackle, but his bold characterization and exuberant comedy remain highly effective.

Miguel Echegaray (1845–1915)

Echegaray's distinguished brother, the dramatist and statesman José, sometime Minister of Public Works and Housing, was eventually to win the Nobel Prize for Literature (1904); but ironically, the Laureate's posthumous fame has been overshadowed by that of his theatrical brother. Miguel himself was an active radical who eventually abandoned politics and the law to devote himself to his chief love, the theatre. Echegaray's output of 110 stage works, including twenty-one zarzuelas, would seem prodigious for a playwright today. His zarzuela texts, all in *género chico* style, are outstanding for their clever versification, imaginative and offbeat choice of subject, as well as unerring popular appeal. He wrote for Bretón and Chapí. His four texts for Vives include the festive *La rabalera* (The Girl from Arrabal, 1907) and the circus drama *Juegos malabares* (1910).

Echegaray's chief legacy came from a congenial collaboration with Caballero late in that composer's career. Their seven *sainetes* center on a trio of masterworks, *El dúo de la africana* (1893), *La viejecita* (1897) and finally *Gigantes y cabezudos* (1898). This last is most worthy to stand as his memorial. In addition to Echegaray's accustomed literary taste, its exuberant carnival atmosphere, tight construction, and poignant topicality (the return of the defeated soldiery from the disastrous Cuban war) make it one of the most distinctive and deep achievements in *género chico* zarzuela.

Luis Mariano de Larra (1830–1901)

Luis was the son of the romantic poet and satirist Mariano José de Larra, who committed suicide in 1837 after the collapse of his domestic life: he had left his wife to elope with a married lady, who promptly rejected him. Young Luis proved an easy target for his father's erstwhile victims, the literary and theatrical reviewers that Mariano José had often lampooned, and his work was always greeted with critical opprobrium, despite popular acclaim. There was yet another family scandal when his sister was responsible for defrauding large numbers of people in a financial scam, and eventually even the public finally turned against poor de Larra, booing and stamping their feet during his first nights.

Eventually he was forced to give up theatre work completely. He left a legacy of workmanlike libretti for the Teatro de la Zarzuela, but undoubtedly his major claim to fame is one, great work with Barbieri, the three-act *El barberillo de Lavapiés* (1874). Taking his cue from José Picón in *Pan y toros*, de Larra provided Barbieri with a fine libretto in which the conventionally aristocratic verse drama is overshadowed by the popular language and characters of Madrid, presented with clarity and simplicity. The consequences of this for the development of zarzuela were to be enormous, but *El barberillo* remains a masterpiece in its own right.

Luis de Olona (1823–73)

Olona studied for the law but soon turned to the more congenial atmosphere of the theatre. He wrote plays, many translated from French originals, and librettos for music theatre flowed thick and fast from the middle of the century. His most important initiative came in 1851, when he banded together with fellow writers such as Camprodón and Ventura de la Vega, the group of composers under Barbieri, and the singer Francisco Salas, to rent the Teatro Circo as a base for a permanent company dedicated to the establishment of Spanish zarzuela. Olona became President, and such was the group's success that the inauguration of the national Teatro de la Zarzuela followed five years later in 1856. Here Olona was again the presiding literary spirit, with Barbieri and Gaztambide most prominent among the musicians.

His most significant literary work was to be with Arrieta and Gaztambide. One of his finest texts for the latter was *El juramento* (1858), which proved a sleeping masterpiece in the 2000 revival at the theatre of its birth. Not surprisingly, Olona's huge workload took its toll, and he more or less retired from active theatre work after 1860. As a tireless proponent for the rebirth of zarzuela his place in history is assured, but the quality of his best work should not be forgotten. Comparable elegance, intelligence and depth of feeling are rarely found in words for music at any period.

Guillermo Perrín (1875–1923) and Miguel de Palacios (1863–1920)

In public character Palacios was serious and moody, Perrín witty and bright. Together they formed an indissoluble literary union, to the extent that many people believed *Perrín y Palacios* to be one writer. The quantity and inconsistent quality of their work made them the butt of many jokes ("At the end opinion was divided, some booed Perrín and others booed Palacios") but their popularity never waned, partly because they steered clear of situations drawn from everyday Madrid life in favor of lighter, more frivolous plots closer to contemporary mainstream operetta. The critics were cruelly harsh; but composers, singers, actors and even scenic painters worshipped them for their canny theatrical know-how, and the public helped them cry all the way to the bank.

They turned out a massive quantity of scripts in all shapes and sizes for leading musicians of the day including Bretón, Chapí and Caballero, as well as younger composers such as Luna. Two *revistas* written for Miguel Nieto, *Certamen nacional* (National Debate, 1888) and *Cuadros disolventes* (1896), were hugely famous in their day. With Gerónimo Giménez, Nieto also furnished the music for one of their most enduring successes, the amusing backstage farce *El barbero de Sevilla* (1901). With one notable exception it is through Vives that their work is best remembered today; they provided him with the repertory stalwarts *Bohemios* (1904) and *La Generala* (1912), as well as all-but-forgotten works such as the intriguingly titled *Miss Australia* (1914).

The exception is their most (in)famous work of all, the biblical skit *La corte de Faraón* (1910), one of many pieces penned for the fertile Vicente Lleó but the only one to stand the test of time. Outrageously popular and eternally controversial (it was banned for blasphemy by the Franco government), *La corte de Faraón* displays the characteristic citric qualities of their best work. As in all good light revue, the humor is silly without being stupid, the satire is genial; above all, the script is tightly constructed and offers succulent theatrical opportunities. Altogether, *Perrín y Palacios* show no sign of losing their public just yet.

Serafín Álvarez Quintero (1871–1938) and Joaquín Álvarez Quintero (1873–1944)

From their very first stage piece, *Gilito* in 1889, *Los hermanos Quintero* were the Golden Boys of Madrid theatre. They always wrote as a partnership. Even after his brother's death Joaquín continued to write in both their names, until his own demise little more than six years later. Like their contemporary Carlos Arniches, they favored the one-act *sainete*. Unlike him, they did not usually base their work on realistic sketches of Madrid, but on scenes of picturesque *costumbrista* (popular life) taken from their native Andalucia or its capital, Seville. On occasion they weren't afraid to tackle contemporary political themes, as in *El buena sombra* (1898, with "Quinito" Valverde), a serious reflection on the disastrous tragedy of the Cuban war against the United States.

Not surprisingly with upward of 200 stage works to their credit over a period of fifty years, they worked with many of the leading composers of three generations. For Chapí they wrote many works including the still-popular *La patria chica* (1907). Caballero, Vives, Guerrero, Luna, Torroba and María

Rodrigo were also numbered among their select clientele. Two of their earlier and more ambitious three-act librettos were adapted and set years later by Sorozábal: a sharply observed version of the Don Juan story, *Los burladores* (1948); and *Las de Caín* (1953), which deals with the comic tribulations of a Madrid family.

Their key collaboration was with Serrano, for whom they wrote in a passionate, romantic style much closer to Italian *verismo* than to the accustomed realism of the *sainete madrileño*. Their successes included the lyrical *La reina mora* (1903), *El mal de amores* (1905) and *La mala sombra* (1906); but even the composer's last, unfinished stagework *La venta de los gatos* (1943) was to a text provided by the Quinteros. The virtues of their work include good taste, solid construction, and shafts of that brooding, poetic imagination which created such a stir in their work for Serrano at the turn of the century.

Federico Romero (1886–1976) and Guillermo Fernández Shaw (1893–1965)

Romero trained as a mining engineer, a calling which adversely affected his health, before becoming a telegrapher. He was involved in the foundation of the national telephone service in 1917 shortly before resigning to pursue his writing career. Even during the long writing partnership with Fernández Shaw, he occasionally wrote with other writers, and after their 1948 split Romero turned again to solo work, notably in *Pepita Romero* and *Aquella canción antigua* (both 1952, for Juan Dotras Vila).

Fernández Shaw was of Scottish and Irish ancestry, a son of Carlos Fernández Shaw, the author of several of the greatest zarzuelas of the Golden Age, as well as de Falla's *La vida breve*. Guillermo trained as a lawyer but quickly gravitated into journalism, publishing poetry in the fashionable periodical *Blanco y negro*. He also worked with others, principally his brother Rafael on *María Manuela* (1941, for Federico Moreno Torroba), and after 1948 they became regular writing partners. *Un día de primavera* (1947) and *El gaitero de Gijón* (1953) for Romo, *La Duquesa del candil* for Jesús Leoz (1949), and *El canastillo de fresas* (1951, Guerrero's last zarzuela) were the finest fruits of this fraternal collaboration.

Romero and Shaw wrote more than seventy libretti together; but from the very first, the wildly popular *La canción del olvido* for José Serrano (1916), their supreme merit was recognized. In addition to zarzuelas, they produced stage versions of dramas by Goethe and Schiller, as well as Rostand's *Cyrano de Bergerac*. The practical influence of these forays into verse drama gives many of their libretti a genuine poetic quality which stands the test of time. Their structures are watertight, their dialogue sleek and richly characterized, and their finest lyrics (such as *"Por el humo le sabe"* from *Doña Francisquita*) have a density and imaginative depth which is rarely found in words specially written for music.

Occasionally they turned to classic theatre for their plots, always to good advantage. This tactic was used to supreme effect in two major works written for Amadeu Vives. *Doña Francisquita* (1923) is a radical reworking of a famous Lope de Vega comedy, and the later *La villana* (1927) a more straightforward adaptation from the same author. For Guerrero they quarried the same Lopean mine with the hugely popular *La rosa del azafrán*; but most of their texts are original, ranging far and wide in time and space over Spanish regional and *madrileño* settings. A brief listing of the best known reads like a history of zarzuela in the mid-twentieth century. For Millán they produced *El dictador* (1923). For Guridi they penned the Basque idyll *El caserío* (1926), *La meiga* (1928) and the later, once popular *Peñamariana* (1944). Luna was given *La moza vieja* (The Old Woman, 1931).

For Torroba the complex classic *Luisa Fernanda* (1932) was followed by a long series of works including the almost equally celebrated *La chulapona* (1934). For Torroba's rival Sorozábal they wrote several librettos including his greatest triumph, the fishing port melodrama *La tabernera del puerto* (1936). After the Civil War they continued to write for both composers. Torroba's *Monte Carmelo* (1939) may be marred for modern tastes by its heavy religiosity, but the comedy scenes are fresh and lively. The more secular pieces they provided for Sorozábal, such as *Cuidado con la pintura* (Wet Paint!, 1939) did not enjoy comparable exposure, or the approval of the authorities. Ultimately, an unhappy feud between these two composers led in 1948 to a cooling in Romero and Shaw's relationship, personal as well as professional; but for the range and consistently imaginative quality of their work the pair stand as the most successful literary partnership in the history of the zarzuela.

Ricardo de la Vega (1839–1910)

As the son of Ventura de la Vega, it is hardly surprising that Ricardo's academic studies and later work as an official for the Ministries of Public Works and Information had to take second place to a career in the theatre. He was also something of an anglophile, like his great novelist contemporary Benito Peréz Galdós, and a regular at the Cafe Inglés, venue of the most famous Madrid *tertulias* during the last quarter of the century.

Very far from following his father's path toward verse drama and the *zarzuela grande*, he was drawn to the world of Ramon de la Cruz, whose brief vignettes of Madrid street life proved fruitful models for a refreshing new style of theatre, the *género chico*, which he developed stylistically worlds away from the parodistic *bufos* presented by the popular writer and entrepreneur Arderius. De la Vega's very first *sainete* was *Frasquito*, written for the young Caballero in 1859; but his talent was fully revealed in collaboration with Chueca and Valverde, and it was with *La canción de la Lola* (1880) that the new genre became a mass mania. This satirical squib was so universally popular that the city authorities feared it might become the focus for popular revolutionary ferment, and bans were imposed.

Other leading composers were understandably keen to hitch their wagons to the rising star, and collaborations with the likes of Barbieri and Chapí followed swiftly. He also worked with Giménez, and provided another success for Chueca and Valverde with *El año pasado por agua* in 1889. However, his greatest and most enduring triumph came in collaboration with a more "establishment" composer: Tomás Bretón. The masterly *sainete La verbena de la Paloma* was written with Chapí in mind, but for contractual reasons he was unable to provide the music. Bretón was handed the jewel, and certainly made the most of it despite his own misgivings. For this one work alone, a fluent mixture of verse and prose, with a large and vivid range of *tipos* (character types) and pithy exploration of Madrid's social and sexual mores, its author's name will survive wherever Spanish is spoken or sung.

Ventura de la Vega (1807–65)

Ventura de la Vega was one of the most important Spanish playwrights of his time. Like other writers of the time he made his mark in the adaptation of French plays, although his versions were often more radical and adventurous than the norm. Among his best straight plays are *El hombre de mundo* (The Man of the World, 1845) and the tragedy *La muerte de Cesar* (The Death of Caesar, 1842), both of which are still occasionally revived. The best of his many zarzuela texts exhibit the same qualities of comic zest, sharp characterization and elegant structure. He wrote most often for Barbieri, and their *Jugar con fuego* (1851) proved a watershed, effectively marking the birth of the romantic zarzuela.

30
Singers

Zarzuela has been important to nearly every great Spanish singer of the last 150 years. Even those globe-trotting *divas* and *divos* who were rarely able to appear in them on stage, such as Conchita Supervía, Victoria de los Ángeles, Hipólito Lázaro and Miguel Fleta regularly included zarzuela *romanzas*, *canciónes* and *dúos* in their recitals and recorded work. The same is true of today's singers, such as José Carreras, María Bayo and Carlos Álvarez. They do not view zarzuela as opera's poor cousin, but as a distinct art form with its own artistic challenges and rewards. The handful discussed below are representative of countless artists who inspired the great *zarzueleros*, and includes some of those who have kept the flame burning into the present day by their studio as much as their stage work.

Lucrecia Arana (1867–1927)

One of the most impressive and famous sopranos of the *género chico* from 1887 until her marriage and retirement in 1907. She created over one hundred leading roles including many for Caballero, notably the "breeches" role of Carlos in *La viejecita* and—perhaps her greatest triumph—Pilar in *Gigantes y cabezudos*. The ample size and musicality of her voice made her idolized by the public.

Faustino Arregui (1904–1964)

Although the size, tonal depth and technical control of his voice could have led to a notable operatic career, the Basque lyric tenor devoted his talents to Spanish zarzuela from his debut in Serrano's *Los de Aragón* (1929) through to his retirement from the stage in the 1950s. An idea of his operatic strength can be gleaned from Vidal in *Luisa Fernanda*, and Leandro in *La tabernera del puerto*—just two of the many fine roles written for him. During the Civil War he worked in Argentina, returning to Spain only after his vocal prime. Perhaps the highlight of his plethora of recordings is the extended selection from *Luisa Fernanda* recorded with Pérez Carpio and Redondo in 1934.

Manuel Ausensi (b. 1919)

One of a very few world-class Spanish baritones, Ausensi's powerful voice and expressive freedom gave him an acclaimed international opera career between the mid-1950s and his retirement in 1969. His huge recorded repertoire of zarzuelas under Argenta and later conductors has kept his name before the public ever since; and though some of his studio work would have benefited from more restraint than his lusty instrument was able to finesse, most of his singing provides musical as well as visceral pleasure. Of the fifty or so zarzuela roles he tackled on LP his comic braggarts such as the Marquis in *Jugar con fuego* are irresistible; though perhaps his brutal but human Juan de Eguía in *La tabernera del puerto* and sensual Pintu in *La pícara molinera* remain his finest legacy.

Teresa Berganza (b. 1935)

Of the select band of internationally famous mezzo-sopranos, Berganza stands out for the consistent intelligence of her music making, wedded to a voice of warm quality and agility throughout its considerable range. Reckoned by many critics to be the classic Carmen of her time, her repertoire of Spanish roles extends far beyond Bizet's gypsy. While still in her teens she became a regular on Argenta's recording roster; and her very first studio role was Doña Simona—hilariously doubled with the Italian beggar boy—in *Agua, azucarillos y aguardiente* (1954). Of her many zarzuela roles perhaps María in *La tempranica* stands out for its intense beauty and nobility; but her extended range allowed her to take on roles more usually associated with sopranos, and the sheer breadth of her work makes up one of the great treasures of the recorded repertoire.

Isobel Bru (c. 1875–?)

The most famous *tiple* (light singing-actress) of *género chico*. She was discovered by Ruperto Chapí, making her debut in the premiere of *El tambor de granaderos* in 1894. Among the many roles she later created were Regina in *La fiesta de San Antón* and Asia in *Agua, azucarillos y aguardiente*; but undoubtedly the high point of her career was the creation of Mari-Pepa in *La revoltosa*, the role which deployed her mercurial stage personality and mellifluous light voice to best effect. She retired from theatre in 1907 and was lost to public view.

Montserrat Caballé (b. 1933)

One of the best-loved sopranos from the last quarter of the twentieth century, Caballé's stage work in zarzuela has been relatively limited, although she was a regular guest star in José Tamayo's touring *Antología* in the 1980s and 90s. Having said which, she is nowhere heard to better advantage than in her complete zarzuela recordings and romanza recitals dating from the 1970s. The recordings of *El pájaro azul* and *La villana* are treasuries of those incomparable floating pianissimos above the stave which are her special signature; and fans who only know Caballé from her Italian opera recordings may be surprised at the extra interpretive fire that comes across in her Spanish-language characterizations.

Plácido Domingo (b. 1941)

Madrid-born Domingo moved to Mexico in 1949 with the zarzuela company of his parents, Plácido Sr. and Pepita Embil, and made his first stage appearance aged sixteen as a baritone in *Gigantes y cabezudos*. His tenor debut as Javier in *Luisa Fernanda* (Veracruz, 1958) proved the base camp for his steady climb to preeminence in an unprecedented variety of roles covering the entire Italian, German and French repertoires, as well as Spanish opera and zarzuela. Inevitably his stage appearances in complete zarzuelas have been few; but his gala concerts with colleagues such as Lorengar and Caballé have done much to open the outside world's eyes to the hidden gems of the repertoire. Complete recordings of *La dolorosa* and *Los Claveles* in his youthful prime (both with Berganza) have been supplemented recently by a rich, weighty Fernando in *Doña Francisquita*; and his scrupulously prepared series of recordings for Auvidis include *Luisa Fernanda*, *La verbena de la Paloma* and *La tabernera del puerto*. Domingo's uniquely honeyed *mezza voce* and brilliant timbre prove especially well suited to that first-ever role, the brooding, heroic Javier.

Plácido Domingo Ferrer (1907–1987)

Born in Tordera (Barcelona), Domingo made his debut in *Los gavilanes* as a member of María Badía's Zaragoza company. His mellifluous lyric baritone and theatrical gifts soon led him to the capital, where he met his wife-to-be Pepita Embil; they became engaged whilst playing opposite one another in Torroba's *Sor Navarra* (1940) and married soon after. Domingo's finest roles included Felipe in *La revoltosa*, Vidal in *Luisa Fernanda*—he was Torroba's favorite exponent of the role—and most of the important baritone roles of Sorozábal, such as Joaquín in *La del manojo de rosas* and the title roles in *Black, el payaso* and *Don Manolito*. In 1950 Domingo and Embil set up their own company in Mexico, which raised artistic standards throughout Spanish-speaking Central America and the Caribbean. By this time Domingo had lost his voice owing to a badly treated throat infection, but he continued to shine in character and acting roles, notably Nogales in *Luisa Fernanda* and Don Matías in *Doña Francisquita*.

Pepita Embil (1918–1994)

Trained under her father and others in San Sebastián and Paris, Embil became one of the leading *tiples* at Madrid's Teatro Calderón directly after the Civil War, later forming her own company with baritone Antonio Medio and creating roles in popular zarzuelas by Guerrero and Jesús Romo. Her work with Pablo Sorozábal included triumphs as Marola in *La tabernera del puerto* and Sofía in *Black, el payaso*, both of which she recorded under the composer. Some years after her marriage to Plácido Domingo Sr. she departed to Mexico, where the couple created a highly successful zarzuela company which nurtured the careers of many singers including their son, Plácido Jr. Embil's memory is held dear for her satisfying vocal richness and discriminating musicality.

María Espinalt (1915–1981)

Barcelona soprano who made her debut aged sixteen at the Liceu, as Gilda in *Rigoletto*. Her great Madrid triumph came a year later as Niña Estrella in *Don Gil de Alcalá*, a rare fusion of radiant voice and youthful purity which made her an overnight sensation. Espinalt's best years came before the onset of the Civil War, and by the late 1940s (after which time, alas, came most of her complete zarzuela recordings) her voice had lost much of its appealing freshness and ease.

Tino Folgar (1892–1983)

One of the finest lyric tenors of the Barcelona school, Folgar created leading roles in *Los Claveles*, Guerrero's *Martierra* and many other works, and enjoyed major successes in *Luisa Fernanda*, *Doña Francisquita* and a host of similar opera and zarzuela revivals. Later in his career he worked in *revista* with Celia Gámez, retiring from the stage in 1952. His reputation as a recording artist centers on the first electric recording of any opera, HMV's famous La Scala *Rigoletto* from 1927; but his delectable, sweet lightness and ear for interpretive detail are at least as well served by his many zarzuela records, of which the *romanzas* from *Los de Aragón* and *La pícara molinera* are outstanding. The *dúo* "Mala mujer" from *Los flamencos* (Vives) with Pérez Carpio stands as an essential zarzuela recording, for its unique brew of wit, vocal allure and theatrical intensity.

Manuel Gas (1905–1995)

Gas began his opera career in Barcelona and Milan, gaining an enviable reputation for his mellifluous, firm lyric bass and charismatic presence. An engagement to play the drunken Simpson soon after the premiere of Sorozábal's *La tabernera del puerto* changed the course of his career, and he devoted himself henceforth to the zarzuela repertoire. An unbroken series of successes in Sorozábal's later pieces, notably as White in *Black, el payaso*, led to national fame; and his stupendous facility in "patter" led Sorozábal to write Guillermo's showstopping description of a soccer goal for him in *Don Manolito*. His popularity and artistic reputation were augmented by his recordings, until inevitable vocal decline led him to retire from the stage in the late 1950s.

Celia Gámez (1908–1992)

Argentine *chanteuse* who came to Madrid in 1925 to appear in a series of variety shows, culminating in Alonso's hugely successful *revista Los castigadoras* of 1927. This triumph was eclipsed four years later by the phenomenon of *Las leandras*, which confirmed Gámez as the brightest star in Spain's popular pre-war firmament. She maintained her regal preeminence for many years, though after 1964 her fame and fortune waned drastically and she retired to Buenos Aires, ending her days in poverty. Her strident, sexy, crushed-glass voice and powerful personality live on in her *revista* recordings, most famously the "standards" from *Las leandras* such as *"Pichi"*, which she set down at various stages of her career.

Felisa Herrero (1905–1962)

Unquestionably the greatest zarzuela soprano of the decade before the Civil War, Herrero was as much esteemed for her rare histrionic gifts as for her superb vocal prowess and individuality. With hindsight the most important of her early creations were Ana-Mari in *El caserío* (1926) and the demanding title role of *La villana* the following year. For Torroba she was Rosario in *La chulapona*, for Sorozábal she played Katiuska opposite Marcos Redondo; and for Guerrero she was a matchless Sagrario in *La rosa del azafrán*. Much of her career after the Civil War was spent in South America, though she returned to Madrid before her death. Her records reveal a thrilling individuality and imagination; and given her courage to sacrifice vocal security for dramatic impact, her reputation as "The Callas of the Zarzuela" is not far from the truth.

Ana-María Iriarte (b. 1927)

Familiar from a huge body of zarzuela recordings made in the Alhambra series under Ataulfo Argenta, Iriarte's highly personal vocal style continues to divide opinion. Those LPs were made at legendary speed, and there's no gainsaying that they reveal technical flaws: a tendency to over-aspiration and throaty delivery result in the squally vocal image which many associate with Iriarte's work.

Yet given proper preparation, a very different singer emerges. Early in her short stage career she appeared in *La Duquesa del candil* (1949) and the original Teatro de la Zarzuela recording reveals a subtly expressive, beautifully placed clear mezzo voice. Her recording of de Falla's *El amor brujo* is equally impressive, and her very early retirement (1960) left only memories of her powerful stage performances, notably as Aurora in *Doña Francisquita* and Cecilia in *Las golondrinas*, both of which she recorded under Argenta.

Alfredo Kraus (1927–1999)

The patrician elegance of his lyric tenor graced the world's opera houses for nearly half a century; yet Kraus' zarzuela work, on stage and in the studio, formed a major part of his career. He made his Teatro de la Zarzuela debut in *Doña Francisquita*, and Fernando remained a signature role—as was Jorge in *Marina*, in which he made his last appearances at the theatre in 1994. His dedication to recorded zarzuela was total, not least through his own label, Carillon, which set down exhilarating performances of *La dolorosa*, *La Generala* and many other repertoire standards—this was one singer who really put his money where his mouth was. His series of Sorozábal zarzuelas for Hispavox (1959 onward) have near-legendary status; his Columbia version of *La bruja* (with Berganza) is another classic. In the twilight of his career, his third and last version of *Doña Francisquita* for Auvidis proved in many ways his best, full of a compelling, subtle artistry which more than compensates for the inevitable loss of his earlier silver brilliance and rock-solid strength. For many, Kraus remains the zarzuela tenor of choice from any era.

Pedro Lavirgen (b. 1930)

The popular dramatic tenor began his career in the chorus of the Teatro de la Zarzuela. When he made his 1959 solo debut in *Marina*, his opulent timbre and stentorian resources made an immediate impact, and his operatic career throughout the 1960s and 70s was internationally applauded. As he never transferred his major stage roles such as Otello and Don José to LP, his art is better remembered through the series of fine zarzuela recordings he made for EMI-Hispavox, including *La dolorosa* and *Doña Francisquita* under Sorozábal as well as the conductor-composer's own *La eterna canción*. Here and elsewhere he generally proved well able to harness his generous tone to the slighter lyric demands of zarzuela; and the results combine vigorous passion and vocal taste in fair proportion.

Pilar Lorengar (1928–1996)

Zaragoza soprano whose international operatic reputation should not be allowed to obscure her fine achievements in zarzuela. Her stage debut was in Guerrero's posthumous *El canastillo de fresas* (1951); and her breathtaking agility, distinctive fast vibrato and pristine warmth throughout her range graced many staple roles in the theatre and on record. She was a vital contributor to Ataulfo Argenta's LP series for Alhambra, and made several classic versions of Sorozábal's works with the composer. Her very wide recorded legacy includes about thirty other complete zarzuela recordings, perhaps most notably her thrilling assumptions of the title roles in *El rey que rabió* and *La calesera*.

Carlos Munguía (b. 1921)

Basque tenor, whose work with the famous Orfeón Donostiarra chorus encouraged him to turn professional in 1950. His quick musicianship and uniquely plangent timbre soon brought him to the attention of Ataulfo Argenta, who recruited him into his Columbia "repertory company" which recorded a multitude of scores between 1954 and 1958. Those priceless records are still held in great affection, though he sang successfully on stage in both opera (including Wagner) and zarzuela until his final retirement in 1986. Munguía's voice was not large, but its steely precision cut through the orchestral web without compromising its very distinctive personality. Never less than efficient, he is at his considerable best in lyric *verismo* roles such as Daniel in *Moros y cristianos*, where his stylish understatement pays great musical dividends.

Ofelia Nieto (1900–1931)

Nieto's sunburst career was launched when she created the title role in Vives' *Maruxa* at the age of fourteen, a wondrous debut preserved in extracts recorded by the Gramophone company. After that, her uncannily resonant and rich voice was almost exclusively heard in opera, although she did record the barcarolle from Serrano's *El carro del sol* and the *dúo* from *El asombro de Damasco* (opposite Marcos Redondo) just before retiring from the stage on her marriage in 1928. The year before her death she ventured once more into the recording studio to record *Maruxa*, opposite her sister Ángeles Ottein (Nieto reversed) and the leading Italian baritone Carlo Galeffi. This was the first virtually complete recording of a major Spanish stage work, and it remains a fine memento of Nieto's powerful, varied artistry.

Ángeles Ottein (1895–1981)

Although Ofelia Nieto's elder sister may not have been so phenomenal of voice, in musicality and pliant, vocal purity she was a great artist in her own right. Her debut three months after her sister's (1914, in *Marina*) catapulted her to almost equal stardom, and during the next forty years she sang widely in opera at home and abroad. Her recorded legacy in zarzuela is at least as impressive, notably in the 1930 *Maruxa*, a haunting selection from *La canción del olvido*, and *Luisa Fernanda* (with Redondo and Vendrell) where her attention to character is as arresting as her vocal artistry. From the mid 1940s she turned to teaching, inspiring a new generation of singers at the Madrid Conservatory including Lorengar and Consuela Rubio.

Antonio Palacios (1890–1972)

The essential comic tenor of the pre-War years, Palacios created a host of roles in *sainete*, *revista* and operetta-zarzuela. Most famous was Cardona in Vives' *Doña Francisquita*; but he proved equally indispensable in many other premieres, not least *La calesera*, *La villana*, *El caserío* and Torroba's *Mesonera de Tordesillas*, as well as in the established *género chico* repertoire. At the start of the Civil War the much-loved artist left for exile in Cuba and Spanish America, where he worked tirelessly on behalf of zarzuela until his death. His cheeky energy and perfect clarity are preserved on many records, notably in highlights from *Doña Francisquita* and original cast excerpts from *La calesera*.

Conchita Panadés (1908–1981)

A much-loved *tiple* or light soprano whose career straddled the Civil War, Panadés worked in Barcelona between 1926 and 1930 before coming to notice in the title role of the first Madrid *Katiuska* (1932). She then toured America with Miguel Fleta's company, returning to Barcelona to create the role of Marola in *La tabernera del puerto*. After the Civil War her creations included the title roles in Alonso's *La zapaterita* and Torroba's *La caramba*. Her vivacious charm and wit come across strongly in many recordings from the 1930s onward, notably *La canción del olvido* with Redondo; in the early days of LP she was still singing comedy roles, such as Catalina in *La rosa del azafrán*, with undiminished success.

Isabel Penagos (b. 1931)

Although her career extended far beyond its boundaries, Penagos' weighty, warmly expressive soprano is usually associated with the zarzuela repertoire. She made her Teatro de la Zarzuela debut in *La tempranica* (1959) and moved easily between opera house and concert hall until retiring from the stage in 1979 to devote herself to teaching, which she has continued to do with conspicuous success at home and abroad. Her musicality is heard to great advantage in the series of fine zarzuela records Penagos made in the late 1960s and early 70s under Sorozábal and others, of which her Katiuska and Ascensión in *La del manojo de rosas* are exemplars of an intelligent and emotionally satisfying artistry.

Dolores Pérez (1930–1982)

The daughter of two successful singers, Pérez initially took her father's matronymic as a stage name, appearing as Lily Berchman throughout the 1950s in opera and zarzuela, at home in Madrid as well as abroad. Her smokily attractive soprano was supported by interpretive gifts of a high order, and her many zarzuela recordings are always compelling dramatically, even if some roles sit uneasily within the weak "break" of the voice. She always gave generously, and perhaps as a result her later career saw her take on more mezzo-soprano roles, such as Aurora in *Doña Francisquita* in which she had a notable success. Many of her recorded interpretations, such as María *La tempranica* and Pilar in *Gigantes y cabezudos* remain *hors concours* for depth of feeling and dramatic involvement; not surprisingly, she proved specially effective in a series of three Lecuona zarzuelas, notably *El cafetal* with Sagi-Vela.

Selíca Pérez Carpio (1900–1984)

Pérez Carpio was encouraged to devote her dramatic talents to zarzuela by Vicente Lleó, who in 1917 gave her a contract to sing in his Valencia theatre. By 1924 she had made top billing in Madrid's Teatro de la Zarzuela in Padilla's *Sol de Sevilla*. Once established as a major star she mixed *revista* and zarzuela work, creating a host of roles including a gently seductive Raquel in *El huésped del Sevillano*. Her later 1920s triumphs included the premiere of *La pícara molinera* and *Los flamencos*. Perhaps the greatest of her later creations were the title roles of *Luisa Fernanda* and *La chulapona*, both for Torroba, but she continued to appear in character and acting roles until 1976. Her high mezzo voice was strong and expressive, and her mesmeric qualities as a singing actress can be heard in several early recordings. They can also, luckily, be seen—in the 1935 film version of *La verbena de la Paloma*, where her Seña Rita comes across with a fresh, essentially modern understatement which is as potent as ever.

Cora Raga (1893–1980)

Raga's vibrant mezzo-soprano possessed much of the dramatic talent of Pérez Carpio and many of the vocal guns of her great operatic contemporary Conchita Supervía. After experiencing her Amneris in *Aida* Amadeu Vives encouraged her to try zarzuela, where her dual strengths made her a stupendous asset as Aurora la Beltrana in the premiere of his *Doña Francisquita* (1923). Many other vocally demanding roles followed and her surviving records show off her tigerish stage persona to tremendous advantage. Raga's graphically frustrated Lotha in *La corte de Faraón* and bitter power as Dolores in *La dolorosa* perhaps have to give best to a matchless Seña Rita in *La verbena de la Paloma*, recorded with Vendrell under Capdevila in 1931.

Marcos Redondo (1893–1976)

An acknowledged world-class singer, Redondo possessed not only an exceptionally beautiful, strong and flexible baritone, but also something far harder to quantify: an air of tender humility. The great Titta Ruffo, hearing the young singer in *Pagliacci*, gave vent to a memorable epithet: "That voice is a first class ticket to glory." So it proved, although a three-month contract to sing zarzuela in Barcelona (1924) led his career along an unexpected path. Triumphant in Millán's *El dictador*, Redondo found the immediacy of the native form very much to his taste; and numerous premieres followed including *La calesera*, *Katiuska* and *La tabernera del puerto*. His recorded legacy is hugely impressive, whether in the *verismo* passions of *Las golondrinas*, the aristocratic romance of Rafael in *La calesera*, or the common humanity of Perico's jota from *El guitarrico*. He continued to make records into the LP era, and retired from the stage in 1957 with one of his favorite roles, Miccone the jester in *La Dogaresa*. A highly popular man of many parts, Redondo even turned his hand to the composition of at least one zarzuela of his own, *La tuna de Alcalá* (The Alcalá Loiterer).

Pepe Romeu (1900–1985)

Although he began and ended his career as a popular stage and film actor, Romeu was encouraged by his friend the great Italian tenor Giacomo Lauri-Volpi to train for the lyric stage. His natural, mellifluous tenor was not without its core of steel, and his actor's intelligence allowed him to make the most of it. All this made him one of the most exciting zarzuela singers throughout the 1920s and 30s, starring in many premieres such as *Los flamencos* (Vives), *La pícara molinera* and as the elegant Enrique in *El último romántico*. Romeu's recordings of the *romanzas* from these last two still come across with that thrilling magnetism which he must have possessed in the theatre.

Toñy Rosado (1923–1996)

Antonia Rosado moved to England with her parents at the start of the Civil War, returning to her home town of Madrid to study at the Conservatory before making her first stage appearance as a mezzo soprano Santuzza in *Cavalleria Rusticana* opposite Gigli in 1946. An extremely successful career as a soprano in both opera and zarzuela succeeded this high-profile debut. Her vocal personality combined great purity and cutting power above the stave with a mezzo's depth of color, held together by reliable technical and musical security. She was a key member of the conductor Argenta's recording team for Columbia-Alhambra, successfully taking most of the weightier soprano assignments such as the "breeches" role of Roberto in *La tempestad* and Regina in *El santo de la Isidra*. Perhaps her finest hour in the recording studio was as Zobeida in *El asombro de Damasco*, an assumption of Tebaldi-like sympathetic vocal beauty.

Emilio Sagi-Barba (1876–1949)

Unlike the younger Redondo he devoted himself to native works almost exclusively, singing Spanish zarzuelas and operas in Cuba before the turn of the century. He devoted his great vocal and dramatic talents to Spanish and Catalan zarzuela, crowning his Madrid reputation as the leading baritone of the day in Usandizaga's *Las golondrinas*, which he and his soprano wife Luisa Vela premiered to ecstatic applause in 1914. Among the many first nights Sagi-Barba blessed during the remaining twenty or so years of his career, Millán's *El dictador*, *La del soto del Parral*, *La rosa del azafrán* and *Luisa Fernanda* stand out. His ample voice has a reedy, clarion cut which is instantly recognizable; and even very late in his career, in the 1932 recorded extracts from *Luisa Fernanda*, it had lost none of its firmness or declamatory power.

Luis Sagi-Vela (b. 1914)

Son of Emilio Sagi-Barba and Luisa Vela, the eighteen-year-old baritone made a sensational Madrid debut as Juan Pedro in *La rosa del azafrán*, which his father had created a mere two years earlier. By 1934 he was famous enough to form his own company, which toured Spain and Spanish America for many years, and to create Joaquín in Sorozábal's epochal *La del manojo de rosas*. The following year he followed this triumph with the third part of the "modern trilogy," Alonso's *Me llaman la presumida*. After the Civil War he premiered Torroba's *Monte Carmelo* and *La caramba* at home, gradually becoming almost as well-known in Spanish America and the United States as in his native Spain. In the late 1940s he turned his attention to opera, singing Alfredo in *La Traviata* amongst other tenor roles. Tenor or baritone? The appeal of Sagi-Vela's cultured voice is its combination of popular, tenorial croon with baritonal depth. He retired from zarzuela in 1960, though his stage career finished seven years later with *Man of La Mancha*. His many records cover the best-known roles in both registers, with very few adaptations. Some find his style mannered, but the beauty, clarity and sheer musical intelligence of his singing—most notably in high-lying baritone roles such as Pablo in *Maruxa*—silences criticism. In 2000, he was still giving zarzuela masterclasses in Madrid, revered as a living legend.

Francisco Salas (1812–1875)

A sonorous bass singer who made his debut in Italian opera and specialized in Rossini's demanding *buffo* roles, Salas' vehement belief in Spanish stage music led him to band together with his friend Gaztambide, Barbieri and writers led by Olona in the group working at the Teatro del Circo around 1850, and as singer-manager of the new Teatro de la Zarzuela after its foundation in 1856. Although the focus of his own stage work was Italian opera he continued to be a mainstay of the romantic zarzuela movement until his death, through his tireless entrepreneurial activities.

Enriqueta Serrano (c. 1911–1958)

Little is known of the 1920s career of this fine comedy singer. Her beauty and comic gift began to attract notice late in the decade; and an appearance with Cora Raga in the *revista La granjera de Arlés* led to a contract to play the *tiple* role of Olga in the 1932 Madrid production of Sorozábal's *Katiuska*, in which she scored a great success—with the composer as much as the public, becoming his wife the following year. Serrano limited her stage engagements after her marriage, though she did appear as the comedy star of many of Sorozábal's succeeding works from *La isla de las perlas* (1933) through to *Brindis* (1955), recording many of these roles before her early death in 1958. Her compelling acting and dance skills were allied to a small but expressive voice, which can be heard not only in the Sorozábal LPs, but also in the 1930 recording of Sul's song in *La corte de Faraón*, in which her *"¡Ay ba!"* is all the more lubricious for being pertly contained.

Emilio Vendrell (1893–1962)

Vendrell began his career as soloist with Barcelona's Orféo Catalá, and created a series of leading roles in Catalan sarsuelas (notably Morera's *Don Joan de Serrallonga*) before coming to Madrid, where his stock rose rapidly. Guerrero tailored *"Flor roja"* in *Los gavilanes* for his fluid tonal beauty, range of vocal colors and impressive dynamic control—three qualities which subsequent tenors have found hard to emulate. He sang Fernando in *Doña Francisquita* more than thirteen hundred times, and his recording of the great *Romanza: "Por el humo se sabe"* remains a model of the singer's art in its attention to verbal as well as musical nuances. Of his later creations, Rafael in *La dolorosa* was outstanding for its brooding intensity and tonal richness; and although by his retirement in 1953 much of his lustrous technique had deserted him, his place is secure as the finest zarzuela tenor of the pre-Civil War era.

Appendix A
Select Discography

This guide to zarzuela recordings lists the most recommendable complete (or nearly complete) versions currently available on CD or cassette. The handful of recordings available with dialogue are noted. One or two pre-LP historical recordings (H) are included, either to plug obvious gaps or because of their intrinsic interest. The modern, digital Auvidis series is currently available worldwide, while the classic BMG and EMI recordings are readily available in Spain. Others listed may be harder to find, but will repay the effort.

Adios a la Bohemia (Sorozábal)
Lorengar, Cesari, Gas, c. Sorozábal *EMI 7243 5 74345 2 2*
Berganza, Ausensi, de Narke, c. Sorozábal *BMG Alhambra WD 74386*

Agua, azucarillos y aguardiente (Chueca)
Tourne, Gabriel, Higueras, García, c. Sorozábal *EMI 5 74152 2*
Rivadeneira, Iriarte, Portillo, Otero, Pérez Carpio, c. Lauret *BMG Alhambra WD71433* [with dialogue]

Alma de Dios (Serrano)
Blancas, Sinova, Martelo, c. Frühbeck de Burgos *BMG Alhambra WD 71587*

Aquella canción antigua (Dotras Vila)
(H) Olaria, Leonís, Abad, Viruete, c. Dotras Vila *Blue Moon BMCD 7517*

Black, el payaso (Sorozábal)
Cesari, Barclay, Kraus, Algorta, Serrano, Fuentes, c. Sorozábal *EMI 7243 5 74227 2 7*

Bohemios (Vives)
Higueras, Lavirgen, García, Farres, c. Sorozábal *EMI 5 74209 2 (2-CD)*
Bayo, Lima, Jericó, Álvarez, c. Ros Marbà *Auvidis Valois V4711*
Ortiz, Martinez, Fuentes, c. Frühbeck de Burgos *BMG Alhambra WD 71434*
(H) Redondo, Racionero, Gonzalo, Zanardi, c. Capdevila *Aria 1015*
Berganza, Munguia, Rosado, Ausensi, Gil, Fernandez, / Argenta (r. 1954)

Cançó d'amor i de guerra (Martínez Valls)
Caballé, Carreras, Decamp, Sardinero, c. Ros Marbà *BMG Alhambra WD 71466*

Cecilia Valdés (Roig)
Sánchez, c. Guerrero *EGREM CD-036*
Varela, Pico, Muñoz, c. Roig *EMI Hispavox 5 73417 2* [extended highlights]
(H) Fernández, Perez, Pujol, Naya. c. Roig *Montilla CDFM 118* [extended highlights] Bayo etc Galicia 50 / Perez

Don Gil de Alcalá (Penella)
Huarte, Berganza, Torrano, Ausensi, Campó, Campos, c. Argenta *BMG Columbia 74321 35972 2 (2-CD)*

Don Manolito (Sorozábal)
Cesari, Langa, Algorta, Serrano, Fuentes, c. Sorozábal *EMI 7243 5 74343 2 4*
Ausensi, Berganza, de Narke, Molina, de la Victoria, Regidor, Frutos, c. Sorozábal *BMG Alhambra WD 71581*

Doña Francisquita (Vives)
Bayo, Kraus, Pierotti, Jericó, c. Ros Marbà *Auvidis Valois V4710 (2-CD)*
Arteta, Domingo, Mirabal, del Portal, c. Roa *Sony Classics S2K 66563 (2-CD)*
Tourné, Higueras, Lavirgen, Gabriel, García, c. Sorozábal *EMI 5 74209 2 (2-CD)*
Kraus, Pérez, Chamorro, del Portal, c. García Asensio *Carillon CAL 21-22 (2-CD)*
Del Campo, Lerer, Aragall, Molina, c. Gardelli *BMG Alhambra WD 71440 (2-CD)*
Kraus, Olaria, Ramade, Perez c. Montario (1960)

El amigo Melquíades (Serrano)
Rivadeneira, Sanchez, Monreal, Portillo, c. Cisneros *BMG Alhambra WD 74393*

El anillo de hierro (Marqués)
Berganza, Munguía, Ausensi, Monreal, c. Lauret *BMG Alhambra WD 74555*

El año pasado por agua (Chueca & Valverde)
Iriarte, Monreal, Luque, c. Cisneros *Columbia BS 7186* [cassette only]

El asombro de Damasco (Luna)
Pérez, Sagi-Vela, Martelo, Ramallé, c. Navarro *Orfeon CDE 231*
Argenta

El baile de Luis Alonso (Giménez)
Rivadeneira, Berganza, Munguía, Monreal, Fernández, c. Argenta *BMG Alhambra WD 71464*

El barberillo de Lavapiés (Barbieri)
Bayo, Casariego, Lanza, Sempere, c. Pérez *Auvidis Valois V4731*
Sagi-Vela, Ramirez, Pérez, Saura, c. Moreno Torroba *EMI 5 74163 2*
Olaria, Berganza, Munguía, Monreal, Maizo, c. Argenta *BMG Alhambra WD 71978*

El barbero de sevilla (Giménez & Nieto)
Dominguez, Ramirez, Villarejo, Pérez Carpio, Ligero, c. Lauret *BMG Alhambra WD 74552* [with some dialogue]

El barquillero (Chapí)
Rosado, Munguía, de Andía, c. Argenta Columbia *BS 7203* [cassette only]

El bateo (Chueca)
Berganza, Monreal, Portillo, de Andia, c. Cisneros *BMG Alhambra WD 74393*

El cabo primero (Caballero)
Monreal, Rosado, Gil, Fernández, Luque, c. Argenta *BMG Alhambra WD 71589*

El cafetal (Lecuona)
Pérez, Sagi-Vela, de Córdoba, Lombay, Lazari, c. Guerrero *Zafiro 33458 2* [highlights]

El canastillo de fresas (Guerrero)
Berchman (Pérez), Leonis, Ausensi, Lorengar, de la Vara, c. Pavon *BMG RCA Classics 74321 33841 2*

El cantar del arriero (Díaz Giles)
Cava, Ausensi, Bermejo, Monreal, c. Lauret *Columbia BS 7213* [cassette only]

El caserío (Guridi)
Pérez, Sagi-Vela, del Monte, c. Moreno Torroba *EMI 7243 5 74156 2 0*
Lorengar, Ausensi, Munguía, Argenta *BMG Alhambra WD 71468*

El chaleco blanco (Chueca)
Iriarte, Monreal, Portillo, c. Argenta *BMG Alhambra WD 74389*

El dúo de la africana (Caballero)
Iriarte, Munguia, Roa, Maldonado, c. Argenta *BMG Alhambra WD 74387*
(H) Raga, Santagostino, Gorgé, Gonzalo, c. Capdevila *Blue Moon BMCD 7520*

El hijo fingido (Rodrigo)
Ramón, Rodríguez, Casariego, Suarez, Rey-Joly, Sánchez, del Portal, Álvarez, López, Haro, c. Roa *EMI Classics 5 57127 2*

El huésped del Sevillano (Guerrero)
Pérez, del Monte, Sarmiento, del Portal, c. Moreno Torroba *EMI 5 74214 2*
Chamorro, Cava, Kraus, del Portal, Pereiro, c. García Navarro *Carillon CAL 24*
Pérez, Silva, Sagi-Vela, Ramallé, c. Navarro *BMG Zafiro 1012-2*
Cava, Bermejo, Munguía, Monreal, c. Cisneros *BMG RCA Classics 74321 33034 2*

EL HUSAR DE LA GUARDIA (Vives/Gimenez)   Lorengar, Ausensi, /Tejada

El mal de amores (Serrano)
Rivas, Uriz, Fondevila, Contreras, Gonzalez, c. Navarro *BMG Alhambra WD 74554*

El niño judío (Luna)
Iriarte, Huarte, Ausensi, Monreal, Portillo, c. Argenta *BMG Alhambra WD 71807*
EL PARAJO AZUL (M. LLAN) 1921 Caballe so/Benito Laurel (1972)
   Carpe, orta, Borras, Sardinero,
El pobre valbuena (Torregrosa & "Quinito" Valverde)
Iriarte, Pérez Carpio, Ligero, Vidal, c. Tejada *Columbia BS 7186* [cassette only, with some dialogue]

El puñao de rosas (Chapí)
Berchman (Pérez), Rubens, Rincón, Moro, Cuevas, Ramallé, c. Navarro *BMG Zafiro 74321 33462 2*
Sinovas, Martínez, Blancas, c. Frühbeck de Burgos *BMG Alhambra WD 74391*
Iriarte, Lorengar, Berganza, Ausensi, Martos, Madrid Sinfin + Madrid CO/Argenta (1954)
El rey que rabió (Chapí)
Sagi-Vela, Cubeiro, Álvarez, Alonso, c. Moreno Torroba *EMI 5 74229 2*
Lorengar, Rosado, Munguía, Ausensi, c. Argenta *BMG Alhambra WD 71806*
(H) Albiach, Isaura, Parra, de León, c. Gelabert *Blue Moon BMCD 7525*

El santo de la Isidra (Torregrosa)
Rosado, Luque, Gil, Campo, Monreal, c. Argenta *BMG Alhambra WD 74392*

El tambor de granaderos (Chapí)
Berganza, Rosado, Luque, c. Argenta *BMG Alhambra WD 71591*

El último romántico (Soutullo & Vert)
Berganza, Rivadeneira, Torrano, Monreal, Gil, c. Cisneros *BMG Alhambra WD 75124*
(1956)
Foc i fum (Rosselló)
Coll, Quetglas, Pons, c. Busquier *BLAU CD 207*

Gigantes y cabezudos (Caballero)
Berchman (Pérez), Cano, c. Montorio/Navarro *BMG Zafiro 50603002*
Iriarte, Munguía, Aldanondo, Erdozain, c. Argenta *BMG Alhambra WD 71465*
(H) Melo, Folgar, Vidal, c. Gelabert *Blue Moon BMCD 7509*
Espinalt, Ternel,   c. Ferrer EMI 7243 5 74155 2
Jugar con fuego (Barbieri)
Lorengar, Ausensi, Munguía, Campo, c. Argenta *BMG Alhambra WD 74556*

Katiuska (Sorozábal)
Penagros, Ausensi, de Victoria, Frutos, Julián, c. Sorozábal *BMG Zafiro 74321 33461 2*
Lorengar, Serrano, Kraus, Cesari, Gas, c. Sorozábal *EMI 7243 5 74161 2 2*
Higueras, Laya, Molina, Blancas, Frutos, c. Sorozábal *BMG Alhambra WD 71585 2* [2CD with dialogue]
(H) Herrero, Ottein, Serrano, Redondo, c. Sorozábal etc. *Blue Moon BMCD 7516* [extended highlights]
Garmendia, Arruabarrena, Catalina, Azpeitia, c. Ocón *aus_Art Records aAr 007*

La alegría de la huerta (Chueca)
Rosado, Munguía, Berganza, Martos, Ortega, c. Argenta *BMG Alhambra WD 71589*
(H) Isaura, Melo, Arnó, Vidal. c. Gelabert *Blue Moon BMCD 7536*

La alsaciana (Guerrero)
Lorengar, Díaz, Ausensi, Munguía, c. Argenta *BMG Alhmabra WD 71591* or *BMG RCA Classics 74321 33034 2*

La boda de Luis Alonso (Giménez)
Rivadeneira, Berganza, Munguía, Monreal, Fernández, c. Argenta *BMG Alhambra WD 71464*

La bruja (Chapí)
Berganza, Kraus, Munguía, Cava, c. Lauret *BMG Alhambra WD 75125 (2-CD)*

La calesera (Alonso)
Lorengar, Berganza, Ausensi, c. Cisneros *BMG Alhambra WD 71810*

La canción del olvido (Serrano)
Castelo, Cesari, Higuero, c. Sorozábal *EMI 5 74157 2*
Martínez, Blancas, Molina, c. Frühbeck de Burgos *BMG Alhambra WD 71436*
Lorengar, Ausensi, Munguía, c. Argenta *BMG RCA Classics 74321 35969 2*

La chula de Pontevedra (Luna & Bru)
Rosado, Rivedeneira, Gil, Ausensi, Monreal, c. Argenta *BMG Alhambra WD 71590*

La chulapona (Torroba)
Lorengar, Berganza, Fagoaga, c. Frühbeck de Burgos *BMG Alhambra WD 71977*

La corte de Faraón (Lleó)
(H) Raga, Serrano, Gonzalo, c. Capdevila *Blue Moon BMCD 7503*
Iriarte, Portillo, Cava, Ligero, c. Argenta *BMG Alhambra WD 71441*
De Cordoba, Ramallé, Aranda, Rincón, c. Navarro *Montilla/Orfeon CDE 226*

La del manojo de rosas (Sorozábal)
Penagos, Ausensi, de la Victoria, Regidor, Rodríguez, c. Sorozábal *BMG Zafiro 74321 33463 2*
Lorengar, Cesari, Serrano, Fuentes, Maroto, c. Sorozábal *EMI 7243 5 74158 2 (2-CD)*
Berganza, Blancas, Laya, Regidor, Molina, c. Sorozábal *BMG Alhambra WD 71583 (2-CD)* [with dialogue]

La del soto del Parral (Soutullo & Vert)
Gulin, Blancas, Ortiz, c. Frühbeck de Burgos *BMG Alhambra WD 71582*
Espinalt, Gual, Meseguer, Panadés, Esteban, Pol, c. Ferrer *EMI 5 74228 2*
Peréz, Sagi-Vela, Aguírre, c. Montorio *Montilla/Orfeon 25CDE-223*

La dogaresa (Millán)
Lorengar, Berganza, Ausensi, Munguía, c. Argenta *BMG RCA Classics WD 71808*

La dolorosa (Serrano)
Lavirgen, Tourné, Catania, Oran, García, c. Sorozábal *EMI 7243 5 74216 2*
Berganza, Cava, Domingo, Contreras, c. García-Navarro *BMG Alhambra WD 71588*
Kraus, Chamorro, Cava, Blancas, del Portal, c. García Asensio *Carillon CAL 30*

La duquesa del candil (Leoz)
(H) Iriarte, E. Leoz, Langa, Ausensi, c. J. G. Leoz *Blue Moon BMCD 7510* [highlights]

La eterna canción (Sorozábal)
Tourné, Higueras, Lavirgen, Cesari, Catania, c. Sorozábal *EMI 7243 5 74344 2 3*

La fama del tartanero (Guerrero)
Cava, Bermejo, Ausensi, Munguía, Monreal, Portillo, c. Lauret *BMG Columbia 74321 33033 2*

La fiesta de San Antón (Torregrosa)
Rosado, Berganza, Monreal, c. Argenta *BMG Alhambra WD 74392*

La gatita blanca (Giménez & Vives)
De Córdoba, Rincón, Cuevas, Ramallé, c. Navarro *BMG Zafiro 74321 33462 2*

La Generala (Vives)
Olaria, Kraus, del Campo, c. Estela *BMG Zafiro 50603037*
Espinalt, Vilardell, Torrento, c. Ferrer *EMI 5 74340 2*

La Gran Vía (Chueca & Valverde)
Domingo, Martín, Moreno, Montiel, c. Roa *RTVE Música 65150*
Mistral, Blancas, Martínez, c. Frühbeck de Burgos *BMG Alhambra WD 71587*
Tourné, Cesari, c. Sorozábal *EMI 7243 5 74152 2*

La leyenda del beso (Soutullo & Vert)
Gulin, Ortiz, Blancas, c. Lauret *BMG Alhambra WD 71463*
Pérez, Águila, de Córdoba, Picaso, Ramalle, c. Estela *Montilla CDFM-93*

La Marchenera (Torroba)
Lorengar, Balparda, Munguía, Ausensi, c. Moreno Torroba *BMG Alhambra WD 75127*

La montería (Guerrero)
Sagi-Vela, Lombay, de Córdoba, Ramallé, c. Navarro *BMG Zafiro ZOR 173*
Huarte, Bermejo, Ausensi, Monreal, c. Cisneros *BMG Columbia 74321 33030 2*

La parranda (Alonso)
Lorengar, Ausensi, Bermejo, Monreal, c. Tejada *BMG Alhambra WD 71467*
Rovira, Redondo, Panadés, Bardaji, c. Delta *EMI 5 74213 2*

Select Discography

La pícara molinera (Luna)
Berganza, Lorengar, Torrano, Ausensi, c. Cisneros *Columbia BS 7216* [cassette only]
(H) Pérez Carpio, Romeu, Redondo, Palacios, c. Puri/Fuentes *Blue Moon BMCD 7535* [extracts]

La picarona (Alonso)
Balparda, Bermejo, Munguía, Ausensi, Monreal, c. Lauret *Columbia BS 7170* [cassette only]
(H) Vazquez, Haro, Hernández, Redondo, Vela, c. Alonso *Blue Moon BMCD 7539* [highlights]

La reina mora (Serrano)
Sinovas, Martinez, Blancas, c. Frühbeck de Burgos *BMG Alhambra WD 74391*

La revoltosa (Chapí)
Rodríguez, Domingo, Garijo, Matilla, Sola, Muñiz, c. Roa *RTVE Música 65150*
Chamorro, Kraus, Rivedeneira, de Cordoba, c. García Asensio *EMI 5 74212 2*
Tourné, Cesari, c. Sorozábal *EMI 7243 5 74212 2*
Iriarte, Ausensi, Rivadeneira, Pérez Carpio, c. Argenta *BMG Alhambra WD 71438*

La rosa del azafrán (Guerrero)
Berganza, Ausensi, Bermejo, Monreal, c. Tejada *BMG Columbia 74321 33031 2*
Penagos, Sardinero, Orán, Blanco, Gil, c. Alonso *BMG Zafiro 1002-2*

La tabernera del puerto (Sorazábal)
Bayo, Domingo, Pons, Baquerizo, c. Pérez *Auvidis Valois V4766*
Barclay, Kraus, Cesari, Algorta, c. Sorozábal *EMI 7243 5 74158 2* (2-CD)
Higueras, Ariza, Ausensi, de Narke, c. Sorozábal *BMG Alhambra 71469* (2-CD) [with dialogue]
Penagos, Molina, Farrés, Catania, c. Sorozábal *BMG Zafiro 1030-2, 1031-2* [only available separately]

La tempestad (Chapí)
Huarte, Pérez, A. Kraus, F. Kraus, c. Estela *Carillon CAL 3* [highlights]

La tempranica (Giménez)
Pérez, Silva, Sagi-Vela, c. Navarro *Montilla/Orfeon 25-CDE 232*

La verbena de la Paloma (Bretón)
Bayo, Domingo, Pierotti, Castejon, c. Ros Marbà *Auvidis Valois V4725*
Tourné, Cesari, Ripolles, Bayod, c. Moreno Torroba *EMI 7243 5 74212 2*
Ausensi, Rivadeneira, Iriarte, Pérez Carpio, Pérez, Ligero, c. Argenta *BMG RCA Classics 74321 35967 2*
Kraus, Rivadeneira, Chamorro, de Córdoba, Campo, c. García Asensio *Carillon CAL19*
Sagi-Vela, Pérez, Ramallé, del Campo, c. Marco *BMG Zafiro 50603039*

La viejecita (Caballero)
(H) Melo, Isaura, Vidal, c. Gelabert *Blue Moon BMCD 7509*

La zapaterita (Alonso)
Ramirez, Meneses, Blancas, c. Moreno Buendia *RCA ND74203*

Las bravías (Chapí)
Iriarte, Bermejo, Monreal, Campos, c. Argenta *Columbia BS 7203* [cassette only]

Las de Caín (Sorozábal)
Tourné, Higueras, Cesari, Catania, García, Frutos, c. Sorozábal *EMI 7243 5 74342 2*

Las golondrinas (Usandizaga)
Cubeiro, Rivas, Sardinero, Alonso, c. Moreno Torroba *EMI 7243 5 74215 2* [extended highlights]
Lorengar, Iriarte, Torres, Munguia, Aldanondo, c. Argenta *BMG Alhambra WD 75126 (2-CD)*
(H) Galeffi, Campiña, Plantada, Gonzalo, c. Capdevila *Blue Moon BMCD 7529 (2-CD)*

Las hilanderas (Serrano)
Uriz, Rivas, Fondevila, Giménez, Contreras, Pons, Gonzalez, c. García-Navarro *BMG Alhambra WD 74554*

Las leandras (Alonso)
(H) Gámez, Vela, c. Alonso *Blue Moon BMCD 7542*
Rubens, Aznar, Moro, c. Montorio *Orfeon/Montilla 25CDE-246*

Las musas latinas (Penella)
Ramallé, Aznar, Aranda, de Córdoba, c. Navarro *Montilla/Orfeon 25-CDE 222*

Los cadetes de la Reina (Luna)
Espinalt, Torrento, Pol, c. Ferrer *EMI 574341 2*

Los de Aragón (Serrano)
Rosado, Munguía, c. Argenta *BMG Alhambra WD 71590*
Kraus, Pérez, del Portal, c. García Asensio *Carillon (Tiempo 11)*

Los Claveles (Serrano)
Berganza, Domingo, Cava, Manzaneda, c. García-Navarro *BMG Alhambra WD 71588*
Espinalt, Civil, Puigsech, Paulet, c. Ferrer *EMI 5 74213 2*
(H) Romo, Simón, Albiach, c. Serrano (?) *Blue Moon BMCD 7510*

Los diamantes de la corona (Barbieri)
Lorengar, Alite, Torrano, Ausensi, Monreal, Campos, c. Argenta *BMG RCA Classics 74321 35973 2*

Los flamencos (Vives)
(H) Pérez Carpio, Romeu, Avelli, Navarro, Palacios, c. (?) *Blue Moon BMCD 7551*

Los gavilanes (Guerrero)
Gulin, Oran, Molina, Blancas, c. Frühbeck de Burgos *BMG Alhambra WD 71432*
Egido, Poblador, Belaza, Ordóñez, c. Blancafort *RTVE Música 65085*
Ausensi, Berganza, Rosado, Munguía, c. Argenta *BMG Columbia 74321 33032 2*
Ripolles, Armentia, Cesari, Lavirgen, c. Moreno Torroba *EMI 7243 5 74154 2*

Los sobrinos del capitán Grant (Caballero)
Cava, Ramirez, Villarejo, Portillo, c. Lauret *BMG Alhambra WD 75123*
[extended highlights]

Luisa Fernanda (Torroba)
Villarroel, Rodrigo, Domingo, Pons, c. Ros Marbà *Auvidis Valois V4759*
Berganza, del Campo, Molina, Blancas, c. Frühbeck de Burgos *BMG Alhambra WD 71437*
Pérez, Lombay, Sierra, Sagi-Vela, c. Estevarena *BMG Zafiro 50603041*
Solá, de los Ángeles Morales, Munguía, c. Argenta *BMG RCA Classics 74321 33105 2*
Tourné, Alsina, Lavirgen, Cesari, c. Moreno Torroba *EMI 7243 5 74153 2* [rev. version]

Maravilla (Torroba)
(H) Vallojera, Sagi-Vela, Durán, Silva. c. Moreno Torroba *Blue Moon BMCD 7526*
[highlights]

María la O (Lecuona)
Pérez, Sagi-Vela, Granados, de Córdoba, López, c. Guerrero *BMG Zafiro 33460 2*
[highlights]
Sánchez, Chacon, c. Romeu *EGREM CD 0122*

Marina (Arrieta)
Bayo, Kraus, Pons, Baquerizo, c. Pérez *Auvidis Valois V4845 (2-CD)*
Álvarez, Kraus, Kraus, Yebra, c. Olmedo *Carillon CD 1-2 (2-CD)*
Canale, Aragall, Blancas, de Narke, c. Frühbeck de Burgos *BMG Alhambra WD 71586 (2) (2-CD)*

Martierra (Guerrero)
(H) Almodóvar, Folgar, de Diso, Pereira, Baldrich, Vela. c. Guerrero (?) *Aria SL 1029*

Maruxa (Vives)
Caballé, Sardinero, Riera, Lavirgen, de Narke, c. García Asensio *BMG Alhambra WD 71584 (2)*
Pérez, Sagi-Vela, Cubeiro, Julián, Gonzalo, c. Moreno Torroba *EMI 7243 5 74212 2*
Rosado, Ausensi, Lorengar, de la Vara, Corbello, c. Argenta *BMG RCA Classics 74321 35970 2*

Me llaman la presumida (Alonso)
(H) Vallojera, Sagi-Vela, c. Alonso *Blue Moon BMCD 7528* [extended highlights]

So / Frühbeck de Burgos ✓

Molinos de viento (Luna)
Lorengar, Ausensi, Munguía, Martos, c. Argenta *BMG Alhambra WD 74388* ✓
Tourné, Cesari, García, Frutos, c. Sorozábal *EMI 7243 5 74226 2* ✓

Berchman, Sagi-Vela, Ramalle c. Navarro ✓

Moros y cristianos (Serrano)
Iriarte, Munguía, c. Argenta *BMG Alhambra WD 74389* ✓

Pan y toros (Barbieri)
Iriarte, Ausensi, Munguia, Dominguez, Campos, Portillo, c. Cisneros *BMG Alhambra WD 74390* [extended highlights] ✓

Rosa la china (Lecuona)
Pérez, Sagi-Vela, de Córdoba, López, c. Guerrero *Zafiro 33457 2* [highlights]

Appendix B
Bibliography

English

Bentivegna, Patricia. *Parody in the Género Chico*. New Orleans: University Press of the South, 2000.

Chase, Gilbert. *The Music of Spain*. New York: Dover Publications, 2d ed. 1959.

Crichton, Ronald. *Falla (BBC Music Guides)*. London: BBC Publications, 1982.

Lamb, Andrew. *150 Years of Popular Musical Theatre*. New Haven and London: Yale University Press, 2000.

Salter, Lionel. "Spain: a Nation in Turbulence." In *Man & Music: the Late Romantic Era from the Mid-Nineteenth Century to World War I*, ed. J. Samson. London: Macmillan, 1991.

Stein, Louise. *Songs of Mortals, Dialogues of the Gods: Music and Theatre in Seventeenth-Century Spain*. Oxford: Clarendon Press, 1993.

Sturman, Janet. *Zarzuela: Spanish Operetta, American Stage*. Chicago and Urbana: University of Illinois Press, 2000.

Webber, Christopher, ed. *Zarzuela! Romanzas (Vols. 1–4)*. Madrid and London: Union Musical Ediciones, 2000

———. *Zarzuela! Website*. Biographies, Synopses and Discography (1998–2002) http://www.nashwan.demon.co.uk/zarzuela.htm (August 1997)

Spanish

Alier, Roger. *El libro de la zarzuela*. Barcelona: Daimon, 1986.

Alonso, José Montero. *Francisco Alonso*. Madrid: Espasa-Calpe, 1987.

———. *Usandizaga*. Madrid: Espasa-Calpe, 1985.

Amat, Carlos Gómez. *Historia de la música española 5. Siglo XIX*. Madrid: Alianza Editorial, 1984

Arozamena, Jesús de. *Jesús Guridi*. Madrid: Nacional, 1967.

Arribas, Ramón Regidor. *Aquellas zarzuelas*. Madrid: Alianza Editorial, 1996.

Burguete, Sol. *Vives*. Madrid: Espasa-Calpe, 1978.

Carabias, Josefina. *El Maestro Guerrero fue así*. Madrid: Biblioteca Nueva, 2001.

Casares Rodicio, Emilio. *Francisco Asenjo Barbieri*. Madrid: ICCMU, 1994.

———, ed. *Historia Gráfica de la Zarzuela (Vol 1, 2 y 3)*. Madrid: ICCMU, 1999, 2000, 2001.

Cortizo, Maria Encina. *Emilio Arrieta. De la ópera a la zarzuela*. Madrid: ICCMU, 1998.

Fernández-Cid, Antonio. *Cien años de teatro musical en España*. Madrid: Real Musical, 1973.

Franco, Manuel García, and Arribas, Ramón Regidor. *La Zarzuela*. Madrid: Acento Editorial, 1997.

Girbal, F. Hernández. *Amadeo Vives, el musico y el hombre*. Madrid: Ediciones Lira, 1971.

———. *Federico Chueca, el alma de Madrid*. Madrid: Ediciones Lira, 1992.

Iberni, Luis G. *Ruperto Chapí*. Madrid: ICCMU, 1995.

Labad, José María Gómez. *El Madrid de la Zarzuela*. Madrid: Editorial Tres, 1983.

Montero, E. *José Padilla*. Madrid: Fundación Banco Exterior, 1990.

Peña y Goñi, Antonio. *España desde la ópera a la zarzuela*. Madrid: Alianza Editorial, 1976.

Ruiz, José López. *Historia del Teatro Apolo y de La verbena de la Paloma*. Madrid: Avapiés, 1994.

Sagardia, Ángel. *Chapí*. Madrid: Espasa-Calpe, 1979.

———. *Luna*. Madrid: Espasa-Calpe, 1978.

Sagarmínaga, Joaquín Martín de. *Diccionario de cantantes líricos españoles*. Madrid: Acento Editorial, 1997.

Sorozábal, Pablo. *Mi vida y mi obra*. Madrid: Fundación Banco Exterior, 1986.

Vila, Jaime Estévez. *Reveriano Soutullo Otero*. Madrid: Alpuerto, 1995.

Vives, Amadeu. *Sofía*. Madrid: Espasa-Calpe, 1973.

Appendix C
Glossary

Alborada: Dawn serenade.

Alhambrismo: Nationalist Spanish musical style developed in the late nineteenth century, drawing on Moorish harmonies, vocal figurations and rhythms, taking its name from the Alhambra in Granada. It is related also to gypsy music.

Baile: Dance of any kind. In zarzuela it sometimes describes a danced *Intermedio**.

Bandurria: A plucked lute. A hybrid of the guitar and cittern, found in Spain and parts of Latin America. Major component of the *rondalla**.

Brindis: Drinking song.

Bufo: Comic. In nineteenth century Madrid the *bufos madrileños* theatre staged light, risqué entertainment corresponding to the Parisian operettas of Offenbach.

Bolero: Popular Spanish dance in triple time, originating in the mid-eighteenth century and often performed by a pair of female dancers with castanets.

Cachucha: Andalusian solo dance in triple time, similar to the *fandango**.

Canción: Song, generally strophic in form and simpler in content than a *romanza**.

Cantables: Sung texts.

Carceleras: Andalusian song, sung by prisoner bewailing their lot. Literally "prison verses".

Castizo: Traditional, typically Spanish, pure Castilian.

Chotis: Popular nineteenth century Madrid dance, deriving from the schottische.

Chulapa: Attractive urban, lower-class girl.

Chulo: Male *chulapa**.

Coloquio: A duologue, in rhymed verse or song.

Comedia: Any comedy drama.

Conga (-o): Cuban communal dance and song.

Contradanza: Spanish (and especially Cuban) version of the eighteenth century French *contredanse*, a courtly square dance in duple time.

Coplas: Couplets, rhyming verses. Broadly applied in zarzuela to strophic songs with comic, satirical or risqué texts, the singular *copla* later identifies a distinct song form, especially popular in Madrid.

Costumbrista: Colorful local customs and costume.

Danza: Formal dance, alternative name for c*ontradanza** in Cuba and the Caribbean.

Danzón: Complex Cuban song or dance, developed from the *contradanza**.

Dúo: Duet.

Estribillo: Refrain of a song, especially a *villancico**.

Espatadanza: Basque "sword dance" in lively 7/4 meter.

Fandango: Triple time dance with castanets.

Fiesta: Public celebration or holiday. A *fiesta de la zarzuela* was the original description of the seventeenth century entertainments at the Zarzuela Palace.

Final: Musical finale to an act or work.

Género chico: The genre of popular, short one-act zarzuelas prevalent from the late nineteenth century onward. Literally, "little genre."

Género grande: Three-act zarzuelas from the mid nineteenth century onward, alternatively called *zarzuela grande** to distinguish them from Grand Opera. Literally, "large genre."

Género ínfimo: Decadent development of the *género chico**, often of a crude or vulgar nature. Literally "inferior genre."

Gitana (-o): Gypsy.

Guajira: Street song, originally Cuban, with rhythmic clapping accompaniment.

Guaracha: Cuban clog dance.

Habanera: Nineteenth century Cuban song and dance form, in moderate duple time with characteristic dotted rhythm, familiar in Spain and France as well as Latin America. The name suggests its association with the Cuban capital, Havana. The French form *habañera* is a well-established solecism.

Humorada: Originally a short, comic skit. *Zarzuela humorada* is sometimes applied to a short, farcical piece of music theatre.

Intermedio: Musical interlude or entr'acte, played between scenes or before an act. Sometimes *interludio*.

Jácara: A popular, notably riotous, song and dance dating from medieval times.

Jota: Popular song and dance. Aragon's classic *jota aragonesa* alternates slow, improvisatory vocal verses with fast, lively refrains in triple time.

Lírica (-o): Sung, or songlike.

Preludio: Overture or prelude to an act.

Madrileña (-o): Woman (man) of Madrid.

Maja (-o): In the late eighteenth and early nineteenth centuries, fashionable young woman (man) from Madrid's lower classes. They often feature in Goya's paintings.

Marcha: March-time music or dance, generally military in style.

Mazurka: Popular triple time urban dance, originally Polish, with dotted rhythm and accent on weak beat of the bar. Alternatively *mazurca*.

Opereta: Nineteenth and twentieth century Spanish music theatre in the style of classic Viennese or French Operetta. Any light zarzuela might be designated *opereta*, especially one with a foreign or fairy-tale setting, but the distinction is often hazy.

Panaderos: Slow, *tango*-like dance, traditionally associated with bread baking.

Pasacalle: Lively, march-like street music, especially associated with Madrid.

Pasatiempo: Light play or zarzuela. Literally "diversion."

Pasodoble: English paso doble or two-step; lively march, with distinctive syncopated rhythm, associated with the bullring but also immensely popular as a street dance in Madrid. Often conflated with *pasacalle*.

Plegaria: A sung prayer, often to the Virgin.

Polaca: Triple time urban dance, especially popular in Madrid, adapted from the polonaise.

Relato: Narrative or story, sung or spoken.

Revista: Revue. Light theatrical genre, originating in late nineteenth century France, which succeeded *Los bufos** in Madrid, and came to rival zarzuela in popular esteem. In its later manifestations the contents were more salacious than satirical.

Romanza: Romantic aria or song.

Rondalla: Traditional street band of mandolin and/or *bandurria** players, associated with weddings, *fiestas** and other celebrations.

Salida: Entry song.

Sardana: Catalonia's famous communal street dance, in march time with a distinctive dotted rhythm.

Sainete: One act comic drama, with or without music, usually with lower-class, urban settings and characters.

Seguidillas: One of the most popular Spanish dances. The *seguidilla* was originally a strophic rhymed verse form. When *seguidillas* are sung and danced to music in 6/8 meter, the plural form is invariably used.

Soledad: Andalusian song, often in melancholy or homesick mood.

Tango: Popular Argentine dance in moderate duple time with dotted rhythm, related to the Cuban *habanera**. Introduced into Spain during the late nineteenth century.

Tanguillo: Fast dance in *tango** style.

Terceto: Trio.

Tertulia: Regular gatherings of artists, musicians, writers and philosophers, often in a specific café or bar.

Tiple: Light soprano or soubrette.

Tonadilla escénica: Short music theatre piece, twenty minutes or so in length, fashionable in late eighteenth and early nineteenth century Madrid theatres and salons. A *tonadilla* (literally "little song") was written for a small number of solo singers, often on a comic or satirical theme, and lightly staged.

Vals: Waltz.

Verbena: Night celebration or *fiesta** on the vigil of a Saint's Day.

Villancico: Classical Spanish poetic form with strophes (*coplas**) and refrain (*estribillo**). In zarzuela, the meaning is more fluid, and may describe any formal or antiquated song or ballad.

Zapateado: Lively Andalusian heel-and-toe dance, in 6/8 meter. The term is also used adjectivally, to describe heel-clicking in any dance.

Zarzuela grande: Three-act zarzuela, alternatively *género grande**.

Zarzuelero: Composer, writer or performer of zarzuela.

Zortzico: Basque dance in moderate 5/8 meter, with strong accents on the second and fourth beats of the bar.

Index

A casarse tocan, 271
Abati, Joaquín 152, 155
Abel y Caín, 53
Acevedo, Emilio, 278
Acis y Galatea, 2
Adam, Adophe: *Le postillon de Lonjumeau*, 274
Adios a la bohemia, 226
Agua, azucarillos y aguardiente, 5, **74–78**, 294, 302
Al fin se casa la Nieves, 48
Albéniz, Isaac, 247, 249, 250, **269**; *Henry Clifford*, 269; *Merlin*, 269; *Pepita Jiménez*, 269
Alhambra (recording company), 9
Alhambrismo (musical movement), 47, 99
Alma de Dios, 191, **192–194**, 292
Alonso, Francisco, 6, **11–26**, 168, 182, 201, 275, 293, 305, 308, 311; *Pólvora sin humo* (pasodoble), 11
Alonso, Manuel Marti, 215
Álvarez, Carlos, 301
Álvarez, Enrique García, 78, 80, 159, 192, 194, 237, 242, 292
Álvarez Quintero, Serafín. *See* Quintero, los hermanos
Álvarez Quintero, Joaquín. *See* Quintero, los hermanos
Amalia Baptista, **289**
Amengual, Antonio. *See* Compañía Lírica Española
Amor y arte, 269

Amores de aldea, 227
Ancelot, Jacques and Decomberousse, Alejo: *La Comtesse d'Egmont*, 40
Andreu, Lorenzo, 227
Anguita, Francisco Serrano, 208, 211
Aquella canción antigua, 278, 297
The Arabian Nights, 152, 155
Aramburu, Silva, 229
Arana, Lucrecia, 107, **301**
Arbós, Fernández, 207
Ardavín, Luis Fernández, 22, 24
Arderius, Francisco, 4, 47, 274, 293, 299
Argenta, Ataulfo, 9, 302, 305, 306, 307, 310
Armas al hombro, 11
Arniches, Carlos, 5, 108, 192, 194, 205, 237, 238, 240, 242, **291–2**, 296
Arregui, Faustino, **301–2**
Arriaga, Juan Crisóstomo, 244
Arrieta, Emilio, 4, **27–31**, 33, 47, 53, 70, 272, 274, 275, 277, 292, 293, 295; *La Conquista de Granada*, 27; *Ildegonda*, 27
Asenjo, Antonio, 162, 164
Asenjo Barbieri, Francisco. *See* Barbieri, Francisco Asenjo
Auber, Daniel: *Si J'etais Roi!*, 271
Ausensi, Manuel, 302
Auvidis Valois (recording company), 9
¡Ave César!, 146
de Ayala, Adelardo López, 28, 30
Aza, Vital, 54, 58, 63, 66, 293

Badía, María, 303
Baixant de la Font del Gat, 285
Balada de Carnaval, 267
Balarrasa (movie), 279
Balart, Gabriel, **269**
Barbieri, Francisco Asenjo, 3, 4, 9, 27, 28, **33–45**, 50, 73, 109, 110, 270, 271, 273, 292, 295, 299, 311; *Il Buontempone*, 33
Baroja, Pío, 226
Baroque zarzuela, 1–2, 9
Barrera Saavedra, Tomás, 277
Basili, Basilio, 3
Bayo, María, 301
Bazin, François, 117
Beethoven, Ludwig van: *Fidelio*, 7; Pastoral Symphony, 72
Benamor, 152, 165
Benavente, Jacinto: *Los intereses creados*, 189
Benavente Ossuna, Duke of, 3
Berchman, Lily. *See* Pérez, Dolores.
Berganza, Teresa, 272, **302**, 303, 306
Berlioz, Hector, 33, 272; Beatrice et Benedict, 80
Bernstein, Leonard, 9; *West Side Story*, 287
Bienvenido Mr. Marshall (movie), 279
Bizet, Georges: *L'Arlésienne*, 70; *Carmen*, 9, 105, 272, 302; *Les Pecheurs de Perles*, 127
Black, el payaso, 207, **208-12**, 303, 304, 305
Blanco y negro (periodical), 297
Boccaccio, Giovanni, 197
Boccherini, Luigi, 3, 5
Bohemios, 249, **250–253**, 256, 262, 267, 296
Bonito país, 48
Brecht, Bertolt: *Die Dreigroschenoper*, 89
Bretón, Tomás, 5, 9, 27, **47–51**, 53, 62, 63, 82, 118, 192, 269, 275, 294, 296, 299; *El apocalipsis*, 47; *En la Alhambra*, 47; *Escenas andaluzas*, 47; *Guzmán el Bueno*, 47; *La Dolores*, 47; *Los amantes de Teruel*, 47; *Salamanca*, 47

Brindis, 312
Britten, Benjamin: *Peter Grimes*, 138
Bru, Enrique, 152, 165
Bru, Isobel, **302**
Buendia, Manuel Moreno, 6

Caballé, Montserrat, 8, **303**
Caballero, Manuel Fernández. *See* Fernández Caballero, Manuel
Cádiz, 73, 90, 275
Calderón de la Barca, Pedro, 1–2
Calleja, Rafael Gómez, 145, **277**
Camín, Alfonso, 164
del Campo, Conrado, 253, 281, 282
Campos, Pérez, 162
Camprodón, Francisco, 28, 45, 115, **292**, 293, 295
Cancionero de Palacio (antique songbook), 33
Cançó d'Amor i de Guerra, 284
Capdevila, Antonio, 309
Capdevila, Luis, 285
Cara al sol, 282
Carnicer, Ramón, 3, 33, 109, 270
Carreño, Anselmo Cuadrado, 19, 21, 198, 201, 212, 215, 218, 221, 232, 235, **292–3**
Carreras, José, 8, 285, 301
Carrión, Miguel Ramos, 28, 31, 54, 57, 58, 63, 66, 67, 70, 74, 77, 85, 86, 100, 104, 105, 108, 292, **293–4**
Caruso, Enrico, 72
casticismo (musical movement), 6, 174, 280
del Castillo, Emilio García, 12, 15, 215
Castro, Francisco Ramos de. *See* Ramos de Castro, Francisco
Catalina, 110, 114
Cecilia Valdés, 289, **290**
Celos aún del aire matan, 1
Cereceda, Guillermo, **270**
Certamen nacional, 296
de Cervantes, Miguel, 72, 130; *Don Quijote*, 72
Chapí y Lorente, Ruperto, 5, 27, 31, 47, 48, 50, **53–72**, 118, 151, 177, 192, 221, 227, 237, 260, 275,

277, 291, 293, 294, 296, 299, 302; *Fantasía morisca*, 53; *La serenata*, 53; *Las naves de Cortés*, 53; *Los ángeles*, 53; *Los gnomos de la Alhambra*, 53; *Margarita la tornera*, 53; *Roger de Flor*, 53
Chaplin, Charlie: *City Lights*, 280
Chateau-Margaux, 91, **108**
Chatrian, Alexandre. *See* Erckmann, Emile
Chueca, Federico, 4, 5, 6, 9, 45, 48, **73–90**, 177, 192, 194, 205, 275, 279, 291, 294, 299
Cimarosa, Domenico: *Il Maestro di Capella*, 149
Cinematógrafo nacional, 118
Circe, 53
Clavé, Josep Anselm, **283**
Colegialas y soldados, 270
Colomer, Conrad, 283
Compañía Lírica Española, 8
Con las de Caín, 275
¿Con quién caso a mi mujer?, 270
costumbrismo, 6
de la Cruz, Ramón, 2–3, 4, 36, 298
Cuadros disolventes, 273, 296
Cuba, 7, 91, 110, 272, **287–90**
Cuidado con la pintura, 298
Cupido y Esculapio, 73
Curro Vargas, **71**

dance forms in zarzuela, 5
de los Ángeles, Victoria, 301
De Valencia al Grao, 145
Debussy, Claude, 117, 208; *La Mer*, 225
Decomberousse, Alejo. *See* Ancelot, Jacques
Delgado, Sinesio, 275
Diana cazadora, 281
Díaz Giles, Fernando, **277–8**; *Danza Siberiana*, 278; *Himno de la Academia de Infantería*, 277; *Rocío*, 278
Dickens, Charles: *A Tale of Two Cities*, 108
Diet, Edmond: *Madame Putifar*, 148
d'Indy, Vincent, 139, 143, 243

Disney, Walt, 140: *The Castaways*, 104
Domingo, Plácido, 8, 9, 185, 225, **303**, 304
Domingo Ferrer, Plácido, 173, **303–4**, 304
Domínguez, Antonio, 83, 84
Don Gil de Alcalá, 185, **186–90**, 304
Don Joan de Serrallonga, **285**, 312
Don Juan Tenorio, 284
Don Lucas del Cigarral, 249, **267**
Don Manolito, **212–5**, 293, 303, 305
Don Simplicio Bobadilla, 271
Doña Francisquita, 6, 25, 136, 143, 181, 250, **253–7**, 262, 266, 297, 298, 303, 304, 306, 308, 309, 312
Donizetti, Gaetano; 28, 110, 115
Dotras Vila, Juan, **278**, 297
Dugi, Emilio, 279
Dukas, Paul, 243
Durón, Sebastian, 2, 9
Dürrenmatt, Friedrich: *Der Besuch*, 126
Dvorak, Antonin, 143

Echegaray, Miguel, 5, 92, 94, 95, 97, 105, 107, 267, **294**
Echegaray, José, 294
Eco y Narciso, 2
El ama, **137**
El amenacer, 109
El amigo Melquíades, 191, **205**, 276, 292
El amor brujo, 306
El anillo de hierro, **272**
El año pasado por agua, 73, **81–2**, 275, 299
El asombro de Damasco, 151, **152–6**, 165, 307, 310
El Ayre Español, 9
El baile de Luis Alonso, 117, 118, **121**
El banco del Retiro, 277
El barberillo de Lavapiés, **34–37**, 44, 295
El barbero de Sevilla, 117, **122**, 273, 296
El barquillero, **71**
El bateo, 74, **83–5**

El batey, 288
El buena sombra, 296
El caballero del amor, 278
El cabo primero, **91**, 108, 137, 291
El cafetal, **288**, 309
El campamento, 271
El canastillo de fresas, 123, **138**, 297, 307
El cant de la Marsellesa, 284
El cantante enmascarado, 278
El cantar del arriero, **278**
El capricho de una Reina, 228
El carro del sol, 307
El caserío, **140–3**, 298, 305, 308
El chaleco blanco, 74, **85–7**, 294
El cimarrón, 289
El clavel rojo, 47
El coche correo, 292
El código penal, 277
El conjuro, 28
El diablo en el poder, 34, **45**
El dictador, 167, 168, **171**, 217, 298, 310, 311
El divo, 278
El domingo de Ramos, 47
El dominó azul, 28, **31**
El duende, 271
El duende azul, 174, 281
El dúo de la africana, 91, **92–5**, 174, 294
El estrago en la fineza, 2
El gaitero, 273
El gaitero de Gijón, 281, 297
El gato montés, 185, 186, 190
El golfo de las Sirenas, 1
El gorro frigio, 273
El grumete, 28, **31**
El guitarrico, 274, 310
El hermano lobo, 185
El hijo del sol, Faetón, 2
El hijo fingido, **281**
El hombre de mundo, 299
El huésped del Sevillano, 72, 123, **127–30**, 137, 309
El húsar de la guardia, 118, 249, **267**
El iluso Cañizares, 277
El jardín de Falerina, 1
El joven piloto, 282

El joven Telémaco, 4, 274
El juramento, **110-14**, 295
El laurel de Apolo, 1
El maestro Campanone, 146, **149**
El mal de amores, **205**, 297
El marqués de Caravaca, 40
El mayoral, 289
El mesón del Pato Rojo, 281
El método Gorritz, 146
El milagro de la Virgen, **72**
El molinero de Subiza, 273
El monaguillo, 272, **273**
El motete, 191
El niño judío, 151, 152, **159–62**, 227
El novio pasado por agua, 271
El pájaro azul, 167, 168, **171**, 303
El Pilar de la victoria, 152
El plato del día, 272
El pobre diablo, 237, 276
El pobre Valbuena, 237, **242**, 276, 292
El pollo Tejada, 191, 276, 292
El postillón de la Rioja, 273, **274**
El pou de la veritat, 284
El primer día feliz, 91
El primer reserva, 237, 276
El príncep del Congo, 284
El Príncipe Bohemio, 167
El puñao de rosas, **72**, 291
El rayo de sol, 270
El reloj de cuco, 47
El reloj de Lucerna, 272, **273**
El renegado, 278
El rey que rabió, 54, **63–7**, 260, 293, 307
El romeral, **278**
El santo de la Isidra, 237, **240–2**, 292, 310
El secreto de la reina, 271
El señor Joaquín, 92, **98–100**, 221
El sobrino del difunto, 73, 275
El sonámbulo, 27
El sueño de una noche de verano, 110
El tambor, 271
El tambor de granaderos, 54, 63, 71, **72**, 302
El tesoro de Golconda, 168
El tulipán de los mares, 269

El último romántico, 228, **236**, 310
El valle de Andorra, 110, **115**
El Versalles madrileño, 228
Embil, Pepita, 173, 303, **304**
EMI (recording company), 9
Emigrantes, 277
Encarna, la misterio, 228
Entre mi mujer y el negro, 34
Entre Sevilla y Triana, 207
Episodios nacionales, 145
Erckmann, Emile and Chatrian, Alexandre: *Le Juif Polonais*, 70
Eslava, Hilarión, 91
Espinalt, María, **304**
Estebanillo, 273
Estellés, Ramón, 90, 276

de Falla, Manuel, 249, 266, **279**, 306; *La vida breve*, 120, 279, 297
Fando, Urbà, 283
Fernández Caballero, Manuel, 5, **91–108**, 137, 145, 174, 191, 221, 275, 287, 291, 293, 294, 296, 299, 301
Ferré, Lluis, 123
Fiesta Nacional, 73
Fleta, Miguel, 152, 277, 301, 308
Foc i Fum, 286
Folgar, Tino, **304**
Follet, 270
Franco, Francisco, 7, 145, 148
Frasquito, 299
Frutos, Luis Pascal, 151, 156, 158, 260, 262
Fuenteovejuna, 6
Fundación Jacinto y Inocencio Guerrero, 124

Galdós, Benito Pérez, 5, 298; *Fortunata y Jacinta*, 73, 90
Galeffi, Carlo, 307
Galván, Eulalia Fernández, 162
Gámez, Celia, 18, 304, **305**
García, Manuel, 270
Gas, Manuel, **304–5**
Gaztambide, Joaquín, 3, 9, 30, 33, **109–15**, 271, 273, 287, 292, 295, 311
género chico, 2, 4–5, 7

género grande, 3–4
Gerhard, Roberto, 249
Gershwin, George, 208
Gigantes y cabezudos, 92, **95–97**, 107, 191, 294, 301, 303, 309
Gigli, Benjamino, 310
Gil, Julián, 91
Gilbert, William Schwenck, xi, 50, 155
Gilito, 296
Giménez, Gerónimo, 85, **117–22**, 249, 267, 273, 279, 299
Giner, Salvador, 145, 185, 191, **270**
The Girl with the Roses, xii. See also *La del manojo de rosas*
Glinka, Mikhail, 34
Goethe, Johann Wolfgang, 297
Golondrina de Madrid, 192
Gómez, Julio, 152
Gounod, Charles, 70
Goya, Francisco, 45, 270
Granados, Enrique, **270**; *Goyescas*, 270
Grenet, Eliseo, 288
Grieg, Edvard, 156
Guerrero, Jacinto, 6, **72**, **123–38**, 173, 189, 279, 296, 297, 298, 304, 305, 306, 312
Guitarras y bandurrias, 228
Guridi, Jesús, **139–144**, 173, 243, 293, 298; *Amaya*, 140; *Diez melodías vascas*, 139; *Euzko Irudiak*, 140, 225; *Homenaje a Walt Disney*, 140; *Sinfonía Pirenaica*, 139; *Una aventura de Don Quijote*, 139
Guridi, Ignacio, 139

Halévy, Jacques Fromental, 115
Handel, Georg Frideric: *Acis and Galatea*, 2, 262
Hernando, Rafael, 109, **270–1**, 273
Herrero, Felisa, 121, **305**
Hidalgo, Juan, 1
Hispavox (recording company), 9
Humperdinck, Engelbert, 269

ICCMU (Instituto Complutense de Ciencias Musicales), 8
Ildara, 274

Inzenga, José, 109, **271**, 273
Iquino, Ignacio F., 194
Iradier, Sebastián **272**; *El arreglito*, 272; *La Paloma*, 272
Iriarte, Ana-María, **305–6**
Irving, Sir Henry, 70
Isabel II, 27
Isidro, Saint, 242
L'Isle, Rouget de, 108

Jackson Veyán, José. *See* Veyán, José Jackson
Jiménez, Jerónimo. *See* Giménez, Gerónimo
Jonson, Ben, 221; *The Devil is an Ass*, 237
Juan Miguel, 280
Juegos malabares, **267**, 294
Jugar con fuego, 3, 34, **37–40**, 45, 299, 302
Justos por pecadores, 272

Kálmán, Emmerich, 208
Katiuska, 171, 207, **215-8**, 225, 305, 308, 310, 312
Koch, Friedrich, 207
Kosmópolis, 278
Kraus, Alfredo, 31, 72, **306**

L'Àliga Roja, 284
L'aplec del Remei, 283
L'art de la Bruixeria, 283
L'illa tranquil·la, 284
La alegre alcaldesa, 279
La alegría de la huerta, 74, **78–80**
La alegría del batallón, **205**, 292
La alsaciana, 123, 133, **137**
La balada de la luz, 249
La banda de trompetas, 237
La banderita, 11
La baraja francesa, 275
La beata, 2
La bejarana, 275
La bengala, 140
La bien amada, 280
La bien ganada, 281
La boda de Luis Alonso, 117, 118, **121**
La bruja, **54–8**, 66, 67, 293, 306

La calesera, 11, **12–15**, 18, 24, 25, 182, 307, 308, 310
La canción de la Lola, 4, 73, 89, **90**, 275, 299
La canción del Ebro, 130
La canción del olvido, 192, **194–8**, 297, 308
La caramba, **182**, 308, 311
La cariñosa, 47
La cautiva, 140, 293
La chavala, **71**
La chula de Pontevedra, 152, **165**
La chulapona, **174–8**, 298, 305, 309
La Clementina, 3
La condesa de la aguja y el dedal, **144**
La conquista de Madrid, **115**
La corte de Faraón, 145, **146–9**, 252, 296, 309, 312
La cortesana de Omán, 118
La del manojo de rosas, 6, 12, 21, 100, 183, 201, 207, **218–21**, 225, 293, 303, 308, 311
La del soto del Parral, 228, **232–6**, 292, 311
La Dogaresa, 167, **168–71**, 310
La dolorosa, xii, 192, **202–4**, 303, 306, 309, 312
La Duquesa del candil, **279**, 297, 306
La España Musical (society), 33
La estrella de Oriente, 277
La eterna canción, **226**, 306
La fama del tartanero, 123, **138**
La fiesta de San Antón, 177, 237, **238–40**, 292, 302
La fiesta del pueblo, 185
La gatita blanca, 118, **122**, 249
La gaviota, 167
La Generala, 133, 249, **257–60**, 296, 306
La Gran Vía, 5, 7, 18, 74, 77, 82, **87–9**, 90, 275
La granjera de Arlés, 282, 312
La Guerra Santa, 28
La Habana de noche, 289
La hechichera en Palacio, 280
La hija de Jefté, 53
La hija del sol, 289
La isla de las perlas, 312

La jardinera, 91
La Legió d'Honor, 284, **285**
La leyenda del beso, 130, 228, **229–32**
La linda tapada, 11, **25**
La llama, 243, **247**
La madrileña, 2
La mala hembra, 279
La mala sombra, **205**, 297
La malquerida, 185
La marcha de Cádiz, 90, 276
La marchenera, 173, **182**
La Marquesa chulapa, 280
La Marsellesa, 91, **108**
La meiga, 140, **144**, 298
La mensajera, 109
La mesonera de Tordesillas, 173
La montería, 123, **131–3**
La morería, 12, 167. See also *La severa*
La moza vieja, 298
La muerte de Agripina, 237
La muerte de Cesar, 299
La mujer de cartón, 277
La niña de los cantares, 11
La Noche (periodical), 145
La noche de San Juan, 275
La paloma del barrio, 227
La parranda, 11, 18, **22–5**
La pastorela, 152, 173
La patria chica, 54, **58–60**, 296
La pícara molinera, 152, **162–5**, 235, 302, 304, 309, 310
La picarona, 11, **25**
La plaza de la catedral, 288
La pradera del canal, 272
La primera del barrio, 249
La púrpura de la rosa, 1, 287
La rabalera, 294
La reina fea, 280
La reina mora, 191, **206**, 297
La república del amor, 146
La revoltosa, 5, 48, 54, **60–3**, 71, 77, 90, 221, 302, 303
La rosa del azafrán, 123, 127, **134–7**, 189, 298, 305, 308, 311
La rubia del Far West, 282
La rumbosa, 12
La Santa Espina, 285
La serranilla, 281
La severa, 167. See also *La morería*
La silla de manos, 277
La tabernera del puerto, 31, 207, **222–5**, 298, 302, 303, 304, 305, 308, 310
La taza de té, 146
La tempestad, 31, 54, **67–70**, 293, 310
La tempranica, 117, **118–21**, 279, 302, 308, 309
La tuna de Alcalá, 310
La vaquerita, 292
La venta de Don Quijote, **72**
La venta de los gatos, 191, 297
La Ventera del Ansó, 284
La verbena de la Paloma, 5, 9, **48–51**, 62, 63, 77, 82, 269, 299, 303, 309
La viejecita, 91, **105–8**, 294, 301
La villana, 136, 249, **263–6**, 298, 303, 305, 308
La vuelta del Corsario, 28
La zapaterita, 12, **25**, 308
de Larra, Luis Mariano, 34, 36, 115, **294**
de Larra, Mariano José, 294
Las bravías, 54, **71**
Las bribonas, 277
Las de Caín, 208, **226**, 297
Las delicias de Capua, 281
Las golondrinas, 235, **244–7**, 306, 310, 311
Las hazañas de un pícaro, 281
Las hijas del Zebedeo, **71**
Las hilanderas, 192, **205**
Las leandras, 12, **15–18**, 305
Las maravillosas, 228
Las musas latinas, 185, **190**
Las percheleras, 47
Las viejas ricas, 282
Las vírgenes paganas, 228
Las zapatillas, 74
de Laserna, Blas, 2
Latymer, Lord. *See* Money-Coutts, Francis Burdett
Lauri-Volpi, Giacomo, 310
Lavirgen, Pedro, **306**
Lázaro, Hipólito, 301

Lecuona, Ernesto, 280, **287–9**, 309; *Danzas Cubanas*, 287; Lecuona's Cuban Boys, 287; *Malagueña*, 288; *Siboney*, 288; *Suite Andalucía*, 288
Lehár, Franz, 161, 164, 167; *Der Graf von Luxemburg*, 146; *Die Lustige Witwe*, 148
Leigh, Mitch: *Man of La Mancha*, 311
Leoncavallo, Ruggero: *La Boheme*, 256; *Pagliacci*, 62, 226, 235, 246, 310
Leonís, Rosario, 162
Leoz, Jesús García, 124, **279**, 297; *Barataria*, 279
Lessing, Gotthold Ephraim: *Minna von Barnhelm*, 114
Lewis, Leopold: *The Bells*, 70
de Literes, Antonio, 2, 9
Lleó y Balbastre, Vicente, **145–8**, 252, 270, 296, 309
Lo somni de la Ignocència, 284
Lola Cruz, 288
López, Félix Máximo, 3
López Monís, Antonio, 168, 171
López Muñoz, Conte de. *See* López Monís, Antonio
Lorengar, Pilar, 123, 303, **306–7**, 308
Lorente, Juan José, 202, 204
Los africanistas, 94
Los amores de la Inés, 279
Los barrios bajos, 73
Los borrachos, 117
Los bufos madrileños, 4, 274, 293
Los burladores, **226**, 297
Los buscadores de oro, 167
Los cachorros, 281
Los cadetes de la Reina, 151, **165**
Los calabreses, 151
Los castigadoras, 305
Los Claveles, 12, 21, 192, **198–201**, 215, 221, 293, 303, 304
Los de Aragón, 191, **205**, 301, 304
Los descamisados, 291
Los diamantes de la corona, 34, **45**, 292
Los diamantes negros, 269
Los flamencos, 249, **267**, 304, 309, 310
Los gavilanes, 123, **124–7**, 133, 137, 303, 312

Los husares del Zar, 47
Los inseperables, 152
Los magyares, 110
Los mendigos, 270
Los puritanos, 276
Los sobrinos del capitán Grant, 91, **100–105**, 287, 293
Los viajes de Gulliver, 118, 249
Los viejos verdes, 280
Los voluntarios, 117
Luca de Tena, Juan Ignacio, 127, 130
Lucio López, Celso, 108, 237, 291
Luisa Fernanda, xii, 6, 143, 174, 177, **178–82**, 298, 302, 303, 304, 308, 309, 311
Luna, Pablo, 6, **151–65**, 167, 168, 173, 227, 235, 260, 296, 298; *The First Kiss*, 155; *Miguelon*, 152; *Una noche en Calatayud*, 152
Luna de mayo, 281
Luzbel, 280

Madrid Conservatory, 27, 33, 47, 53, 73, 109, 123, 139, 227, 228, 237, 272, 275, 277, 279, 281, 282, 308, 310
Manent, Nicolau, **284**
Manso, Juanita, 145
Maravilla, 182
Mari-Eli, 140, 225
María Belén Chacón, 289
Maria de la O (Quiroga), 280
María del Carmen, 270
María la O (Lecuona), 288, **289**
María la tempranica (Torroba), 121. *See also La tempranica*
María Manuela, **183**
Marina, **28–31**, 70, 292, 293, 306, 307
Marqués, Miguel, **272–3**; *Primera lágrima*, 272
Martierra, **138**, 304
Martín, José Ramos, 124, 126, 131, 133
Martín y Soler, Vicente, 2
Martínez Sierra, Gregorio and María Lejarraga, 244, 246, 247; *Saltimbanquis*, 246
Martínez Valls, Rafael, **284–5**

Maruxa, 249, **260–2**, 267, 307, 308, 311
The Marx Brothers: *A Night at the Opera*, 94
Mascagni, Pietro: *Cavalleria Rusticana*, 62, 235, 310
Massenet, Jules, 252
Mazza, Giuseppe: *La prova di una opera seria*, 149
Me llaman la presumida, 12, **19–22**, 201, 221, 293, 311
Medio, Antonio, 304
Mendelssohn-Bartholdy, Felix, 72
Mendi Mendiyan, 243
Mesonera de Tordesillas, 308
Messiaen, Olivier: *Turangalîla*, 140
Mestres, Apel·les, 270
Mexico, 7, 110, 115
Meyerbeer, Giacomo, 70: *L'Africaine*, 92, 94, 95
Millán, Rafael, 12, **167–71**, 217, 298, 310, 311
Mirentxu, 140
Misón, Luis 2
Miss Australia, 296
Molinos de viento, 151, 152, 156, 158, 165, **167–171**, 260
Money-Coutts, Francis Burdett, 269
Monte Carmelo, 174, **183**, 298, 311
Monterde, Pilar, 162
Moreno Torroba, Federico, 6, 121, 143, 152, **173–183**, 280, 296, 297, 298, 303, 305, 308, 309, 311; *Concierto flamenco*, 173; *Concierto ibérico*, 173; *El poeta*, 174; *La Virgen de Mayo*, 174; *María la tempranica*, 121; *Sonatina*, 173
Morera, Enric, **285**, 312; *Tassarba*, 285
Mori, Victor, 285
Moros y cristianos, 191, **206**, 307
Mozart, Wolfgang Amadeus, 3; *Die Zauberflöte*, 269
Munguía, Carlos, **307**
Murger, Henri: *Scenes de la Vie de Bohème*, 252
Musetta, 151
Música clásica, **72**
Música, luz y alegría, 11

de Nebra, José, 2, 9
Ni Amor se libra de amor, 2
Nieto, Miguel, 117, 122, 273, 280, 296
Nieto, Ofelia, **307**
Nin, Joaquín, 287
Niña Rita, 288
Noche de verbena, 249

Offenbach, Jacques, xi, 122; *La Belle Hélène*, 146, 148, 274; *Le Pont des Soupirs*, 171
de Olona, Luis, 3, 109, 110, 114, 115, 271, **295**, 311
opéra comique, 66; *La Rose de Péronne*, 114
operetta-zarzuela, 6
Orféo Catalá, 249, 312
Orfeón Donostiarra, 307
Ortega, María, 228
Ottein, Ángeles, **307–8**
Oudrid, Cristóbal, 4, 28, 33, 109, 271, 272, **273–4**; *El sitio de Zaragoza*, 274
Oviedo Festival, 8
Oxford Theatre (London): *The First Kiss*, 152, 155

Pacini, Giovanni: *Saffo*, 117
Padilla, José, **279–80**, 309; *El relicario*, 280; *La violetera*, 280; *Valencia*, 280
de Palacios, Miguel, 145, 146, 250, 257, **295–6**
Palacios, Antonio **308**
Palazón, Rafael, 91
Pan y toros, 4, 34, 36, **40–5**, 270, 295
Panadés, Conchita, **308**
Paso, Antonio, 78, 80, 83, 84, 152, 155, 159
Paso Díaz, Antonio, 229
Pedrell, Felipe, 173, 249, 266, 279, 283; *Els Pirineus*, 283
Peña y Goñi, Antonio, 114, 272
Penagos, Isabel, **308**
Peñamariana, 140, 298
Penella, Manuel, **185–90**, 191, 270
Penella Raga, Manuel, 185
Pepe-Hillo, 270

Pepita Romero, 297
Pérez y Gonzalez, Felipe, 87, 89
Pérez, Dolores, **309**
Pérez Carpio, Selíca, 121, 302, 304, **309**
Pérez Galdós, Benito. *See* Galdós, Benito Pérez
Pergolesi, Giovanni Battista: *La Serva Padrona*, 2
Perrín, Guillermo, 145, 146, 250, 257, **295-6**
Philip IV, 1
Piazzolla, Astor: *María de Buenos Aires*, 287
Picarol, 270
Picón, José, 40, 44, 295
Ponchielli, Amilcare, 27
Por seguir a una mujer, 109, 271
Prats, Jaime: Cuban Jazz Band, 289
Prats, Rodrigo, **289**; *Una rosa de Francia*, 289; *Misa Cubana*, 289
Puccini, Giacomo, 192, 208, 240, 249, 252; *La Boheme*, 256; *Madama Butterfly*, 231; *Manon Lescaut*, 189; *Turandot*, 162
Pulido, Delfín, 121

¿Qué sabes tú?, 282
Quintana, Félix, 292
Quintero, Los hermanos, 58, 60, 191, 205, 226, **296-7**
Quiroga, Manuel López, **280**

Raga, Cora, **309**, 312
Ramos Carrión, Miguel. *See* Carrión, Miguel Ramos
Ramos de Castro, Francisco, 19, 21, 201, 218, **293**
Ramos Martín, José. *See* Martín, José Ramos
Ravel, Maurice, 227, 287
Redondo, Marcos, 302, 305, 307, 308, **310**, 311
Reoyo, Enrique, 127, 130, 229
Respighi, Ottorino, 140
revista, 5, 6, 18, 122
Rodrigo, Joaquín, 174, **280-1**; *Concierto de Aranjuez*, 174, 280
Rodrigo, María, **281**, 297

Rogel, José, 4, **274**, 275
Roig, Gonzalo, 287, **289-90**
de Rojas, Francisco: *Entre bobos anda el juego*, 267
Román, Luis Martínez, 12, 15
Román, José Muñoz, 15
Romanza húngara, 278
Romea, Julián 98, 100, 118, 120
Romero, Federico, 6, 134, 136, 140, 143, 144, 171, 174, 177, 178, 181, 183, 194, 197, 222, 225, 253, 256, 263, 267, 281, **297-8**
Romeu, Pepe, **310**
Romo, Jesús, **281**, 297, 304
Rosa la China, **288**
Rosa la pantalonera, 12
Rosado, Toñy (Antonia), **310**
Rosaura, 174
Rosillo, Ernesto, **281-2**, 292
Rosselló I Sintes, Francesc D'Assís, **286**
Rossini, Gioachino, 3, 115, 122; *Guillaume Tell*, 273; *Il Barbiere di Siviglia*, 36-7
Rostand, Edmond: *Cyrano de Bergerac*, 297
Rubio, Consuela, 308
Ruffo, Titta, 310

Sagi, Emilio, 8
Sagi-Barba, Emilio, 171, **311**
Sagi-Vela, Luis, 309, **311**
sainete, 2, 4-5
Saint-Saëns, Charles Camille, 227
Salas, Francisco, 109, 295, **311-12**
Saldoni, Baltasar, 270
Salir el amor del mundo, 2
San Antonio de la Florida, 269
San Franco de Sena, 28
de Sarasate, Pablo, 58
sarsuela (Catalan), **283-6**
Schiller, Johann Christoph Friedrich, 297
Schipa, Tito, 277
Schöenberg, Arnold, 207
Scribe, Eugène, 45, 115
Segovia, Andrés, 173
Serrano, José, 6, 9, 12, 72, 92, 97, 168, **191-206**, 215, 270, 276, 277, 292, 293, 297, 301, 307

Serrano, Emilio, **274–5**, 281; *Doña Juana la Loca*, 275
Serrano, Enriqueta, **312**
de Sevilla, Luis Fernández, 198, 201, 212, 215, 232, 235, **292–3**
SGAE. *See* Sociedad General de Autores y Editores
Shakespeare, William, 110; *All's Well That Ends Well*, 197; *The Taming of the Shrew*, 71
Shaw Guillermo Fernández, 6, 134, 136, 140, 143, 144, 171, 174, 177, 178, 181, 183, 194, 197, 222, 225, 253, 256, 263, 267, 281, **297–8**
Shaw, Carlos Fernández, 60, 63, 71, 297
Shaw, Rafael Fernández, 297
Shostakovich, Dmitri: "Leningrad" Symphony, 208
¡Si yo fuera rey!, **271**
Silva, José López, 60, 63, 71, 292
Simón, Andrés Marín, 228
Smetana, Bedrich, 266
Sociedad General de Autores de España, 53, 173
Sociedad General de Autores y Editores (SGAE), xii, 8. *See also* Sociedad General de Autores de España
Sol de Sevilla, 309
Soler, Almerinda, 67
Solera, Temistocle, 27
Song of the Volga Boatmen, 218
Sor Navarra, 303
Soriano, Agustín Pérez, **274**
Sorozábal, Pablo, xii, 5, 6, 9, 12, 21, 22, 31, 100, 171, 173, 183, 201, **207–226**, 269, 275, 293, 297, 298, 303, 304, 305, 306, 307, 308, 311, 312; *¡Ay tierra vasca!*, 207; *Capricho español*, 207; *Dos Apuntes Vascos*, 207; *Gernika*, 207; *Juan José*, 208; *Maite*, 207; *Suite vasca*, 207; *Symphonic Variations on a Basque Theme*, 207; *Victoriana* (ballet), 207
Sorozábal Serrano, Pablo, 226

Soutullo, Reveriano, 130, 162, **227–36**, 293; *Puenteáreas* (pasodoble), 227; *Vigo*, 227
Strauss, Johann Jr., 37
Stravinsky, Igor: *The Rake's Progress*, 40
Sullivan, Arthur, xi, 9, 262; *The Mikado*, 155; *The Pirates of Penzance*, 37; *The Rose of Persia*, 155
Supervía, Conchita, 205, 301, 309
von Suppé, Franz: *Boccaccio*, 270
Swift, Jonathan: *Gulliver's Travels*, 118

Talismán, 250
Tamayo, José: *Antología de la Zarzuela*, 8, 303
Tamberlick, Enrico, 30, 31, 53
Teatro Apolo, 5, 47, 74, 117, 123, 164, 237
Teatro Calderón, 304
Teatro Cervantes (Granada), 11
Teatro Cómico, 11
Teatro de la Cruz, 33, 109
Teatro de la Zarzuela, 3, 8, 9, 27, 33, 47, 67, 84, 110, 114, 117, 133, 151, 167, 178, 249, 272, 273, 281, 284, 295, 306, 308, 309, 311
Teatro de Variedades, 73, 91
Teatro del Circo, 3, 33, 109, 110, 151, 273, 295, 311
Teatro Eslava, 145, 146
Teatro Español, 109
Teatro Ideal, 151
Teatro Lope de Vega, 91
Teatro Novedades, 11
Teatro Real, 27, 30, 53, 54, 91, 109, 253
Telemann, Georg Philipp: *Pimpinone*, 2
Tellaeche, José, 25
Tellería, Juan, **282**
Tennyson, Alfred Lord: *The Idylls of the King*, 249
Thomas, Ambroise, 117
Thomas, Brandon: *Charley's Aunt*, 107
Toldrá, Eduardo, **286**; *El giravolt de Maig*, 286
Tonadilla escénica, 2–3, 4, 36, 72

Torregrosa, Tomás López, 177, **237–42**, 275, 276, 292
de Torrejón y Velasco, Tomás, 1, 287
Torres del Álamo, Angel, 162, 164
Torroba, Federico Moreno. *See* Moreno Torroba, Federico
Trafalgar, 117
Tres madres para una hija, 91
¡Tribulaciones!, 109
Turina, Joaquín, 143

Ufisa Film Corporation, 139
Un día de primavera, 281, 297
Una vieja, **110**, 115, 292
United States: zarzuela in, 7
Usandizaga, José María, **243–7**, 282, 311; *Dans la Mer*, 243; *Hassan y Melihah*, 243; *Obertura Sinfónica*, 243; *Rhapsody on 3 Basque Popular Songs*, 243; *String Quartet Op. 31*, 243; *Suite in A*, 243
Usandizaga, Ramón, 243, 246, 247

Vaccai, Nicola, 27
Valverde, Joaquín, 5, 48, 73–4, 81–2, 87–89, 90, **275**, 276, 299
Valverde Sanjuan, Joaquín ("Quinito"), 90, 191, 205, 237, 242, **275–6**, 277, 280, 292, 296; *L'Amour en Espagne*, 276; *Clavelitos*, 276; *The Land of Joy*, 276; *A Night in Spain*, 276
Vega, Emilio, 228
de Vega, Lope, 6, 266, 281, 298; *El perro del hortelano*, 136, 189; *Fuenteovejuna*, 6, 136; *La discreta enamorada*, 256; *Peribáñez y el Comendador de Ocaña*, 266
de la Vega, Ricardo, 4, 6, 48, 50, 63, 81, 82, 90, 298, 299
de la Vega, Ventura, 3, 37, 40, 295, 298, 299

de la Vega, Ventura (grandson), 279
Vela, Luisa, 311
Vendrell, Emilio, 285, 308, 309, **312**
Veralet, pare i fill, del comerç de Barcelona, 284
Verdi, Giuseppe, 50; *Aida*, 146, 148, 309; *I Due Foscari*, 171; *Un Giorno di Regno*, 109; *Otello*, 31; *Rigoletto*, 70, 171, 304; *La Traviata*, 311
verismo, 92, 192, 244, 246, 297
Verne, Jules: *Les Enfants du capitaine Grant*, 104; *Miguel Strogoff*, 28
Vert, Juan, 130, **227–36**, 293
Veyán, José Jackson, 108
Viento es la dicha de Amor, 2
Villaverde, Cirilo, 290
Vives, Amadeu, 6, 25, 118, 122, 133, 136, 143, 145, 181, **249–67**, 279, 286, 294, 296, 298, 304, 307, 308, 309, 310; *Artús*, 249; *L'emigrant*, 249; *Sofía* (autobiography), 250
Voltaire (François-Marie Arouet): *Candide*, 104, 287

Wagner, Richard, 50, 110; *Der Fliegende Holländer*, 70; *Lohengrin*, 148, 273; *Tristan und Isolde*, 225; Hans Sachs, 143
Weill, Kurt, 208; *Die Dreigroschenoper*, 89

Yradier, Sebastián. *See* Iradier, Sebastián

de Zamora, Antonio, 2
zarzuela grande, 3–4
Zarzuela! website, xii
Zimmermann, Bernd Alois: *Die Soldaten*, 285
Zorilla y Moral, José: *Don Juan Tenorio*, 284

About the Author

Christopher Webber is an English writer, actor and stage director. His original stage works include *Tatyana*; *Love and Politics*; *Dr Sullivan and Mr Gilbert*; *A Flower and a Kiss* (for Welsh National Opera); and *Green Tea* based on the story by Sheridan Le Fanu, which has been shortlisted for a Guinness Award. He is also the author of the best-selling *Bluff Your Way At the Races*, and co-author (with Peter Gammond) of *Bluff Your Way in Opera*.

As an actor he has worked consistently in British theatre, film and television. He has been a part of Sir Alan Ayckbourn's company in Scarborough, England; gave the British regional and European premieres of Alan Bennett's *A Chip in the Sugar*, and created the role of Owl in the first-ever staging of A. A. Milne's *Winnie The Pooh* in London's West End. Among many productions as a stage director around the world was a highly praised *The Mikado* for the D'Oyly Carte Opera Company which was seen throughout Britain and in Los Angeles.

His Internet site *Zarzuela!* (from 1997) is the prime global resource for information on Spanish music theatre, and recently he has been concentrating on the form as writer and performer. The global Spanish newspaper *El País* called him "our unofficial cultural ambassador," and his 1999 stage version of Sorozábal's classic *La del manojo de rosas* as *The Girl with the Roses* was enthusiastically reviewed, notably by London's *The Times*. His versions of Serrano's *La dolorosa* and Torroba's *Luisa Fernanda* for the Santa Fe Opera have enjoyed highly successful tours from fall 1998.

He was dramaturge for the Super Ichiza Company's production of *La dolorosa* in Nagoya, Japan; wrote program articles for Plácido Domingo's Royal Opera Zarzuela Gala in London and for Calixto Bieito's production of *La verbena de la Paloma* at the Edinburgh Festival; has translated and edited four volumes of zarzuela *romanzas* for Union Músical Editores; and has written entries on romantic and modern Iberian and Latin American music and composers for the Oxford Companion to Music.

www.zarzuela.net